Forgotten Peace

VIOLENCE IN LATIN AMERICAN HISTORY
Edited by Pablo Piccato, Federico Finchelstein, and Paul Gillingham

1. *Uruguay, 1968: Student Activism from Global Counterculture to Molotov Cocktails,*
   by Vania Markarian

2. *While the City Sleeps: A History of Pistoleros, Policemen, and the Crime Beat in Buenos Aires
   before Perón,* by Lila Caimari

3. *Forgotten Peace: Reform, Violence, and the Making of Contemporary Colombia,*
   by Robert A. Karl

4. *A History of Infamy: Crime, Truth, and Justice in Mexico,* by Pablo Piccato

5. *Death in the City: Suicide and the Social Imaginary in Modern Mexico,* by Kathryn A. Sloan

Forgotten Peace

*Reform, Violence, and the Making of
Contemporary Colombia*

———

Robert A. Karl

UNIVERSITY OF CALIFORNIA PRESS

University of California Press, one of the most distinguished university presses in the United States, enriches lives around the world by advancing scholarship in the humanities, social sciences, and natural sciences. Its activities are supported by the UC Press Foundation and by philanthropic contributions from individuals and institutions. For more information, visit www.ucpress.edu.

University of California Press
Oakland, California

Library of Congress Cataloging-in-Publication Data

Names: Karl, Robert A., 1981– author.
Title: Forgotten peace : reform, violence, and the making of contemporary Colombia / Robert A. Karl.
Description: Oakland, California : University of California Press, 2017 | Includes bibliographical references and index.
Identifiers: LCCN 2016046167 (print) | LCCN 2016046544 (ebook) | ISBN 978-0-520-29392-2 (cloth : alk. paper) | ISBN 978-0-520-29393-9 (pbk. : alk. paper) | ISBN 978-0-520-96724-3 (ebook)
Subjects: LCSH: Violence—Colombia—History—20th century. | Peace-building—Colombia—History—20th century. | Social problems—Colombia—20th century. | Insurgency—Colombia. | Colombia—History—1946–1974.
Classification: LCC HN310.Z9 V54 2017 (print) | LCC HN310.Z9 (ebook) | DDC 303.609861—dc23
LC record available at https://lccn.loc.gov/2016046167

Manufactured in the United States of America

25 24 23 22 21 20 19 18 17
10 9 8 7 6 5 4 3 2 1

To Beth, for the audacities, to be sure, but for the rest even more

This ... tale of blood and martyrdom, of madness and cruelty, may never properly be history.

—ALBERTO LLERAS CAMARGO, 1955

CONTENTS

List of Illustrations   ix
Acknowledgments   xi

Introduction: Peace and Violence in Colombian History   1

1. Messenger of a New Colombia   15

2. Encounters with Violence, 1957–1958   38

3. The Making of the Creole Peace, 1958–1960   63

4. Peace and Violence, 1959–1960   95

5. Reformist Paths, 1960–1964   120

6. Books and Bandits, 1962–1964   148

7. Confrontation, 1963–1966   182

Epilogue: The Making of "La Violencia"   215

A Note on Citations, Institutional Abbreviations, and Archives   227
Notes   233
Bibliography   293
Index   309

ILLUSTRATIONS

MAPS

1. Colombia, c. 1960   *xvi*
2. Gran Tolima   *7*
3. Important sites of peace and violence, 1958–1965   *39*
4. Counties where partisan majority flipped, 1946–1958   *53*
5. Gran Tolima's frontier Communist communities, 1953–1965   *58*
6. Monthly homicides attributed to partisan violence, Tolima, 1958   *73*
7. Counties with peace pacts negotiated by the National Investigatory Commission, 1958   *76*
8. State-of-siege departments and distribution of Agrarian Bank rehabilitation loans (as of June 1959)   *80*
9. Roadway attacks, 1962   *156*

FIGURES

1. Alberto Lleras Camargo, 1962   *17*
2. Father Germán Guzmán Campos with unidentified young combatants, 1958   *51*
3. The National Investigatory Commission visits southern Tolima, August 1958   *56*
4. Gaitania (Ataco), 1964   *59*
5. The National Investigatory Commission visits El Pato, 1958   *60*
6. Liberal leaders visit southern Tolima's Communists, September 1957   *70*

ix

7. Monthly homicides attributed to partisan violence, January 1957–
   April 1959   *72*
8. Jorge Villamil with former Liberal combatants, El Pato, 1960s   *93*
9. Monthly homicides attributed to partisan violence, January 1957–
   December 1960   *99*
10. Orlando Fals Borda and Father Camilo Torres Restrepo   *131*
11. "The Decisive Match": "The 'National' Team against 'Los Violentos'"   *161*
12. Monthly homicides attributed to partisan violence and banditry,
    January 1957–December 1964   *178*
13. Martín Camargo among *desplazados* from El Pato, 1964   *186*
14. Ceremony marking the government occupation of Marquetalia,
    June 1964   *196*
15. Army troops with residents of Marquetalia, 1964   *200*

ACKNOWLEDGMENTS

My first years of work on Latin America unfolded under the sign of two counter-insurgency wars. I departed the United States for my college study-abroad program on the night of September 10, 2001. I spent those next three anxious months in London, researching British counterinsurgency during the Malayan Emergency, while the United States occupied Afghanistan. Two years later, as I finished a thesis on U.S. counterinsurgency and development policy in 1960s Latin America, my graduate school recruiting visit coincided with protests against the pending U.S. invasion of Iraq. The resulting fascination with the projection of U.S. power eventually drew me to study Colombia. I arrived in Bogotá to begin my research a few weeks before Álvaro Uribe's second inauguration, as the war against the FARC had already begun to turn. Early the next year, the U.S. troop surge in Iraq ramping up, I would write the first kernel of a dissertation on the origins of the FARC.

Yet if my intellectual interests had thus emerged hand-in-hand with events in the wider world, my attraction to the topic of (counter)insurgency eventually waned alongside counterinsurgency's fall from grace. By the start of 2012, counterinsurgency was on its way out as the favored doctrine of the U.S. military; in August, the Colombian government and the FARC had announced an agenda for peace negotiations. By then three years out from the dissertation, still searching for a path forward to the book, I arrived at the question of peace at the precise moment that Colombia's attentions shifted away from counterinsurgency toward the possibility of peace. I likewise finished revising this book just weeks after Colombian voters rejected the October 2, 2016, referendum on peace with the FARC. Though I counted among those who fervently wished for a different outcome, this extraordinary coincidence of timing underscores the importance of thinking about the mutual constitution of ideas and practices of violence and peace.

I have, of course, accumulated no small number of debts over this past decade and a half. As a confirmed archive rat, my first thanks must go to the numerous archives and libraries where I conducted research for what became this book. Several institutions and people deserve extra praise. The Archivo General de la Nación became my home-away-from-home in Bogotá, thanks in large part to the generous support of Mauricio Tovar, and to my fellow researchers, including Adriana Rodríguez, my archival fairy godmother. Fabio González Castro has been my man at the AGN, research assistant, Bogotá fixer, and—most importantly—great friend. Armando Moreno opened up his home in Ibagué, facilitated my research, and has tracked down a number of leads since. Gabriel Escalante Guzmán and Nelly Flórez Cabeza welcomed me to the Archivo Central e Histórico, Universidad Nacional, and the Archivo Histórico de Ibagué. Back in the States, Michael Evans made possible a short but productive visit to the National Security Archive. Some of the material from the JFK Library used in this book dates back to my days as an archival intern under Stephen Plotkin, who remains a backer of my work. Thanks also go to the staffs of the Biblioteca Darío Echandía in Ibagué, the Biblioteca Luis Angel Arango in Bogotá, the Law School Library and Widener Library at Harvard University, and Firestone Library at Princeton University.

Research for this book was generously funded by Fulbright Colombia; the Lyndon Baines Johnson Library Foundation; the David Rockefeller Center for Latin American Studies and Weatherhead Center for International Affairs at Harvard; and the History Department, Program in Latin American Studies, and University Committee on Research in the Humanities and Social Sciences at Princeton. I was among the last in a long line of scholars of Colombia to experience Consuelo Valdivieso's expert support at the Fulbright Commission. At Princeton, Judy Hanson and Debbie Macy have helped things to move with as little administrative friction as possible. Princeton's paid parental leave policy made it possible for to me complete this book while also caring for my daughters and supporting my wife's career.

My professors at Dartmouth College taught me how to be a historian and planted the seeds for this book. Marysa Navarro told me long ago that my undergraduate thesis topic could be a doctoral dissertation. I am so proud to get to share the book with her now. Agnes Lugo-Ortiz, the late Bob Russell, John Watanabe, and especially Emilio Kourí further helped to stoke my interest in Latin America.

It is a testament to my graduate advisors that they did not blink when I switched countries in my third semester at Harvard. I owe an incalculable debt to John Womack Jr., who introduced me to Colombia and taught me to embrace a diversity of approaches and cultivate a deep appreciation for unnoticed detail. John Coatsworth got me thinking across big scales. Mary Roldán's breadth of knowledge about Colombia, to say nothing of her scholarly and personal brilliance, continues to inspire. I am also fortunate to have learned from Jorge Domínguez, Carrie Elkins, and Akira Iriye.

The intellectual environment of Princeton's History Department allowed this project to take its current shape. Jeremy Adelman pushed me to turn an overly long dissertation into a single book, and provided me a new toolkit with which to think about Latin America. Michael Gordin and Erika Milam offered extensive comments on two very different versions of the project; conversations with Michael, as well as with Marni Sandweiss and Sean Wilentz, inspired key elements of the book's final structure. I benefited too from the feedback of my junior-faculty writing group—Alec Dun, Caley Horan, Matt Karp, Jon Levy, Beth Lew-Williams, Rosina Lozano, Rebecca Rix, and Wendy Warren—as well as from comments from Joe Fronczak, Shel Garon, Phil Nord, Keith Wailoo, and Max Weiss. Bill Jordan has been a model chair, unfailingly generous to an entire generation of assistant professors. Margot Canaday, Vera Candiani, Molly Greene, Katja Guenther, Josh Guild, Dirk Hartog, Alison Isenberg, Kevin Kruse, Mike Laffan, Yair Mintzker, Brad Simpson, and Jack Tannous have also helped to make these last seven years so enriching and humane. Outside of Dickinson Hall, I am grateful for the support of Bruno Carvalho, Miguel Centeno, Rubén Gallo, Pedro Meira Monteiro, and Meredith Martin.

The opportunity to work with outstanding students has been one of my greatest privileges at Princeton. Teaching undergraduate courses has refined my thinking about topics big and small, while even that oft-dreaded task of preparing lectures has made my writing clearer. In addition to their comments on the book's chapters, interactions with graduate students José Argueta Funes, Teresa Davis, Valeria López Fadul, Allen Kim, Martín Marimón, Edgar Melgar, Iwa Nawrocki, Andrea Oñate-Madrazo, Fidel Tavárez, Melissa Teixeira, Paula Vedoveli, and Kim Worthington have been fundamental to my approach to our field. Three other students deserve a particular word of thanks: Diana Andrade Melgarejo, for conversations on Colombian political history and for her indispensable work locating sources in Bogotá; Margarita Fajardo Hernández, for our shared enthusiasm for Colombia and *letrados;* and Jessica Mack, for helping me to think more deeply about issues of memory.

My fellow *colombianistas* have been a constant source of encouragement and insight. Without Abbey Steele, I might have never started to think about displacement; her fondness for the tale of Tirofijo and his fourteen cousins also encouraged me to tell a good story. A. Ricardo López has meanwhile been a better friend and interlocutor than I could have ever hoped for. I owe every Colombian listed here—and plenty of others—an enormous debt for their faith in my study of their country, but none more than Ricardo. Hardly a week has gone by without an exchange with him about the progress of our research, a discussion of a translation, or news of some archival find. I am also grateful to Tico Braun, Óscar Calvo Isaza, Alex Fattal, Jorge González Jácome, Daniel Gutiérrez Ardila, Catherine LeGrand, Catalina Muñoz, Amy Offner, Joanne Rappaport, Lukas Rehm, Jim

Robinson, Joshua Rosenthal, Susana Romero, Eduardo Sáenz Rovner, María Paula Saffón Sanín, Rebecca Tally, Winifred Tate, Brett Troyan, and Victor Uribe-Uran. The usual provisos about errors apply.

One benefit to working on what David Bushnell once called "the least studied of the major Latin American countries" has been the need to seek feedback from scholars of other parts of the region. Audiences at the Congreso de la Asociación de Colombianistas; Latin American Studies Association congresses in Toronto and New York; American Historical Association and Conference on Latin American History annual meetings in Boston and Washington; Columbia University; the University of Toronto; the Program in Latin American Studies and Rewriting the History of the Latin American Left workshop at Princeton; Harvard's David Rockefeller Center for Latin American Studies; the University of Chicago Latin American History Workshop; the New York City Latin American History Workshop; the Universidad Nacional de Colombia, sede Medellín; and the Universidad de Antioquia provided feedback on various pieces of the project. I have also benefited immeasurably from the guidance and input of Isaac Campos, Oliver Dinius, Thomas Field, Browdie Fischer, Mark Healy, Emilio Kourí, Sarah Osten, Hillel Soifer, and Rachel StJohn.

After years of helping me with various spatial history endeavors, T. Wangyal Shawa transformed my rough maps into their polished final versions. Fabio González Castro, Thomas Irby, Amanda Mitchell, and Jeffrey Williamson helped me to assemble the data, while Jean Bauer assisted with coding for the online maps. Alexandra Gürel conducted research at the Rockefeller Archive Center. I am profoundly grateful to Rocío Londoño Botero, Víctor Eduardo Prado Delgado, and Vicente Silva Vargas for allowing me to reproduce this book's images; and to Danilo Pizarro and his colleagues at *El Tiempo* for sifting through seven thousand photographs to find a suitable image of Alberto Lleras.

This book is lucky to have a home in the Violence in Latin American History series. Pablo Piccato deserves a special word of gratitude, for his comments on the manuscript and our wide-ranging, enjoyable conversations in New York. Margaret Chowning, Paul Gootenberg, and an anonymous reviewer likewise offered pivotal feedback that greatly improved the project. Kate Marshall at the University of California Press not only helped to usher the book into being but also shaped several of its arguments in key ways. Also at the Press, Bradley Depew patiently led me through the first stages of the publishing process, while Kate Hoffman and Tom Sullivan took care of the rest. Sue Carter provided expert copyediting, Jen Burton the index.

My last debts are the greatest. Jon Hollander and Victor Roberts have been fixtures in my life for longer than I can remember. Friends from Dartmouth have accompanied me from the Upper Valley to London and Boyacá. Thanks especially to Dave, Andy, *los Jon,* and *los Pete.* My Harvard classmates, Edward Baring,

Denise Ho, Hal Jones, Miles Rodríguez, and Sergio Silva Castañeda among them, continue to be an essential part of my professional and personal worlds. Roberto Antonio Hernández remains one of the most giving people I have ever met, above all for the honor of making me Sebastián's godfather.

Baker and Stringer Bell were present for more of the writing of this book than any being on two legs. Though we have ended up spread across the world as adults, I am grateful that my brother, sister, and I have become such friends. The Rabbitts and Canellis embraced me from the first moment I met them, making me part of the big Irish and Italian families I never had. My own parents gave me every opportunity, and, crucially, instilled in me not just an appreciation for reading but also the kind of patience that ended up being so useful in the archives.

I am glad that those days were largely behind me by the time that I met Beth Rabbitt. She has still had to live with this book for longer than she ever expected, but she has made the whole thing—and so much else—possible. Along with our daughters Phoebe and Maeve, who came along toward the end of this book, Beth has pulled me out of my own head, out of the past and into the present. They are the greatest joys I have ever known. *Las amo.*

MAP 1. Colombia, c. 1960.

Introduction

Peace and Violence in Colombian History

Colombia, more than any other country in Latin America, a region famed for its revolutions and dictatorships, is synonymous with "violence." The global imagination envisages Colombia as a land of kidnappings and assassinations, the domain of brutal cocaine kingpins. Scholars examining Colombian history frequently analyze violence as an unyielding constant, positing that the nineteenth-century civil wars fought between the Liberal and Conservative parties established "inherited hatreds," party identities, the narrative goes, that endured longer in Colombia than anywhere else in Latin America. This idiosyncrasy is said to have borne disastrous consequences after 1945, when Liberal and Conservative peasants seemingly returned to the nineteenth century, hacking each other to death with machetes in an apparently pointless internecine affair called simply "La Violencia"—The Violence.[1] Actors of all political commitments identify this conflict's final stage as the incubator of the Revolutionary Armed Forces of Colombia (FARC; Fuerzas Armadas Revolucionarias de Colombia), whose historical demands for land later merged with the exigencies of the drug trade to sustain the world's longest-running insurgency.[2] Yet, as prominent as this reputation for violence is, scholars seeking to explain the origins and persistence of violence in Colombia must square it with the country's claim to one of Latin America's longest traditions of democratic governance, as well as its occasional status as a hemispheric model for socioeconomic development.[3]

This book explores how Colombians grappled with violence during and after the period known as La Violencia. It demonstrates that, far from enjoying widespread usage during the era it defines, "La Violencia" only came into being in the mid-1960s, the result of alienation from a nearly decade-long experiment with democratization and social reform which thus failed to define Colombia's recent past. The emergence of "La Violencia" as a temporal concept is moreover the story of the FARC's creation, for the latter formed less out of the politics of 1960s revolution than from disillusionment with that same intervening period of democratic and reformist projects. In evolving into an institution and an idea central to narratives of violence in Colombia, the FARC and La Violencia obscured their shared origins in the optimistic, collective steps that politicians, intellectuals, and rural folk had taken against violence in a promising moment from the late 1950s into the 1960s.

The history of how this moment became a forgotten peace is thus emblematic of how societies seek to move beyond collective violence, and how that search molds notions of belonging—local, regional, and national—as well as understandings of the past. The case of midcentury Colombia shows how a process of political transition unfolds hand in hand with the creation of that transition's possibilities and closures, of how the process is experienced and remembered. In building peace while contemplating violence, rural and urban Colombians arrived at new representations of their regions in the nation, and of their nation in the world. Even in a country so associated with violence, the drive for peace is an equally fundamental component of contemporary history.

The inseparability of peace from violence was a familiar concept to midcentury Colombians. As he sat down in 1962 to write the final pages of what would quickly become Colombian social science's most famous study of violence, Germán Guzmán Campos reflected on the linkage between violence and peace. The middle-aged priest had already woven into most of the book's chapters his personal knowledge on the subject of violence—anecdotes of atrocity and loss gleaned from tours through the countryside, along with his measured observations about the depth of human failings. But when he wrote the epilogue to *La violencia en Colombia* (*Violence in Colombia*), he turned to consider his role in the political transition that had transpired during the five years since Colombia had exited authoritarian rule. "It's been thought," Guzmán commented, "that [we should] write up ... the immense effort realized [against violence] since May 10, 1957 to present as a second volume that could well be called 'How Peace Was Made.'"[4]

Forgotten Peace attempts Guzmán's ultimately unrealized tale, chronicling how peace was made. Amidst a broader national move toward democracy, Colombians inside and outside the state collaborated on a far-ranging experiment in peace-making that was without parallel in post-1945 Latin America.[5] If their internal conflict in the first decade of the postwar era had been the hemisphere's worst since the Mexican Revolution of 1910, Guzmán's fellow Colombians nonetheless remained undaunted as they then aspired to mount a multipronged peace-building effort equal to the task.[6] As Guzmán's reference to the overthrow of the dictatorship on May 10, 1957, made clear, the confluence of state and popular initiatives in favor of peace was inseparable from Colombia's new democratic framework.

In the language of the era, Colombians might have called this a creole peace (*una paz criolla*)—a homegrown set of improvised approaches, "adapt[ed] to local circumstances," that did not follow any imported model.[7] Decades before human rights and transitional justice cohered as global regimes, Colombians devised analogous practices to address the legacies of internal conflict and political authoritarianism. Guzmán, for instance, participated in a government-appointed commission that exceeded its vague initial mandate, moving from its charged task of investigating "the causes and current situations of violence" to an active role negotiating dozens of local peace pacts as well as gathering the recollections of tens of thousands of people affected by state violence and partisan fighting—a monumental undertaking that yielded insights which would both inform state policy and eventually form the basis of Guzmán and his collaborators' classic work, *La violencia en Colombia*.

This experience of the creole peace poses challenges to other studies on how countries confront the violence of their recent pasts. Though midcentury Colombia's exact configuration of democracy, justice, and human rights differed from those seen in subsequent contexts, the transition that unfolded there between 1957 and 1966 featured many of the practices around political legitimacy and memory associated with the "third-wave" democratization that commenced in Latin America, Asia, and Eastern Europe after 1970.[8] This is not to say that the creole peace represents part of a lost genealogy of human rights or transitional justice.[9] But it does help us to decenter the North Atlantic countries in debates over rights, violence, and state responsibility, and to see such postauthoritarian procedures not simply as reactions to the military dictatorships of the 1970s.[10] Furthermore, by moving the study of transitions to an earlier era, and by adopting an expansive definition of "transition" that includes issues of development and lived politics along with formal elements of democratization, we can better comprehend the fate of democracy in Latin America over the rest of the twentieth century. Doing so allows us as well to historicize the very categories with which we think through these political processes.

Transitions were at the heart of global attentions as the 1950s neared a close. The mood contained no small amount of unease. "We are situated between two worlds, one dead, the other hardly born; and our fate is chaos for a generation," the Liberal man of letters Alberto Lleras Camargo proclaimed at the end of 1958.[11] Anticolonial wars in Africa and Asia portended a new world map delineated by liberation, while population growth and demands for the material benefits of modern life—a so-called revolution of rising expectations—placed new demands on states everywhere.[12] Across Latin America, a crisis in the economic model of agricultural exports and internal manufactures triggered the fall of various authoritarian governments, including Colombia's in 1957. Well into the 1960s, continuing economic uncertainties would cast a shadow over the prospects of political stability and dampen the chances of potential policy responses to the revolution of rising expectations.[13]

At the same time, these political openings and socioeconomic transformations also originated substantial hopefulness. Colombia's democratic transition was guided by the National Front (Frente Nacional), a power-sharing coalition intended to remove the Conservative-Liberal antagonisms that had triggered the bloodshed of the previous decade by making state institutions the patrimony of all Colombians, rather than that of members of a single party.[14] "It will be seen [if the National Front's first president] is indeed the most intelligent of all the Presidents," dozens of inhabitants of the rural Sumapaz zone near Bogotá wrote in a 1959 petition. "And [if] all that Politicking ends, and there's work . . . soon people will start to see cash roll in, and we and the Government will be put out of our misery. . . . we will make a just, great, and peaceable country."[15] Under the National Front, its founders and advocates hoped, democratic institutions and the traditional parties would enable dialogue, thus encouraging pluralism; and government representatives would work with citizens to establish equitable standards of living.

Midcentury Colombians had a word for this aspirational combination of political and social citizenship: *convivencia*. The term is generally translated as "coexistence," such as coexistence between the Liberal and Conservative parties. Its meaning is nonetheless richer, implying both "the politics of civility" and the material conditions for democratic exchanges to prosper.[16] When Lleras, the architect of the National Front and its inaugural president, spoke in 1957 of eliminating violence, he described a goal "above and beyond pacification[:] peace, which is order and *convivencia*."[17]

In narrating this Colombian pursuit of *convivencia*, *Forgotten Peace* follows political leaders, intellectuals, and rural peoples over the course of a decade as they interacted across different scales and spaces on the question of violence. To make sense of the encounters between these three sets of actors, *Forgotten Peace* adopts a variegated methodological approach, combining a biographical focus on individual actors with analysis of broader trends in public discourse; mapping spatial patterns of violence and political change while also drawing on research in national and regional archives and periodicals, as well as a careful rereading of classic texts from Colombian social science such as Guzmán and his collaborators' *La violencia en Colombia*. The nature of archival sources from this period means that the narrative focuses more on men than women, and more on Liberal men at that. Though the effort to extirpate violence transcended partisan identity, Liberals were nonetheless behind many of the most important initiatives for peace.

"Any study of the Violencia," leading historian Gonzalo Sánchez G. remarked in the mid-1980s, "should begin (and this has not been done) with a reconstruction of the genealogy and implications of the manifold meanings of the term itself."[18] "Violence" is inherently a shorthand for a wide array of practices, a fact that midcentury Colombians were well aware of as they struggled to classify the diversity of death and destruction that their country faced. Beginning in the mid-1940s, state repression set off scattered urban uprisings, persistent rural conflict, and economically motivated predations against life and property. This was "an undeclared civil war," Lleras remarked; a "confused national catastrophe that we have generically referred to, for lack of a more precise name, as *la violencia*," explained a prominent intellectual in 1962.[19] Historians have been quick to assume the interchangeability of this intellectual's "*la violencia*" and the "Violencia" that Sánchez wrote of a quarter-century later. Nevertheless, close examination of contemporary usage indicates that "*la violencia*" very often meant the "technique of violence," as Guzmán's collaborator, the sociologist Orlando Fals Borda, defined it.[20] Only from the mid-1960s did Colombians begin to employ "La Violencia" as a designation for a precise block of time. The distinction is crucial to understanding how the political and intellectual commitments of Fals's cohort of social scientists were transformed into a dominant version of Colombia's national history—a manifestation of the disillusionment that grew out of the democratic opening of the late 1950s.

In order to follow the trajectory of the concept of La Violencia as it developed out of larger political, social, and intellectual contexts, *Forgotten Peace* adopts four interwoven lines of analysis and narration. The first is a focus on politicians, men of letters (*letrados*), and inhabitants of the provinces. Midcentury Colombians conceptualized these actors into separate "countries" (*países*), expressions of Colombia's perceived social divisions. Employing such vernacular categories captures the imaginaries that guided Colombians' public interactions, much as the use of "creole" and "*convivencia*" enables an appreciation of sensibilities toward particular political issues.

The drama of the early National Front period lies less in the telling of a single grand story than in the frictions and convergences that resulted as these different groups of Colombians, each with their own pieces of the larger puzzle, came into contact. This book's chapters all open with one such encounter: the delivery and reception of a speech on agrarian development, a homecoming that led to the writing of an emblematic song, an ambush, and an ill-fated bureaucratic expedition to the countryside. Every encounter demonstrates how social distance or shared regional ancestry could yield misreading or comprehension.[21] Violence and peace impelled urban and rural peoples across Colombia's landscapes, and into contact with each other's images of region and nation.

Scale and space represent the second and third means of analyzing peace and violence. Questions of scale are essential but often overlooked in our study of the past, be it in Latin America or other areas of the world.[22] Recent scholarship on the second half of the twentieth century has emphasized the influence of a "global Cold War" on political and social struggles in Latin America.[23] To be certain, midcentury Colombians frequently pivoted to the level of the global, evoking transnational ideas or reaching out to international backers. But to "assum[e] that the global (or transnational) perspective is relevant and telling" risks overlooking essential components of local, regional, and national experience.[24] *Forgotten Peace* therefore concentrates on these smaller scales. More significantly, in place of a framework that positions local and regional history as national history's opposites, the book emphasizes how these scales intersected at frequent intervals, as Colombians shifted between them rhetorically and physically.

Rethinking the regional scale is particularly meaningful for Colombian history, and brings us to the matter of space. As the longer period of peace begun in the late 1950s came crashing down in the early 1980s, the casualty of an exploding cocaine trade and expanding armed groups, Gonzalo Sánchez and his generation of *letrados* spread out across the country. Blindfolded and driven out of Bogotá under the cover of darkness by mysterious contacts, journalists made the grueling trek to the remote headquarters of the resurgent FARC, an experience that underscored in a visceral fashion the country's dizzying spatial heterogeneity.[25] Academics, and historians in particular, meanwhile commenced a search for the roots and contexts of Colombia's burgeoning crisis, a process of inquiry that entailed a turn to the regions and a return to the idea of La Violencia, the intellectual tool inherited from the *letrados* of the 1960s. Infused with a commitment to resolve the country's predicament, and nourished by rich oral and archival materials related to local political and social life, the ensuing regional literature remains an indispensible guide to twentieth-century Colombia.[26]

While this book builds on such testimonials and regional studies, it also endeavors to escape one of the limitations present in that earlier scholarship's consideration of space. For much of the twentieth century, regional civil and military authorities practiced an exaggerated sovereignty: tightly bound to their jurisdictions, they could not effectively pursue armed groups that constantly moved across administrative borders, striking in one department (*departamento*) before slipping back over the line to relative safety.[27] In largely adhering to departmental boundaries, scholars of Colombia have unintentionally replicated this predicament, missing an opportunity to identify how regional elements contributed to a larger whole, in particular through the mediating role of the central state and other national institutions.

The story of Colombia's forgotten peace is best told against an alternate, vernacular backdrop, one defined by the circulation of people and goods rather than legally prescribed perimeters. The decisive theater for politics in the 1950s and '60s was a macro-region of central and southern Colombia known as Gran (Greater) Tolima. Stretching from the peaks of the central Andean *cordillera* (range), across the valley of the upper Magdalena River, the country's great arterial waterway, to the eastern slope of the eastern Andes—an area roughly the size of the Commonwealth of Pennsylvania or the country of North Korea—Gran Tolima encompasses the present-day departments of Tolima and Huila, together with sections of the neighboring departments of Cauca, Meta, and Caquetá (map 2).[28] If in one sense

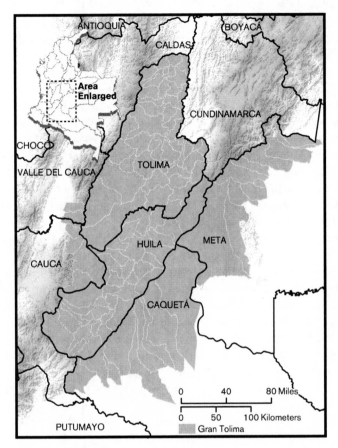

MAP 2. Gran Tolima.

Bogotá's hinterland, Gran Tolima was also composed of a series of overlapping centers and peripheries that stretched from the national capital to provincial capitals, and from there to smaller towns and tiny villages. These, in turn, anchored expanses of farmland and forest—be they occupied by the large-scale, capital-intensive operations in tobacco, rice, and cotton which dominated the lowlands of the Magdalena River plain, the coffee plantings which ruled higher altitudes, or the enormous tracts of unclaimed public lands (*tierras baldías*) which drew settlers (*colonos*) to Gran Tolima's internal agricultural frontiers. Gran Tolima was home to urban and rural spaces, even as the region itself represented a province relative to Bogotá, the nation's political and economic metropolis.

Though its origins as a single administrative unit in the nineteenth century helped to give rise to a common notion of cultural belonging, Gran Tolima was nevertheless far from unified. At the same time that Colombians were casting their ideas and appeals across multiple spatial scales, their encounters over the issue of violence occurred across variegated physical terrain. Ties of economic exchange peeled localities away from their putative administrative capitals, complicating the exercise of political sovereignty. This regional patchwork of social, economic, and political relations was fundamentally linked to topography, to the ways in which Andean escarpments impeded human movement and interaction. Outside of the sunbaked flatlands that immediately surround the Magdalena River, moving through Gran Tolima horizontally was nearly impossible without extensive climbing or descending. To paraphrase the anthropologist Michael Taussig, to contemplate Colombia requires learning to think about space in not two dimensions but four, tracing the Andes's rises and folds, as well as accounting for the ways space stretches the experience of time.[29]

Eager to rebuild their lives and their regions, midcentury Colombians looked to Bogotá and the provincial capitals for the assistance they felt they deserved, both as citizens generally and as victims of violence specifically. Then as now, overcoming the limitations of their physical environment ranked as a priority for Gran Tolima's residents. The chapters that follow are therefore replete with a persistent clamor for new or better roads, projects that would redefine the links between the local, regional, and national by easing the financial and human costs of commerce and governance, or by converting jungle into farmland to the benefit of all Colombians. These calls became all the more insistent by the late 1950s, animated not solely by the imperatives of material devastation, but by the renewed expectation of the state's obligations that followed the democratic opening and first stirrings of the creole peace. In the provocative assessment of historian Herbert Braun, "It is as though the state's often feeble presence made [Colombians] yearn for it all the more."[30]

As the National Front took shape, there was little doubt that the department of Tolima would be the focal point of state and citizen energies directed at the question of violence—"the object of the entire Republic's deepest, most intense, and most effectual concern," as Lleras proclaimed.[31] Abutted by five other departments, adjacent to Bogotá—which meant both the potential for scrutiny from the central state and proximity to radical political influences—Tolima had transformed since the late 1940s from early hotspot to leading theater of disorder. The presence of coffee cultivation in its manifold forms—established small plots in the north; large estates in the east and south; and emergent plots on the demographically dynamic but unruly frontier in the east, west, and furthest south—moreover fostered commensurate varieties of violence, from isolated robbery (which could well reflect Liberal-Conservative antagonisms) to pitched battles involving hundreds of armed fighters.[32] As a British diplomat explained to his superiors in 1958, "Tolima represents in many respects, and in accentuated form, an amalgam of the troubles and problems which affect Colombia as a whole."[33]

While *Forgotten Peace* foregrounds the idea of peace in Colombian history, it also accounts for where and how violence took place (violence-as-practice), and how we inherited the frameworks with which we think about violence (violence-as-idea). These categories of practice and idea are not intended to align with binaries of bottom-up/top-down and rural/urban: as the story of the forgotten peace shows, violence was practiced not only by people of the fields (*campesinos*), but also by the state; and provincial folk thought about their experiences in ways that inspired social scientists.[34] In other words, this book asks the question of how Colombians spoke of violence, and how those ideas and debates influenced and were influenced by the wider political arena.

For urban Colombians, violence seemed primarily a problem of knowledge: before they could hope to eradicate violence as a widespread practice in public life, they first had to comprehend its origins and scope. This process occupies much of chapters 1 and 2, which focus on Alberto Lleras Camargo and Father Germán Guzmán Campos as representatives of the countries of politics and letters. The product of an era in which Colombia had not been associated with violence, Lleras's commitment to partisan *convivencia* helped to engineer Colombia's return to electoral democracy in 1957. The subsequent removal of restrictions on the exchange of information and the exercise of dialogue made easier the task of formulating ideas about violence. In the freer and more expectant atmosphere that followed, men of letters—journalists, lawyers, clerics, military officers, and above all social scientists—could engage in a broad conversation about violence and Colombia's other "national problems." Furthermore, democratization opened the way for Guzmán and other members of the lettered class to journey out to the countryside to survey firsthand how violence had functioned and how it might be resolved. Cumulatively, these acts of talking about and studying violence also introduced new conceptualizations of region and nation. Even the basic step of identifying violence as a *national* problem suggested the instrumental role of violence in nation-making.

Expanding notions of violence-as-idea—realizations about the collective political and economic causes of violence, as well as acknowledgment of its social effects—subsequently catalyzed a campaign toward peace, the subject of chapters 2 and 3. However, as they sought to move Colombia from violence to peace, officials and *letrados* from Bogotá quickly discovered that they did not have a monopoly on violence-as-idea. To borrow a famous description of Colombian politics, the search for solutions reached beyond "conversations among gentlemen" in the capital.[35] The combined weight of economic crisis, a decade of sharp inter-elite feuds over the shape of the Colombian polity and nation, and provincial violence threw open the political system to other players and additional kinds of exchanges. Across the public sphere—in rural village plazas as well as in the formal halls of political power, on the printed page, and over the airwaves—debates over past and present forms of violence shaped state policy. By voicing their own memories of violence, or by choosing to continue employing violence in their public interactions, provincial Colombians enacted a determinant role in the molding of national responses to the question of violence. In the same way that urban Colombians engaged in scaling, drafting fresh schemes of region or nation, provincial Colombians selectively invoked regional identity or national citizenship in order to strengthen their position at the local level. In doing so, they redefined the meaning of each of these scales and the relationship between them.

When Father Guzmán and other representatives of the state arrived in Gran Tolima in 1958, they discovered yet another way in which the region instantiated broader trends. Hundreds of thousands of people there—like hundreds of thousands more throughout Colombia—had been forced to abandon their homes after violence-as-practice began to spread in the mid-1940s onward. In time, the most famous of these *desplazados* (displaced) would be a young man known by many names: Pedro Antonio Marín, Manuel Marulanda Vélez, Tirofijo (Sureshot). A middling provincial Liberal who had found refuge in the ranks of the Colombian Communist Party (Partido Comunista de Colombia), Marulanda would go on to renown as the founder of the FARC. But before that, he figured among the tens of thousands of Colombians from the *país nacional*—that country outside the lettered and political classes—who participated in one way or another in the creole peace. As chapter 3 details, the Lleras administration's political pardon and agrarian lending program extended to frontier Communists such as Marulanda an opportunity to restore their rights and livelihoods. Though Latin American historians have concentrated on the grander utopian visions of geopolitical insurgency and revolutionary politics that took shape after the Cuban revolution of 1959, the crux of Colombian politics remained in these local, regional, and national contexts.

Placing peace alongside violence accordingly entails a sweeping reinterpretation of not only Colombian history but also the Latin American 1960s—ostensibly an era of revolutionary violence. A focus on peace reveals a greater coherence to the words and decisions of well-known historical figures such as Marulanda. At the same time, imagining a history of peace allows for an expanded range of historical actors and repertoires of behavior, beyond those that commonly concern historians of the place known as the Third World. Popular agency, especially in rural settings, is often coded strictly in terms of resistance, be it to the state or landowner interests.[36] Those same political and economic elites receive relatively little examination in local and national histories, despite the fact that, as historian Louise Walker notes, such "historical actors . . . are squarely at the forefront of the extant historical record."[37] The propensity to treat the state and elites in one-dimensional terms is particularly pronounced in Colombian historiography, which portrays the National Front as the end of politics. The pact, historian Marco Palacios writes, "banished controversy": the terms of power sharing reduced election results to a foregone conclusion, while a unified elite class ensured that social reforms would be a nonstarter.[38] The outcome, according to this line of thought, was the perpetuation of violence into the future, as *guerrillas* such as the FARC fought what the group's organizers called an "oligarchy that illegally holds on to power."[39]

Marulanda's changing relationship with the state from the creole peace to the FARC owed much to the mutual transformations of ideas and practices of violence. In key moments of the transition, violence-as-practice in the countryside—particular forms of homicide in specific spatial contexts—intersected with political events in the capital to shape notions of peace and violence. One such instance came about during the very formation of the creole peace in 1959–60, when returning *desplazados* were met with threats and assassination. The ensuing political row over partisan responsibility for the bloodshed prompted a *convivencia*-minded Lleras to placate opposition Conservatives by reducing his administration's outreach to the provinces. Chapter 4 explores how, for Marulanda and others, the consequent change in relations with the government seemed to demand a return to physical force. Yet Marulanda never fully abandoned dialogue, in particular the dialogue offered by the mechanism of law—that "ostensibly neutral medium for people of different cultural worlds, different social endowments, different material circumstances . . . to deal with their conflicts."[40] For still others, the path forward from the creole peace would entail a deepening of social reform.

Although various indicators of violence continued to fall, the practice of peace proceeded differently at the local, regional, and national levels after 1960. In Bogotá, a fresh vision of *convivencia* took hold, the creation of a new class of *letrado*. Led by the thirty-something Fals, social scientists pioneered developmentalist policies that picked up where the Lleras administration's initiatives to "rehabilitate" rural Colombia had left off. By cataloging the country's social realities and designing state agencies to meet the perceived needs of the *país nacional*—thus hopefully eliminating the structural causes of violence—these social scientists advanced their own variant of *convivencia*. Their applied scientific knowledge and role in a growing government apparatus moreover placed them at the forefront of global developmentalism—an ideology advocating state-led programs to improve economic performance and human welfare. The *letrados'* engagement with city and countryside, with the nation and the transnational, is the subject of chapter 5.

Chapter 6 gives the biography of *La violencia en Colombia*, Colombian social science's crowning intellectual achievement of the 1960s. The work's first volume both furnished a new language to describe the violence of the past and shaped the politics of the transition. In addition to publicizing the previously unaired tales of violence and displacement collected by Father Guzmán, *La violencia en Colombia* provided Fals a forum to present novel variants of violence-as-idea. For instance, Fals began to put the term "violence" in quotation marks, a demarcation that resignified it as a temporal category rather than as a generic "technique." However modest a step, it signaled the sort of intellectual experimentation necessary for the evolution of "*la violencia*" into "La Violencia."

La Violencia was also a profound if veiled proclamation of political disenchantment. This thread of Fals and Guzmán's story is woven through the book's final chapters, alongside discussion of changing urban and rural ideas and practices of violence. Contact with Colombia's local communities first exposed Fals and his colleagues to the frustrated expectations set in motion by the promises of democratization and development. The social scientists' sense of their place in the nation received a more dramatic jolt thanks to the release of *La violencia en Colombia*, whose telling of Conservative-led state repression in the 1940s kindled as never before debates over the parties' responsibility for the violence of the recent past. The Conservative idea that violence was rooted in the pathologies of a base rural sector gained wider political and social acceptance thanks to the 1962 concurrence of a frightening form of violence-as-practice with political discussions in Bogotá. However, here practice and ideas entered a more pronounced feedback loop than they had in 1959: as public opinion decried "bandit" attacks that seemed to threaten the moral precepts and geographic linkages that made Colombia a country, dialogue and reform lost currency as potential policies. More and more, violence seemed a constant in Colombia's recent past. The creole peace became increasingly transformed into a forgotten peace.

Colombia's transition thus reached a crucial juncture in 1962. Electoral politics, academic theories about violence, and events in the countryside all collided to alter the linkages between politicians, *letrados,* and rural folk that had constituted the creole peace. Although peace did not come to an end in 1962, its meaning came increasingly under question at various scales. Already embittered by the toll that Conservative politicking was exacting on their development work, Fals and Guzmán began to turn away from public life, a process reflected in the concepts they coined after 1964. A set of *letrados* within the Colombian military meanwhile spearheaded new policies that aspired to put a definitive end to collective violence in Gran Tolima. The final two chapters of this book outline how, even where this "banditry" did not directly erode local and regional forms of *convivencia,* military-led pacification between 1962 and 1964 often stripped out the hopefulness present in the creole peace of the previous years.

Chapter 7 concentrates on the place of Colombian Communism within the redefinition of democracy, *convivencia,* and reform in the countryside. The construction of the FARC out of this convergence would cement Marulanda's status as Colombia's best-known frontier Communist. However, Marulanda exemplified but one of many possible paths for Gran Tolima's Communists between 1962 and 1965. In concert with regional elites, Bogotá's social scientists, and select military officers, many of Marulanda's comrades chased peaceable solutions to displacement and development until the end.

The absence of these actors and repertoires from accounts of the FARC's creation highlights a final step in the creole peace's fade from memory. As the product of Marulanda's alienation from the National Front experiment, the FARC's formation represented a rural counterpart to Fals's La Violencia. At times, the frontier Communists' grievances signaled a desire for self-directed livelihoods, as well as for respect, objectives that these men shared with countless other country people in Colombia. Yet the elevation of Gran Tolima's disparate Communists to the level of the international and national (*Revolutionary* Armed Forces *of Colombia*) also required a minimization of Marulanda's own history during Colombia's transition, in subordination to the message of "revolution" brought by a handful of Communist *letrados* from the city. The experience of Colombia's midcentury peace ultimately generated ideas of unceasing violence that concealed the very possibility of transition.

Forgotten Peace offers a Colombian vantage on global processes of transition, development, and knowledge formation in the 1950s and '60s. It reveals the human history behind our categories of understanding, the embeddedness of ideas in specific social formations. The mid- to late 1960s are famed in global consciousness for the decision of some historical actors to formulate radical critiques, if not to drop out of politics entirely.[41] But less examined in Latin America and elsewhere is how those actors' scholarly authority or influence in political life has fundamentally framed our approach to the contemporary world.[42]

La Violencia is one such inheritance. Critics of the National Front have long panned the coalition as a "pact of forgetting" which foreclosed the possibility of meaningful conversations about midcentury violence.[43] Yet to the extent it ever existed in practice, that pact took shape not in 1958 but in 1962, when the controversy around *La violencia en Colombia* prompted political and lettered elites to seek a change in the rules of politics. And as Argentine sociologist Elizabeth Jelin argues, "Slogans such as 'memory against oblivion'... hide an opposition between distinct and rival memories."[44] The idea of La Violencia was indeed encoded with memories, specifically the sense of loss felt by Orlando Fals Borda and his colleagues. The democratic opening of the late 1950s created accounts of the recent past that represented a closing in terms of memory, as social scientists imperceptibly erected an enduring version of national history.

Reconstructing the genealogy of La Violencia out of the encounters of urban and rural Colombians grants a voice to the men and women of the *país nacional* whose lives and deaths are partially concealed by both the term "La Violencia" and the FARC's telling of its origins. Country folk, no less than intellectuals and government officials, directed Colombia's debates over peace and violence. Their struggles, and the effects these had on the direction of national life, populate much of this book. In any given moment, they chose violence or peace—a decision that Colombians currently face with renewed intensity as they speak seriously once more of peace. Many of the issues that Colombia now contemplates—the place of victims' voices in reconciliation, the resolution of forced displacement, the payment of reparations for losses suffered—have their parallels in history, however seldom remembered these are. The tale of "how peace was made" in the 1950s and '60s suggests the fragility of any attempt to move beyond violence, but to an even greater extent, its potential.

Messenger of a New Colombia

The morning's scenes offered a living tableau of the interpretation that he was about to deliver, a portrait of a nation "unbalanced in space . . . [and] in time."[1] Alberto Lleras Camargo had commenced the two-hundredth day of his presidency with a tour through the sprawling hillside complex of Popular Cultural Action (ACPO; Acción Cultural Popular), the Colombian Catholic Church's most dynamic social initiative. Before viewing the facility's state-of-the-art radio equipment, the technological heart of ACPO's educational and spiritual outreach, Lleras met with a select group of young rural leaders who had come to ACPO's classrooms from across Colombia's Andean heartland. Their stories of home, of communities beset by sickness and isolation, and their aspirations for uplift, underscored for Lleras the necessity of national solidarity with the countryside. "You all," he remarked, "are the messengers of a new Colombia, the Colombia that we all vehemently desire."[2]

We have no record of what the largely anonymous students whom Lleras addressed made of his words. But the speech that Lleras recited later that day—on the obligations that government, large landowners, and *campesinos* had to one another; on their collective task of leveling the nation's inequities—roused excited comment in various corners of Colombia's social and physical landscape. Broadcast through the air by ACPO's powerful transmitters, and in print by many of the country's leading publications, within a matter of days Lleras' speech entered public consciousness as a penetrating summation of the president's agenda.[3] For a struggling but socially minded landowner in the coffee zones of southern Caldas, Lleras's words rejuvenated hope that bureaucrats would concede to his designs for a land reform in miniature. One of Colombia's most distinguished lawyers took

Lleras's talk of responsibility as a rallying cry for his profession, an invitation to "throw ourselves into the task of promoting better understanding between all citizens, whose equal rights are frequently prone to violation by . . . elements whose [sole] rationale is force."[4]

The setting and the diffusion of Lleras's oration signaled, no less than did the content of his message, the negation of force and a confirmation of rights. For the better part of the preceding decade, Colombia's legislative institutions had lain dormant, shuttered under a constitutional state of siege that at times also silenced the country's press. Lleras's weekend tour through the highlands northeast of Bogotá, culminating in his appearance at ACPO, reaffirmed Colombia's recent emergence from this authoritarianism. As Lleras's retinue rubbed elbows with ACPO's cassocked priests under a brilliant Andean sky, the president carved out time to speak with delegates of the recently reconvened local municipal council.[5] If Lleras's visit substantiated the deep relationship between the Catholic Church and the Colombian state, so too did his presence and words recast that Sunday in February as a celebration of temporal power and an expanding, democratic public sphere.

Before reconstructing the story of the creole peace, this book first introduces the larger tale of Colombian politics. Few figures were as closely linked to the arc of the twentieth century—not solely the changing fortunes of administrations or parties, but also the relationship between words and power—as Alberto Lleras. Part of a generation of lettered Colombians who did not initially conceive of their nation as a place of violence, Lleras labored to maintain *convivencia* in Colombian public life as well as global diplomacy. The shepherd of Colombia's democratization and the primary exponent of the reformist possibilities that accompanied the transition, Alberto Lleras emerged in the late 1950s as the paramount messenger of a new Colombia (figure 1). But just as Lleras's path indicated the will of many Colombians to move beyond force in all their affairs, so too did it expose the limits of urban Colombians' engagement with the countryside—a divergence at the heart of struggles over violence, peace, and nation.

THE LIFE AND TIMES OF ALBERTO LLERAS CAMARGO, 1906–1947

When Colombian Liberals spoke of politics, they commonly invoked two lexicons. The first was the language of party, which identified Colombians as belonging to the Liberal and Conservative parties, the two great collectivities of public life. The second lexicon became popularized in the middle third of the twentieth century by the Liberal politician Jorge Eliécer Gaitán. Even as he operated within the bipartisan logic, Gaitán's humble origins led him to conceive of Colombia as divided into distinct corporate bodies. The largest of these, the *país nacional*, represented the popular, organic nation. The destiny of this authentic Colombia was

FIGURE 1. Alberto Lleras Camargo, 1962. *El Tiempo.*

in turn steered by the *país político,* the gentlemanly country of politics that ruled from the halls of power in Bogotá.[6]

Though Gaitán never spoke of it, it is possible to discern a third division within his schema. The *país letrado,* the lettered country, was the smallest of the three, a virtual subset of the country of politics. Like their brethren in the *país político,* the writers, journalists, and lawyers of the *país letrado* idolized the capacity of words both to describe and to transform the world around them. Working in different genres, from the printed newspaper page to the composition and exercise of the law, these men slid fluidly in and out of the *país político* as circumstance and personal predilection dictated.[7]

Alberto Lleras Camargo straddled the border between these countries of letters and politics. In the estimation of Colombia's most famous journalist-turned-writer, Gabriel García Márquez—a native of the Caribbean coast who normally possessed little patience for the upland *país político*—Lleras was "a great writer who was twice president of the Republic."[8] Yet Lleras started life distant from even the *país letrado.* Born on the hardscrabble outskirts of Bogotá in 1906, Lleras ultimately relied on a family birthright to escape his parents' "nomadic poverty." While Alberto's father Felipe toiled on the marginal lands of rented farms, other relatives carried on the family vocation as schoolteachers. With Felipe's death in 1915, these uncles and cousins eased Alberto's entry into the capital city and its lettered circles. This move to the heart of Bogotá, which Colombians styled the "Athens of South America," allowed Alberto to immerse himself in the written word. As he later described, he now had the opportunity to indulge already evident "literary passions" that otherwise "would have drowned amidst *haciendas* [estates] and country chores."[9]

In addition to learning alongside the children of the *país político* in Bogotá's best schools, Alberto gained familiarity with the intertwined histories of his family, party, and nation. Alberto's grandfather, Lorenzo María Lleras, had entered politics in the late 1820s as a devotee of Francisco de Paula Santander, Colombia's hero of independence and early president. Over subsequent decades, Lorenzo María's attachment matured into a deep identification with the Liberal Party, which claimed descent from Santander. At the same time, however, Lorenzo María stayed largely apart from the civil wars that consumed many Liberals and Conservatives, instead embodying the civic tradition associated with Santander. From prolonged stints in newspaper publishing and education, Lorenzo María evolved into a man of laws in his own right. His hand showed in the 1851 abolition of slavery and the establishment of church-state separation in the 1863 constitution—two of the Liberal Party's signature accomplishments of the nineteenth century.[10]

As he contemplated Lorenzo María Lleras's legacies, the young Alberto also had to face up to the final act of Colombia's nineteenth century. The War of a Thousand Days, which ended four years before Alberto's birth, had confirmed the Conservatives' unmaking of Lorenzo María's Colombia. In the 1880s, the Conservative Party overturned the 1863 constitution, imposing—in alliance with the Catholic Church—a new order that survived an armed challenge from the Liberals at the turn of the century. The Liberals' defeat in the War of a Thousand Days left the party largely excluded from national political life, and the Lleras family consigned to posts on the lower rungs of the education system.[11]

Such political strictures helped to funnel Alberto Lleras into the *país letrado*. However, his decision to turn to journalism was ultimately his own. In an echo of his grandfather's precocity, Lleras published his first newspaper article before his eighteenth birthday. Within two years, further displays of mettle won Lleras a paid position at *El Espectador,* one of the two main newspapers associated with the Liberal Party. The arrangement opened doors for the thin, unassuming teenager, plunging him deeper into the newspaper scene and bringing him into contact with influential politicians. He simultaneously emerged as a spokesman for his "new" generation of *letrados, los nuevos,* who sought to infuse the country's intellectual and political currents with novel styles in order to "[raise public life] above small ambitions and crude appetites."[12] After four decades, the so-called "Conservative hegemony" appeared decadent and ripe for critique.

Other sectors of Liberalism meanwhile geared for a more frontal challenge against Conservative rule. This position's maximum proponent was Alfonso López Pumarejo, the scion of a top Colombian banking clan. López's life tightly tracked the era's politics: his birth preceded the centralist constitution of 1886 by mere months, and by the 1920s his political activism fed into the growing travails of the Conservative regime. When the 1930 presidential contest came into view, López dared his party to discard its recent policy of electoral abstention and take on the Conservatives. Lleras received a preview of this argument when he met with López in Paris in 1929. Lleras had left Colombia for Buenos Aires two years earlier in search of new journalistic frontiers. The success he made for himself abroad only increased his stock back home. By the time of his conversation with López, the Liberals' flagship newspaper, El Tiempo, had already extended him an offer to return. The combination of personal entreaties from Eduardo Santos, the paper's editor, and López proved irresistible. The twenty-three-year old Lleras, whom El Tiempo hailed as "perhaps the most brilliant representative of the young Colombian intellectual generation," returned to take his place in the countries of letters and politics.[13]

Lleras found Colombia in the midst of monumental changes. Months after his homecoming, the Liberal presidential candidate beat a divided Conservative field, returning the Liberal Party to power for the first time in nearly half a century. To Lleras, this epochal shift paled next to the accelerating pace of history itself. If his semi-rural childhood had recalled the sixteenth century, and stories of his grandfather the nineteenth, after 1930 Lleras perceived the twentieth century developing in earnest. The unequal distribution of industrialization and urbanization—what Lleras's ACPO speech would call "a disequilibrium in space . . . [and] in time"— quickly emerged as one of his central preoccupations.[14] These would be, moreover, essential problems in the quest for development throughout Latin America.

Though the advent of a historical disjuncture after 1930 disquieted Lleras, he found solace in another conception of time. Lleras reckoned that national life moved through an unbreaking sequence of generations. The inception of the "Liberal Republic" in 1930 and Alfonso López Pumarejo's election four years later signified the ascension of López's generation, one senior to Lleras's. Yet López overwhelmingly turned to los nuevos to direct his reformist project, dubbed the "Revolution on the March" (Revolución en Marcha). Looking years afterward at a 1935 photograph of López with his cabinet, García Márquez observed that none of the nine ministers equaled the age of the forty-eight-year old López, who "possess[ed] the mischievous air of a precocious father among his illegitimate sons."[15]

For the young men of letters and politics in that photograph, the Revolution on the March presented a chance to put their impulse for national renovation into practice. In his memoirs, Lleras remembered these years with López as "the best

part of my life, without any doubt." To borrow a later formulation of García Márquez's, "Liberalism . . . [became] not simply a political party but rather a mentality,
a new point of view toward the nation's problems." "Back then, we had a feeling . . .
of [r]enaissance," Lleras admitted. "We saw ourselves resuming the legacy of the
golden days of struggle against colonialism, fanaticism, the dullness and tarnish
on Colombian life . . . [it] was an inversion [of decades of Conservative custom]."[16]

Lleras's enthusiasm stemmed in part from López's preferred methods. "He
loathed physical force in the affairs of state and never resorted to it outside of [gov-
ernment]," Lleras explained in his 1959 eulogy for López.[17] Adopting a strategy that
called to Lleras's mind the best traditions of their party, the Revolution on the
March followed legislative avenues to transformation. A 1936 constitutional reform
revived the state's separation from the Catholic Church, while also fundamentally
expanding the state's powers relative to society and the economy. In response to
mobilization by urban and rural workers, the governments of the Liberal Republic
had already commenced debate on labor and agrarian reform. The constitutional
reform now defined work and landed property in terms of their contribution to the
social good, granting the state the legal authority to structure market relations.[18] To
Lleras, these steps marked the fulfillment of priorities fit for the twentieth century.

Though generational disagreements on these precepts restricted the content
and real-world reach of Liberal reforms, they did nothing to impede Lleras's rap-
port with López.[19] Lleras was unchallenged as López's most faithful disciple; their
relationship ranked as the most influential of Lleras's life. Under López's tutelage,
Lleras greatly enlarged his portfolio of activities in the *país político*. To be certain,
the president enlisted Lleras's clarity of thought and prose in conventional tasks.
As López's secretary within the Liberal Party early in the 1930s, and then within
the presidential palace, Lleras continued to hammer away at a typewriter on
speeches and policy declarations. He also advanced López's platform by periodi-
cally stepping back into the editorial rooms of Liberal newspapers.[20]

The real maturation came in Lleras's facility with the spoken word. In 1931,
Lleras was elected to Congress and then selected to preside over the House of Representatives. His interventions before his colleagues benefited as much from his
carefully crafted statements as from his authoritative speaking style. Lleras's slight
frame belied a surprisingly forceful baritone voice enhanced by the precise, classic
Spanish diction of Bogotá. President López put this attribute to good use, too, by
twice appointing Lleras as his interior minister (the youngest in Colombian history). Lleras thus became, in addition to the head of the state's most important
ministry, the face of the administration's actions before Congress and the public.[21]

Lleras commenced a final pursuit in the 1930s, one that combined his dedication
to civil political exchange and legal frameworks. Beginning in 1933, at the same
conference where Franklin D. Roosevelt announced his Good Neighbor policy,
Lleras attended hemispheric congresses contemplating changes to the existing

pan-American system. Lleras's time in Argentina had awakened an interest in inter-Americanism, a principle whose legal mechanisms were now being formalized. In the words of Lleras's primary biographer, exposure to this making of international diplomacy and law made Lleras into "the Good Neighbor" par excellence. Lleras saw national sovereignty and non-aggression as extensions of the democratic ideals he was working for within Colombia. Inter-Americanism therefore became another of his abiding concerns; in time, Lleras would become a foundational, global figure in the movement for regional solidarity and cooperation.[22]

For Liberals of Lleras's generation, exposure to the wider world in the 1930s and '40s served to bolster the notion of Colombia and the Americas as a space of peace. Observing firsthand the rising tide of unfreedom in Europe sharpened these *letrados'* notions of nationhood. Writing in his journal from Berlin in late August 1939, Gregorio Hernández de Alba, a boyhood classmate of Lleras's who had come to Europe to study ethnography, reflected that "never before in any city have I felt myself to be such a stranger . . . A stranger because of the language, because of the spirit. . . . In the back-and-forth of European politics, in the lack of conscience of these civilized peoples, in the tragedy that is upon us, that weighs on the air and on my Colombia, my wild America, where we still have peace, where we still live freely without obstruction, where the ethics and morality of people still have meaning."[23] This was a romantic portrait of Latin America, grounded in urban lifeways. But Hernández de Alba's understanding of peace was entirely suited to the cresting wave of democratic, Liberal politics in Colombia.

And even in the global calamity that followed, Alberto Lleras remained fixed on the possibilities of peace. In early 1945, he embarked on the most frenetic months of his overseas career. With the end of the world war in sight, Latin American representatives gathered in Mexico City to discuss "problems of war and peace." The February conference was in many regards a rehearsal for the founding meeting of the United Nations, scheduled for San Francisco just weeks later. Indeed, for Lleras—head of the Colombian delegation—plans for the United Nations overshadowed the Mexico City proceedings. Though they would fail to win over enough votes to halt the Allied powers' domination over the U.N., the Colombian delegation eventually succeeded in adding language to the U.N. Charter that privileged "pacific settlement of local disputes through . . . regional arrangements or . . . regional agencies"—the possibility of a hemispheric iteration of "the universal system of peace and security."[24] Enshrined in international law, the inter-American system could endure in the postwar world.

The situation back in Colombia remained close to Lleras's thoughts throughout this exhausting stretch of months. Mexico City's thin mountain air and San Francisco's morning fog injected small reminders of Bogotá into the conference proceedings. As he went about drafting a public summary of the U.N. delegation's accomplishments, Lleras made sure to incorporate an admonition to the *país político.* "Nothing will prosper," he warned, "in an atmosphere of personalist, aggressive politics, where cooperation and collective labors are considered humiliating acts and rebellion is held in the highest public esteem." "Colombia has been advancing until now a foreign policy born . . . directly from its internal politics," Lleras concluded, "and it would be a grievous catastrophe for this republic, the better portion of its international aspirations for law, peace, justice, and security fulfilled, to have that foreign policy no longer coincide with the domestic, destroyed and disrupted by periodic convulsions."[25]

Lleras's accusations cast a broad critique. He certainly had in mind anti-López Liberals, who had cooled the reforms of the Revolution on the March.[26] However, to a greater extent, Lleras's words targeted the Conservative most associated with the polarization settling into the country of politics. Laureano Gómez was in many ways his party's foil to López: three years younger than López, Laureano also caused political headaches for the creaky Conservative regime of the early 1920s. Common cause against the political establishment had in fact prompted a young Lleras, at López's urging, to make his first political speech a public defense of Gómez.[27]

The 1930s brought out a very different Gómez. Known for his fiery style and a personality sufficiently forceful to grant him first-name recognition, Laureano gained a new moniker early in the Liberal Republic: "The Monster." The reforms of López's Revolution on the March redoubled the firestorm of criticism that Laureano and other prominent Conservatives unleashed after their party's 1930 electoral defeat. Taking an opposite approach from Hernández de Alba, Conservatives projected the clash between right and left extremisms in Europe onto events in Colombia, reading the Revolution on the March as a vehicle for Communist infiltration. From the pages of his newspaper *El Siglo,* Laureano issued forth a constant stream of denunciations, attacking López's government on everything from Conservative voting rights to the president's personal finances.[28]

The possibility of a second López presidency ignited Laureano's most unbridled fulminations. As Lleras put it afterward, Laureano threatened "civil war if the [Liberal] candidate selected is not satisfactory to Conservatism. Civil war if the constitution of 1936 is not abrogated. Civil war if guarantees to Colombia's workers are not terminated. Civil war if, in the end, the Conservative Party is not allowed to govern the Republic as it pleases." The intimidation continued through the remainder of 1940. From New York, where he had lived since leaving office in 1938, López worried to Lleras that Laureano's latest statements sought "to provoke and excuse in advance an [assassination] attempt against my person."[29] Violence threatened to reach into the highest levels of the *país político.*

In spite of López's resulting hesitation, the residue of past ambition—combined with the encouragement of devoted partisans like Lleras—proved weighty enough to pull him back into Colombian politics. López cruised to an easy reelection in 1942. Doubts and regrets nonetheless resurfaced rapidly. The social bases of the

Revolution on the March, never consolidated in the 1930s, turned on López as he sought to manage the world war's economic and political repercussions by tacking to the center. From the right, Laureano and the Conservatives afforded the president no quarter, pummeling him on a pair of alleged scandals. Chastened, López sought to resign. When Congress rejected this attempt, López requested leave from the presidency, hoping that his temporary departure from the political scene would calm the situation.[30]

The government's difficulties instead mounted. "It seems to me that we are rapidly entering into the national crisis that we have spent so much time discussing," López said to Lleras in a February 1944 cable from New York. After Congress again denied López the possibility of permanent exit, he had little choice but to reassume the presidency in May 1944. His presence detonated Colombia's conspiratorial atmosphere; when López traveled to the southwestern city of Pasto in July, mutinous army units squirreled him away.[31]

In Bogotá, pro-López forces in the government scrambled to contain this unprecedented military challenge to civilian authority. Darío Echandía, the stately forty-eight-year-old Tolima native who had held power during López's self-imposed exile, once more assumed the mantle of constitutional authority. Lleras hurried down from Medellín, and an hour after nightfall took to the radio to read statements of loyalty from senior military officers. So commanding was Lleras's performance, so reassuring his voice, that decades later García Márquez remembered Lleras as having "maintained the country in an air of calm and confidence throughout the entire day, until the rebellion was defeated."[32]

The aura of credibility that surrounded Lleras during the Pasto uprising soon translated into unanticipated responsibility. Colombia's democracy survived an armed threat only to fall victim to the worst vices of the country of politics: with the 1946 election approaching, and López politically debilitated, Liberal Party leaders turned their attentions almost exclusively to the presidential contest. Amidst this internal discord, in July 1945 Liberals in Congress finally consented to López's third offer of resignation. To replace him, they selected Lleras, fresh off his triumph in San Francisco. Even as he solemnly assumed the presidential sash, Lleras remained an outsider, a Liberal who brought a proven capacity to govern mixed with an evident aversion to the *país político*'s politicking ways.[33]

Just past his fortieth birthday, Lleras contemplated an impossible task: to serve as president in a labyrinth of others' making. The impartiality expected of him amplified his own high standards, leaving him with a feeling of total isolation. Moreover, as Lleras confided to Eduardo Santos, the Liberals' divisions left the Conservative Party with its "best opportunities since 1930." Lleras stood adamant that his government would afford the Conservatives every possible guarantee. "They will get them," he told Santos, "even if it costs me my life. And at the very least, I am conscious that it will cost me my reputation among my co-partisans.

I will also do everything necessary to guarantee a peaceful transition of power, if [the Conservatives] win."[34]

Win the Conservatives did. Though the Liberals outpolled the Conservative Party by more than 230,000 votes, the split Liberal presidential ticket ceded the outcome to the opposition. Though they retained control of Congress and the judiciary, Liberals had suffered their own 1930. However, to Lleras's shock, the peaceful transition of power seemed a reality. In a radio address three days after the election, Lleras simultaneously implored his countrymen to eschew acts of force and congratulated them for their upstanding behavior to date. Allowing himself some of the rhetorical adornment that had long since disappeared from his writing, Lleras ended by saying that "it is as if assuming accidental representation of the Motherland [Patria] makes one better, more thoroughly, connect with it, in its dazzling grandeur."[35] The concerns which Lleras had expressed ahead of the election morphed into a cautious optimism that appealed to what Lleras saw as Colombians' best instincts.

By contrast, Lleras's fatalistic prediction about his own fate came to pass. Blame for the Liberal defeat cascaded down on the outgoing president, as prominent party members denounced Lleras for capitulating to the Conservatives and not using the mechanisms of government as instruments to perpetuate Liberal power. His public persona battered and his duty fulfilled, Lleras immediately commenced his retreat from the country of politics. After founding *Semana*, a pioneering national weekly news magazine, Lleras received an offer to head the Pan-American Union. The disconnect between Colombia's internal and external politics that Lleras had identified in San Francisco seemed wider than ever. Lleras therefore shifted scales, decamping from Bogotá to Washington to take up the work of building "democracy between nations."[36]

THE RELUCTANT EXILE, 1947–1957

More than at any other time of his life, over the remainder of the 1940s Alberto Lleras lived as a citizen of the Americas. The intense pace of building hemispheric institutions provided a welcome distraction from affairs back home. Lleras had, besides, few sources of information to draw upon. The 1946 election left the Liberal Party in disarray, leading many notables to join Lleras in exile. Domestic and international newspapers similarly remained transfixed on the country's high political drama.[37] Lleras's urban myopia was thus of a piece with that of the *país político*.

Outside of Bogotá's gaze, the 1946 election had unleashed energies quite contrary to those acclaimed by Lleras before his departure. Across Andean Colombia, provincial Conservatives seized on their party's resumption of power to settle scores with local Liberals. The highest concentration of these clashes erupted in the highlands that stretch northeast from Bogotá some three hundred miles to the Venezuelan border, an area where Conservatives had been subjected to similar treatment by jubilant Liberals at the end of the Conservative hegemony in 1930. However, the new Conservative terror came to far surpass any antecedent. It furthermore became more systematic as midterm elections approached, and departmental and local Conservative political appointees opted to rig the results through violent forms of electioneering. Rural Liberals found their political lives increasingly flattened, as Conservative officials and their deputized civilian posses blocked Liberals from entering town centers on election days, stripped them of their citizenship cards, and subjected them to outright beatings and assassinations.[38]

Usually at arm's length, these two worlds—the diplomatic sphere occupied by Lleras, with its consecration of ideals of mutual security, and a burgeoning violence-as-practice in provincial Colombia—collided spectacularly in 1948. In early April, Lleras and the cream of the Americas' political and diplomatic elite arrived in Bogotá to formalize a new inter-American alliance. Representatives of the twenty-one American nations ultimately did arrive at a charter for the Organization of American States (OAS). Violence nevertheless interrupted the proceedings: early in the afternoon of April 9, just blocks north of the capitol, a gunman fired four bullets into Jorge Eliécer Gaitán. Lleras's one-time companion in the literary groups that nurtured *los nuevos,* Gaitán had become Colombia's most thrilling politician, the rare figure whose language aspired to transcend the basic cleavage of party. It had been Gaitán's insurgent candidacy that tipped the 1946 election in favor of the Conservatives; and until April 9 it was Gaitán who seemed to be the future of the Liberal Party.[39]

In response to their idol's death, Bogotá's popular classes—Gaitán's *país nacional*—took to the streets to express their grief and rage, burning, smashing, and looting central Bogotá. In towns up and down the rest of the country, radical Liberals and militants from smaller left parties lashed out at the symbols of Conservative rule and Catholic authority. The net result was a dramatic escalation in the scope of violence, as Conservative police and paramilitary forces meted out revenge against what they more and more saw as godless, upstart Liberals. Violence extended into even the *país político,* which—Laureano Gómez notwithstanding—had managed to preserve a modicum of its old, orderly rules. Liberal collaboration with the Conservative government, begun in 1946 and reinscribed in the confused aftermath of the Gaitán assassination, frayed as the 1950 presidential election approached. A shootout on the floor of Congress seventeen months after Gaitán's death left one Liberal representative dead and another, who had been in Mexico City with Lleras, with a mortal wound through his leg.[40]

The unsustainable timbre of Colombian politics jolted Alberto Lleras into a rare intervention from abroad. "For three years I have kept silent on the Colombian political situation," the OAS secretary general wrote from his Washington office in the aftermath of the firefight. "The position with which the American governments honor me and honor Colombia obliges me to not interfere in the political struggle, which in spite of its rare violence nonetheless developed within constitutional channels and with good prospects for a normal outcome. Today this situation appears to have changed." Lleras implored Colombians to rise above the Liberal-Conservative rift by forming an "unyielding and majoritarian party of patriots" that would "halt those who enact violence" and stave off "catastrophe."[41] Lleras's political inheritance—the legacy of laws imparted by his grandfather and the aversion to violence that marked Alberto as a child of the early twentieth century—seemed at grave risk. At the same time, however, that same set of convictions beckoned as a path out of the fearful night of partisan conflict.

Where Lleras dreamed of bipartisan cooperation, party leaders enmeshed in the thick of the political fight considered only partisan advantage. In order to overcome the Liberals' continued if shrinking congressional majority, which threatened him with impeachment, President Mariano Ospina Pérez carried out a constitutional coup against his own rule in early November 1949. By closing Congress and other public bodies, this declaration of a state of siege paved the way for one-party rule. Laureano won an uncontested presidential election a short time later. With the "high-priest of political sectarianism" in control of his party and the state, the situation in the countryside deteriorated markedly; a later survey calculated that fifty thousand people died in 1950. Not only did violence against Liberals spike, but in far-flung pockets of the country, an armed Liberal resistance began to take shape.[42] Writing after his first visit to Colombia a little over a decade later, British historian Eric Hobsbawm ventured that Colombia had experienced "what is probably the greatest armed mobilization of peasants (as guerillas [sic], brigands or self-defence groups) in the recent history of the western hemisphere."[43] The Colombia that Lleras had known was no more.

Lleras meanwhile remained absorbed by his duties in Washington. The censorship regime imposed by the state of siege placed additional limits on news coming out of Colombia. "I haven't learned anything distinct from the press clippings [a contact] sent me," Lleras explained to Eduardo Santos in early 1952. Reflecting on the ideas of violence presented in *El Siglo*, Lleras added that "I saw the . . . editorial which divides the country between the bandits and the good guys, and which two days later gets corrected. I can't figure out for myself what happened and I see from what *El Tiempo* says that no one can explain it there either."[44]

Lleras found himself torn. On the one hand, he styled himself an "exile . . . from public life," swearing to a Liberal colleague that "I have the irrevocable intention to not return to active political participation in the rest of my days." On the other hand, Lleras had never shed the patriotic wistfulness that had compelled him to abandon Buenos Aires in his twenties. This feeling was only made worse by Colombia's diversion into authoritarianism. "I am obsessed with the idea of returning," he wrote to Santos in the closing hours of 1952. "I feel obligated to do something." The germ of an idea was coming into being: Lleras envisioned what he termed "democratic education . . . partaking in the reestablishment of new conditions by means of a constant contribution to the formation of a democratic public opinion."[45] The country of letters presented Lleras with a means of correcting what seemed Colombia's deviant course.

A confluence of fortuitous happenstance and ill omen eventually opened the way for Lleras to reenter Colombia. Content at having guided the OAS through its inaugural six years, Lleras used the American states' 1954 gathering—their first since Bogotá—to announce his resignation. At roughly the same time, the recently founded University of the Andes in Bogotá invited Lleras to assume its rectorship. Though Lleras had originally foreseen journalism as the best avenue to repay his outstanding debt to Colombia, he happily accepted the offer. According to one of Lleras's biographers, the former president and international statesman "[thought] he had finally found the lost paradise of his youth." As the university expanded its footprint on a verdant, hilly "corner of Bogotá," Lleras shared with a confidant that "all this has me extraordinarily excited." Fund-raising for the school moreover introduced Lleras to top Colombian industrialists, a connection that would later bear fruit at a critical juncture.[46]

Political changes at the national level further enabled Lleras's reappearance in Bogotá. Laureano's aspirations to redesign the constitution along corporatist lines, as well as his refusal to rein in militant provincial Conservatives, had triggered a military coup in June 1953. The new government of General Gustavo Rojas Pinilla portrayed this intervention in politics as a temporary measure. Its initial pledges to curtail partisan fighting, end the state of siege, and return the country to democratic constitutional rule ensured it the support of sectors of the Conservative Party, as well as the Liberal leadership.[47] Within the year, Rojas made good on his word through amnesty policies that attracted tens of thousands of combatants, many of whom demobilized in dramatic public ceremonies. Large swaths of the country, above all on the Eastern Plains (Llanos Orientales), enjoyed a newfound calm.[48]

Whatever these initial achievements, Rojas's image as the purveyor of justice and peace floundered over the course of 1955. The government first made clear to the nation that the state of siege would in fact remain in place indefinitely, as a means to ensure peace and the enactment of the popular will. It then organized the grandest yet most absurd conventional military campaign attempted since the onset of interparty strife. In response to reports that fighters associated with the Colombian Communist Party had concentrated in the mountainous eastern Tolima county (*municipio*) of Villarrica, the Colombian Armed Forces evacuated much of the civilian population before unleashing tanks and the military's own napalm concoction against entrenched local fighters. Despite the government's vastly superior firepower, the offensive bogged down, generating ever larger casualties. With the government facing a security crisis of its own choosing, Rojas dissimulated: even as the government claimed success in Tolima, it cited the recrudescence of partisan conflict as a reason to perpetuate the state of siege.[49] It similarly used *El Tiempo*'s reporting on violence as an excuse to order the newspaper's closure.[50]

If Alberto Lleras had been able to stomach the thought of living under Rojas's rule, the expanding curtailment of democracy pushed him to revoke his vows to himself. Barely a year had passed since his return to Colombia, but in the last months of 1955 the former president stepped back into the public spotlight. Shaking the rust off his pen, Lleras rejoined the pages of *El Espectador.*[51] Through a series of smartly vitriolic and thoughtfully reflective columns, he took the government (whose head he rarely mentioned by name) to task for its excesses. Authoritarianism exacted a heavy toll on Colombia, Lleras argued. Rojas's increasingly personalist government was "incompatible" with nearly every desirable institution and practice: "A free press . . . the parties . . . public corporations [i.e., legislatures] . . . moderate budgets . . . a level commercial balance . . . the nation's foreign prestige . . . And so, one by one," Lleras reckoned, "the ills that the nation feels and bitterly bears, match with the strict necessities of the regime."[52]

Lleras reserved his harshest criticism for Rojas's abuse of emergency powers. Lleras's time away from politics prompted no small amount of soul-searching, particularly regarding his own experience with the state of siege. President López's 1944 abduction had also triggered the declaration of a state of siege, which Lleras and other officials prolonged for three additional months in order to give Congress time to consider all the emergency decrees issued during the crisis. Mortified that the Rojas government now cited this extension as precedent, Lleras admitted in December 1955 that he had "arrived at the conviction that what we did [in 1944] was wrong . . . it opened a fissure for the entrance of a State of Siege without any limits."[53] His generation of Liberals' "contribution to the contemporary history of Colombia," Lleras wrote mournfully, "is a sole institution, imposed on a pained and frightened nation: the State of Siege."[54] This self-reflection would fundamentally orient Lleras's approach to democracy and violence after his eventual return to politics.

In the meantime, his earlier political career took on a different valence. What had been a liability in 1946 evolved by 1956 into an asset. Their options for political action increasingly constrained, Lleras's fellow Liberals now saw virtue in his commitment to dealing with the Conservatives. At a March 1956 political convention, Liberals selected Lleras as the party's sole leader. His mission would be to seek rapprochement with the Conservatives, on terms suggested by Alfonso López Pumarejo, who was himself enjoying renewed viability within the party.[55]

Though his reentry into the *país político* was complete, Lleras expressed no remorse. He had, after all, received his copartisans' consent to pursue the "party of patriots" that he had called for in 1949. And, improbably, there were indications from Spain that the exiled Laureano Gómez would be open to the proposal. However, despite Lleras's entreaties with Laureano's followers in Colombia, months passed without a response from Laureano himself. Lleras finally resolved to travel to Europe to speak with Laureano in person.[56]

Neither Laureano nor Lleras, nor any of Laureano's aides, left behind a record of the two exiles' encounter in the Valencian seaside community of Benidorm. Photographs show Laureano supporting his weight with a cane, his face looking older than his years. The ocean air had not been enough to arrest further declines in Laureano's health following a 1951 heart attack. Regardless, what Laureano termed "perfect tranquility, calm, and space" had produced a profound reassessment of Colombia's desired political system. "I have been given [the opportunity] to reconsider many events," Laureano later explained to a group of disciples, "arriving at a clear vision of that which constituted the great error of my life and glimps[ing] its terrible consequences in the destruction of the republic."[57]

Conciliatory statements aside, previous battles had left their imprint on Laureano. Partisan fault lines over the recent past formed immediately. As he and Lleras collaborated at Benidorm on a joint statement of purpose, Laureano promoted a characteristically Conservative idea of violence, framing rural unrest as "banditry, [an] atrocious phenomenon which scorns morality and the law." Lleras ceded this minor point, agreeing to denounce "banditry" in a section of the annoucement "repudiat[ing] violence." Elsewhere, however, Lleras turned back Laureano's attempt to promulgate language describing "violence" as "a means of political struggle adopted by Liberalism since 1930." To cast his "impartial regime" as the victim of Liberal machinations, Lleras warned Laureano, risked "a frenzied polemic about Liberalism's responsibilities in the violence . . . which could spoil our intentions."[58] This tiff previewed the debates over the past that would animate Colombian politics within and beyond the *país político* for the better part of the next decade.

Nevertheless, the overall July 1956 Benidorm accord reflected an impulse to *convivencia*. (The accord's opening lines, which refer to Laureano and Lleras in the third person, suggest Lleras's journalistic touch.) The accord aimed to restore Colombians' "common civic patrimony" through "a government or series of governments of broad coalition between the two parties" that would also return the country to constitutional rule and the exercise of popular sovereignty. Furthermore, the bipartisan coalition would seek "to give the people not only the reconquest of their lost liberty, but also a concrete vision . . . of the possibilities the immense majority of Colombians have to obtain a radical improvement in their living conditions."[59] More than is generally appreciated, then, Lleras and Laureano gestured to the social content of the government they hoped would replace Rojas. Developmental reforms would accompany the transition from authoritarianism.

The work of winning adherents to the Benidorm accord fell to Lleras. Lleras and López's combined authority ensured that his own party leadership presented no problem. By contrast, outside of Laureano's camp, the splintered Conservative Party required greater convincing.[60] Shifting economic currents would ease Lleras's task somewhat. Slackening global demand for commodities had already begun to squeeze Latin American economies, raising the stakes for governments throughout the region. The demands of balancing social and economic constituencies had brought Argentina's Juan Domingo Perón crashing from power in 1955, and as Lleras journeyed back from Spain at the end of July 1956, Peru's military ruler also faced ouster. Yet Rojas refused to alter his administration's spendthrift policies or refrain from lining his own pockets, in spite of falling prices for coffee, Colombia's dominant export. The parallels were not lost on observers. "Colombia is in for rough weather," a U.S. businessman in Colombia remarked to diplomats. "When the coffee market goes to pot a real crisis will develop, and each month brings this closer."[61]

Contingent as well as conjunctural developments conspired against Rojas. Within weeks of Benidorm, an escalating series of missteps by the president further facilitated Lleras's political work. In the predawn hours of August 7, Colombia's independence day, a military convoy stocked with a thousand-plus crates of dynamite exploded in downtown Cali. As a stunned nation weighed the damages— which amounted to over a thousand dead and staggering material losses—Rojas took to the airwaves to denounce the accident as an act of "political sabotage" by the opposition and the Communists.[62]

Lleras could scarcely believe his good fortune. "It is nice to put faith in the stupidity of others from time to time," he stated in a letter to Laureano six days later. "The public reaction against this piece of nonsense was very encouraging . . . What matters is to pull people out of their complacency and let the SIC [Colombian Intelligence Service] take care of the rest. Its persecutions will bring them closer to our cause, which I am convinced now more than ever is shared by the totality of the country."[63]

Lleras's calculation would prove prophetic, but not before Rojas stumbled again. The Cali tragedy stirred up rumors that military commanders had booted Rojas from the presidential palace. This story line about intramilitary frictions gained traction at the end of January 1957, with a *Time* article stating that Rojas had been demoted to "a kind of chairman of the board." Though untrue, the accusation provoked Rojas, who had assimilated too well the example of Perón's deposition by his former military colleagues. Even as his censors held the offending issue of *Time* from circulation, Rojas browbeat his top subordinates into publicly affirming the extension of his presidency for the 1958–62 term. The dictatorship's pliant, extracongressional legislature reconvened weeks later to grant a legal veneer to the maneuver, prompting the U.S. Embassy to comment that the "break in 'constitutional continuity' seems complete."[64]

With the issue forced, Lleras and Laureano's Civil Front (Frente Civil) shifted to an openly oppositional stance. In fulfillment of their party's commitment that a Conservative would stand for the coalition, Lleras and fellow Liberal notables joined with Conservative leaders to nominate Guillermo León Valencia as the parties' candidate to oppose Rojas. The government retorted by detaining Lleras and other prominent Liberals as they set out to campaign for Valencia. This counter-move catalyzed the response that Lleras had predicted eight months earlier, as thousands of urban Colombians took to the streets in protest.[65]

These men and women had their own reasons for turning out against Rojas. University students in Bogotá, for instance, carried memories of classmates gunned down by the army during demonstrations three years earlier. The students' willingness to turn out on the streets, risking even death, was all the more striking to contemporaries because they had come of age in an authoritarian Colombia. Here, one commentator described approvingly, was "a generation that reached 21 years of age without a citizenship card [cédula de ciudadanía] and since adolescence has fought against totalitarian systems of government, making it difficult to reconcile the thesis of the books they studied, which described a democratic Republic, and the certainty [that] jail and rifle[s] [could waiting be] around any corner." Germán Arciniegas, Colombia's most internationally renowned intellectual and one of Lleras's fellow nuevos, would agree that "this is a generation that has suffered what we did not endure. [In] this perturbation of the free order which gives it [its] name ... it defended its ideals with dead that we did not have."[66] Known in some circles as the "generation of midcentury," maligned in others as the carefree "Coca-Cola generation," young Colombians were earning for themselves the enduring designation of the "generation of the state of siege."

Other city residents felt pain primarily in their pocketbooks. While a continued slide in coffee prices added to the general economic malaise, beginning in 1956 the cost of living increased by nearly 20 percent. Various Conservative leaders predicted that this "economic situation would topple [Rojas], but there was no need to push him politically." Lleras took the opposite stance, wryly joking that "I, being less of a Marxist, believe that it's necessary to keep explaining to the people that the economic situation was created by Rojas [through his inflationary budgets and corruption]. If not, we run the risk that they will attribute it to divine providence."[67]

As the pace of events accelerated, urban Colombians left nothing to chance. Popular displays of resistance hit a crescendo in early May, after Valencia himself was arrested. One of the largest demonstrations saw forty thousand people, perhaps a quarter of the city's population, turn out in the Caldas coffee hub of Pereira. Colombia's bourgeoisie—Lleras's onetime sponsors at the University of the Andes—likewise decided that it was time for Rojas to go. In a vigorous display of their organizational muscle, leading businessmen assembled a general strike that shuttered newspapers, schools, banks, and other businesses in major cities.[68]

The endgame came quickly. As the government's security forces ratcheted up repression against the public protests, the Civil Front rejected Rojas's overtures. Within the government, the old rumors became reality; senior military officers worked throughout the night to convince Rojas of the necessity of leaving office. (The hurriedly arranged handover of $15,000 sealed the deal.) The news of Rojas's abdication attracted a thunderous popular response: in its first report on May 10, hours after Rojas departed the country, the U.S. Embassy reported that Bogotá was "delirious with joy." [69]

An old aphorism reentered Colombian consciousness: "Colombia is a sterile land for dictatorship." [70] But how was democracy to be rebuilt? "Returning to the republic is not going to be an easy thing," Lleras counseled in a June speech. [71] The challenges facing the democratic transition were twofold. First, it remained for the parties to hammer out their coalition and realize the promise of *convivencia*. Second was the reestablishment of regular constitutional rule. Many conceived of this latter issue as the most pressing, for the democratization process rested on shaky juridical ground: the constitution made no allowance for a multiperson body to govern Colombia, as a *junta* of Rojas's five top commanders was now doing. [72]

While dealing with the political side of the transition, Alberto Lleras also furnished a framework through which these legal uncertainties could be resolved. Looking to recalibrate bipartisan rapprochement in the wake of Rojas's departure, Lleras returned to Spain in mid-July to negotiate again with Laureano. At Sitges, outside of Barcelona, the two signed a second agreement that reiterated and built upon the joint statement reached the prior summer. Neither man left behind an account of this meeting either, but the final product shows Lleras's hand even more than does Benidorm. The Sitges pact repeated Benidorm's denunciations of violence and of the dictatorship's sins, focusing on a return to the constitution. Positing that "it would be foolish [to return to democracy only to have] the struggle for predominance between Conservatives and Liberals reopen," the pact then prescribed designs to institutionalize *convivencia*. In order to strip partisanship out of state affairs, Lleras proposed the establishment of a meritocratic civil service. He also recommended that Congress and the presidential cabinet be divided equally between the parties for twelve years. A "very simple and concrete" popular vote would decide the constitutional revisions necessary to implement the plan. [73]

The party chiefs thus handed the transition a solid blueprint. The *junta* saw the popular plebiscite as a means to establish its legal authority until the regular 1958 presidential elections. Backers of the Civil Front were more effusive. Laureano's son and political heir Álvaro Gómez proclaimed that the Sitges agreement sought to resolve "the problems of an entire generation." The recently revived *El Tiempo* celebrated the pact as the outline of a "new Colombia." The *país nacional* concurred: upon Lleras's return from Sitges, his car from the airport up to central

Bogotá found roads choked with enthusiastic well-wishers assembled more than a dozen deep on either side.[74]

After four years without electoral politics, and eight years without full bipartisan participation in elections, Colombia's public sphere roared back to life. Popular mobilization during "the days of May" had demonstrated the urban *país nacional's* stake in the country's direction. The plebiscite now offered them the opportunity to enshrine the vision of a bipartisan, democratic Colombia as the law of the land. The outpouring was stunning: over 72 percent of eligible Colombians voted, the highest figure in the nation's history. The "yes" camp garnered 95 percent of the ballots cast.[75] In the minds of many Colombians, the confirmation of democracy marked a turning point in the nation's entire history, what Lleras denominated the "inauguration" of Colombia's "Second Republic."[76]

This shorthand for democratic renewal, and not La Violencia, would be into the 1960s the term by which urban Colombians described their era. It signaled the hope of Colombia's transition as much as La Violencia would represent that feeling's disappearance. News of anti-authoritarian struggles in neighboring countries further nourished Colombians' optimism at the start of 1958. When Venezuela's dictatorship collapsed in late January, one Bogotá radio news program (*radioperiódico*) announced that the "triumph is not simply a step forward in the history of our sister country, but one in the history of the whole continent. The fall of the despots continues on its unalterable course, until ours is a continent for liberty and the juridical-constitutional order."[77]

The plebiscite's triumph also brought practical implications for political *convivencia*. For one, it underlined politicians' cooperation with non-Rojas sectors of the military, a process that culminated in the abandonment of the term "Civil Front" in favor of the more inclusive "National Front."[78] Second, whereas Sitges had proposed establishing Conservative-Liberal parity in the legislative and executive branches, the plebiscite extended it to the judiciary, consequently putting an end to the possibility of "hegemonic [i.e., one-party] governments." As the leader of the *junta* described it, the vote thus "fix[ed] the indispensable bases to guarantee the mutual tolerance of our traditional parties and the transformation of their political customs."[79] Colombians had evidently found the formula to eliminate partisan violence.

While the new year of 1958 dawned with the formal rules of democracy settled, the political scene was growing increasingly turbid. Laureano's triumphant return to Colombia in early October 1957 wrecked the Liberal-Conservative deals struck in the heat of the anti-Rojas struggle six months earlier. Exile had mellowed Laureano's opinions toward the Liberals, but he seethed with unalloyed hatred at those Conservatives who had betrayed him to Rojas in 1953. So long as Laureano remained in Spain, Lleras had shown himself capable of keeping The Monster's fangs in check. Now, the U.S. ambassador found Lleras to be "pessimistic and cynical," "very outspoken about the folly, the venom and the danger of Laureano's course." Lleras anticipated that Laureano would maintain the political following to make good on his anger, which "was obsessed by one thought: to get revenge on his political enemies—nothing else mattered." Two favorite enemies, along with one fresh target, most attracted Laureano's ire. Laureano's predecessor, Mariano Ospina Pérez, and the hierarchy of the Catholic Church had alternately orchestrated and endorsed the 1953 coup. Laureano's gripe with Guillermo León Valencia, the Civil Front's presidential choice, only dated to Valencia's recent sidling up to Ospina Pérez. For the time being, though, derailing Valencia's candidacy mattered more than old scores. Nearly as soon as he stepped off the plane, Laureano insisted to Lleras that Valencia had to go.[80]

Other Colombians joined Laureano in this sentiment, though for different reasons. Valencia's personal bravery in early 1957 merely patched over his reputation as the Conservatives' enfant terrible. Valencia could seemingly do no right as the transition advanced. Embarrassing gaffes on both domestic and international affairs left many questioning the appropriateness of Valencia's candidacy. "We won't say anymore that Dr. Valencia is an ignorant fool," the hosts of the Conservative-run Bogotá radio news show *Orientación* told their listeners in early 1958. "It is Dr. Valencia [himself] who insists in making [us all] think that he is an ignorant fool."[81] The political class would return to this assessment in the years to come.

Lleras and other Liberal leaders resigned themselves to Valencia's fate after the March congressional elections. In this first test of the National Front, Laureano's slate won 59 percent of the Conservative vote. Such domination, a senior U.S. State Department official remarked, confirmed Laureano as the National Front's "kingmaker." Liberals consented to Laureano's dictate; Valencia was out as the coalition's presidential pick. However, this result left few observers content. Speaking on a Conservative radio program, one commentator observed that "we . . . face a tremendous dilemma: the imposition of a candidate, or the salvation of the motherland. It has already been seen that the two things don't work simultaneously."[82]

Among the possible solutions that materialized in the weeks following was a proposal for Lleras Camargo to assume the presidential candidacy. This option seemed simultaneously viable and explosive. Colombian military intelligence officers estimated that the move would have the support of business interests, but warned that it would incite provincial Conservative bosses to violence or prompt the dissolution of the partisan pacts. The U.S. Embassy guessed that these grim scenarios would lead Lleras to turn down the candidacy, "in [the] interests [of] preserving bipartisanship and avoiding political strife."[83]

Lleras did nothing to court the presidential mantle. Necessity, not ambition, had dragged him out of the private life he had pledged to live upon returning to Colombia in 1955. Practical considerations now magnified his continued reluctance: the entire pact with Laureano was premised on a Conservative occupying the presidential palace from 1958 to 1962. Gómez was furthermore proving to be an erratic and unreliable partner.[84]

Amidst this uncertainty, outside social groups pulled Lleras and Laureano along. By mid-April, business interests in Medellín—the country's most powerful regional bourgeoisie, and key organizers of the days of May—launched a pro-Lleras campaign. Urban Liberals in particular leapt at the chance to express their political sentiments: more than one hundred thousand people congregated in Medellín to hear Lleras speak on April 20. Lleras played along with the hypotheticals, suggesting that in exchange for a Liberal candidate in 1958, the parties alternate the presidency and their pact be extended from twelve to sixteen years (which would guarantee a Conservative for the final term). It was a crucial gambit to gain Conservative support, and by April 24, a majority of Conservative congressmen had committed their backing. Lleras finally yielded to the pressure that night. As his acceptance speech filled the airwaves, U.S. diplomats reported that "central Bogota [was] jammed with joyously shouting crowds and [a] mammoth impromptu[u] motorcade honking familiar dot-dot-dash for liberty and Lleras." The scene, they added, was "reminiscent of May 10."[85]

There were ten days left before the election.

DEMOCRACY, DEVELOPMENT, AND VIOLENCE

Uncertainty persisted through the middle months of 1958. "Very early in the morning of July 26," a U.S. Embassy officer awoke to "impromptu celebrations and tootling horns all over" Bogotá. The diplomat "alertly tumbled out of bed onto the streets thinking the much rumored new coup attempt had finally struck." Only later did he discover that the commotion had been sparked by news that a Pereira native had won Colombia's first Miss Universe title.[86]

In many regards, Alberto Lleras's election as the National Front's first president contained reasons for hope. Officials in Washington, for example, expressed surprise that Lleras carried the largely Conservative department of Antioquia by a margin of nine-to-one. Lleras, by contrast, was less sanguine. Just before the August inauguration, U.S. diplomats said that "Lleras of late has seemed much concerned with the magnitude of the problems he will have to face." Lleras publicly declared that he felt "overwhelm[ed] by the almost physical weight of [this] responsibility," while the radio program *Orientación* commiserated that "the task that President Lleras Camargo has before him is certainly one of the least enviable in the world."[87]

Three sets of problems loomed largest. The first, civilian-military relations, was the most direct outgrowth of the dictatorship's collapse. Two days before the May 4 election, midlevel military officers joined in a coup attempt with small numbers of radical Conservatives. Though the uprising collapsed within hours due to "a lack of coordination, bungling and a few strokes of sheer luck," it drove home for

Lleras the importance of completing the separation of the military from politics.[88] The president-elect therefore delivered a strident speech on the military's place in the Second Republic. As if to highlight his thin frame, Lleras stated that "[this] fragile civil symbol will be . . . the symbol of the national will. It can be broken with a grimace, with a gesture, without any effort. But if it is broken, the history of the republic, the honor of the Armed Forces will be broken with it." In exchange for the military abstaining from politics, and thus retaining its honor, Lleras promised that the political class would not intervene in the armed forces' internal affairs. The speech, widely considered his most influential, won him the enduring loyalty of the military command.[89]

Management of the economy represented Lleras's second great challenge. Public as well as personal austerity became administration watchwords. In conjunction with the International Monetary Fund and the World Bank, which had previously suspended operations in Colombia because of Rojas's economic mismanagement, Lleras imposed what he termed "the simple application of good sense and the most orthodox economic norms," restraining imports and trimming certain state subsidies. By late 1959, U.S. officials would laud the Lleras government for "sustained performance" they found "outstanding, and possibly without equal in any other Latin American country faced with similar problems."[90] Though Latin America had not fully exited the economic conditions that had contributed to the democratic wave, for the time being Colombia was through the most politically taxing phase.

Economic stabilization also offered Lleras Camargo a forum to articulate his larger vision for the nation. The presidential inauguration of August 7, 1958, was "on the whole [an event] of quiet satisfaction, with nothing like the wild jubilation which exploded when Lleras originally accepted the nomination." Lleras termed the event "an example of austerity," which the country would need to emulate in order to escape from the deficits left by Rojas. (*Time*'s coverage highlighted the absence of champagne from the inauguration festivities.) In subsequent months, pro–National Front radio programs reinforced this message, highlighting the contrast between Lleras's famously modest lifestyle and the avarice demonstrated by the Rojas family.[91] Lleras thus became the National Front's moral center, as well as its architect.

By his estimation, Lleras inherited a country burdened by "the damages of 150 years of feudalism, injustice, faulty administrative and social arrangements, neglected popular education, misery and backwardness, sectarianism and violence, suitably topped off by an irresponsible and voracious dictatorship."[92] Economic belt-tightening would resolve the most recent issues. Larger questions of development required a renewal of the ideologies and practices of state that had sprung from the Revolution on the March. At the first meeting of Lleras's cabinet, his Liberal finance minister laid out a sweeping outline of the administration's "economic and social policy." The government's overarching objective, he explained, would be to "facilitate relations between citizens and the State," to "correct . . . extant inequalities and try . . . to orient the energies of the country toward the achievement of clear objectives for the general interest."[93] The reformist inclinations of Lleras's generation had a new lease on life.

The third and final challenge involved the modification of Colombia's political culture, to root out violence-as-practice. "*Convivencia,* peace, [and] solidarity between Colombians are mere expectations," Lleras noted ahead of the inauguration. "Hatreds, reprisals, impassioned words, and brutal acts are, still, unfortunately, the atrocious daily reality." To break this cycle, Colombians' relationship to the state would have to undergo a transformation, such that government would become "a site of confluence between the governed, and not the center of their disputes and the reason for their battles." Lleras warned that without "the acclimatization of certain political customs of moderation that have only appeared for extremely short moments in Colombian public life . . . democracy is a fiction."[94]

The National Front agreements had started to return the *país político* to the civil practices of *convivencia*. In and along the paved streets, monumental squares, and ornate lyceums of the countries of letters and politics—the urban spaces where Lleras had mounted his campaign for an inclusive, stable Colombia—"the new climate of *convivencia* [was] palpable," *Semana* reported in early 1959.[95] Yet as his speech before the microphones of ACPO suggests, Lleras had other topographies in mind as he commenced his second presidency. "We have signed the peace, but not solely for the cities or for ourselves, but principally so that it flows mercifully over the countryside," Lleras said weeks into the transition. "There lie the most innocent victims of . . . political hegemony and of its fatal consequence, dictatorship."[96] During his successive exiles from the country of politics and Colombia itself, Lleras had lamented the collective ignorance of the *país político* toward rural Colombia's plight. In order to undo the damage wrought by partisan and military excess—to live up to his former ideal of Colombia as a space for peace—Lleras's Second Republic would first have to reckon with the nature of violence in the provinces.

Encounters with Violence, 1957–1958

Once the local boy's words rose over the excited chorus of voices surrounding him, Germán Guzmán Campos found himself completely transported. The physical journey to La Herrera, at the far edge of Tolima (map 3), had already placed the bespectacled priest close to the mountains of his birth. The men who led Father Guzmán through the woods around the village likewise called up his own peasant origins. Yet it was the gaggle of children who trailed Guzmán around La Herrera that most affected the onetime school director. La Herrera's adults narrated how, fewer than two years earlier, government planes had blanketed the area with flyers requesting collaboration, an act followed four days later by a reprehensible surprise. As La Herrera's schoolchildren lined up one morning for school, the same aircraft rained machine-gun rounds down on the assembly. Community leaders produced the empty shell casings for Guzmán, also pointing out the grottoes the children had carved in order to continue their studies in safety. The most lasting memento of the episode proved to be the coarse words of one of those children, which Guzmán recorded in his notebook and would return to years later. "Those sons of swine fired at us," the boy had piped up. "Those damned [swine] killed a lady while she was defending a kid. The leaflets were a trick, we believed them and they almost fucked us. Now, as soon as we hear them, we fly to the shelters." [1]

Village by village, story by story, tales such as this came to comprise an alternative body of knowledge about Colombia's midcentury violence. For urban Colombians, the excitement that accompanied the country's return to democracy in 1957–58 was joined by frank realization of how little they knew about "national problems," violence foremost among them. "The truth," one of the *junta* generals commented, "is that each of us Colombians unfortunately has a distinct concept of

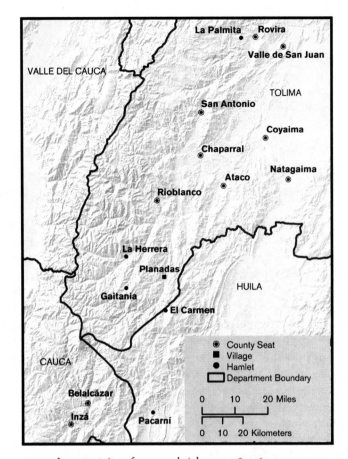

MAP 3. Important sites of peace and violence, 1958–1965.

violence [*la violencia*]." [2] With the veil of censorship lifted, observers inside and outside the state engaged in sociological, ethnological, economic, and partisan readings of violence. While these converged on select points of agreement regarding the origins and consequences of violence, no unified explanation emerged. The frightening resurgence of violence-as-practice in the countryside, especially across Tolima, only served to intensify the search for solutions.

Father Guzmán's passage through places like La Herrera marked the apogee of this quest. The debate over violence in Bogotá generated rumbles of discontent from the provinces, where expectation generated by democratization mixed with resentment over the capital's condescension. "We were inhabitants of those zones and suffered violence in the flesh," a group of nearly two hundred residents of eastern Tolima proclaimed in May 1958, "and we know 'the causes' that you now want to investigate."[3] Through a capacity to listen to such voices—an openness character-istic of the democratic conjuncture—Guzmán and other government emissaries assuaged hard feelings by forging the most significant urban-rural linkages of the transition. The texture of the provinces' experience in the 1940s and '50s conse-quently entered the public sphere, altering Colombians' understandings of nation-hood and political possibilities.

THE PROBLEM OF VIOLENCE

President-elect Alberto Lleras Camargo's anxieties about the economy and parti-san relations stemmed largely from the fact that the true depth of Colombia's chal-lenges lay obscured by authoritarianism's shadow. In addition to censoring the press outright, Rojas had consistently refused to reveal the reasons behind the con-tinuation of the state of siege. The result, Lleras wrote in late 1955, was that "the state of siege has created an atmosphere of falsehood and unreality." In a deep affront to Lleras's democratic and journalistic sensibilities, the Rojas government cited disruptions to "public order" as the basis for the curtailment of democratic-constitutional rule while simultaneously denying the Colombian public any details on those disorders. "Colombians keep up daily on incidents in Indochina's civil war . . . [but] are unaware what goes on in Tolima," groused Lleras.[4] International news was more readily at hand than information from Bogotá's hinterland.

Colombia's gradual transition away from military dictatorship threw open prospects for dialogue, if not revelation, about crucial national problems.[5] For-merly latent discoveries bubbled to the surface in the months after Rojas's ouster, granting the country of politics and a nascent, technocratic *letrado* class a more complete portrait of the nation. Truth-telling would encompass a range of national problems, of which violence was only the most prominent. Moreover, this process did not solely provide fodder for policy debates: a direct retort to the practices of the Rojas era, such public airings contributed to the basic configuration of Colom-bia's reemergent democratic sphere.

The most influential disclosures came from one of the numerous foreign experts contracted by Colombian governments after 1945, as international development began to coalesce as a field of investigation and practice. In Rojas's second year in office, his administration invited to Colombia the Dominican priest and noted humanist-social scientist Father Louis-Joseph Lebret. Having cut his teeth organiz-ing and carrying out social planning in his native France during the Depression and World War II, Lebret had subsequently served as an adviser to the Brazilian govern-ment, first steps in what would coalesce into a formative relationship with Latin America and the Third World. In Colombia between December 1954 and June 1956, Lebret and a team of researchers from his Économie et Humanisme group carried out an ambitious sociological study of living conditions in forty-five rural and thirteen urban communities. The fieldwork yielded statistical evidence of Colombia's preponderant level of "underdevelopment," as well as an admonition from Lebret on the ruling elite's "technical insufficiency, lack of historical consciousness, and hermetic egoism." Horrified, Rojas's advisers buried the Lebret report.[6]

Come the democratic transition, Lebret's work offered Colombian leaders a double utility. For the *junta*, allowing the report to enter the public sphere would underline the distinction between the discredited Rojas and the armed forces as an institution. For civilians, Lebret's "double technical and religious authority" presented an unmatched window onto local socioeconomic conditions as well as a possible road map for government policy. By September 1958, a full year before the two-volume *Study on Colombia's Development Conditions* entered its official ten-thousand-copy run, Lebret's findings began to spread through government and civil circles.[7] The 1960s would see the Lebret report remain a cornerstone of Colombians' debates on (under)development, a blueprint for reformers and fodder for critics of the National Front's developmentalist choices.[8]

While Lebret's status as an outsider magnified the reception of his inquiry, it likewise limited his contributions. *Development Conditions* amalgamated Colombia out of a sampling of communities. By largely skipping the regional, the report omitted the scale at which many Colombians conceived of their own country.[9] More importantly, Lebret replicated the fundamental error of his cohort of development specialists, glossing over the economic and social disruptions wrought by partisan violence and its offshoots.[10] The imperative to construct Colombia as a subject accessible to expert intervention, together with prevalent disciplinary methodologies, compelled Lebret to emphasize markers of human welfare and inequality, characteristics that Colombia shared with the other Latin American, Asian, and African nations that Lebret knew firsthand.[11] Colombia's "state of violence" received only passing mention as a "difficult[y] of the current period of [socioeconomic] transition."[12]

For the most part, Colombians' own arguments about the connection between violence and socioeconomic conditions remained at a high level of generality. One widespread school of thought conceived of violence as the "effect of penury, illiteracy, endemic diseases," century-old maladies made worse by the acceleration of population growth.[13] (Lleras's constant references to demography and the dislocations of modernization betrayed some affinity with this argument.) Sociological inquiry also mixed readily with other intellectual currents. In November 1957, sensing "there is [an] atmosphere . . . [for a seminar] on violence," officials at the Ministry of Education convened nearly three dozen of the nation's most promising teachers "to realize as dispassionate, objective, and complete a study as possible . . . [on] the causes that produced and have sustained [violence]." The seminar's final report, issued seven months later, opened with a long exposition on racial theory. "Anthropological factors of [an] ethnic order," the report read, "contribute markedly to the establishment of a favorable environment for violence to flourish with relative ease in the Colombian." In other words, the country's inhabitants had "inherited" those cultural traits—"warlike spirit," "extreme ambitions and passions, and inclination for vengeance," and "physical resistance"—characteristic of the its foundational "aboriginal . . . Spanish . . . [and] African . . . elements." The report continued with explanations of how Colombia's physical and sociological environments served to reinforce these tendencies toward violence.[14]

The issue of causality was but one side of the problem of violence. Colombians sought as well to grasp the scope and consequences of their national "tragedy," and by the time of Lleras's May 1958 election, a preliminary arithmetic began to congeal.[15] "It is now time that we get to know our dead," Gonzalo Canal Ramírez indicated in a February opinion piece. A peripheral but exceptionally versatile member of the *país letrado*—polyglot lawyer, prolific writer and publisher, sometime bureaucrat—Canal Ramírez enjoyed close ties to the military establishment, which left him uniquely qualified to guide his compatriots into a quantitative discussion. He went on during the transition's first months to unveil a number of little-circulated armed forces and press estimates of the conflict's human and economic costs. He simultaneously worked in alternative veins. Soon after May 10, the *junta* had tasked Canal Ramírez with assessing conditions in the countryside, a mission it conceived as a precursor to rural reconstruction programs. Those policies never materialized under the interim military government, casualties of the compressed time frame and limited economic resources of the democratization process. By contrast, Canal Ramírez converted the interviews and stories he had gathered on his tour into a twenty-one-minute cinematic dramatization of "a peasant region before, during, and after the violence." The film *This Was My Village* (*Esta fue mi vereda*) reached nearly a half-million theatergoers.[16]

Lacking the scholarly imprimatur of a Lebret, and eclipsed by subsequent attempts to investigate rural violence, Canal Ramírez's diverse 1958 oeuvre quickly faded from collective consciousness. However, he would return as an expert voice on violence. His works moreover foreshadowed two of his contemporaries' central concerns around the violence question. The first involved a diffuse consensus regarding what Canal Ramírez called "macabre statistics." His implication that up to two hundred thousand Colombians had died in partisan clashes since the late 1940s aligned with concurrent estimates being formulated privately by various domestic and international observers. Indeed, even as scholars in later decades aspired to greater precision, combing through government homicide statistics and designing field surveys, they too would converge around the two hundred thousand mark.[17]

For Canal Ramírez and many of his contemporaries, the number of dead indexed the degree of the nation's moral deficiency.[18] There was nonetheless a second, surer measure of Colombia's ongoing crisis, one that Canal Ramírez admitted "has struck

[most] at my conscience."[19] The fates of the dead had already been fixed. By contrast, there were legions of other country people whose lives had been upended, their uncertain futures loaded with peril and the possibility of redemption. As Colombians contemplated the problem of violence at start of the National Front era, these victims of forced displacement—*desplazados,* separated from their homes by dangers imagined and real—represented the crux of the national predicament.

Colombian commentators and officials therefore also began to take stock of displacement's human and economic costs, though they attained less consensus than on the death toll. Canal Ramírez put the number of displaced at eight hundred thousand, four times the number of dead and perhaps 6 percent of the nation's population. A 1959 U.S. government study meanwhile proposed a figure twice as large.[20] These numbers were necessarily speculative, particularly given the impossibility of disentangling forced displacement from economic opportunity as accelerators of rural-to-urban migration. Regardless, few would have contested Canal Ramírez's assessment that the displacement phenomenon reached "alarming proportions."[21]

Given the paucity of reliable data, one study on displacement grabbed immediate and enduring authority. On the basis of surveys carried out in 1957, Tolima officials stated that more than 320,000 people—fully 42 percent of the department's residents—had experienced displacement between 1949 and 1957. Over forty thousand properties were abandoned over the same span, the great majority by owners who were motivated not by direct threats but by "fear." "Political violence," the report's authors concluded, "was superseded by violence as a corrupt commercial enterprise, as a new source of rights and obligations."[22]

This, then, was the state of understanding about Colombia's "undeclared civil war" as the National Front commenced. Advancing on the one hand a host of statistics, urban and urbane men like Canal Ramírez grasped that violence extended beyond the Liberal-Conservative conflict. Displacement highlighted how violence had come to form a nexus with issues of property. Any continuation of the status quo therefore not only imperiled the citizenship rights of *desplazados* but also stood to exacerbate Colombia's crisis of political economy. The loss of goods and land through theft and displacement lowered agricultural output, undermined commerce, and helped to fuel consumer price increases.[23] To limit social dissatisfaction and the possibility that the National Front might meet the fate of its predecessor, as well as to fulfill Lleras's commitment to equity, responses would need to be found to ongoing rural bloodletting and to the plight of the displaced.

The transition's widespread spirit of inquiry and disclosure was inseparable from Alberto Lleras Camargo. The politically independent newsweekly *Semana* perceived so much of Lleras in the salutary new national ethos that it hatched the term *"llerismo,"* "a nonconformist, critical intellectual position that tries to scrutinize Colombian problems with clarity, and that always looks to present solutions to the crises that it uncovers." This phenomenon was sufficiently widespread, *Semana* further explained, that one did not have to be a supporter of the government to be a practitioner of *llerismo*.[24]

Lleras himself put forward what proved to be the transition's most consequential step toward scrutiny and solution. In early February 1958, Lleras joined a who's-who of Liberal and Conservative notables at the capitol to advise the *junta* on national policy. By the time his turn to speak arrived, Lleras had grown tired of petty sniping among the Conservatives surrounding him. For weeks, ecclesiastical and political leaders had engaged in pointed deliberation on the origins of violence.[25] But the assembled Conservatives seemed content to rehash an ill-advised comment about partisan conflict that Guillermo León Valencia—who was not now even present—had made a month earlier.

Lleras perhaps sensed as well that the gathering would be this new body's last. The postauthoritarian process was at that moment running out of steam, its civilian principals consigned to endless committees as the unresolved presidential succession loomed on the horizon. Out in the countryside, people continued to die at an alarming rate; the final two months of 1957 had been the year's worst, with 870 homicides attributed to partisan causes. A weary Lleras thus ventured that "neither Dr. Laureano Gómez nor I can do anything else to prevent more bloodshed ... we have done everything within our powers." As an alternative, Lleras suggested that the government convene "a special commission of penologists and experts on social questions to investigate the true causes of the violence, in the very places that it thrives, and to establish possible remedies capable of putting an end to it."[26]

Proposals for an investigatory commission had circulated in Liberal circles in preceding months, but the combination of evolving political circumstances and Lleras's prestige now compelled the government to action.[27] This was a characteristic moment where Lleras captured broader currents of political thought. Over the months that followed, the country's political direction more certain, bureaucrats drafted legislation to give life to Lleras's rudimentary idea. The maturing national conversation on displacement and the violence-property nexus also echoed unmistakably in their labor. The National Investigatory Commission on the Causes and Current Situations of Violence in the National Territory (Comisión Nacional Investigadora de las Causas y Situaciones Presentes de Violencia en el Territorio Nacional) would audit conditions in "departments or regions most affected by disorder and delinquency." Its goal would be to formulate "recommendations dedicated to methodically solving the situations analyzed, giving preference to those involving injustice created by intimidation or force, as well as those related to the dispossession of property and the displacement of people."[28]

The creation of the commission laid bare the latent political perils of dealing with Colombia's recent past. Cognizant that the commission might implicate Conservatives within the National Front coalition, the *junta* built in safeguards: according to the commission's founding statute, the commission's findings would be kept "classified" unless the government determined that their "partial or full" publication was "advisable for the interests of the country and the public peace."[29] However, this stipulation represented insufficient guarantee for Conservatives. Rather than fulfill the requirements and spirit of parity, numerous Conservative candidates declined their nominations to the commission. In the end, the commission included only one Conservative alongside its two Liberal representatives.[30]

Despite this setback, the *junta* found other ways to make the commission politically advantageous. In line with Lleras's initial proposal, the commission included two parish priests and two military officers. It thus glorified the coalition that had toppled Rojas on May 10. The priests' presence moreover augmented the commission's moral gravitas, while the inclusion of both active and retired army officers curried favor with the military establishment.[31]

Two commissioners in particular possessed impeccable credentials as advocates of *convivencia*. The first, the jocular former secretary general of the Liberal Party, Otto Morales Benítez, had served late the previous year as Lleras's personal envoy to long-demobilized Liberal fighters on the Eastern Plains. Well known for his troubleshooting skills, Morales Benítez, whom *Semana* termed a "full-time optimist," would serve as Lleras's labor minister in subsequent years.[32] The second was Father Germán Guzmán Campos, the parish priest of El Líbano, Tolima's top coffee town. Where Morales Benítez and the commission's other civilian appointees brought a deep knowledge of the law, the Chaparral-born priest's vocation lay in education. Being a clergyman—and a Conservative one at that—in a Liberal bastion such as Ibagué had encouraged a twenty-something Guzmán to go out of his way to build relationship with Liberals in order to ensure the success of his educational projects. (The work had also brought him into close contact with then-education minister Jorge Eliécer Gaitán in 1940.)[33] Guzmán's appointment held a certain geographic logic, as his Tolima connections complemented those that Morales Benítez and Absalón Fernández de Soto—the commission's other Liberal member—enjoyed with their native Caldas and Valle del Cauca.

Of far greater significance, however, were the lessons of Guzmán's ministry. His postings to northern Tolima included Armero, where his predecessor had been decapitated by furious Liberals in the rumor-filled hours after Gaitán's April 1948 murder, and now Líbano, the "epicenter of violence" in that section of the department. Guzmán thus possessed, as he explained in a 1984 presentation, "a moral obligation, deeply personal, to do what I could to halt the violence, for having felt its multiform horror."[34]

Guzmán's experience fixed a practical course for the commission, which in its first weeks fumbled for a suitable approach to the task ahead. The commission's ungainly full name suggests something of the unrefined impulse behind it. Without direct national or international precedents to replicate, the commission initially looked to the leading edge of social science for direction. Several of the commission's members, for instance, turned immediately to Lebret's blockbuster survey.[35]

Word that the commissioners were sitting in Bogotá, leafing through reams of paper, was met with indignation in the provinces. When one of the *junta* generals remarked to *El Tiempo* that "we wished for all Colombians to be aware of what violence signified, of its catastrophic consequences," one regional newspaper snapped back that "the Colombian people are well-informed of what the violence is and has been." Writing from the sweltering port of Girardot, which had received huge inflows of refugees fleeing violence across the Magdalena River in Tolima, the paper's editors critiqued the government's approach: "Violence cannot continue to be combatted with fabrications, nor admonitions, nor such insubstantial declarations to the press . . . it is essential, urgent, and pressing that the government takes action, but that it takes action as it should do, because what it has been doing up to now is nothing. Commissions, delegations, special envoys, reports, written warnings, projects, good procedures, decrees, etc. There has been all that in abundance. But in practice, nothing."[36]

By late June, the commission had abandoned its preliminary intention "to advance [its own] sociological study of the violence." Guzmán catalyzed the shift, arguing to his colleagues that "we start from an apparently trivial truth: to hunt tigers you must go to where there are tigers. If we want to investigate and halt the violence, we go to where there are violent offenders and we speak to them wherever they are." Thus convinced, the commission resolved "to analyze exhaustively the proximate, immediate, and concrete causes of the violence . . . [in order] to propose equally proximate . . . immediate and, above all, practical solutions."[37] The inclination toward sociological inquiry would ultimately return, decisively molding the commission's second act in the 1960s. But oriented by Guzmán, the commission first departed the city for the provinces, to construct from up close an idea of violence.

DESARMANDO LOS ESPÍRITUS

In contemplating the scope and nature of Colombia's recent violence, as well as the prospects of peace, the *país político* ran into uncomfortable questions about the limits of its authority. Pacts between select national leaders of the Liberal and Conservative parties furnished no guarantee that regional and local party representatives would adhere to the pledge of *convivencia*. Thus, when Lleras spoke in his inaugural about "national conciliation and the pacification of the spirits [as] fundamental objectives of the new system," there could be no assumption that the two were automatically linked.[38] Though some in the *país político* arrogated to themselves the mantle of "natural leaders" (*jefes naturales*), the extent of their influence remained murky, the political lives of party rank-and-file virtually inscrutable.

Perhaps the sole certainty that the *país político* did possess was the notion that rural peoples were easily moved to hate. As a leading Liberal rationalized to a U.S. Embassy official, "Two opposing politicians can make bitter speeches against the other's party in the Congress and when it is all over they will congratulate each other. But heard over the radio in the rural countryside, where bitterness is deep and historic, it will move opposing elements to violence."[39]

By 1958, substantial doubt existed around whether this mechanism could function in reverse.[40] The mounting weight of events militated against any simplistic correlation between party discipline and the issue of peace. "Laureano Gomez had a very strong hold on his adherents," Lleras had assured the U.S. ambassador in August 1957, "and a word from him had been sufficient to prevent further violence by his adherents." However, subsequent partisan confrontations highlighted how more direct political work would be required to bridge scales, between the messaging of national politicians and the actions of local party members.[41]

Interparty relations remained raw even in urban areas. Such was the case with Tolima's capital, Ibagué, where outgrowths of the department's violence coagulated into distinct forms. To a greater extent than many places in the region, Ibagué's location captured in miniature the topographic diversity of Gran Tolima. Bounding the city on three sides, so close as to seem within reach, stretched the wooded foothills of the central Andes. To the east, Ibagué's small plateau opened up on to the Magdalena Valley, such that the light of each day's rising sun underscored the more tropical climes of the lower altitudes.

Ibagué similarly mirrored midcentury Colombia's bifurcated sociopolitical environment. At the same time that officials in Bogotá sponsored the modernist renovation of Ibagué's core, the municipality as a whole strained under the weight of another, unplanned transformation. "New neighborhoods have sprouted like aching appendices, practically overnight, from the continuous influx of exiles," a Liberal observer complained at the end of the 1950s. Ibagué's natural gravity as a capital, along with its proximity to north-south and east-west routes across the Magdalena Valley and central Andes, made it a magnet for displaced residents of Gran Tolima and neighboring Caldas. This convergence contributed to an explosion in the city's population: somewhere shy of 100,000 souls in 1951, by the start of the National Front period Ibagué counted nearly 130,000 inhabitants. The spectacle of migrants living in ramshackle arrangements, short on basic services and economic prospects, was not unique to Ibagué. However, as another Liberal politician observed, Tolima's capital lacked the industrial development of a Cali or Bogotá. The city thus endured a relatively low level of development, including what some claimed was the worst housing deficit in the nation. These realities were made worse by what locals perceived as the indifference of the national government to provincial affairs.[42]

Ibagué's malaise also evinced a specifically partisan tinge. As many in the department understood, and officials from Bogotá would soon discover, Tolima's displacement was a predominantly Liberal phenomenon. As a result, Ibagué, already in the 1940s the Liberal capital of a department dominated by Liberals, saw its partisan majority expand in step with its general population.[43] The resulting mixture of partisan, political, and social grievances came to a head shortly after midnight on a late January Sunday in 1958, when two brothers cruised just past the updated heart of Ibagué to the city's southwestern edge. As these young Liberals stepped across the threshold of the Bar Bombay, they announced their arrival with loud cheers for their party, a bold public declaration of identity that drew derision from a pair of plainclothes policemen drinking at the bar. Once the ensuing scuffle had spilled onto the street, the brothers grabbed weapons they had left in their truck. Though one brother got off a single round, the policemen proved the quicker, or at least the better, shots.[44]

Ibagué's institutions and partisan publics each responded in their own way to the brothers' murders. Within thirty-six hours, the political fallout from the shooting absorbed nearly all of the city's energies, as the regular bustle of Ibagué's cramped streets redirected itself to meetings and marches. Business and Liberal leaders descended on the seat of Tolima's government, just a few hundred meters from the Bar Bombay. Ibagué's powerful merchant and transport associations had already spearheaded a paralyzing civic strike, while the departmental Liberal Directorate was helping to organize a funeral for the brothers that would bring five thousand people to the streets the following day. These "eruptions of collective indignation" not only succeeded in extracting concessions from the chastened Conservative governor, including the confinement of the police to their barracks, but also drew the presence of four cabinet ministers from Bogotá. After twelve hours of "tense and pessimistic" roundtable talks between national and departmental officials, Liberal chiefs and various Conservative factions, Ibagué's business interests agreed to lift the economic stoppage before it completed its second full day. The parties' representatives meanwhile restated their rejection of "any [act of] violence, individual or collective," as they made a general recommitment to the precepts of the National Front.[45]

Faced with a provocation like the brothers' deaths, Liberals outside the negotiations had greater difficulty maintaining their composure. For weeks, Ibagué's Liberal majority had complained about the presence of shadowy opponents of the National Front from other parts of the country, who had targeted several Liberals in the capital. This newest episode represented the final straw. The afternoon following the shooting, on a commercial avenue teeming with locals left aimless by the civic shutdown, Liberals caught wind of two Conservatives a block apart. It is unclear whether these men themselves committed the indiscretion of hurling party slogans, or if someone on the street recognized one of them as a Conservative boss from a town three hours to the north, who had arrived in Ibagué the previous day. Embittered and likely a little bored, Liberals in the vicinity set upon the men with rocks and cudgels, until army patrols came onto the scene. The assaults may have paradoxically contributed to defusing the overall situation; citing "the stirred-up mood and with the goal of preventing skirmishes," businessmen and Liberal politicians canceled a planned mass rally later that afternoon. Conservative groups played it less safe the next day, convening a demonstration in support of the governor that, as many feared, attracted a "Liberal counter-demonstration." With both crowds occupying adjacent sections of the main plaza, occasionally surging toward one another "in a hostile manner," it took "the immediate intervention of the Army, the brigade commander, and the governor to avert a [greater] clash."[46] In the subsequent days, as rumors of a massacre in rural western Tolima circulated through the city and exacerbated its "war of nerves," the governor implored "the department's citizenry to remain calm and have confidence that it is possible, through the action of the government and the parties, to exorcise [this] phase of violence in Tolima and return the department to peace."[47]

The affair surrounding the brothers' death typified two fundamental components of the violence problem at the start of the National Front. The first was the central role played by sectarian elements within the state apparatus. It was no mistake that Ibagué's Liberal and business leaders made "the immediate purging of the police" one of their central demands, or that the presence of official government vehicles in the Conservative rally grated Liberal sensibilities.[48] Indeed, the post-1946 Conservatization of the state emerged as a significant concern across Colombia by the late 1950s. "It is worth remembering," a lawyer from southern Caldas explained to the *junta* in June 1958, "that even though May 10 was a date that we all applauded, [it] has not been made effective everywhere." The lawyer decried in particular the complicity of government appointees in acts of bloodshed, warning that such "official causes [of violence] have still not been corrected."[49]

The second issue involved Ibagué's tense atmosphere after the killings. Reporters referred repeatedly to the city's "stirred-up mood," an image that appeared in various guises throughout the Colombian political imaginary of the era. Beginning with his 1958 inaugural address, Alberto Lleras cited "the pacification of the spirits" as one of the primary objectives of his presidency. Other government officials spoke of "*desarmando los espíritus*"—literally, disarming the spirits.[50] This constellation of concepts orbited a common dilemma: How could seemingly ingrained patterns of thought and behavior be reined in? How could Colombians learn to look beyond the so-called inherited hatreds of party identity in order to live together civilly?[51] Peace was an intellectual, even spiritual, proposition. How

Colombians responded would be central to conceptions of political community, particularly as *letrados* and politicans traversed localities and regions in search of answers about Colombia as a whole.

FROM VIOLENCE TO PEACE

Later in the twentieth century, throughout Latin America and the rest of the world, such questions of state repression and the construction of *convivencia* would go by different designations. Establishing the truth about state-sponsored terror, it came to be believed, would facilitate national reconciliation and consolidate a stable base for postauthoritarian democratic politics.[52] In grappling with these issues amidst Colombia's transition, the National Investigatory Commission on the Causes and Current Situations of Violence in the National Territory represented an indirect antecedent to those truth commissions.

However, aside from the notion that the reality of violence was to be found outside Bogotá—Father Guzmán's dictum that "to hunt tigers you must go to where there are tigers"—the commission possessed little sense of how to carry out its mission. Such want of firm methodological direction would rapidly prove an asset, for it opened the commissioners up to improvisation. Over five kinetic months, from late June to late November 1958, the commission wound its way through Gran Tolima and the middle Magdalena and upper Cauca river valleys, building procedure as it went. In Guzmán's telling, "The reality we encountered when we came into contact with the people, the civilians, the military men, the combatants [*guerrilleros*], guided us toward lines of action" (figure 2).[53]

"Contact with the people" occurred on a scale that at times astonished Guzmán and his companions. Guzmán related in an interview how "people . . . in some principal cities and in others of lesser importance flocked to speak to us [in] impressive [numbers], forcing us to hold sessions that lasted well into the night." In Ibagué and other regional hubs mushrooming with new migrants, the commissioners carried out "open interviews" in public plazas, accumulated written accounts, and convened forums with city notables.[54] Through such interactions, the commission came to model Colombia's reemergent civic sphere.

The true sources of revelation were found in the countryside. While "situations of violence" concentrated a great many *desplazados* into cities such as Ibagué, they also acted centrifugally, casting many more Colombians out to the peripheries. Such patterns were hardly new to Colombia; the onset of partisan hostilities after the 1946 election had instead altered extant forms of physical mobility in social and economic life. Like other agrarian societies, antebellum Gran Tolima and other Colombian regions had been worlds in motion. On any given day, farmers transported livestock from outlying farms into town centers for sale and slaughter, while families shuttled between kinsmen spread across multicounty diasporas.

FIGURE 2. Father Germán Guzmán Campos (center) with unidentified young combatants, 1958. Guzmán Campos, Fals Borda, and
Umaña Luna, *La violencia en Colombia,* 2nd ed., vol. 1.

What made central and southern Colombia distinct were the vast unclaimed
lands of the internal frontier, spaces where generations of Colombians had headed in
search of a modest life for themselves. Amidst the mountainous fastness of southern
Tolima, the National Investigatory Commission came across an emblematic incarnation of this process, a Liberal who much impressed Guzmán. Born thirty-five
years earlier in the Roncesvalles village of Santa Elena, Leopoldo García had lived a
peripatetic existence on the eastern slope of the central *cordillera.* At age eleven,
García and his four brothers accompanied their father to Rioblanco, where the family substituted work on another's farm for labor on their own. In place of school and
mandatory military service, García tended the owner's animals and assisted in *tum-
bando monte,* the work of converting untitled hillsides into farmland.[55]

Armed partisan confrontation ripped this world apart from the inside out. Threats of beating and assassination, if not those acts themselves, infused mobility with a shattering urgency.[56] Even more than the loss of life, the transposal of human and commercial circuits disrupted the fabric of Gran Tolima. Farm-dwelling Colombians emptied out of the countryside for safer quarters. By 1953, for instance, roughly a fifth of the thirty-seven thousand people in Chaparral, southern Tolima's most prosperous coffee county and Guzmán's hometown (map 3), had taken refuge in the county seat.[57] Untold others made their way into the hills. Amidst such mass comings and goings, families and business partners lost track of one another. A later judicial tribunal heard from a shopkeeper in northernmost Tolima who had logged outstanding debts of nearly 15,000 pesos. Of the twenty-one customers responsible for that money, he knew only three who had died. The remainder had fled the county for parts unknown, leaving the shopkeeper to shoulder a huge financial loss.[58]

In order to reconstruct accountability for violence, the National Investigatory Commission found itself following these trails of displacement. As it immersed itself ever deeper in the countryside, the nature of evidence transformed. In urban and rural settings, the displaced were both eyewitnesses to the atrocities visited upon others—spokesmen for the dead—and a special class of victims unto themselves. Most of the information that they could provide about "the causes and present situations of violence" was internal, embodied in their persons or borne in the form of memories. However, closer to the sites of violence in the countryside, *desplazados* could also point the commission to more tangible forms of attestation. In Rovira (map 3), villagers guided the commissioners to a mass grave containing seventeen corpses. Farther to the south, in La Herrera, Rioblanco's most remote settlement, Liberals presented Guzmán with the talismans of the school attack, their most visceral ordeal.[59]

By September 1958, such tales of displacement and survival began to coalesce into a discernible narrative. The commission's arrival in southern Tolima proved decisive, perhaps less for the quantity of stories collected—the commission had already accumulated thousands—than for the clarity of the Liberal experience there. At the very limits of Tolima, above which lay the forbidding tropical-alpine moors (*páramos*) that separated the Magdalena Valley from the Cauca, a picture materialized of not just the entire region but also the whole country. In his notebook, Father Guzmán recorded the first of three interpretative cuts that he would take at "violence" over the next decade. Violence, he determined, had commenced in the late 1940s as a conscious strategy by Conservative officials to ensure their party's "electoral expansion." Only subsequently did this original sin spawn a host of other maladies, embedding hostility in rural society and kicking off a wave of "crime that strangled the country."[60]

Colombia's electoral map provides arresting corroboration of Guzmán's argument about Conservative electioneering. Between 1946 and 1958, the Conservative

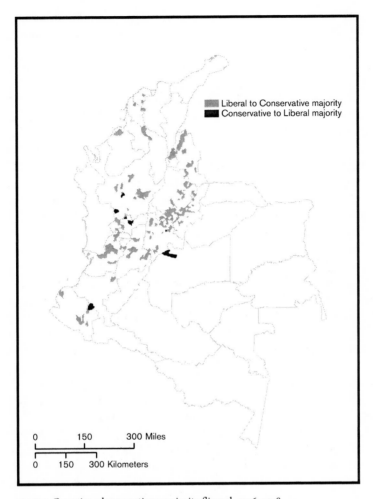

MAP 4. Counties where partisan majority flipped, 1946–1958.

Party expanded the number of counties where it represented a majority of the elec-
torate from 246 to 365, fully half of Colombia's 735 counties. In central and eastern
Tolima, and to an even greater extent in Valle del Cauca and the eastern Andean
departments (map 4), a total of 125 counties that had been majority Liberal in 1946
passed to Conservative control. (Just seven Conservative counties underwent an
equivalent process of Liberalization.) The stickiness of partisan identity meant that
such changes did not come about through programmatic appeals or regular campaigning, but rather through targeted harassment in the 1940s and more generalized violence in the 1950s.[61] In the decade after 1945, Colombia underwent a process

of partisan homogenization, whereby members of the parties flocked to the relative safety of living alongside their copartisans. This was not a local or even a regional phenomenon; Conservative-led violence was national in scope.[62]

Liberals in the provinces and Bogotá had long pointed to Conservative political designs as the spark behind violence.[63] Guzmán's conclusions may not therefore have looked radically dissimilar. The difference instead lay in the nature of the evidence available to him. Rather than relying on secondhand anecdotes or news condensed into the abbreviated form of telegrams, the commission had journeyed for weeks through a landscape that contained such durable reminders of violence as Rovira's mass grave.[64] For Guzmán, the proof was unimpeachable. What was more, the authority of local memories and artifacts came in sharp contrast to the incriminating actions of local political appointees: notwithstanding the commission's statutory power to review government records, in advance of the commissioners' arrival, intransigent Conservative agents—fearing either prosecution or simply exposure—frequently destroyed police files that implicated their copartisans.[65]

Guzmán was no stranger to the notion of "violence and persecution" being visited upon Liberals "for the sole sin of being Liberals," as one *desplazado* described it.[66] In 1952, El Líbano, the priest's later posting, had endured a massive act of collective punishment: in retaliation for an assassination attempt against the governor of Tolima and the son of Colombia's acting president, the army mounted a massive reprisal that killed as many as fifteen hundred people and demolished an estimated one thousand dwellings across the county's central swath. Guzmán would go on to declare that "the area that should be considered the most completely devastated of any seen during the [commission's] investigation."[67]

Yet despite this previous exposure, Guzmán was unprepared for what else the commission's tour revealed. Displacement, the commission discovered, had altered the evolution of Colombia's conflict; violence paradoxically carried within it the possibility of individual and social redemption. Once more, the Liberal Leopoldo García exemplified larger currents. When asked by Guzmán "How did the violence begin?," García explained that after six years of working alongside his father and brothers in Rioblanco, "1949 arrived and some commissions started up, led by . . . civilians . . . of the opposing party. They carried out the first assaults." In order to stay clear of these Conservative raids, García turned to the coffee trade. Leading mule trains between Rioblanco and Chaparral carried the added benefit of greater financial reward than farming. "But then," García recalled grimly, "the police arrived in Rioblanco."[68]

The entrance into southern Tolima of what Liberals called *chulavitas*—the most brutal breed of Conservative thugs, fighters motivated by an anti-Liberal creed and the prospect of public-sector employment—meant that danger had become inescapable.[69] García resolved that "I would prefer to die rather than to keep being humiliated by the *chulavita*." He therefore approached Gerardo Loaiza, a prosperous Rioblanco *campesino* "who already directed the resistance in these parts." At the time, Loaiza counted fewer than twenty followers, among them four of his sons. "At first we did nothing but run," García confessed, "but in the end we met up with . . . many others and we resolved to take up the offensive."[70] Unable to appeal to the regional or central government, frontier Liberals turned to their own practice of violence.

This would-be Liberal resistance stumbled out of the gate. A theater of legendary martial exploits since the arrival of the Spanish, southern Tolima had not been touched by war for decades; what locals defined as their "warrior and patriotic tradition" held out little in the way of practical guidance on how to organize. The men around Gerardo Loaiza therefore made themselves into what they thought a fighting force should look like. García reflected on these early steps with some bemusement. If the creation of a classic military hierarchy was a logical step for the Liberals to take, the accompanying measures were more difficult to iron out. Fighters mustered up a hodgepodge of uniforms; noms de guerre were likewise handed out haphazardly. "I don't know why," García told Guzmán, but "they named me 'Peligro' [Danger]."[71]

The Liberals' limited experience was most evident when it came time to define their program. Though they fashioned their struggle against the Conservatives as a "revolution," Peligro explained that "we were so crude, so ignorant, that we wrote 'revolution' with an upper-case 'b.' It was Ignacio Parra who taught us to write that word with a lower-case 'v.' I remember that well." At once appreciative and able to see the humor in the situation, Parra's comrades elevated the former Herrera schoolteacher to the position of "ideologue of the movement" and pegged him with the nickname "Revolución."[72]

In the interviews that he imparted to the National Investigatory Commission and an *El Tiempo* reporter in late August 1958 (figure 3), Peligro spoke freely about the evolution and advances of the makeshift Liberal army. He was less forthcoming about many of the losses: as the reporter sat down with Peligro amidst the burned-out houses of La Herrera, he noted that the candle illuminating their dialogue also "establish[ed] an imaginary frontier between what happened and what is narrated." In particular, Peligro glossed over the deaths of three of his four brothers.[73]

The impulse to forget was nevertheless far from total. Unlike the absence of other personal details, Peligro's narrative came back again and again to the issue of betrayal, which comprised a particularly potent form of memory. A portion of his enmity was directed at the military government, whose arrival had generated a cycle of expectations that was then incrementally dashed. The pronouncement of amnesty and guarantees in 1953 allowed Liberal combatants to descend from the recesses of Rioblanco and resume residency in villages such as La Herrera or on once-abandoned farms. By 1954, Gerardo Loaiza was complaining that the Rojas

FIGURE 3. The National Investigatory Commission visits southern Tolima, August 1958. Otto Morales Benítez (second from right) with Leopoldo García, alias Peligro (third from right); Germán Dussán, alias Santander (right); and other Liberal combatants in the plaza of La Herrera (Rioblanco). Guzmán Campos, Fals Borda, and Umaña Luna, *La violencia en Colombia,* 2nd ed., vol. 1.

government had not made good on pledges of financial and material support to rebuild the countryside. Local Conservatives resumed their depredations against the restored Liberal population, an inauspicious sign that portended outright aggression by the army itself in mid-1956. In the collective memory of Liberal combatants, this was "the big violence, that of planes, bombs, shrapnel, that of the toughest raids we ever saw." (Among these was the aerial attack against Herrera's schoolchildren.) Peligro reflected that "they were twenty times more numerous than us, and equipped with everything. I don't know how we held them off."[74]

Father Guzmán might not have been able to answer this question, but his meeting with Peligro made clear to him the larger meanings and potentialities of the Liberal resistance. "Combat changes you," Peligro told his guests. The priest concurred: Peligro was "a pure *campesino,* thrown into violence," a trial that awoke "an incredible talent."[75] When he wrote more expansively in the early 1960s about the commission's travels, Guzmán remained consistent on this point. A veritable "new way of being for the peasant man" had been realized. The people of the Colombian countryside found in their own ranks their true natural leaders. Moreover, they were expressing a deep desire to leave behind the armed resistance that had defined so much of their lives for the previous decade.[76]

The formula for reconciliation and forgiveness drew on patriotic and Christian idioms. Contact with the commission helped to drive home for provincial Colombians their role in the project of national betterment. It also gave them opportunities for absolution: following the commission's four-plus hour conversation with the leaders of La Herrera, the commission's other priest held mass for a good portion of the community's members, Liberals and Conservatives both.[77] The spectacle of patriotic fellowship would have been inseparable in Guzmán's mind from that of Christian fellowship. We know little about popular attitudes on Catholic forgiveness, but the confessions which preceded mass likely allowed the faithful to set things right with their God.[78] Perhaps they regarded as their penance the trials of martyrdom that they had already endured.

Guzmán's estimates about the capacities of rural Colombians did not stay confined to Liberals. Days after the commission left the Rioblanco Liberal commanders, it paid a visit to Teodoro Tacumá, a Conservative fighter whose group operated in the Magdalena lowlands of south-central Tolima. Though Guzmán trafficked in the racial assumptions present in others' ideas of violence, seeing Tacumá as the living incarnation of his indigenous ancestors' martial prowess, he could not help but be impressed by the man's willingness to sustain his family through other means. Holding his youngest daughter in his arms, Tacumá decried "war" and detailed how the time had come to abandon the fight, and turn instead to the pursuits of a simple man of the fields.[79]

Even more captivating to Guzmán were the exploits of a group that occupied a central place in Peligro's chronicle. For a time early in the 1950s, Loaiza's Liberals had made common cause against the *chulavitas* with another command operating in southern Tolima. This front was a oddity in Colombia's bipartisan system, the offspring of struggles which had gripped Chaparral's immense coffee estates starting in the 1930s, when cadres from the recently formed Colombian Communist Party sided with agricultural workers in the latter's push to win concessions from the coffee magnates. The terms and terrain of this class conflict shifted definitively with the Conservative restoration of 1946; systematic persecution from landlords and their allies in the state forced the *comunes*, as the Communists became known colloquially, to seek haven in the wilds of southern Tolima. It was there that they would soon meet the Loaizas.[80]

The union was not to last. Liberals bristled at the *comunes*' collectivist practices, which placed captured arms—both a military necessity and a crucial status symbol—under common ownership and centralized control over the bodies of local women, denying Liberal commanders what they had until then treated as their prerogative. Thus opened, Guzmán would later write, "an insurmountable chasm of hatred." The fissures radiated in all directions: some in the Liberal ranks

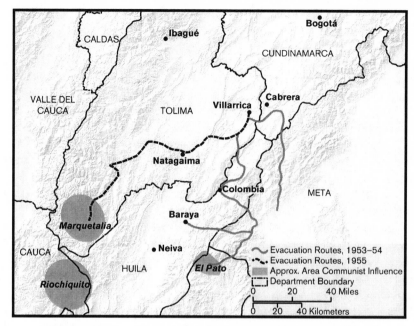

MAP 5. Gran Tolima's frontier Communist communities, 1953–1965. Adapted from Londoño Botero, *Juan de la Cruz Varela*, 485; González Arias, *Espacios de exclusión*, 167.

identified a certain laudable discipline within the *comunes* and abandoned the party of their birth. This was the second betrayal that stuck with Peligro, who from 1951 made war against the *comunes* and the treasonous "dirty" Liberals (*sucios*), hostilities that would deepen even after Peligro's "orthodox," or "clean," Liberals (*limpios*) made their peace with the military in 1953.[81]

Confronted by pressure on every side, *comunes* and *sucios* struck out for fresh horizons. Many continued in a familiar vein, following the courses of rivers and streams higher into the Andes in search of refuge. A few dozen others engaged in a perilous journey across the Tolima plains, traveling only under cover of darkness, to join another hotspot of agrarian struggle and Communist organizing in eastern Tolima (map 5). It was precisely the arrival of these seasoned combatants from the southern part of the department that occasioned the army's scorched-earth campaign against Villarrica in 1955, a hammer blow that dispersed to the winds the five thousand families who had formerly comprised one of Colombia's most thriving frontier colonization zones. In turn, hundreds of these families, their numbers thinned by constant assault from hunger and the elements, joined the *comunes* on an epic march out of the Magdalena Valley, across the eastern Andes, and down into the sparsely populated eastern piedmont (map 5).[82]

FIGURE 4. Gaitania (Ataco), 1964. Prado Delgado, *Sur del Tolima*, 200.

These trails, too, the National Investigatory Commission pursued. Technology collapsed distance in ways impossible for the *desplazados* themselves; transport in government airplanes and helicopters frequently allowed the commissioners to cover in hours distances that might have taken days on muleback or on foot.[83] As a result, the commission visited more of Gran Tolima's far-flung Communist settlements than any party representative had ever managed. Upon reaching Gaitania, the Ataco frontier hamlet that served as an entryway to the zone of Marquetalia (figure 4; map 5), soon to be Colombia's most famous Communist colony, the commission identified an uncommon refuge that welcomed people of all political stripes. Though Guzmán noted that new arrivals "must submit themselves to a protective, paternalistic communism, which obligates them every Monday to attend a conference with the political commissar responsible for the task of indoctrination," he acknowledged that "it is undeniable that while they lived side by side [*convivían*] ... [in nearby areas] blues and reds [i.e., Conservatives and Liberals] killed one another like beasts."[84]

Guzmán discerned still more to praise seventy-odd miles to the east at El Pato, a settlement along the Caquetá-Huila border (map 5). Communal effort by these survivors of the trek from Villarrica had yielded a handsome collection of sturdy dwellings (figure 5), which seemed impressive in comparison to the flimsy lodgings the commission had viewed in other *desplazado* communities.[85] The buildings also did more than provide protection from the oppressive tropical sun and punishing rains characteristic of the El Pato River basin; one housed the sole library that the commission came across in all of its travels. Hearing the origin story of the

FIGURE 5. The National Investigatory Commission visits El Pato, 1958. Guzmán (back row, third from right) with alias Richard (right). Guzmán Campos, Fals Borda, and Umaña Luna, *La violencia en Colombia*, 2nd ed., vol. 1.

community must have called to Guzmán's mind a jumble of biblical references, for here were refugees who had left a corner of Villarrica called Galilea to embark on their own version of Exodus. "That march," Guzmán concluded, "was a heroic feat of our people." [86]

Communist, Conservative, Liberal—the National Investigatory Commission's catholic approach revealed to Guzmán and other commissioners what seemed like fundamental truths about Colombia as a nation. The central import of this process of realization was not located in the details of stories of loss and perseverance, incredible though these may have been. Instead, the commission's work uncovered an unseen potentiality: Colombians' capacity to reconcile with the state and with one another in spite of the scars of violence. Traversing Gran Tolima redefined for the commissioners both ideas of violence and the meanings of politics. According to Guzmán, many of the commission's interview subjects hailed it as "the first time that [the state] come[s] to ask us what happened to us; to talk without deception;

to speak to us of peace without sending bullets our way afterward." [87] The Liberal commissioner Absalón Fernández de Soto proudly explained that the commission "has managed to break the self-imposed silence of the people, who feared to speak out of fear of retaliation on the part of the bandits. The people have conveyed their misfortunes to the members of the Commission and it seems as if this single deed—that of being able to speak—is ample demonstration that no one yearns for peace like the citizens who have suffered the scourge of violence." [88]

To be certain, a portion of Fernández de Soto's diagnosis was overly optimistic, for the commission frequently found its capacity to break silences to be partial at best. (A group of foreign visitors learned that "in one village alone 75 widows appeared before the commission to complain of the loss of their husbands and their land. No one would admit to the slightest idea of the identity of the killers.")[89] Fernández de Soto's statement is nonetheless revealing. First, Fernández acknowledged provincial Colombians as "citizens," an indication that the central state could engage with them in terms of rights and obligations, rather than dismissing violence as the product of an irrational rural society, as later historiography would mantain.[90] Second, the statement nods at a shared yearning for peace as a basis for future action.

A metamorphosis in the commission's work had commenced. In its first month, the press and political observers generally referred to the body as the "Violence Commission." However, as the commissioners entered Tolima in August, a subtle change in language took place and commentators began speaking of the "Peace Commission," a designation that persists to the present day.[91] By bringing Colombians into conversation, the commission's presence had from the start exhibited *convivencia* as an acceptable form of sociability. Now, fully swayed by the attitudes of those they encountered, the commissioners moved to formalize the promise of peace. *Desarmando los espíritus* had meanings beyond literal disarmament: *desarmar* could also signify persuasion, the act of winning over or placating someone.

This shift from memory-work to peace-work would further bring into relief the distinctiveness of both the National Investigatory Commission and the phenomenon it was sent to uncover. In contrast to the military authoritarianism that would grip other Latin American countries in ensuing decades, above all in the Southern Cone, Conservative-sponsored state violence had never eliminated armed challenges to the government—resistance that it had itself generated.[92] The deployment of coercion diffused the practice; in the absence of formal and informal representative institutions, Liberals (and Communists) themselves picked up weapons, generating a new dynamic of violence. Guzmán erred on this point when he later wrote that "the armed forces . . . cleared out once their objectives had been met, leaving the men of the rural sphere enmeshed in a merciless mutual vendetta within their regions." [93] Only in the 1950s had the military become a major actor in the armed conflict. The foundational moment of violence for Leopoldo García and countless others instead came at the hand of the *chulavitas*, private actors operating with the blessing of the Conservative government. Colombia had undergone a "privatization of the public realm" that only intensified with time.[94]

This situation remained very much in place when the National Investigatory Commission entered the countryside. Though democratic institutions had begun to function anew, the reconstruction of a regional or national common good, above the interest of party, had to contend with sometimes ongoing violence. By piecing together memories scattered by violence and displacement, as the "truth commissions" of the late twentieth century would do, the commission could contribute to new understandings of community.[95]

Yet it would be wrong to claim genealogical affiliation between the commission and those subsequent investigatory bodies. The commission's broader significance instead lies in the way it highlights the contingent creation of all postauthoritarian and postconflict campaigns to uncover the truth of recent violence. Furthermore, the shape of Colombia's postauthoritarian order was more malleable than those in the more famous Southern Cone cases, because peace remained to be achieved; no side in Colombia's indeterminate wars had been able to claim outright victory. As a result, the commission's findings would also play a fundamental role in ongoing public debates over violence. The exigencies of Colombia's particular forms of violence meant that the commission would undertake peace-making alongside memory-work—a combination which would alter the course of the democratic transition.

3

The Making of the Creole Peace, 1958–1960

As Jorge Villamil Cordovez descended the eastern Andean range and made his way up the Magdalena Valley from Bogotá, his mood better matched the capital's eternal gloom than it did his increasingly tropical surroundings. The Christmas season—the dapper young surgeon and aspiring composer's usual excuse for returning to his native Huila—was still weeks away. Villamil went instead to tend to his father's failing health. The uncertainties and insecurity plaguing southern Colombia had for years prevented the elder Jorge Villamil from visiting the coffee bushes and cedar trees of his vast plantation in easternmost Huila. Now, on the verge of his seventy-fifth year, Gran Tolima's greatest coffee baron was consigned to wait out his final days in the departmental capital of Neiva.

In addition to the more immediate apprehensions surrounding his father's demise, Jorge Villamil Cordovez carried back within himself an older set of anxieties. Music had permeated his childhood, thanks as much to the workers who labored for Don Jorge as to the legendary record collection his parents' wealth had afforded the household. Yet after half a lifetime away from Huila, Villamil worried that his desire to express through song his longing for his native region would risk being interpreted as an unacceptable departure from his medical studies, an affront to the proper social customs (*buenas costumbres*) that his father had strictly enforced.

Villamil's homecoming began to dispel these fears. A month before the patriarch's death, a local trio serenaded the Villamil house with three original compositions by Jorge the younger. His father—whose exacting ear had long intimidated Jorge and his six older sisters—greeted Villamil's brave showing with a smile and praise.[1]

Fortified by his father's approval, Villamil embarked on a new song. The milieu of Gran Tolima provided no shortage of material. Already in Bogotá, Villamil had observed firsthand the sense of optimism that accompanied the fall of the dicta-torship. In Neiva these seven months later, he heard tell of a particular, regional manifestation of hope: the departure from urban areas of rural folk who had been displaced from their farms and now felt safe enough to return. As they sat around Don Jorge's bed, Villamil's relatives shared the family's personal connection to this drama, news that the impoverished and persecuted country inhabitants who years earlier had occupied the margins of Don Jorge's estate were laying aside their arms.[2]

Such sentiments and stories resonated keenly with Villamil family lore. Parti-san persecution, and then exodus, had fixed the destinies of Villamil's grandfather and father, leading the former to his death on a Tolima battlefield in 1885 and the latter eventually to fortune. Embracing these tales, along with the contemporary accounts circulating through Neiva's streets, Jorge Villamil set about composing a ballad of loss and possibility. Arranged to the quick guitar strummings of the *bam-buco*, Andean Colombia's foremost folk music genre, "The Return of José Dolores" ("El Retorno de José Dolores") layered regional nostalgia on the human travails of José Dolores, Gran Tolima's allegorical peasant.[3]

Vuelvo solo y vengo triste	I return alone and arrive melancholy
me llamo José Dolores	my name is José Dolores
vuelvo a mi tierra querida	I return to my beloved land
a calmar mis sinsabores	to soothe my heartaches
vuelvo a mi tierra querida	I return to my beloved land
a calmar mis sinsabores.	to soothe my heartaches.
Quiero volver a vivir	I want to live once more
esas tardes campesinas	those country afternoons
con su paz tradicional	with their traditional peace
en el Tolima y el Huila.	in Tolima and Huila.
Oír resonar tiples	To hear *tiples*[4]
y guitarras en la llanura,	and guitars resounding over the plain
grato repicar, cual canción de paz	[what a] pleasing ring, that song of peace
de alegres campanas.	from cheerful bells.
Quiero perdonar y olvidar mis penas	I want to forgive and forget my sorrows
Deseo trabajar, por mi patria nueva	I wish to work, for my new *patria*
oír repicar, cual canción de paz	to hear ring, that song of peace
de alegres campanas.	from cheerful bells.
Retorno de la ciudad	Return from the city
solo, lleno de optimismo	alone, full of optimism
a levantar sobre escombros,	to raise over the rubble
la choza, aquí en mis dominios	a hut, here on my lands
a levantar sobre escombros,	to raise over the rubble
la choza, aquí en mis dominios.[5]	a hut, here on my lands.

"The Return of José Dolores" represented an anthem for its moment in Colombian history. By the time the song first gained public recognition that following Christmas of 1958, the phenomenon of repatriation that Villamil discerned had grown to significant proportions both within and beyond Gran Tolima. Tens of thousands of Colombians like José Dolores made their way back to their lands during the first months of the National Front, encouraged by the national political climate, by rhetorical and substantive moves toward a more participatory politics.[6] This return across space also involved a double trip through time: a reckoning with memories of the past and the possibility of envisioning a future. Repatriation reproduced at an individual or family level many of the dynamics of the democratic transition.

The many returns of these real-life José Dolores unfolded within and contributed to the creole peace. As Alberto Lleras Camargo took office, state and provincial actors deepened the range of negotiations and reforms initiated during the early democratic transition, solidifying the "truce" of 1957–58.[7] Amidst continued institution building, Colombians from all political stripes endeavored to cast violence out of the public realm, to fill Colombia's newly redemocratized political space with practices and cultures of peace. Provincial elites and backcountry leaders frequently made common ground on the question of regional and local progress, a confluence that defined the creole peace as not simply the absence of physical force, but also as a project for *convivencia* and an equitable prosperity.

Over the past four decades, Colombian observers have come to see the closing years of the 1950s as merely a pause in an otherwise continuously bloody national story. By contrast, neither Alberto Lleras nor José Dolores could have predicted the fate of the creole peace that both helped to build. Contemporaries certainly recognized that their quest to carve out new channels of state-citizen relations often faltered in the face of entrenched ways of doing politics. The creole peace was also a spatially uneven affair, never encompassing all of Gran Tolima or other regions.

Nevertheless, the enterprise of peace—a diverse set of responses to Colombia's diverse varieties of violence—seized Colombians' imaginations. It became the primary referent of politics in central and southern Colombia, as well as the anchor of people's expectations toward the state. The peace was homegrown not only because it originated within national boundaries but also because it developed in part from the initiatives of local and regional actors. By enabling civil interactions over questions of citizenship, the creole peace extended the process of democratization, allowing rural groups a greater say in the direction of local affairs and providing them with new means to connect to their regions and nation. Though negotiations between the government and rural armed actors helped to create momentum, there was no formal peace process. Imperfect and partial though it might have been, the peace was itself the process.

PATHS TO PEACE, 1957–1958

As the National Investigatory Commission produced new forms of knowledge about violence, its encounters with provincial Colombians yielded a different sort of novelty for the multiple publics who participated in them from the other side. The fact of the commission's presence signaled interest from far-off authorities, a vindication of the energies and lives expended by rural residents during years of conflict.[8] As the official representative of the state, the commission carried an unmatched weight. Nonetheless, the commission was but one in a series of recent interlocutors to elicit this sentiment. Indeed, earlier preliminary contacts between state officials, party delegates, and people in the countryside made possible key elements of the commissioners' stopover in La Herrera.

Peace had been a tricky proposition in Tolima during the later Rojas years. The department slid into a dark period in the aftermath of the 1955 assault on Villarrica, as the army widened its crackdown to both sides of the Magdalena Valley.[9] For party leaders anxious to halt the bloodshed, the government's position marked the epitome of authoritarian caprice; regional military officials might attempt negotiation only to be undermined by Bogotá. For instance, despite the fact that Tolima's military governor had sanctioned the convening of a high-level bipartisan "alliance for peace" in Ibagué, agents of the Colombian Intelligence Service (Servicio de Inteligencia Colombiana) responded by raiding the Liberal Party's Bogotá's headquarters in search of "subversive [material]." Censors then barred recently appointed party head Alberto Lleras from publishing a response to this outrage. "I am exasperated by the impossibility that an absurd and blundering tyranny imposes on all good citizens [who would] work for the good of the country, for peace and conciliation between Colombians," former president Eduardo Santos wrote to Lleras. "That the current dictatorship has guaranteed peace is one of the lies [the country] is living."[10] British diplomats later concurred with Lleras's assessment that the state of siege, the basis of Rojas's rule, depended upon continued upheaval in Tolima.[11]

Resistance from men like Peligro introduced the first cracks in the government's policy, an opening that would widen as the dictatorship tottered. "With the situation [in southern Tolima] stalemated" thanks to *limpio* defiance, and the presidential succession crisis underway, military officers and Liberal chiefs launched a renewed peace venture under more promising circumstances. While a newly appointed military governor wielded a carrot and gentler stick, arresting some Liberal commanders and offering guarantees to the rest, government aircraft transported the leading lights of Tolima Liberalism into Chaparral, from whence they departed on muleback for the punishing ride to Rioblanco (map 3).[12] The contrast between these representatives of the *país político* and their rough country hosts was not lost on the participants. At the head of the Liberal Party delegation was the severe fifty-something Rafael Parga Cortés, who had only lived in Colombia for part of his adult life. Born in England to an expatriate banker, the Oxford-educated "Lord Parga" still exhibited a notable accent. Peligro later admitted that "we accepted [Parga's] proposal [for peace], despite sometimes not being able to understand the language he spoke."[13]

Parga's presence nonetheless carried an unmistakable message. For much of the previous decade, provincial Liberals far removed and seemingly ignored by their "natural chiefs" in Bogotá had fought and suffered in the name of the party and its ideals, ill-defined though these may have been. (One analyst hazarded that for most of Tolima's inhabitants, "Liberalism is a spiritual position more than a philosophical idea.")[14] The arrival of such high-level delegations into Liberal-held territory in 1957 affirmed not only the value of the *limpios'* struggle but also the authority that they themselves had created.[15] Though Parga surely did not see Peligro as his equal, this illiterate son of a farmer was a man to be reckoned with.

Southern Tolima's Liberals garnered additional redress in the months that followed. As soon as the dictatorship crumbled in May 1957, the *junta* certified the extension of talks between party delegates and rural fighters. These discussions further reinforced the air of calm that had settled over sections of Tolima, which in turn permitted the government to close dozens of military outposts and withdraw a thousand troops from the department (steps made all the more desirable by Bogotá's desperate fiscal situation).[16] The *limpios* had already come down from the hills to resume life in villages like La Herrera, a change that would eventually make possible the Peace Commission's visit. With the army's departure, Liberal fighters and other residents of Tolima could also move through a landscape with fewer reminders of the state's repressive presence.

The scene was set for a final act of confirmation. In late August 1957, Liberal commanders convened a "supreme council" that once more drew the attendance of the departmental party leadership. Though the politicians hoped to keep an eye on the proceedings of their copartisans, they were more likely motivated by a sense of party and regional solidarity, a shared aspiration of peace. How, after all, could these Liberal notables have hoped to subordinate Peligro and his men? As the journalist who had met Peligro wrote, the *limpios* "had won . . . a peace very much their own." Self-assured of their position, the commanders used the council to ratify their previous military structure, which they retitled the National Liberal Revolutionary Movement of Southern Tolima (Movimiento Liberal Nacional Revolucionario del Sur del Tolima). However grandiose that designation, the council's other business concerned itself with wholly local priorities. The movement proclaimed its own legal code, which imposed controls on the movement of peoples and goods, established sanctions for infractions, and set up mechanisms for social projects. The code additionally prohibited alcohol from movement territory, a not-uncommon practice in Colombia, and one born less from of any sense of moralism than from a pragmatic assessment about the preconditions for order.[17]

While the August council capped the collective ascendency of southern Tolima's Liberals, it also marked a coronation of sorts for Peligro, who was made the movement's sole brigadier general. Gerardo Loaiza, the "man with the big pants" when Leopoldo García first committed to fight the Conservatives, still held sway closer to Rioblanco. Nonetheless, warring against so many foes had dimmed the man's vitality and cost him the lives of two of his sons.[18] The realities of geography ensured that Peligro would hold little more than titular authority over the loose confederation of other movement generals, each with his own slice of the mountains. Peligro would be, however, the most visible leader when Father Guzmán and his companions arrived at Rioblanco the following year.

The formation of the National Liberal Revolutionary Movement marked but one example of the rural political process that accompanied Colombia's democratization and that set the country apart from post-1970 Latin American transitions. Scenes like Peligro's meeting with Parga played out across the country from mid-1957: from the heat-baked Eastern Plains of Casanare and Meta, to the mist-ensconced mountains of the Sumapaz zone south of Bogotá, to the jungles of Huila and Caquetá, top government and party officials met with some of the country's most renowned combatants—not only Liberal, but also Communist. A surge of petitions followed.[19] The *limpios'* appeal, composed at the beginning of 1958, is representative. Citing their "condition as citizens," Peligro and nearly fifty of his followers expressed to the *junta* their hopes for "this new [post-plebiscite] Constitutional phase." Their demands centered on the institutional reforms they felt the state should undertake: fuller participation for Liberals in the presidential cabinet; the end of military trials for civilians; and the establishment of parity within both the police and the government's preeminent rural lending agency, the Agrarian, Industrial, and Mining Bank (Caja de Crédito Agrario, Industrial y Minero). These reversals of dictatorship-era practices, the *limpios* argued, would expand democratic protections and provide the basis for a new state policy toward the countryside, which would include as well schools and the loosening of Agrarian Bank loan requirements.[20]

Whether or not framed explicitly in terms of citizenship, these petitions demonstrated clear expectations of the state. Their authors would remain consistent in the structure and content of their missives over subsequent years, indicating how seriously they took both the genre of petitioning and the issues they chose to bring to the capital's attention. In their own way, the petitions were an act of *convivencia,* a statement that confirmed civility as a component of citizenship alongside rights and responsibilities.[21] Such patterns of claims-making moreover indicate that purported ideological differences between "clean" Liberals and Communists had less salience than elements of a shared regional political culture. Whatever their party alliances, Gran Tolima's rural inhabitants frequently expressed a common set of demands—for roads, loans, and the return of abandoned or stolen lands—and evinced a similar attentiveness to shifting political opportunities.

The difference between Liberals and Communists instead lay in the institutional networks they had access to as political life resumed in 1957. Pinched though the Liberal Party had been by legal and extralegal measures under successive Conservative and military governments, the Communist Party had absorbed the brunt of political prohibition. Faced on one side with an outright ban on its existence, the party had endured a sustained assault against its miniscule membership. The urban Communist Party leadership therefore began the democratic transition looking to rebuild its organization, including links with those in the countryside who had fought under the party's name.[22] Rather than moving to adopt an insurrectionary position, as a Cold War–centered narrative might assume, Colombia's Communists were one in a wide spectrum of actors to welcome the political possibilities opened by democratization.[23]

With the significant but little-documented exception of Lord Parga's visit with Marquetalia's Communists around the time of the National Liberal Revolutionary Movement of Southern Tolima's founding conference (figure 6), Communism's marginality meant that contacts between Gran Tolima's rural Communists and the government generally materialized months after Liberal combatants had commenced their own negotiations. Subsequent contacts frequently occurred through the auspices of influential regional Liberals. The *país político* possessed many such men, white-collar Bogotá professionals linked to the provinces by family ties and agricultural holdings. Having snapped up huge tracts of public lands on the peripheries of Huila and Caquetá, Gran Tolima's representatives in this stratum exemplified the entrepreneurial frontier spirit on a grand scale. At crucial moments during the transition, they served as key intermediaries between capitals and the regions. Motivated on the one hand to protect their investments, they demonstrated too an interest in advancing regional progress, a role which would lead them into contact with far more modest frontier settlers.

Elite envoys often had to overcome substantial isolation and mistrust in these encounters. Sometime in 1957 or 1958, Gentil Quintero Luna, a Huila lawyer who would soon ascend to the upper echelons of the department's coffee planters, dodged police patrols to undertake a four-hour hike up to the outer reaches of El Pato (map 5). Shortly after midnight, dozens of men with shotguns slung over their shoulders forced Quintero to come to a halt. At first unconvinced by Quintero's explanations of "how the political parties had put an end to political violence for the good of the nation," these Liberals-turned-Communists eventually agreed to meet with Huila's military governor after Quintero assertively pledged his own life as guarantee for theirs.[24] Much as the "men of the mountain" perceived their visitors' presence as a mark of respect, so too did they themselves afford respect to the boldness of these outsiders.[25]

The frontier Communists took seriously the potential inherent in the transition to the Second Republic. They benefited as much as the *limpios* from the army's

FIGURE 6. Liberal leaders visit southern Tolima's Communists, September 1957. Rafael Parga Cortés (fourth from left); Fermín Charry Rincón, alias Charro Negro (fifth from left); Pedro Antonio Marín, alias Manuel Marulanda Vélez, alias Tirofijo (fourth from right). Rocío Londoño Botero, personal archive.

partial mid-1957 withdrawal from Tolima. But more than that, *convivencia* seemed to be carrying in on the evening breeze. As a result, on Christmas eve 1957, residents of Gran Tolima's Communist settlements gathered at Marquetalia to consummate the push toward new forms of sociability. Going a step farther than the *limpios,* the Communists abolished the military ranks that had structured their collective lives for the better part of the past decade. Individually, too, the former fighters regained something of their past selves, as each dispensed with the nom de guerre endowed by the war.[26]

However, such rites did not completely efface the memorialization of struggle and sacrifice. Among those Liberals who had joined the Communist Party was the Loaizas's kinsman Pedro Antonio Marín, a taciturn Caldas native born in 1930—year of the Liberals' great electoral triumph. When he threw in his lot with the Communists, Marín's new spiritual fathers rebaptized him Manuel Marulanda Vélez, after a cofounder of the Communist Party's Medellín branch who had been tortured to death by the Colombian Intelligence Service in 1950. Marín/Marulanda welcomed the change, hoping that the name would supersede the alias imposed on him during the war—Tirofijo, or Sureshot, a sobriquet he despised (figure 6).[27] When a fresh moment of self-reinvention arrived at Christmas 1957, Tirofijo opted to remain Manuel Marulanda Vélez rather than reclaim his birth name.

A season in these men's lives had nevertheless come to a conclusion. Amidst tears, the majority of fighters residing around Marquetalia opted to return to their homes in Valle del Cauca, Caldas, and other portions of the country. The two hundred who remained set to work carving out their futures from the steep, foggy slopes of the region's forests.[28]

DEEPENING THE TRUCE, 1958

The partial dissolution of the Communist movement at Marquetalia typified a broader process that transpired across Colombia after the removal of Rojas. "The democratic restoration was in itself a valuable factor in the recuperation of amity," a senior military officer would write in his memoirs.[29] In a signal of hope—if not confidence—in the country's direction, thousands of displaced Colombians elected to return to their places of origin in the later months of 1957. This was the process that inspired Jorge Villamil to pen "The Return of José Dolores" during the same weeks when so many Marquetalia residents departed.

Villamil's optimistic take on repatriation was somewhat premature. The fortunes of these early José Dolores were far from assured. The cultural production more fitting in terms of tone was Gonzalo Canal Ramírez's short film *This Was My Village,* which the perpetually crotchety Canal Ramírez ended on a downbeat note, the film's nameless protagonist riding alone past the empty homes and abandoned fields of a land "invaded" by "weeds and crosses."[30]

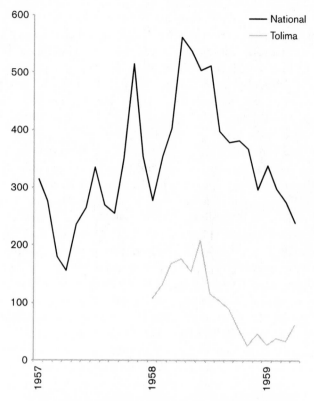

FIGURE 7. Monthly homicides attributed to partisan violence, January 1957–April 1959. Based on a database in my possession; data from Colombian and U.S. government sources.

For the José Dolores of 1957–58, dangers more alive than ghosts populated the paths home. Confrontation with the memory of loss mattered rather less than the ongoing prospect of harm.[31] With the exception of a drop in January, Colombia's partisan homicide figures remained above 350 per month from October 1957 well into 1958 (figure 7). Though it housed just over 6 percent of the country's population, Tolima accounted for as much as 40 percent of the national death toll during this period.[32] The de facto "truce" declared by *limpios* and Communists—the department's most formidable armed groups—had pacified the south, but other areas endured violence that clustered around three practices vital to Colombians' sense of identity: democratic elections, coffee cultivation, and transportation. First, the 1958 elections stirred up partisan spirits, producing a series of fatalities that sapped the democratic triumphalism espoused by many National Front backers. Second, this electoral violence overlapped with the largest of the year's two

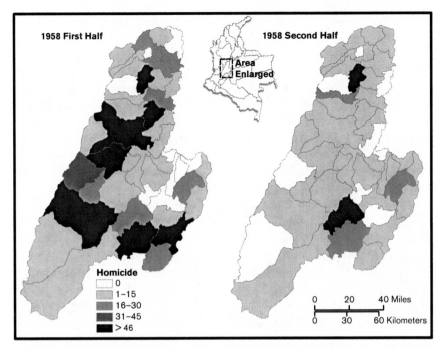

MAP 6. Monthly homicides attributed to partisan violence, Tolima, 1958. An interactive version of this map can be viewed at rakarl.com/research/forgotten-peace. Based on a database in my possession; data from Colombian government and press sources.

coffee harvests, which contributed its own surge in crimes against property and human integrity all along the central Andes in northern and central Tolima (map 6).[33] By April, over 70 percent of Tolima's counties witnessed murders or assaults, a distribution substantially above that of the preceding months.

Virtually no activity in the coffee republic seemed safe. A third practice, intermunicipal bus transport, a mainstay of daily life, came under repeated assault in May and June. In separate incidents in Alvarado and rural Ibagué, each in the predawn hours, gunmen halted a pair of buses and proceeded to rob the passengers before despatching dozens with machete blows and small-arms fire. The scope of the massacres, and the assailants' disregard for the party affiliations of their victims, shocked commentators. Taking up the motif of movement, an *El Tiempo* editorial called on Colombians to back unreservedly the "anti-violence . . . policy" of the National Front, whose "great [reason] for being . . . has been to guarantee concord and to make possible the transition [lit., crossing] toward democracy along the secure paths of *convivencia*." In the absence of such a patriotic gesture, the newspaper warned, "barbarity . . . is crushing our dignity and conscience, shaming us in front of outsiders and humiliating us before ourselves."[34] Violence cast regional and national identity into doubt.

Humiliation also described the feeling of numerous repatriated *desplazados,* who found themselves forced to flee anew in the face of these electoral and apolitical trends in violence.[35] The original act of displacement generally advanced in stages, from farm to village, where the displaced might have family, and from there on to a larger town and perhaps ultimately a city such as Ibagué or Bogotá.[36] To relive this drama through a second round of displacement could provoke a deep questioning of self, a multifold act evident in a 1958 complaint from the central Tolima county of Valle de San Juan (map 5). Emasculated by their separation from their lands and by their consequent inability to provide as "fathers of large families," the thirteen signers of the complaint, who had been forced to seek refuge in Valle's villages, also felt diminished in relationship to the state. "We challenge all those who would reproach us for being poor citizens," the men wrote. They were not beneath meeting their obligations, proclaiming a willingness "to go to prison, if we . . . have committed violent crimes or [offenses] against property." They were nevertheless more pointed in invoking the other side of citizenship—the language of rights. "We too have rights," their letter concluded, "and for that reason we request justice . . . we can no longer continue waiting for hunger to advance over our homes."[37]

Other sentiments of longing found more lyrical expression, as a *bambuco* collected by Guzmán indicated:

A mí denme un aguardiente	Go ahead and give me an *aguardiente*
Un aguardiente de caña	A sugarcane brandy
De las cañas de mis valles	From the cane of my valleys
y el anís de mis montañas	and the anise of my mountains
No me den trago extranjero	Don't give me a drink from outside
que es caro y no sabe a bueno	that's pricey and doesn't taste as good
y porque yo quiero siempre	for, I will always love best
lo de mi tierra primero.[38]	that which comes from my land.

The chances of these José Dolores ultimately depended on the confluence of energies from center and periphery. Much as had occurred after May 1957, Alberto Lleras's August 1958 inauguration witnessed a certain amount of democratic optimism. However, the crucial distinction in this second phase of the transition lay in the fact that urban and provincial Colombians, individually and jointly, had elaborated more sophisticated means to talk about and act against violence. With no additional elections on the immediate horizon, political continuity, absent in 1957–58, afforded these ideas and practices more space in which to unfold.

The primary institutional expression of *convivencia* in the provinces remained the National Investigatory Commission, which hit its stride in Tolima just as the wheels of government in Bogotá were retooling for the Lleras era. The commission's adoption of a peace-making role for itself reinforced, rather than originated, micro and macro tendencies. In the former category, departmental and county partisan leaders across the country had begun to commit their organizations to peace.[39] On a broader scale, the passing of the election and coffee seasons helped to drive homicide levels down from their midyear highs (figure 7).

Even so, when Father Guzmán wrote in 1962 that "the immense effort realized [against violence] since May 10, 1957 . . . could well be called 'How Peace Was Made,'" he had in mind his commission's contribution. Beginning in late July, and then in earnest from late August, the commission reached fifty-two local pacts between armed groups and between these and the government (map 7). The commissioners had no script to follow, nor even, evidently, any direct instructions from Bogotá on the structure or content of the agreements. The hunt for tigers, which had led them into the countryside in the first place, now prompted them to improvise mechanisms for peace-making.

The local pacts additionally highlighted the Peace Commission's capacity to redraw scales: while many negotiations were realized locally, the reverse could also take place, with the periphery coming to the center. Two days after Guzmán met the National Liberal Revolutionary Movement on its home turf, the same aircraft that had carried him brought Liberal and Conservative chiefs from the area to Ibagué. After the commission presented Liberal governor Darío Echandía with the movement's "proposal for peace," Ataco's senior Liberal commander signed "an agreement of friendship" with Conservatives from a nearby village. Both sides "pledged as well to cooperate with the government in the pacification of the department." "Complete calm" ruled in Ataco, Chaparral, and Rioblanco, Echandía informed Bogotá in mid-September. "The insurgents at arms," he cabled the Interior Ministry, "have carried out what they promised."[40]

A review of spatial trends in violence indicates that Echandía perceived patterns already months old. Southern Tolima had been largely peaceful over the course of the year (map 6), due to the existing truce. The potential import of the commission's peace-work was more evident in the southeastern portion of the department, which had been ablaze prior to the commissioners' arrival. Whole villages disappeared in flames across Natagaima during the middle months of 1958, as reprisal attacks consumed neighboring Liberal and Conservative communities. The most extreme episode sent six hundred Conservative survivors staggering up the Magdalena Valley to Neiva; government officials reported no adult men among the refugees.[41] This localized violence also spilled over into surrounding counties. An early September massacre of twenty-four people in southern Coyaima, just over the line from Natagaima, represented Tolima's single greatest loss of life that month.[42]

The interventions of the Peace Commission ensured that the Coyaima attack was by then a rarity. August's death toll in Tolima was half of July's; October's half

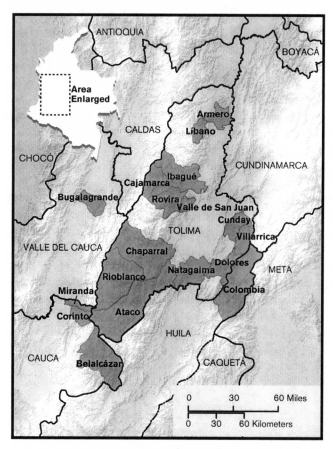

MAP 7. Counties with peace pacts negotiated by the National
Investigatory Commission, 1958. Partial listing of the fifty-two total
pacts. Some counties witnessed multiple pacts. Based on data from
memorandum, Echandía to Interior Ministry; Molano, *Amnistía y
violencia*, 68; "Los pactos han sido eficaces," 2.

of August's; and November's half of October's (figure 7). By the end of the year, the
Colombian Intelligence Service testified that "the most complete atmosphere of
rehabilitation and peace reigns in the majority of regions in [Tolima]."[43] Because
Tolima had accounted for such a high percentage of national homicides, President
Lleras was able to project a positive assessment via an early December radio
address. There were still "many reasons for concern," Lleras confirmed, "but also
concrete causes for optimism. Alongside a new, appalling crime that cuts short the

life of fifty defenseless Colombians, there is the extension of peace to regions that until yesterday seemed unpardonably lost." [44]

In the end, this progress in the anti-violence campaign pitted the commission's peace-work against its memory-work. The two functions were not in themselves contradictory; the commissioners continued to uncover accounts of violence even as they orchestrated peace pacts. (Such was the case with the Conservative "Indian" Teodoro Tacumá, whose adherence in early September was essential for the pacification of the zone around Natagaima.) However, save Guzmán, who would stay on in a consultancy role for another few months, the commission ceased operations before year's end, shortly after informing Lleras that the country had been "practically pacified." [45] This rather abrupt finale left the commission's findings unpackaged, the memories and voices of the thousands of Colombians it interviewed without a full public airing.

Indeed, in further contrast to the truth commissions of the late twentieth century, the Peace Commission produced no final report.[46] Here, too, Colombians had no script to follow, no international norms around truth and reconciliation to which to conform. The improvised format of the commission's tour also played into the absence of a report: between what were essentially four regional circuits, the commissioners opted to repair to Bogotá to conclave with Lleras and his senior cabinet ministers on how the commission's germinal "practical solutions" could be implemented.[47] "Circumstances," Guzmán told an interviewer in the 1980s, "indicated that we should present incremental reports to the President." A preference for delivering these findings orally likely limited their subsequent dissemination.[48]

We can also trace the absence of a final commission report to partisan disagreements over the origins of violence in Colombia's recent past, particularly given Lleras's later abundance of caution on similar issues. On the surface, politicians and the press treated the commission as a triumph. In the first national radio address of his presidency, for instance, Lleras declared that the commission "has [provided] for the government an orientation whose value we cannot exaggerate . . . my impression is that for the first time in ten years someone has reached the very crux of the social, political, economic, and moral problem of this inexpressible tragedy." [49] A comprehensive, national idea of violence had come into being.

Within the país político, by contrast, the specifics of the commission's recommendations were more contentious. On the basis of the evidence it uncovered, the commission arrived at "the certainty that the violence had been undertaken by a Conservative government against the Liberal Party." The commissioners therefore pushed Lleras to modify the state's fundamental rural institutions, the Agrarian Bank and the semi-official National Federation of Coffee Growers (FEDECAFE; Federación Nacional de Cafeteros), in order to remove the discrimination these had practiced against Liberals since 1946.[50] Such steps would have fulfiled the demands of the limpios and other provincial actors, but cogovernment with the

Conservatives effectively prevented Lleras from adopting them outright. However, provincial realities—namely the nature of recent violence—would ultimately guide his administration's policies toward many of these same outcomes.

In the immediate term, the commission buttressed within Lleras's administration what amounted to a Liberal idea of violence. Contrary to a good number of their countrymen, who perceived Colombia's experience over the previous decade as "a gigantic wave of criminality, of the most cruel and monstrous characteristics that any country has ever seen," Lleras and his advisors observed "an internal war" sparked by "partisan hostility" that had only gradually transformed into "economically motivated violence" and "out-and-out delinquency." Such emphasis on "the civil content" of Colombia's upheaval allowed the administration to justify an antiviolence policy based on "persuasion and systems of conciliation" as "the only possible path to peace."[51] Bogotá's diagnosis of violence as the result of partisan and socioeconomic grievances also permitted the Lleras administration to pursue developmental reforms. For the next two years, endeavors to build upon the commission's discoveries and initial steps toward *convivencia* would define Lleras's presidency.

REHABILITATION AS NATIONAL POLICY

Three men—all three of them Liberals, all three from Colombia's Andean core—would steer Bogotá's new policy toward the provinces. Their brief was at once outwardly directed and inward looking. On the one hand, the Lleras administration faced a modification of the state's relationship to its citizens, including a determination of how the government would relate to those who had engaged in violence.[52] In the words of one of its architects, the government looked to grant "people the opportunity to obtain a complete rehabilitation, stripping them of the hatreds and retaliations that differentiated them for so many years."[53] The rehabilitation of Colombia as a nation would begin at the level of the individual. On the other hand, this entire enterprise demanded adjustments to the structure of the state itself. Democratization would need to be followed by the creation of responsive, representative institutions.

The first driver of this undertaking was none other than Alberto Lleras. The president's vision of democratic institutionalism established the bounds of his government's rehabilitation project, while his pursuit of bipartisanship set its tone. Atop the docket was the restoration of normal democratic rule. Within weeks of taking office, Lleras ended Colombia's constitutional state of siege. For the first time in nearly nine years, governance would take place through the functioning of the three branches of state. With abuses of the state of siege having ranked as one of Lleras's main complaints during his return to journalism and politics in the mid-1950s, his own later reliance on the state of siege provoked evident discomfort. When confronted in December 1958 by rumors of an impending coup—a threat amplified by Gustavo Rojas Pinilla's October return from his post-ouster exile—Lleras reestablished a state of siege nationwide. In announcing the decision, Lleras advertised that "there will never be, nor has there been in my already long public career, a decision taken with more repugnance." The passing of the threat and the reversal of the total state of siege six weeks later must have come as an enormous relief.[54]

The state of siege was not without its uses. A strict application of state-of-siege powers, Lleras explained elsewhere, represented "an extremely modest instrument for the preservation of public order and the defense of a weak democracy."[55] (By contrast, under emergency authority Lleras's Conservative and military predecessors had unleashed a blizzard of conflicting regulations on subjects ranging from labor and tax policy to penal procedure.)[56] Lleras therefore saw fit to maintain the state of siege in Tolima, Huila, Cauca, Valle del Cauca, and Caldas (map 8), where extraordinary executive powers could be applied against persistent rural strife.

Gran Tolima and the three departments to its west would henceforth represent the locus of rehabilitation. To administer Bogotá's course of action, Lleras established (via extraordinary decree) a parallel cabinet, the Special Rehabilitation Commission (Comisión Especial de Rehabilitación). From its inception in early September 1958 until December 1960, the Rehabilitation Commission coordinated with existing ministries; the small, independent Office of Rehabilitation (Oficina de Rehabilitación); and departmental affiliates.[57] (This chapter will hereafter refer to "rehabilitation" as the general task of reconstruction, and to "Rehabilitación" as its institutional expression.) Management of Rehabilitación went to José Gómez Pinzón, a stern Liberal engineer three years Lleras's junior. Gómez Pinzón was a natural pick, the political operator to Lleras' statesman. A crucial player in organizing the business community's actions against Rojas in May 1957, Gómez Pinzón not only knew his way around the government contracting process from both sides but also had a reputation for getting things done in a country with its own reputation for red tape and inefficiency.[58] His hard-charging style gained additional impetus by virtue of the state of siege; Rehabilitación's special legal regime allowed officials to circumvent the usual rules for government contracts.[59]

Rehabilitación had massive sums to allocate. The government appropriated 25 million pesos in separate funding for rehabilitation in 1958, a sum that ballooned in 1959 to almost 67.6 million pesos—the equivalent of roughly $25.5 and $69 million in 2016 U.S. dollars. This "considerable budget," as one minister termed it, equaled perhaps 5 percent of the central state's spending—a sizeable figure made all the more considerable by Colombia's ongoing economic crisis. Rehabilitación received more funding than nearly half of the country's thirteen ministries.[60] Such outlays would permit the government to "irrigate . . . with money" those regions that had undergone some of Colombia's sharpest violence, Gómez Pinzón

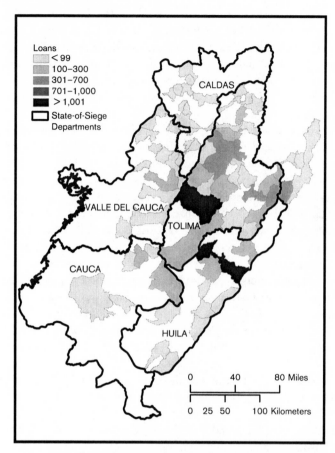

MAP 8. State-of-siege departments and distribution of Agrarian Bank rehabilitation loans (as of June 1959). Based on data from "Prestamos de Rehabilitacion y cupos asignados (nuevos y renovaciones)," June 17, 1959, AGN.PR.SG.303.9.5–6.

explained.[61] A portion of spending would go toward expanding the state's territorial reach, through initiatives including improved radio communications systems, the formation of mounted police units capable of pursuing suspects across the rough terrain of the backcountry, and the addition of extra prosecuting judges to augment an overwhelmed judiciary.[62] Though the Lleras administration's conceptualization of violence centered on partisan causes, it still recognized the presence of high levels of apolitical criminality.

Historians have tended to highlight these rehabilitation programs as an embodiment of the Colombian elite's interest in pacification through repression. To be certain, as Gonzalo Sánchez G. has written, concentrated flashes of violence pushed the Rehabilitation Commission to debate moving money from other rehabilitation projects to bolster police forces.[63] Nonetheless, the most substantial share of Rehabilitación's monies went toward improving social welfare. In education, for instance, Rehabilitación funded the construction of schools for nearly twenty-five thousand students, bolstering Tolima's enrollment capacity by more than 20 percent.[64]

Such long-term investments in Colombia's future were seen as especially vital given the distortions wrought by violence on an entire generation of rural children, who might well themselves become Colombia's next offenders. The president was among the first to articulate this concern, as he spoke of "a generation that does not know other modes of relation, nor another type of life, nor work other than criminal action, nor any prospect [*expectativa*] beyond killing or dying."[65] The image of this generation fused together one of Alberto Lleras's guiding intellectual frameworks—that of generational turnover—with one of his perennial preoccupations—demographic growth. Other Colombians shared Lleras's attention to the subject; the fates of Colombia's newest generation would become an important and politically consequential trope in the gradual evolution of the term "La Violencia" over the first half of the National Front period.

Rehabilitación additionally presented the Lleras administration with an agile, well-funded means to tackle the broader issue of underdevelopment. The Rehabilitation Commission sponsored fourteen pilot All-Purpose Teams (Equipos Polivalentes), thus giving form to one of Father Lebret's central proposals. By bringing doctors, engineers, topographers, agronomists, home improvement specialists, and nurses to some of Colombia's poorest counties, the teams sought to raise socioeconomic indicators at the local level.[66] In this way, Lleras's government connected the problem of development to the problem of violence more explicitly than Lebret himself had.

Addressing underdevelopment through such technical means also presented the *país político* with an opportunity to address long-running anxieties about the work, cleanliness, and morality of the poor.[67] The teams, to say nothing of the very term "rehabilitation," betrayed the *país político*'s simultaneous impulse to better the stock of Colombia's inhabitants. So entrenched was this preference that Lleras's subordinates apparently saw nothing wrong in using terminology that had been employed by Rojas's government, which had run its own Office of Rehabilitation and Aid (Oficina de Rehabilitación y Socorro).

This emphasis on the *país nacional* aligned perfectly with the strategy of advancing development through physical infrastructure. Rehabilitación's second-largest line item entailed the creation of some ten thousand jobs, the vast majority of them in public works construction.[68] These road and airstrip projects intentionally eschewed mechanized labor in favor of sponsoring as many paid positions as possible. Of particular interest were the generation of employment outside of the coffee harvest season (which explains the concentration of a third of the jobs in Caldas, Colombia's leading coffee region) and the inclusion of former combatants. Road construction would thus foster market and political integration, meeting the unending local clamor for roads while also "connect[ing] the capital with centers of violence." At the same time, officials expected that construction jobs would lure potential troublemakers away from crime.[69] Unable to resist the pun, *Semana* wrote that "The road leads to peace."[70]

Rehabilitación's local development projects corresponded to an idea of violence grounded in social explanations. Yet to succeed, the larger undertaking of rehabilitation would also need to deal with politics, namely the relationship between the state and the governed. As Lleras pronounced in his first speech on rehabilitation, "There is another rehabilitation, not of things destroyed, but of people who want to live in peace, join the Nation, and cannot find a path to do so."[71] However necessary, though, this part of the democratic transition had to face up to lingering realities of partisan opinion. Lleras would manage these as best he could; throughout his presidency, he remained exceedingly mindful of his position as head of a coalition, refusing to take actions that might endanger the National Front. In attempting to prevent partisan animosities from spilling out from Bogotá into the provinces, Lleras could advance *convivencia* within the country of politics to the detriment of the transition in the countryside. Depending on its political locus, *convivencia* was at the heart of the creole peace and also one of its limitations.

An early, crucial iteration of Lleras's wariness occurred in late October 1958, far from the public eye. The presidential cabinet briefly considered a sweeping amnesty for "political crimes" that would have excluded only crimes of "military rebellion and those committed by public functionaries."[72] Given the Conservative Party's use of the bureaucracy to exact a violent partisan agenda a decade earlier, this last provision would have provoked ferocious opposition from Conservatives in Congress, possibly risking the survival of the National Front. The cabinet thus temporarily abandoned the possibility of pushing the proposal through legislative channels, and instead utilized presidential powers to promulgate a more modest and—owing to the limited state of siege—geographically constrained pardon, issued as Decree 0328 of November 28, 1958.[73] The measure conditionally suspended legal penalties against people who had committed crimes "in connection with an attack or defense of the Government or the struggle between the political parties," provided that the crimes had taken place in the state-of-siege departments before October 15, 1958, and that the applicants did not re-offend.[74]

Decree 0328 was an important acknowledgment by the Lleras administration of its predecessors' role in the violence of the previous decade-plus. It sheds light too onto midcentury ideas of justice. While a frank admission of the state's incapacity to prosecute the "gigantic wave of criminality" Colombia had witnessed, the pardon also grew out of enduring practices of justice. Colombia's criminal code imposed periods of imprisonment short of life for major crimes, and the judicial system often institutionalized Christian mercy. In 1950, for instance, the Conservative government decreed a 20 percent reduction in the length of all prison sentences in celebration of a Catholic Jubilee Year.[75] Rather than charging people with common crimes committed in the context of partisan conflict, the Lleras government recognized the legitimacy of some of those forms of violence and presented people an opportunity to rehabilitate themselves, their regions, and their nation.

Moreover, if the government's adaptation of Lebret's All-Purpose Teams represented the Colombianization of a foreign import, the pardon, like the Peace Commission, defined creole innovation. In a period without strong international precedents for truth and justice amidst transition, Colombians experimented with their own solutions. In the estimation of the head of the clemency tribunals (*tribunales de gracia*) that administered Decree 0328, the pardon "broke the traditional molds for clemency options" and achieved an ingenious, wholly "Colombian formula for our national reality."[76] Lleras and his two ranking ministers eventually described the pardon as "an audacious . . . experiment to obtain the pacification of territories where for very many years there was not only an absence of tranquility, but [where] public authorities and the forces of order also lacked access."[77] Even sociologist Alfredo Molano, who would become a leading critic of the National Front by the end of the century, allows that the "[pardon] decree was broad and generous, and viewed in relation to the rehabilitation programs, opened the road for an important sector of those at arms to reintegrate themselves to economic and social life."[78]

A final step in the erection of Rehabilitación—one which linked the Rehabilitation Commission, created in September, to the November pardon—originated with Gómez Pinzón and the third luminary of rehabilitation, Darío Echandía. Tolima's most famous living Liberal after former president Alfonso López Pumarejo, Echandía had occupied the governor's post in Ibagué since before the start of Lleras's term. Insights from the Peace Commission, from rural commanders who journeyed to the capital, and from other inhabitants of Tolima left Echandía with a precise picture of how to go about building *convivencia*. He also possessed, unique among the *país político*, personal awareness of the pain inflicted by unjust governments and "sectarian cruelty," two of the major themes of his gubernatorial inauguration speech. While walking the streets of Bogotá on the eve of the 1949 presidential election, then–Liberal Party candidate Echandía and his entourage came under fire from Conservative policemen. The shooting not only led to a Liberal withdrawal from electoral politics until 1958; it also forever marked the Echandía family, fatally striking down one of Darío's six younger brothers.[79]

During ministerial discussions of the pardon in October and November 1958, Echandía and Gómez Pinzón took subtle but significant steps to structure the reintegration process. The Agrarian Bank had previously begun making special, government-backed loans to residents of Tolima affected by violence. As the bank contemplated expanding the credit program to the other state-of-siege departments, Echandía and Gómez Pinzón successfully lobbied it to permit "the provision of credit resources not only to those negatively affected [*damnificados*] strictly speaking, but also and simultaneously to those who could be classified as perpetrators [*damnificantes*], so long as they could demonstrate serious intentions to rejoin the path of peace and hard work, and so long as they were individuals whom the Governors ... had not indicated as individuals reluctant to celebrate peace agreements or [individuals] still disruptive of the public order."[80]

The expansion of the rehabilitation loan program handed officials a powerful tool to entice former fighters to embrace *convivencia*. Straight away, Echandía and other Tolima bureaucrats obtained preferentially large loans for major Liberal fighters who wished to buy farms or return to their families' former lands. The weightiest case involved Colombia's most infamous "bandit," twenty-three-year-old Teófilo Rojas, alias Chispas (Sparks), the exemplar of the countryside's lost generation. Top Tolima officials handled a 50,000-peso transaction to purchase for Chispas what would have been a sizeable farm in his native Rovira. Word of the deal prompted an influential Conservative combatant in a neighboring county to request similar assistance. Echandía recommended that Bogotá approve the deal in the expectation that it would help to pacify the zone.[81] Agrarian Bank records indicate the government made a half-dozen of these mega-loans in Tolima.[82]

Overall, rehabilitation loans comprised Rehabilitación's single greatest appropriation during the first year of Lleras's presidency.[83] Around 85 percent of the loans—over 37 million pesos' worth—went to rural people through the Agrarian Bank. By January 1960, the bank had made over eleven thousand loans, with the average recipient seeing 3,700 pesos. While this paled in comparison to the odd 50,000-peso amount, these loans represented a modest contribution to rural Colombians seeking to reestablish themselves in agricultural pursuits.[84]

Who were these Colombians? Though no comprehensive list exists, records demonstrate that rehabilitation loans aggregated to certain collectivities, even as many of rehabilitation's offerings formally went to individual Colombians. More than 41 percent of the nearly sixty-six hundred Agrarian Bank loans granted in Tolima, and more than a quarter of the loans dispensed nationally, passed through the bank branch in Chaparral (map 8). So great was the demand that the Agrarian Bank exceeded its 3-million-peso budget for Chaparral by almost 190 percent.[85] This heavy draw on Chaparral's bank originated not so much from residents of the county itself as from people in Chaparral's regional partners to the south—Ataco and above all Rioblanco, both of which lacked state services of their own.

In other words, Chaparral's Agrarian Bank served the ranks of the National Liberal Revolutionary Movement.[86] Throughout Tolima, and in other departments as well, state assistance to victims of violence concentrated in Liberal hands. There is no indication that this outcome stemmed from conscious policy decisions. Instead, the predominance of Conservative-sponsored state repression as a form of violence after 1946 shaped the structure of postconflict rehabilitation after 1958. In spite of Lleras's conciliatory position toward the Conservatives, the Peace Commission's recommendation to redress Liberals had come to pass.

The case of Chispas is instructive. The horrors experienced by the young Teófilo Rojas reflected a larger Conservative campaign against Rovira's Liberals. Targeted because of their partisan identity, or driven off their coffee farms under the guise of political animosity, the local Liberal majority fled the county. (Chispas recounted to the Peace Commission how "seeing [my neighbors'] houses burn" and the sound of "my mother and little siblings crying from hunger in the woods" pained him more than the five rifle rounds that had passed through his body.) Conservatives, who had accounted for perhaps a third of Rovira's voting population in 1946, represented 90 percent by 1958.[87] Chispas would be in good company in trying to return home to a remade Rovira: the Agrarian Bank made its third-largest number of loans there. Of the ten counties to receive the greatest quantity of loans, another four underwent similar levels of Conservatization. Though Jorge Villamil intended "The Return of José Dolores" to speak for all the peoples of Gran Tolima, José Dolores would likely have been a Liberal.

State initiatives and popular desires fused into a creole peace across central and southwestern Colombia between late 1958 and early 1960. One measure can be seen in homicide statistics (figure 7), which stayed low in Tolima and continued to decline across the rest of Colombia. Qualitative accounts speak even more meaningfully of the transformation: when Echandía left the governorship in early May 1959, he was applauded for having made good on his initial promise that residents of Tolima would regain their past security.[88] Further to the south, Cauca's Rehabilitación director reported late the following year that the Cauca-Huila-Tolima border zone of Tierradentro (surrounding Riochiquito, map 5) enjoyed "a climate of peace and tranquility . . . through the Rehabilitation Plan." Military officials came to a similar conclusion.[89]

For thousands of Colombians—Conservative, Liberal, and Communist alike—the creole peace involved a return to old occupations and once familiar lands. During the last months of 1958, a second round of *desplazado* repatriation commenced across an arc stretching from the northeastern highlands, through Gran Tolima, to Valle del Cauca in the southwest. Although it is impossible to calculate the precise scale, the phenomenon included tens of thousands of Colombians, by all measures substantially exceeding the levels of return of 1957/early 1958. Repatriation saw its greatest proportions in devastated southern Tolima, where the peace pacts of September 1958 had made special mention of the rights that people now had to return.

In offering some resolution to the question of forced displacement, rehabilitation addressed one of the crucial tests for Lleras's new citizenship regime. If the government could ensure the return of *desplazados* or assist them in resettling on Colombia's internal frontiers, it would remove what was seen as a significant source of tension at the local level.[90] The Lleras government also anticipated that reinstalling agriculturalists on their lands would bolster the cause of social equity nationally by both reducing strains on overstressed urban areas and lowering the cost of living through increased agricultural production. Peace would go hand in hand with broader advances in development, all to fortify the democratic transition.

Desplazado repatriation brought with it a final, unanticipated benefit as well. Returning *desplazados* likely transmitted attitudes about *convivencia* that they had acquired in the local urban centers (*cabeceras*) or larger cities where they sought refuge. As *Semana* indicated in March 1959, urban areas were relatively dense sites of activity and opinion related to democratization. Repatriation may have worked to diffuse the language and practice of the Second Republic to other sections of the country.[91]

REHABILITATION AND LOCAL PRIORITIES

At a minimum, the creole peace granted new space for the pursuit, and often realization, of local priorities. Significantly, the possibilities that rehabilitation opened for the reconstruction of rural life were not limited to the bipartisan fold: Communists wasted little time in expressing their desire to reintegrate into national life. In the same week that Echandía joined the Peace Commission to host Liberal and Conservative commanders in Ibagué, two figures—Pedro Antonio Marín/Manuel Marulanda Vélez/Tirofijo, from Marquetalia, and Ciro Trujillo Castaño, leader of Communists who had taken up residence in Tierradentro—declared their support for the Lleras government. "We are not interested in armed struggles," their manifesto read, "and we are disposed to collaborate in every way we can, with the enterprise of pacification which the current government of doctor Alberto Lleras Camargo has undertaken." Adopting the language of the moment, Marulanda, Ciro, and two of their top lieutenants presented themselves as "ex" combatants, interested in working for the "common good" to build "the new republic."[92]

The promise of Colombia's renovated political order came to the frontier shortly thereafter, when the Peace Commission made a visit to Ciro in the area of Tierradentro known as Riochiquito (map 5). Through the joint auspices of the local county's civil and religious officials, Ciro conferred with his Liberal rivals from across the border in Tolima. As more than two hundred of their fighters demobilized, the commanders "propos[ed] as a standard of action respect for each and every one of the rights of our fellow citizens, regardless of politics." The end of the session seemed to portend the possibility of the new sociability, as the "friendly laughter" of the commission's jovial head, Otto Morales Benítez, "sparked . . . multitudinous guffaws" from all the attendees (see also figure 3).[93]

The better part of a year had passed since Gran Tolima's Communists had held their Christmas demobilization. The onetime combatants had spent much of that time getting back in touch with the land. Jaime Guaraca, then a twenty-six-year old inhabitant of Marquetalia, detailed decades later how "eight or ten men came together one day to work where one comrade was, another the next day, and so on, until the mountain was opened up . . . the region . . . consolidated, everyone with his little plot."[94] Such labors bespoke what was conventional and yet distinguishing about Marquetalia and its sister communities. Colombian frontier colonists had relied on collaborative labor, particularly in the early stages of settlement, since at least the mid-nineteenth century.[95] Communist Party practice systematized this tradition, ensuring the oversight of collective energies by a central authority within each community.[96] Amidst the uncertainties of the frontier and the disruptions of war, it was this promise of internal discipline, rather than any goal of national power through proletarian revolution, that attracted men like Pedro Antonio Marín to the ranks of the Communist Party. As Claudio Lomnitz has recently argued for the case of early twentieth-century Mexican anarchism, agrarian Communism in midcentury Colombia was born largely out of the lived experience of solidarity.[97]

The subsiding of local tensions allowed frontier Communists to turn their attentions away from conflict. In Marulanda's estimation, the Communists entered into the process of "constructing another world, in a situation of peace, in which it was thought that arms were unnecessary . . . [and] words sufficed."[98] Ciro explained to a contingent of government magistrates in 1961 that "we have in this territory, in spite of our poverty, a strong effort that we can say our neighbors do not have agriculturally." Some time afterward, he would conclude that "within just a few years, we had built [at Riochiquito] a Peasant Movement exemplary in its organization, in its forms of self-governance, in its work ethic . . . we showed how far a people organized to direct its own destiny can reach."[99]

As the revivified environment of 1958–59 rendered alternative trajectories conceivable, it simultaneously reintroduced old habits. The residents of Marquetalia resumed the rhythms of their former lives. Local repertoires of movement would no longer be limited to forced night marches or displacement driven by fear. On the cusp of his twenties a decade earlier, Pedro Antonio Marín had found his calling on the road, purveying lumber and other goods up and down the length of middle Cauca Valley. The Conservative terror that swept through these towns after Gaitán's assassination truncated this wayfaring, compelling Marín to reverse his previous wanderings and cautiously make his way through an unanticipated world where words were insufficient and arms necessary. The spectacles and dread of these six hundred days seared into Marín's mind as he spent the subsequent six months hiding out in the bush above an uncle's farm, turning over in his head all that he had witnessed and heard. Yet neither these two years of flight nor the seven years of hardships, losses, and betrayals that followed as Marín/Marulanda took up arms against the Conservatives could erase the remembrance of his young adulthood.[100] With the onset of the Second Republic, Marulanda returned to favored pursuits, wending his way through southern Tolima and northern Huila to do business. Though history has styled Marulanda a "peasant," his life better fit the mold of a backwoods entrepreneur: toiling in the soil interested him less than pasturing cattle on rented lands closer to the road.[101] Taken jointly, the elements of sustentation that Marulanda pieced together in 1958–59—control over his own property and labor, diverse engagement with the local economy—constituted a rural ideal. The struggles of Colombian country people have long centered around "efforts . . . to be in, though not of, the market," to borrow a phrase from historian Michael Jiménez.[102] José Dolores would have found much that was familiar and fulfilling in Marulanda's existence.

He would also have recognized many of the difficulties. Pierre Gilhodès, one of the shrewdest foreign scholars of Colombia, once observed that the Communist enclaves remained marginal commercial enterprises, beset by the same shortages of credit and other inputs that faced frontier colonists throughout Colombia.[103] To counter these limitations, the residents of Marquetalia, Riochiquito, and El Pato turned to the state's offerings no less than did their neighbors from the traditional parties. Alongside their commitment to the discourses and practices of *convivencia,* the creole Communists joined other inhabitants of central Colombia to participate in the full array of rehabilitation programs.

Individual, community, and regional advancement all beckoned. Fermín Charry Rincón, alias Charro Negro (Black Horseman), the leader of the Marquetalia Communists and a member of the Communist Party Central Committee (figure 6), received loans to purchase a few head of cattle, along with a film projector, which he transported around southern Tolima to show movies. Marulanda further supplemented his livelihood with a stint as foreman of a Rehabilitación-funded road-building crew seeking to connect Gaitania with the nearby Huila village of El Carmen (map 3). The project offered local Communists a daily wage and access to basic medical care, as well as the realization of a long-desired step in regional economic integration.[104] Knocking down trees, blasting out rocks, and digging a road out of the muck granted a sense of contributing to the larger whole, expanding the country's productive span into what had formerly been wilderness. Colombians called this *"haciendo patria"*—making the motherland.[105]

Opponents of the Communists gave these labors a different read. The most famous version of this critique, articulated in 1961, imagined the Communist colonization fronts as veritable "independent republics," areas outside of the Colombian nation.[106] Colombian scholars writing from the late twentieth century largely concurred, deciding that the Communists' "armed colonization" represented an alternative state formation project.[107] By contrast, the experience of 1958–59 demonstrates how the government in fact underwrote the Communists' vision of rural life at a vital juncture. All actors strove for equilibrium: the Lleras administration's peace policy required the adherence of all former combatants, including the creole Communists, while the Communists came to count on material support from the government.

This arrangement was not merely a ceasefire between former adversaries, but illustrated the recombination of political and social relations within the creole peace. For *convivencia* to flourish, sociability required a certain degree of equity. As this order took shape, the collective effort outweighed potential frictions between, on the one hand, rural peoples' definition of belonging and obligation, and, on the other, the moralizing impulse present in the state's reworking of citizenship. However, the making of the creole peace also often revealed the *país político*'s propensities toward self-serving politicking rather than high-minded politics. In this way, rural Colombians' experience with the creole peace typified the challenges facing twentieth-century Latin American democracy.

REHABILITATION AND REGIONAL POLITICS

Like others in Tierradentro, the Valencia Dussán brothers marked time through two catastrophes. In late 1950, the army descended on eastern Cauca in retribution for locals having lynched a handful of abusive Conservative appointees. As over a hundred locals lay dead, the Valencia Dussán brothers fled their farms in the upper stretches of Belalcázar. Four years on, the army conducted another foray into the county's peripheries, clearing out one set of indigenous residents and inadvertently opening the way for Ciro's Communists to enter Tierradentro from the north. Blocked from their parcels, the Valencia Dussán settled in Belalcázar's county seat (map 3).[108]

Belalcázar was a far cry from the nameless city that Jorge Villamil imagined as a refuge for the uprooted José Dolores. Tierradentro's indigenous majority ensured that the village saw more than its share of visiting anthropologists, but otherwise, like the rest of Tierradentro, Belalcázar suffered from a smothering remoteness. Crammed between a hillside and the scree-lined banks of the Páez River, Belalcázar's thousand-odd inhabitants were located a bone-jarring day's ride over the central Andes from their departmental capital.[109] Occasional breaks in the valley's seemingly unending cloud cover revealed the Nevado del Huila, the Colombian Andes' tallest peak.

Over the first half of the National Front, Belalcázar's inhabitants let forth a stream of correspondence to Bogotá, their words straining to puncture this isolation. The outside world seemed tantalizingly close in the last months of 1958, both figuratively and physically, as the Peace Commission passed through eastern Cauca and Rehabilitación began to dole out road construction contracts. By January 1959, however, the Valencia Dussáns and more than eighty residents of Belalcázar felt compelled to type out a letter to President Lleras.

The moment did not call for the accessing of deeper memories. In contrast to their later correspondence, the petitioners did not reach back to the reference points of 1950 and 1954. Nor did they invoke their status as displaced people, or make any mention of the Communists up the mountain. Perhaps airing their stories to the Peace Commission a couple of months earlier had sufficed. They now saw fit merely to refer, obliquely, to their "martyred region" (a common refrain in Colombia at the time). The petitioners' grievances bore a decidedly more recent vintage. Their account focused on how the government's embryonic rehabilitation campaign had not yet arrived in Tierradentro. The town's residents still awaited the farming equipment, medical assistance, and other services which they claimed that the Peace Commission had pledged to them. Moreover, such sins of omission rankled less than a sin of commission. Rehabilitación-funded projects were not benefiting locals, the Valencia Dussáns and their neighbors explained, because politicians in the departmental capital of Popayán had filled construction crews with their followers. Belalcázar remained peripheral in every sense. The petitioners therefore plaintively asked the point of "rehabilitating people who in the utmost truth . . . lived pleasant days in the cities while we inhabitants of this region tasted times of bitter weeping and pain. We question how this is rehabilitation." [110]

Such complaints about the clientelist capture of state resources long predate the National Front era, a fact which casts a certain timelessness over the Belalcázar petition. [111] However, the stakes of these political contests had shifted by the late 1950s. First, unprecedented levels of investment would be required if the countryside were to recover from the ravages of internal conflict. Second, if the reimagining of the state that lay at the heart of the National Front project were to become reality, political leaders would need to ensure that, in the words of one government agency, "the particular interest . . . cede[s] to the general interest." [112] Appropriation of the state by the Conservative Party had been a fundamental driver of violence in the 1940s; the Tierradentro petition suggests how the ongoing machinations of both the parties sapped confidence in the meaning of citizenship during the democratic transition. "When everything is saturated with politicking [politiquería]," a prominent Tolima lawyer lamented at the start of the National Front, "the judgments and reasonings that we make about different aspects of national life are false and spurious." [113] The contradictory measures taken by regional politicians during the creole peace demonstrate how provincial parties could simultaneously operate in concert with the state and in favor of their own interests. Partisan action could thus contribute to both the advancement and detriment of the public good, which the parties also claimed a role in defining.

Rehabilitación quickly became a target for partisan appetites. The irrigation of money was a boon to public administration in the departments, some of which stood in "open bankruptcy." Tolima, which still relied on regressive alcohol and cigarette taxes for over 70 percent of its revenues, hit such insolvency by 1958 that it was temporarily forced to take out commercial bank loans to sustain its low levels of services. The depth of this fiscal emergency, combined with the scale of the violence problem, translated into 25 million pesos of Rehabilitación funding for Tolima in 1958–59, the most of any department.[114] Financial infusions into the regions could not help but attract the attention of politicians, particularly those factions which had not been in the military government's good graces.[115]

The back-and-forth between national and regional political interests played out in often paradoxical ways. For instance, José Gómez Pinzón and Rehabilitación's regional officials tussled for months with Huila governor Felio Andrade Manrique, who appeared to be funneling Rehabilitación-financed contracts to his copartisans in violation of National Front parity rules.[116] Despite such maneuvering, Andrade Manrique—a rising star in Laureano Gómez's wing of the Conservative Party—elsewhere showed himself to be flexibly pragmatic in constructing an inclusive framework for peace. His record in favor of *convivencia* dated back to his stint as top subordinate to Huila's military governor during the early democratic transition. Andrade Manrique had been among those who had parleyed with the men of El Pato under the good offices of Gentil Quintero Luna, and once appointed governor himself by Lleras, he had to make good on the department's pledges of material support to El Pato, on its eastern border. Plans advanced to rebuild the neglected primary road out to this frontier community—and to do so using local labor—as well as to have the government assume the cost of teachers for a new school.[117]

Where favoritism for his own party did not factor in, Andrade Manrique exercised his maximum powers under the law. The equity of *convivencia,* in other words, was more convenient in some realms than others. In May 1959, Fermín Charry Rincón, the Black Horseman of Marquetalia, paired up with El Pato military commander José Alfonso Castañeda, alias Richard (figure 5), to request that Andrade Manrique suspend judicial proceedings against their followers.[118] Separate jurisdictions within the state apparatus held differing opinions on the matter: one of the military clemency tribunals handling the pardon ruled against Charry, Manuel Marulanda, and Ciro Trujillo, ordering them to submit to sanctions handed down against them by a 1957 Cali court-martial.[119] But, calculating that regional peace warranted intercession, Andrade Manrique exercised his authority under Decree 0328 to overrule the clemency tribunal. Later that same year, Andrade Manrique would intervene once more, objecting to the refusal of the Huila Ranching Development Fund (Fondo Ganadero) to award Charry a loan to purchase cattle. All pardoned fighters, he reasoned, should receive equal treatment, regardless of their political affiliation.[120]

A little-known figure in Colombian history, at the start of the National Front Felio Andrade Manrique demonstrated better than most the paradoxical nature of political power. For all the centralism supposedly inherent in Colombia's constitutional order, authority remained diffuse: even as power brokers in Bogotá such as José Gómez Pinzón tried to claim for the central state control over public affairs, political appointees like Andrade Manrique remained indispensable components of the governing process. Andrade Manrique's actions often lived up to the twentieth-century Colombian aphorism "to govern is to appoint" (*gobernar es nombrar*). The Conservative nonetheless played a significant role in assembling regional and local pieces of the creole peace. The particular interest of party could well exist alongside, rather than in outright opposition to, the general interest of state or public. Through the idiosyncrasies of the bipartisan system, Colombia's was a democracy in spite of itself.[121]

THE CREOLE PEACE AND THE MAKING OF REGIONAL IDENTITY

In addition to a school and roads, the rehabilitation of the Huila-Caquetá border required—as settlers there made clear to both Andrade Manrique and the Peace Commission—the extension of medical services to the area's hundreds of inhabitatnts. To staff the health post at El Pato, Governor Andrade turned to his copartisan and peer Jorge Villamil. Just a few months removed from his medical apprenticeship in Bogotá, Villamil had already made a name for himself as a doctor in Neiva. Andrade guessed too that Villamil's ties to eastern Huila would help to humanize the government's presence. And so it was that through his role in the creole peace, Villamil reconnected not solely to his corner of Gran Tolima, but also to country folk who provided living reminders of his childhood (figure 8). The dividends for Villamil's calling as a musician would not be not far off.[122]

As the creole peace deepened, Gran Tolima's elite began to propagate revitalized forms of expression and Christian forgiveness, notions present in Villamil's "The Return of José Dolores" ("to hear ring, that song of peace / from cheerful bells").[123] The campaign drew strength from across the region's political classes, demonstrating how some of elite *convivencia*'s old ties of affection had survived the 1940s and '50s. Sensing an opening, Adriano Tribín Piedrahita, one of central Tolima's top Conservative political bosses and the originator of the short-lived 1956 Alliance for Peace, revived discarded proposals for a cultural festival in Ibagué.[124] Part act of municipal boosterism, part signal that "the city . . . has determined how to overcome an era that has been written in blood," the plan initially encountered resistance from Lord Rafael Parga. The Liberal had only recently taken over the governorship from Darío Echandía and felt insecure against what he feared was political scheming against his administration. Tribín deployed all the tools of his trade to win his case. When a public rally failed to sway Parga's mind, Tribín contacted Echandía, who put in a good word with Alberto Lleras.

FIGURE 8. Jorge Villamil (second from right) with former Liberal combatants, El Pato, 1960s. Vicente Silva Vargas, personal archive.

Though it was Parga who set up the ensuing audience with his copartisan Lleras for the two sides to air their arguments, he had already been outflanked. In a meeting at Echandía's Bogotá house following the president's enthusiastic approval of the festival, the host tried to smooth over Parga's feelings. "Work together, my dear Rafi," Tribín remembered Echandía saying in the intimate tone of social equals, "because the solution to Tolima's ills could be there [in Tribín's proposal]. Healing through the spirit was a recommendation of the ancient philosophers."[125]

The spirits were now not just to be pacified, but instead put to productive uses. Ibagué's first Folkloric Festival (Festival Folclórico) went ahead in June 1959, catalyzing widespread interest throughout Gran Tolima. Similar events to honor regional culture, exalt the achievement of peace, stimulate tourism, and generally energize "progress" popped up in cities and small villages beginning the following year.[126] Even political campaigns joined the craze, with local party members composing *bambucos* that connected their national candidates to the cause of peace.[127]

The creole peace thus established centerpieces of Gran Tolima's identity. Outside of Ibagué, the most important festival took place in Neiva, the brainchild of Felio Andrade Manrique and Jorge Villamil. Their thought was to officialize Gran Tolima's traditional late June celebrations for St. John, which had been abandoned years earlier because of rural insecurity. Villamil, whose fame as a composer was outstripping his medical career, began the process by helping to survey popular dances in Neiva's urban and rural peripheries. This search for the "authentic" Gran Tolima marked the first step in the eventual formalization of the fancy dress and swirling choreography of a modified *bambuco* that became a centerpiece of Gran Tolima's regional culture.[128] Even as Colombians' pursuit of *convivencia* forged new linkages between the local, the regional, and the national, it redefined the scales themselves.

Though Gran Tolima's folkloric celebrations remain landmark events, they have been decoupled from the history of the democratic transition that birthed them. With the passage of time, for instance, the folkloric movement's patrician origins faded from consciousness.[129] More significantly, the experience of peace generated positive associations, crowding out alternate recollections of the past. Jorge Villamil continued to pen songs about Gran Tolima, but unlike "The Return of José Dolores," these portrayed an ahistorical region, rather than a region at a specific moment in time. The context of that song's creation passed into the background as well.[130]

The many returns of José Dolores enabled both peace and the possibility of its unmaking. The reversal of displacement, so central to the creole peace, also sparked fresh fissures in the countryside, at a moment when Colombians felt that peace had seemingly only commenced. This violence-as-practice and its political ramifications would, over the long run, further alter the ways in which Colombians remembered the creole peace. In the short run, they endangered the pursuit of *convivencia*. The original Ibagué Folkloric Festival, for instance, briefly confronted postponement amidst sharp anxieties over a new wave of rural violence. In deciding to go ahead with the festival, city and regional officials concurred with the head of Ibagué's tourism board, who rationalized "that if the dead deserve reverent respect, governments have more serious commitments to the living."[131] It was a fitting summation of all of Colombia's strivings toward *convivencia,* and of the ways in which violence and peace ran together through Colombian history.

4

Peace and Violence, 1959–1960

The Luisa River brought small blessings to a small place. A couple of miles upstream from the main bridge into Valle de San Juan, where the waters pooled deepest and townspeople gathered on weekends to cool off, the Luisa filtered thinly through its rocky bed. Close by, the county's northernmost roadway traced a parallel course. In the stretches where the two passed nearest to each other, the hint of a breeze from the Luisa offered passersby a momentary respite from the local routine of tending to cattle pastures and cornfields.[1]

Grinding though those tasks were, the opportunity to return to such a familiar routine came to represent something of a relief for Pedro Susunaga and his copartisans. Fear of Conservative violence had years earlier concentrated Valle's Liberal residents in town and village, where they witnessed their families' well-being deteriorate alongside the county's underfunded public works. The creole peace gradually reopened rural sections of Valle, allowing the Susunaga clan and their partisan kin to take stock of what needed to be done on their farms. Work was progressing by the middle months of 1960, as Valle's Liberal families and their laborers began to recover the habits that had defined, seemingly forever, this impoverished corner of central Tolima (map 3).

However, in one of the department's smallest counties, the resumption of routine easily attracted unwanted attention. So it resulted, one late afternoon in July 1960, that a truck filled with Valle Liberals came to a jarring stop as it bounced along the narrow dirt track. Round after round of bullets, fired from a nearby rise, slammed into the vehicle and its passengers. The eight military personnel who rode alongside them served little of their intended purpose: so thoroughly pinned down was the entire twenty-man company that only two—one soldier and one civilian—mustered any resistance. By the time two other trucks—themselves filled with Liberal landowners and armed government escorts—happened onto the scene, five Liberals and two soldiers lay dead. The toll would rise thanks to deaths among the seven wounded, as well as the shooting of one of three suspected attackers, whom the army quickly located, armed and out of breath.[2]

This massacre does not readily fit into later ideas about Colombia's midcentury violence. To quote historian Malcolm Deas, "Violent acts do not show up well against a background of violence." A single incident in a little-known part of the country is easily "drowned in the general noise."[3] The absence of colorfully named protagonists like Peligro or Charro Negro has helped to obscure the visibility of the Valle attack, as has the fact that the attackers did not commit the close-quarters mutilation that has often drawn morbid fascination to partisan killings.[4]

Beneath the surface, however, events in Valle de San Juan reveal the combination of partisan animosities and disputes over property that inflected Colombian politics in 1959–60. Much as the practice of violence since the 1940s substantially determined the contours of the Lleras administration's rehabilitation effort, the structure of the creole peace molded subsequent outbreaks of partisan hostility. While regional and national homicide levels continued their overall downward trend, the returns of many displaced José Dolores precipitated locally intense breakdowns of *convivencia*. This was not "political violence" per se: rather than a struggle over control of the state or the direction of public policy, collective conflict instead remained grounded in local rationales, often the pursuit of retribution for injuries suffered weeks or even years earlier.

In many localities in Gran Tolima and beyond, the creole peace stopped feeling like so much of a peace. The larger connections of party identity moreover meant that local acts carried regional and national implications. The distinct dynamics of violence that arose in mid-1959 emboldened the National Front's Conservative critics in Congress: already angered by the direction of Rehabilitación and the idea of violence that justified it, opposition Conservatives condemned the government for what they alleged was the Liberal administration's part in fostering bloodshed. Stung by the highly public backlash, officials in Bogotá scaled back rehabilitation's political and material offerings.

Fallout from this decision settled in distinct ways over Gran Tolima. One strategy saw an increasing turn toward the realm of law. Across the three branches of Colombia's government, officials labored to come up with reforms that would untangle the nexus of violence and property—defusing disputes over abandoned or stolen lands and ensuring firmer juridical grounds for the displaced to return—within the democratic framework espoused by Alberto Lleras Camargo. Tolima's Liberals concurrently impressed on the government the need to fulfill its promises of citizenship.

At the heart of these interactions lay the question of how Colombian society could move beyond violence to establish responsibility and implement restitution. Officials and provincial folk thus debated the state's liability for its predecessors' failings in the 1940s and '50s. However, far from confirming that the *país político* and *país letrado* held dominion over the law, its invocation around issues of land and responsibility revealed provincial reworkings of legal precepts that went against Bogotá's objectives. The process points to how much recognition of law's power pervaded throughout Colombian society.[5] Though the resulting frictions did not result in a wholesale challenge to the established political and legal order, they did trigger consequential redirection of state programs toward the countryside. Popular conceptions of the state—of the responsibilities that formal rules and agencies possessed as arbiters of national belonging—would force reform to take on new guises.

A different pattern meanwhile formed on Gran Tolima's peripheries, where the fluidity of the frontier and the fierce warfare of the 1950s left political life sharply fragmented. As the ties between Bogotá and the countryside that had been established under rehabilitation dissipated, and the fabric of *convivencia* in southern Tolima began to unravel, communities began to speciate along different lines of sociability. Leaders of the National Liberal Revolutionary Movement of Southern Tolima moved into confrontation with one another and the central government, while their Communist rivals decried the deterioration of their own relationship to the state.

This would become a mythical moment in the origin story of the FARC, but if we return to the original event, rural Communists' words and deeds speak to a political universe distant from ideas of revolutionary violence. The *país nacional's* choices around peace and violence were rarely absolute: as various Liberal commanders opted for civic political action over a return to force, Marquetalia's Communists, led by Manuel Marulanda Vélez/Tirofijo, decried the terms by which they were being forced from Colombia's Second Republic. These were no Cold War conflicts; an international scale of analysis cannot explain the pace of political developments on Gran Tolima's frontiers in 1960.

Colombia's transition was instead undergoing an internal evolution. The flip side of Colombians' *expectativas*—a word that translates as both "hopes" and "expectations"—was beginning to manifest itself. The politics of expectation that surrounded *convivencia* from 1957 to 1959 began to shade progressively toward frustration. The longer story of the creole peace refracts through these two possibilities: lettered realms of reform and law, on the one hand; and a possible return to violence, on the other. This chapter considers the kernel of Marulanda's grievances with Colombia's political order; the subsequent two chapters introduce the work and gradual alienation of a new type of *letrado*. Chapter 7 tells how the fates of these two sets of actors intertwined during the final phase of the democratic transition, bringing about the FARC and the idea of "La Violencia."

FISHING AT NIGHT, 1959–1960

Talk of peace and violence in 1959 frequently hinged on contrasting uses of a ubiquitous slogan. When he assumed Tolima's governorship months earlier, Darío Echandía pledged that "all *opitas* [inhabitants of Gran Tolima] may [once more] fish at night without someone shooting at them."[6] Powerful in its simplicity, the image of "fishing at night" became a metric by which both parties measured progress in the anti-violence campaign.[7] By late March, sectors of the Conservative press antagonistic to the National Front used the line to parody Echandía, arguing that an uptick in killings meant that "it [was] no longer possible to fish at night in Tolima."[8] In contrast, a May *El Tiempo* cartoon portrayed a fisherman, silhouetted by a brilliant moon, thanking the outgoing governor on behalf of the people of Tolima.[9]

El Tiempo's revival of Echandía's famous phrase highlighted how tenuous Bogotá's connection to the provinces remained, for in that precise moment the invocation rang somewhat hollow. Violent deaths nearly tripled between April and May, as Tolima came to account for nearly half of the country's partisan homicides (figure 9). The succeeding months were less bloody, but the murder rate hovered around pre–National Front levels. This violence-as-practice did not necessarily exceed the highs of the previous year. Instead, the timing and types of violence bore an intimate relationship to displacement, which sat at the core of the creole peace. This violence moreover came at a particularly crucial moment in the development of the National Front. The confluence of on-the-ground events with political debates over the course of rehabilitation would, in other words, mold the options open to Lleras and his officials, and consequently the potential range of interactions between *desplazados* and the state over citizenship and property.

The experience of 1958 strongly informed officials' ideas about 1959's violence and how it could be stopped. Concerns that the coffee harvest would once more destabilize public order led Echandía and Huila's Felio Andrade Manrique to declare extraordinary measures against coffee trafficking beginning in March.[10] Lleras took to the national airwaves to deplore "[the] many depraved people who go around, with a pistol in [their] pocket and little inclination for honest work, looking for confrontations and [the] easy life."[11] Driving coffee growers off their lands right before the harvest, or murdering them to seize the beans, struck many Colombians as the height of parasitic "banditry."

Ultimately more consequential than criminal violence was aggression connected to *desplazado* repatriation, a pattern which would gradually and only partially come into focus for contemporaries. The season's defining event proved to be the May 9 massacre of twenty-five Conservatives—men, women, and children—in

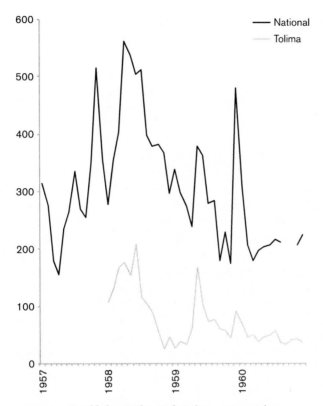

FIGURE 9. Monthly homicides attributed to partisan violence,
January 1957–December 1960.

the Rovira village of La Palmita (map 3).[12] Eleven more massacres took place in
Tolima over the rest of May, with another eight following in June—fully half the
department's yearly total of large-scale homicides.[13] The majority of these attacks
targeted Liberals living in counties that had undergone a high degree of Conservatization since 1946. Few massacres seem to have involved ambushes of intercity
buses, the type of attack that had caused much consternation in 1958. Overall,
then, violence was frequently employed in contexts involving recently returned
desplazados. The successful repatriation process that began in late 1958 put more
Colombians, particularly Liberals, in harm's way, and not solely in Tolima.[14] Furthermore, massacres of Conservatives during these months also frequently took
place in heavily Conservative counties, a distribution which indicates that the
massacres were carried out by mobile Liberal bands seeking to avenge the recent
killings of their party brethren, either by their own account or on behalf of local
Liberals.[15]

Such was the case with the La Palmita attack, which demonstrates not only the dynamics of midcentury partisan violence but also the basic functioning of party linkages. The massacre followed the May 7 murder of a Liberal on the other side of Rovira.[16] Rather than existing as something external to social relations, vengeance deepened pathways for the performance of party identity:[17] at the man's funeral in La Palmita on May 8, his kin conversed with an influential local Liberal politician, who in turn seems to have connected the family with an armed band from outside the village.[18]

By midmorning on May 9, a Saturday, the inhabitants of La Palmita had long since commenced the day's chores.[19] Though they recognized only a few of the several dozen figures in military uniforms who entered the village, they later testified to the presence of a pair of the dead Liberal's relatives, who guided the men into the center of the community. The outsiders were practiced at their craft: they appeared in no rush as they moved through the village, shooting and then mutilating victims here and there, lining up workers on the patio of a local notable's home before coolly killing four and robbing the residence. Two tactics common to assaults of this era further aided their progress: the men's use of uniforms largely disarmed locals' suspicions, and with the murdered Liberals' kinsmen playing the role of signalers (*señaladores*), it was simple to identify targets and call out to some by name.[20] La Palmita was also of sufficient size that even those residents who heard the first volleys of rifle fire were eventually taken by surprise; in their statements to investigators, survivors recounted no screams; simply the sound of gunfire and the interlopers' shouts.

The afterlives of the La Palmita massacre suggest how acts of collective violence acquire varying meanings as people move to commemorate them. La Palmita warranted inclusion three years later in a list "atrocious" massacres complied by Father Guzmán; and in 1970, a Tolima judge ranked it as "possibly one of the gravest cases registered in this country's history of violence." [21] In placing a massacre—a single incident—alongside like occurrences, these classifications helped to create "violence" as a comparative typology, one which flattened broad distinctions in place and political circumstance.

If we instead consider violence-as-practice more systematically, La Palmita figured as a link in a longer chain, a contextually rich episode that influenced regional and national politics. Because a man murdered elsewhere in the county existed within networks of identity and exchange, his death reverberated through those same connections, across physical and social distance. The ensuing La Palmita massacre in turn sparked an electric public response, stirring up central Tolima's partisan spirits. Militant Conservatives from neighboring San Antonio and Valle de San Juan—which with Rovira formed a block of the department's most heavily Conservatized counties (maps 3 and 4)—flocked to attend their copartisans' funeral. Reprisal attacks against Liberals began almost immediately, including

clear across the Magdalena Valley. To contain the crisis, the departmental government hastened to obtain declarations of fealty to the National Front from demobilized Liberal commanders in southern Tolima. Party leaders in Valle de San Juan
restated the terms of the peace pact they had signed during the Peace Commission's visit eight months earlier.[22]

This charged post-Rovira environment meant peril for Tolima's displaced.
Within the county itself, a thousand Liberal families fearful of what might follow
the massacre made arrangements to leave.[23] Government offices began to receive a
new round of complaints from other central Tolima *desplazados* who found themselves displaced anew or unable to return.[24] Liberal ex-combatants in the south
meanwhile took the opportunity to cite a lack of guarantees for the displaced as a
form of impunity that continued to incite violence.[25]

The national political environment constrained the Lleras administration's
responses to both this wave of popular demands and the proposals that followed
from other corners of government. The Rovira attack could not have come at a less
opportune time in the capital's political debate. In April, anti–National Front Conservatives had begun to mount an assault on rehabilitation, arguing that the Lleras
administration was enacting "systematic" discrimination against Conservatives.
Rather than "construct[ing] the nation" or "sow[ing] seeds of *convivencia* and
peace," Santander Conservative senator Hernando Sorzano González argued that
the Liberal government was fostering "foundations of rancor and hate."[26]

Factions within the National Front sprang to defend rehabilitation and Lleras's
entire governance project. Senator Álvaro Goméz Hurtado, Laureano's son, justified
the November 1958 pardon as "an emerging therapeutic, like the policy of the
National Front, which cannot be attacked or distorted . . . because it must not be
forgotten that this bridge of *convivencia* was sought and this experiment arrived at,
because there were two political nations [*países políticos*], antagonistic, independent,
and adversarial." The National Front's policies, Gómez asserted, still needed time to
develop; bureaucratic parity and presidential alternation awaited implementation.
Nevertheless, "from the irreconcilable, feral spectacle of yesterday, a plain of slow but
certain recuperation has been reached, where the parties already coexist, under the
protection of the National Front, which, without exaggeration, has done miracles."[27]

The La Palmita massacre heightened the rancor of this congressional debate.
Another opposition senator let loose a barrage of allegations, calling new governor
Rafael Parga Cortés "chief of the bandits" and fuming that "in Tolima it's true that
you can hunt Conservatives." The following day the senator threw a glass of water
at a rival who called him out for lying.[28] Though such a display of pique did not rise
to the level of the fatal 1949 shootout between the parties, neither was Congress
living up to Lleras's vision for an elevated political discourse.

La Palmita provided critics their most graphic evidence to date that the government was denying Conservatives rehabilitation aid, confiscating their weapons,

and leaving them at the mercy of "amnestied" Liberal "bandits."[29] Sorzano González decried not only the fact that "bandits" were being "granted amnesty and pardon, presented land parcels . . . and had the abundance of rehabilitation poured over them," but also that they were "made partners in authority in the zones they controlled and continue to control."[30] From the opposition's perspective, the government was not expanding its presence through rehabilitation, but rather ceding its authority to the perpetrators of violence.

Sentiments against rehabilitation found echo among Conservative rank-and-file, including backers of Laureano's who ostensibly supported collaboration with the Liberal Party. Days after La Palmita, Conservatives from the department of Meta denounced "[the] wave [of] murders [against] humble Conservative *campesinos* [in] Tolima." "Amnesty and money encourage bandits [who] live outside our democratic laws," the Conservatives added in a telegram to Lleras. "We request justice."[31] Weeks later, Conservative interior minister Guillermo Amaya Ramírez received a delegation of women from different Conservative factions who complained that "the benefits of Rehabilitación are benefiting solely people of a certain political affiliation [i.e., Liberals]."[32] Pro-Laureano Conservatives from San Antonio meanwhile protested the actions of the Rehabilitación office in Ibagué, which they said had acted against or ignored Conservatives pursuing just land deals.[33] Party identity had begun to reassert itself in the provinces.

Two strains of a Conservative critique of violence thus commanded increasing attention from May 1959. The first, which emanated mainly from the *país político,* focused more on the past. Because violent acts committed by Liberals since the 1930s had not been anything other than criminal, the premise of rehabilitation was to be rejected outright. The problem of violence could not have a political solution. The second strain found fault in the execution of rehabilitation, namely the preferential treatment supposedly extended by the Liberal-led administration to its copartisans. Where the second strain doubted the conduct of the National Front, the first went beyond attacking rehabilitation, Lleras' signature policy, and instead denied the possibility of collaboration with the Liberal Party.

These Conservative critiques gathered force as the National Front approached its first anniversary in power and disclosures about Rehabilitación came to light. News that Chispas, one of the most reviled figures in all of Colombia, had received Rehabilitación funds confirmed Conservatives' worst fears, particularly when he was (by all indications wrongly) implicated in the May 9 La Palmita massacre.[34] *El Clarín,* a Conservative-aligned radio news program in Medellín, reported that Chispas had received over 150,000 pesos from Echandía. The money, broadcasters claimed, allowed the "bandit" to buy an airplane, "by means of [which] he has evaded justice and travels from region to region, studying and planning new armed assaults against defenseless peasants." *El Clarín* concluded that "all press observers in Bogotá, both domestic and foreign, affirm . . . that the height of barbarity has been reached, and that the banditry that exists today does not have precedent in history, not through any government; above all, never before have bandits been encouraged in the way that they are now favored."[35] The newspaper *La República*, owned by former president Mariano Ospina Pérez, went on to compare Colombia's "most inhumane, most sadistic, most perverse" banditry to the Mau Mau insurgency that had struck Kenya earlier in the decade.[36] The reference to far-off Africa tapped into the racialized assumptions about Colombia's own violence held by *La República*'s well-heeled urban readership. The paper's appeal to that audience's self-styled cosmopolitanism may have also drawn on a worldliness born of the silver screen: in preceding years Bogotá's moviegoers had been treated to several foreign thrillers about Mau Mau.[37] Far from being distant in space, the prospect of racial savagery was vivid in urban collective consciousness.

Fed by partisan grievances and imaginaries of violence, the controversy over rehabilitation marked a watershed in politics and policy. Whether motivated to extend old feuds with Laureano Gómez, as Ospina's faction was; or radically opposed to the Liberal Party and its version of democratic coexistence, Conservatives outside the National Front pact seized the reins of public debate away from the administration in mid-1959. At the end of May the government declared that the pardon program would end on June 25, 1959, a decision historians Gonzalo Sánchez G. and Donny Meertens have termed "an important victory for the hard-liners."[38] In the provinces, governors received a flurry of last-minute pardon applications.[39]

The rollback of rehabilitation swiftly gathered steam, with new charges against Rehabilitación piling on. As with Chispas, condemnation tended to focus on individual perpetrators rather than aggregate patterns. However, in contrast to what had been the largely manufactured hysteria around Chispas, in June and July the administration admitted that Rehabilitación officials in the departments had acted negligently or worse.[40] In the most notorious instance, government officials appeared to have aided a Liberal with outstanding criminal charges against him, in the process using peace as a cover to advance their personal economic interests.[41] Conservative fears about pro-Liberal government discrimination suddenly gained an evidentiary base.

The Lleras administration's defenders sought to put a positive spin on disputes over rehabilitation, presenting them as a sign of Colombia's democratic vigor. "Opposition is necessary for . . . good government," *El Tiempo*'s publisher wrote in a July column. "And not only that [opposition] which is called constructive and honest, but also that which is unjust, malevolent, untruthful or motivated by wicked passions and fierce and insatiable [clientelist] appetites."[42] The administration mounted a complementary, full-throated justification of its decisions. The Conservative and Liberal governors of the five state-of-siege departments marched before the Liberal press to unveil the pardon's high success rate and to deny charges that Rehabilitación loans had been made according to partisan criteria.[43] From the presidential palace, Lleras and his interior and justice ministers released a public letter denouncing irregularities committed by provincial oficials and claiming the pardon as a step that extended, rather than ceded, the government's authority.[44]

Within the government, however, Lleras's advisors anguished over their response. The Rehabilitation Commission fretted that accusations against lower-level bureaucrats might impinge on Lleras's prestige, the basis of so much of the government's progress. Even the normally hands-off Lleras instructed the commission to find a solution. His adamant desire to remain conciliatory also cast a continuous shadow over the commission's proceedings.[45]

Despite the administration's brave public showing, the damage had been done. The commission ultimately opted to shut down its departmental affiliates, and the administration soon scaled back the larger rehabilitation effort as well, for a lack of resources. The pool of funds available to the Agrarian Bank for Rehabilitación loans ran out in the second half of 1959, and some on the commission worried that shallow government coffers could not handle additional popular requests for aid. This argument beat out concerns that ending Rehabilitación would leave important government programs with the clay-footed ministries, and by July, Lleras set the end of 1959 as the deadline for the administrative devolution of Rehabilitación's functions. In September, the commission began to meet less regularly and convene fewer ministers to oversee Rehabilitación.[46]

Lleras's quick concession to the opposition on rehabilitation showed the limits of his political style. His stint as interim president in 1945–46 had lasted just twelve months; by the time the Rehabilitación controversy commenced, more than a year had transpired since his assumption of the National Front's candidacy. Never a political player built for the long haul, Lleras had already by mid-1959 begun to exhibit signs of exhaustion. His critics in Colombia had long knocked him for what they cast as his cosmopolitan arrogance, which gave off a sentiment that Colombia was too small for him. They had a point: when he perceived his country-men as insufficiently committed to the national enterprise as he defined it, Lleras would reproach them, going so far as to threaten his resignation from public office.[47] Without other means to respond to the Conservative challenge of mid-1959, and desirous to preserve the National Front pact as a form of *convivencia,* Lleras revised his administration's defining policy.

Even with the end of its first act, however, rehabilitation remained the keystone of Colombian politics. Underscoring the extent to which Lleras had been too hasty, numerous regional and local actors proved faster to forgive any faults in Bogotá's programs. Formal political bodies, including the Caldas departmental assembly and Tolima's congressional delegation, petitioned the government to reinstitute Rehabilitación loans. Temporary institutions also cropped up to join the lobbying.[48] The leaders of Riochiquito, El Pato, and Marquetalia came together as well, in an uncommon moment of regional cooperation. The breadth of their

September 1959 petition indicates the extent to which the Communists had embraced rehabilitation: in addition to requesting general support for colonization movements, the Communists requested that Rehabilitación loans and road investments be made permanent, that frontier lands be distributed for free, and that the pardon be extended.[49]

The fatal blow to Rehabilitación in its original form arrived when the National Front reached its first milestone: the midterm congressional elections of March 1960. Later chroniclers of the National Front era would largely overlook the elections' issues and outcome, in spite of the fact that the contests shifted the very composition of Colombia's ruling coalition.[50] Many contemporaries, by contrast, recognized and even anticipated this swing within the Conservative Party. Months before the vote, British diplomats found that Laureano's backing of Lleras Camargo had "caused a wave of extremist [C]onservative reaction."[51] Within this general backlash, rehabilitation appeared as a recurrent campaign device for opposition Conservatives.[52] A prominent Jesuit close to the Conservative Party went so far as to tell U.S. diplomats that the election results were "a direct protest against the rehabilitation policy." However, the victory of Ospina Pérez and his allies would not push the party toward the resumption of large-scale violence-as-practice. The embassy's Jesuit informant instead felt "certain that one of the primary conditions laid down by Ospina for collaboration with the Lleras regime would be a reversal of the rehabilitation policy."[53] With Rehabilitación already undergoing dismantlement, an obvious target would be José Gómez Pinzón. He left the government in July 1960, just ahead of the new congressional session and what many felt was sure to be harsh Conservative criticism.[54]

The 1960 election transformed *convivencia*'s manifestations. Out as national policy was rehabilitation, a specific expression and enactment of coexistence between Colombians. In respecting what amounted to a referendum within the Conservative Party (the results within his own party ranks would be consequential, though less dramatically so), Lleras privileged a separate meaning of *convivencia*. The resiliency of the Colombian political system—a constitutional regime established in 1886 and a party system birthed earlier in that century—rested on its capacity to absorb dissident elements of the *país político*.[55] From March 1960, Lleras went along with a fresh set of partners from the opposite party, while Laureano's disciples continued to present themselves as the true executors of the original spirit behind the National Front. The Liberal-Conservative coalition endured, albeit in modified form.

As for the countryside, neither the violence of 1959 nor the 1960 election overturned another enactment of *convivencia*. Indeed, the irony of the period between mid-1959 and early 1960—the outbreak of violence against returning *desplazados,* the consequent Conservative condemnation of rehabilitation, and the gradual curtailment of Rehabilitación—was that the creole peace continued to advance.

Monthly homicides reached their previous low; 1960 witnessed virtually no seasonal bump during the coffee harvest (figure 9).[56] *Desplazado* repatriation flows in fact increased across many parts of Tolima after 1959's midyear spike in homicides. The return of the displaced, *El Tiempo* wrote in mid-1960, was a "symptom of peace and the revival of the economy." It moreover demonstrated that hateful partisan "passion never . . . acquired a state of permanency, a determinate position in historical events." Violence, the newspaper concluded, represented "a dreadful historical episode, but no more than an episode."[57]

Scale increasingly mattered for how peace was understood. From the vantage of Liberal Bogotá, violence had ceased to define Colombia. Gran Tolima and other regions continued to see marked improvements in security. It was at the subregional level—clusters of villages within counties, clusters of counties within or across departments—that the practice of peace could most seem suspect. These local experiences would eventually facilitate Colombians' adoption of the term "La Violencia," but as the 1960s started, their ideas about violence lacked the unity across scale and time that "La Violencia" implied.

THE RESPONSIBILITY OF THE STATE, 1959–1961

The fading of rehabilitation signified the end of only one set of practices by which Colombians could rectify injuries suffered at the hands of the government and fellow citizens. At the national level, the promise of mediation through the law—however imperfect this proved to be in practice—became a more visible component in Colombians' hunt for remedy and legitimation—the democratic transition, broadly conceived.[58] The organs of government contributed to this process by elaborating a legal and institutional matrix that became more sophisticated over time. President Lleras and his advisors invested particular stock in this turn toward the realm of law. Spurned by the political controversy over Rehabilitación, administration officials saw legalistic solutions to the problem of violence as a strategy above partisan reproach. This approach would run into internal limitations because of a conflict between specific reforms and an emphasis on formal democratic institutions. Constituencies within the government were also obliged to modify their designs when it turned out that Colombians outside the state took cues from the administration's lead. Provincial Colombians, who aspired have the state make amends for the losses caused by mass violence, matched Bogotá's increased reliance on legal arguments after 1960.

The effects of violence on landholding represented one area where the tentative policy steps of the early Lleras administration evolved toward more sophisticated legal solutions. Officials agreed early on about the importance of resolution to displacement and outright dispossession (*despojo*). Seeing the redress of land disputes "as the foundation for the tasks of pacification," Interior Minister Amaya

Ramírez told an early session of the Rehabilitation Commission that the government had an "obligation . . . to assist those property owners given that they are incapable of defending their rights in an opportune manner."[59] His successor, Jorge Enrique Gutiérrez Anzola, invoked the essence of Lleras's governing project when he referred to the need for the "reestablishment of law and equity" where property rights had been altered by force.[60] At the same time, figures in the administration and Congress also cast their glances ahead to a comprehensive, national agrarian reform, to resolve "the paradox that in a nation of farmers and ranchers, there is land without men and men without land."[61]

Tackling the so-called agrarian question would therefore entail a mixture of frontier colonization, redistribution, and the resolution of local land disputes stemming from violence. One expansive early initiative came via an ambitious rural development law directing 10 percent of all national bank deposits to the Agrarian Bank, which would then grant priority funding to *desplazado* resettlement programs.[62] The bill was nevertheless an indirect attack on displacement and dispossession; Lleras's ministers wrung their hands over the prospect of stimulating local violence by encouraging *desplazado* repatriation.[63] It took the pleas of Echandía and other departmental officials to get the administration to take greater action, in the form of a May 1959 decree suspending the statutes of limitation on civil cases involving forced land sales in Tolima and selected counties elsewhere in the state-of-siege zone.[64] Though Colombians' legal options thus expanded, few people could have relished the prospect of a slow, expensive journey through the notoriously cumbersome court system. Provincial inhabitants and officials consequently hatched informal and institutionalized practices that allowed people from opposing parties to swap properties in communities that were now politically homogenized.[65] The enactment of these "friendly compromises" (*arreglos amistosos/amigables*) brought the principles of *convivencia* into the agrarian question and suggested a model for future policies favoring negotiation over litigation.

Over the last months of 1959, after the polemic over Rehabilitación had subsided, calls mounted for the government to issue emergency legislation "that would allow for the rapid and equitable solution of conflict over property and land possession in zones affected by violence."[66] Laudable as the end might be, Lleras refused to budge on the means. Rather than taking unilateral action under the state of siege and thus potentially introducing a precedent of "legislat[ing] on property by means of a . . . decree," his ministers deferred to Congress.[67] Finally, after more than a year of deliberation, Congress obliged the administration's efforts at the end of 1959, approving two bills "to prevent the economic exploitation of violence." Law 201 took the rare step of reforming Colombia's civil code, nullifying contracts in the state-of-siege departments under the assumption that fear had "deprive[d] the victim of the necessary liberty" to realize a just transaction.[68] Commentators judged the measure "one of the most important" of the legislative session.[69]

The other bill, Law 124, meanwhile showed that for all the partisan vitriol that Rehabilitación endured in mid-1959, postconflict reconstruction programs still held broad appeal. More moderate members of Congress, perhaps assuaged by the administration's willingness to scale back Rehabilitación and to remove any semblance of Liberal favoritism, voiced concern that ending rehabilitation altogether would mean the waste of monies already spent. Law 124 therefore established the legal foundation to extend postviolence recovery programs for two additional years.[70]

With these pieces in place, officials in Bogotá started 1960 with a fresh slate of options. Interior Minister Gutiérrez Anzola explicated to his Rehabilitation Commission colleagues the administration's pivot, "stress[ing] the importance of attending in this second phase of rehabilitation to . . . the question of lands and . . . of people."[71] The administration would alter the scale of rehabilitation on two levels: while Rehabilitación's operations would transfer to regular government agencies as planned, additional programs would be directed at individual Colombians rather than the departments.

The lawyers of the *país letrado,* previously frustrated at their incapacity to resolve displacement and dispossession, perceived that their day had finally come. The impulse to restore order to Colombia's property regime was beyond partisan fault. The legislative groundwork of late 1959 also brought government action out from under the shadow of the mid-1940s, the moment when Lleras and his cohort had inadvertently prototyped a wider application of state-of-siege powers. By granting the president additional decree powers under a constitutional provision (Article 76) separate from that governing the state of siege (Article 121), Law 124 provided ministers with the justification Lleras had required to advance land initiatives outside of the legislative process. Within months, eight Conciliation and Equity Tribunals (Tribunales de Conciliación y Equidad) went to work in the five state-of-siege departments.[72]

It seemed that the lettered authority of law could now be brought to the provinces with special force. For the high-ranking, mainly provincial magistrates named to the tribunals, the tribunals' creation augured a singular chance to help build a "new justice," bringing the promise of *convivencia* to a section of national life where it was sorely needed.[73] As their name suggested, the tribunals granted people the possibility of achieving "equitable solutions" outside of the civil court system. To realize this goal, one observer explained, the tribunals' magistrates "sought to apply equity above all, through merely conciliatory means, without considering any legal procedure or criteria, beyond what one would expect from an official who through his knowledge and experience is in a capacity to issue a [just] decision or propose a [just] solution."[74] As if this confirmation of the magistrates' legal expertise were not enough, the tribunals gave adventurous lawyers the opportunity to step into the countryside to encounter for themselves the realities of "political and common crime."[75] For bureaucrats in Bogotá, the tribunals represented a forum in which the lessons of past shortcomings could be applied. In contrast to the "friendly" agreements pursued improvisationally in 1958–59, the tribunals received a modicum of coercive authority, namely the ability to order holds on properties.[76] When it became clear that many litigants lacked the money to settle conciliations, the state stepped in with 2 million pesos of funding for loans, transferred from Rehabilitación to the Agrarian Bank.[77]

Hundreds if not thousands of Colombians put their faith in the state and the tribunals as a legal mechanism for conflict resolution. To be certain, the tribunals were far from perfect for the dispossessed: even once the magistrates gained the ability to traverse their jurisdictions, tribunal offices were rooted in place—places the displaced often no longer occupied. Bringing a claim before a tribunal could therefore require costly and potentially dangerous trips back across space. Yet in their approximately nineteen months of operation, the tribunals accepted over 2,700 cases, achieving conciliations in at least 1,340.[78] Citizens and clergy from outside the state-of-siege zone looked on enviously, petitioning Bogotá to add tribunals in their home departments.[79]

Proud though the tribunal magistrates might be of their mission, the work of reaching conciliations and encouraging equity taxed them intellectually and professionally. "New justice" was not easily reconcilable with the sheer diversity of property relationships that the magistrates encountered: mortgaged lands, lands on indigenous reservations, and properties held by third or fourth parties. The world outside of the *país letrado* was messier than many conceived possible. The magistrates also ran into forms of localized power that obstructed their work and threatened their professional status. The Pereira tribunal complained to Bogotá in February 1961 how "unscrupulous charlatan lawyers have wanted to capitalize on the people who come to this [d]ependency . . . it is pitiful to see how individuals in extreme poverty have [such country lawyers; *tinterillos*] handle their claims, for which they have had to pay an onerous sum of money."[80] To ensure that poverty did not get in the way of access to their new civil justice, as well as to police the bounds of the legal profession against unlicensed provincial practitioners, various tribunals—with sanction from the Rehabilitation Commission—blocked outside lawyers from participating in their sessions.[81]

Such jealous defense of the authority to lay claim over law points to how the legacy of Spanish imperial administration, and a tradition of civilian governance in which both Conservatives and Liberals traced their parties' origins back to the lawmakers of the early nineteenth century, imbued the country with a pervasive culture of legalistic discourse and practice.[82] Provincial Colombians' advocacy through the language of law was especially visible when it came to the issue of the state's responsibility relative to violence. Colombians not only drew up claims that borrowed concepts from law; they also actualized the state's obligations in their own lives. This process of claims-making would have an important bearing on the fate of the tribunals as well as on Lleras's broader rehabilitation policy and popular sentiments about Colombia's democracy. In the end, then, two confrontations between competing visions of legal order influenced rehabilitation's "second phase." The first, which took place within the upper confines of national and regional government, placed the restoration of regular constitutional rule against extraordinary measures to reform the violence-property nexus. The second confrontation involved capital and province, state and citizen, and how each pairing should interact over the violence of the past.

Calls for the state to compensate provincial Colombians for the damages that violence had caused them in the 1940s and '50s emanated from private citizens and elected representatives, Liberals and Conservatives alike. Displacement—and the property losses it often entailed—stood centrally in their formulations. In its first communiqué to Bogotá after the fall of Rojas, the National Liberal Revolutionary Movement of Southern Tolima had framed its request for the expansion of credit to frontier settlers as an act of "compensation that the State owes them for the protection it failed to provide them at the proper time, because of which they were displaced."[83] Months later, a Conservative congressman from Meta began advancing proposals to indemnify *desplazados* affected there between 1956 and 1958.[84]

Reparation requests could also intersect with existing strains of regional resentment toward Bogotá. While a sizeable portion of rehabilitation spending flowed into Tolima, departmental politicians expressed concern that Tolima was actively suffering as national officials focused on other parts of the country. A Conservative member of Ibagué's municipal council eventually introduced a motion to "request that [the central government] not solely bestow [upon Tolima] its legitimate rights as they relate to the distribution of State resources for the increase of national production, [because] in this case [it] would not strictly speaking be [an] increase but [the] recuperation of [Tolima's] wealth, destroyed more by fault of the State than of [Tolima's] own children." The proposal carried easily.[85]

Similar expectations toward the central state increasingly circulated in provincial newspapers, materialized in provincial legislative chambers, and—in the form of letters and telegrams—trickled into Bogotá over the course of 1959. It fell largely to the Office of Rehabilitation to formulate the administration's response. José Gómez Pinzón staked out the government's argument, saying that "it [is] impossible to correct from the [state's position] all of the ravages of ten long years of violence and barbarity. The people thought—and continue to think—that the government was going to settle on making restitution of their lost goods. . . . we [are] only going to help them reconstruct their lives."[86] In addition to this contention—that the scope of the problem lay beyond the state's capacity, save for Rehabilitación's indirect contributions—Gómez Pinzón and his aides, along with some members of Congress, parried requests for direct reparations with indications that the government lacked the legislative grounds to make such payments, and that any such policy might be unconstitutional besides.[87]

However, even as the executive branch sought shelter behind constitutional law, other legal realms held out the possibility of resolution for the aggrieved. Two and a half months into Lleras's term, the Supreme Court delivered a blockbuster opinion on the state's involvement in violence. The case concerned a 1949 event supersaturated with partisan connotations. Within a week of President Ospina's November 1949 declaration of the state of siege, a squad of thirty armed Conservatives from counties around Antioquia's capital entered the town of Rionegro, where they proceeded to sack and burn the colonial-era buildings on one side of the plaza. Rionegro occupied a unique place in Liberal history: "the Mecca of Antioquia Liberalism," according to Father Guzmán, the town had hosted the convention that produced Colombia's 1863 constitution—the apex of nineteenth-century liberal doctrine—and had also briefly been home to José María Córdova, a hero of the independence struggle who eventually died opposing the authoritarian turn of Simón Bolívar, spiritual father of the Conservative Party. Córdova's dwelling went up in flames during the Conservatives' 1949 incursion, which seemed calculated to confirm the central government's recent exclusion of the Liberal Party from the public sphere.[88]

Over the next nine years, judges ruled time and time again against Rionegro's officials and their regional and national superiors. Not only had the unfamiliar and brand-new Conservative county executive failed to oppose the attackers, but also, days beforehand, he and his underlings fired shots at a crowd of Rionegro's most illustrious denizens. (Prophetically, one of the bullets lodged in the shoulder of the town's Córdova statue.) Pleas for protection from local Liberals, Conservatives, and clergy fell on deaf ears in Medellín, and when confronted with judicial proceedings over their actions and inactions, Rionegro's officials offered no justification. A 1950 court-martial therefore convicted Rionegro's county executive and his subordinates on criminal charges; a regional tribunal later held the departmental and national governments accountable for civil damages. It was this latter decision that the Supreme Court ratified in 1958.[89]

Though the court's ruling largely concerned a procedural matter, the Rionegro decision touched on wider legal rationales. El Tiempo remarked in its initial coverage that "[this] is the first time that the irresponsibility of the government [in selecting officials] has been sanctioned in this manner."[90] The Rionegro ruling drew on jurisprudence regarding "the responsibility of the state," an interpretation of civil statutes that allowed the state to be found liable for the commissions or omissions of its agents.[91] Judges in Medellín and Bogotá ordered the Antioquia and national governments to compensate victims of the Rionegro assault for "moral and material harm."

This notion of the responsibility of the state carries significant implications for comprehending the outcome of early agrarian reforms. Colombia's civil code would likely have made many people familiar with the idea of moral and material harm.[92] This awareness helped to shape Colombians' engagement with rehabilitation programs. Though Colombian law made no formal provision for the payment of reparations to victims, a sizeable number of Rehabilitación loan recipients proceeded as they believed was just, treating government assistance as a de facto form of reparation. As a frustrated state bank official explained to a senior government lawyer in 1961, a majority of borrowers ultimately refused to make payments. "The transaction was not a loan," the official reported these people as arguing, "but rather *a donation by the State to in part make reparations for . . . the damages suffered.*"[93] Such reasoning need not have been guided by word of specific court decisions like the Rionegro ruling. Nor did it necessarily reflect mere "naive intuitions of fairness." Instead, provincial Colombians acted on a "juridical imagination" informed by the broader exercise of law in regional life.[94]

The accumulated influence of such claims on the state would go on to have far-reaching repercussions for the scope of the Lleras government's agrarian initiatives. By 1961, the Agrarian Bank had been burned by high default rates in three specialized programs related to violence: one in 1948, one in 1953, and the rehabilitation push of 1958–59.[95] Fearing that further defaults would decapitalize it, the bank fulfilled but a fraction of the loans necessary for the Conciliation and Equity Tribunals to complete conciliations. So consuming was this nervousness that bank administrators admitted years afterward that they had never loaned out over 75 percent of the 2 million pesos the Agrarian Bank had received to assist the tribunals.[96]

Reformism under the Second Republic generated a particular politics of expectation. Bureaucratic skittishness impinged on far more than the range of programs carried out by government agencies. It additionally helped to color popular impressions of the state. Only eight months after the government added the Agrarian Bank as a partner to the tribunals, Lleras's newest interior minister groused that the bank's miserliness "created a dangerous discontentment because people think that the Government has made an offer that it cannot carry out."[97] This attitude had in fact existed before 1961, stemming in part from the overall democratization process; as one of the Liberal Party's brightest young leaders noted to the U.S. Embassy in 1959, "There is always a tendency for people to expect that the achievement or restoration of democratic government will automatically provide the answer to all ills."[98] While a not insubstantial number of Conservatives and others had believed that the military government of 1953–57 held the keys to liberating Colombia from such difficulties, a greater portion of Colombians committed themselves to Alberto Lleras's democratic projects.[99] The creole peace was but one demonstration of Colombians' faith in the possibility of the "new Colombia" that Lleras described.

The interlocked crises of the the creole peace and rehabilitation inspired questioning within Tolima about the relationship between popular aspirations, the aspirations of the political class, and the capabilities of the state. One Liberal observer asked what good Rehabilitación had even accomplished, if all it had done was build roads that *desplazados* could never travel on because conditions were too dangerous.[100] He similarly assailed the state's inability to protect property rights, which he cited as "a permanent threat to peace and public tranquility."[101] The publishers of the left-leaning Ibagué Liberal newspaper *Tribuna* expressed a like concern about what they saw as government inaction, and about the rights and ruin of the displaced. *Tribuna*'s commentary through mid-1959 crystallized by September into an impassioned treatise on the nature of Colombian citizenship and democracy. "With [*desplazados*] being unable to return," *Tribuna*'s editors wrote, "it is not possible to talk sensibly of legal order, of [a] government of laws, and the return of institutions." Events had overtaken the government, which had proven incapable of exercising its authority. Nor, the editors concluded, had political leaders delivered, as they and government bureaucrats

> presented to our exiles the reestablishment of political rights, within the restrictions of the state of siege, as the great conquest of the National Front. This reestablishment arrives when the *campesino* had lost property rights *en masse*.
>
> What the *campesino* wants the government and his leaders to know is that he can live without political rights, as he has never in the history of the country been able to enjoy them fully. What he cannot endure is the lack of bread, housing, and a guarantee for his work.[102]

This tension between political and social rights—between the formalities of the democratic transition and the lived experience of reform—appeared anew as the Lleras administration weighed its rural policy. As an extraordinary measure, the Conciliation and Equity Tribunals depended on the prolongation of the state of siege. In October 1960, with homicides hovering around their lowest point in three and a half years (figure 9), Lleras polled his governors on the advisability of returning the country to normal constitutional rule. Nearly all of them thought a six-month continuation was advisable, to assist further pacification and the task of repatriating the displaced.[103] By contrast, Lleras's ministers shortly thereafter opted to end rehabilitation as a distinct branch of the state, citing the importance of "the reestablishment of institutional normalcy."[104] Ever the democrat, Lleras continued in this latter direction, lifting the state of siege on January 1, 1962. The administration thus opted to strengthen political and civil rights, under the guise of completing the return to democratic normalcy, at the expense of a particular means of strengthening the guarantees to property and livelihood implied in social citizenship.

Although the end of the state of siege marked the fulfillment of one of the National Front's basic rationales, in the provinces, the measure carried practical consequences that bore further on opinions toward Bogotá. The Conciliation and Equity Tribunals had engendered new expectations around civil and social rights. Their disappearance, a man in Caldas told officials, represented the infliction of "grave damages against an infinite number of exiles." [105] Another Caldas resident— a former tribunal claimant—worried that his property deeds would wind up lost in the byzantine maze of provincial and capital bureaucracies. [106]

Colombians' evolving frustration toward the state in the early 1960s had little to do with the restrictions on political competition imposed by bureaucratic parity and presidential alternation, an argument that would later become prevalent in depictions of the National Front. [107] Provincial reaction to the end of the state of siege and the closure of the tribunals epitomized how disillusionment sprouted from a mixed medium of rights and expectations. Politics did not take place solely at the ballot box. Instead, Colombians anticipated equitable access to land, legal guarantees, and state services ranging from police protection to agricultural assistance. And precisely because Colombians took seriously Lleras's talk of inclusive belonging and prosperity, attitudes had farther to fall.

THE AFTERMATH OF REHABILITATION
IN SOUTHERN TOLIMA

Amidst national conversations over the state's responsibilities, the residents of southern Tolima engaged in separate but not unrelated debates about the state's role on the frontier. Events in southern Tolima typified how the end of rehabilitation could trigger explosive if inconclusive reorderings of the local political arrangements created since 1957. The key episode—indeed, what became the best-known act of violence during the Second Republic—was the January 1960 assassination of Marquetalia's Fermín Charry Rincón/Charro Negro. In subsequent retellings by Pedro Antonio Marín/Manuel Marulanda Vélez/Tirofijo and others, the shooting of southern Tolima's top Communist chief evinced collusion between the *comunes*' bitterest rival and a central state set on eliminating rural leaders. [108] The assassination would be transformed into usable myth, an allegory for frictions between the Colombian government and the countryside, and evidence of violence's centrality in Colombian history.

But before the formation of the FARC, what did rural Communists think of the assassination, as the gun smoke faded and meanings began to accrue to the fresh memory of the event? The circumstances of Charry's death, and the heart-pounding confusion of the hours and days that followed, speak not to coordinated state action, but to unanticipated decisions, fragmented political authority, and hundreds of stolen cattle. The contentious dynamics of interparty relations meant that recourse to violence had greater currency on this frontier than in other areas of Gran Tolima, including other Communist communities. Nonetheless, returning to the armed path was a final resort for Marulanda, and a defensive one at that. In the early 1960s, Marulanda fought not to spark a revolution against the Second Republic, but to preserve his place within it.

The primary instigator behind southern Tolima's destabilization was José María Oviedo, alias Mariachi, the troubadour of frontier warfare. Oviedo, who turned thirty-two the day of Charry's shooting, jumped out to visitors as the most outgoing figure they met in the area; his musical aptitude, especially his fondness for Mexican *rancheras,* had smoothed his entrance into the Liberal-Communist resistance in 1952 (where he received his nickname) and charmed the National Investigatory Commission in 1958. Mariachi broke with the *comunes* on his own accord before adhering to the command of Gerardo Loaiza and Leopoldo García, where he closed out the war with the rank of general. Though he was formally outranked by García/Peligro, geographic fortune had left Mariachi in control of Planadas, Ataco's most prosperous jurisdiction (map 3).[109]

Mariachi flaunted his newfound power like no other commander. Lord Parga Cortés, who met him during Mariachi's trips to Ibagué, found him "very ambitious."[110] As Tolima's armed groups pledged peace through the National Investigatory Commission, numerous commanders demonstrated their partnership with the state by handing over men suspected of cattle theft and other crimes. Mariachi went above and beyond in this de facto cogovernance, outfitting his men in police uniforms and having them sally forth to bully the Communists in nearby Gaitania (map 3).[111] To enhance further his self-styled image as southern Tolima's predominant broker, Mariachi negotiated with the government "a sort of monitored freedom" for Chispas, making possible the latter's purchase of a Rovira farm and the employment of his men on Rehabilitación works. "We chiefs of the old *guerrillas* imposed a new order," Mariachi bragged to a reporter in the early days of 1960.[112]

That order was nevertheless slipping out of Mariachi's control. Three circumstances, two of them at least partially of Mariachi's choosing, began to unravel his successes. The first was the dissolution of his sponsorship of Chispas. Regional army officers bore a strident enmity toward Chispas, who had hunted soldiers with far greater facility than vice versa. Refusing to trust Chispas's commitment to rehabilitate himself, the army stepped up harassment of the young Liberal in the wake of the May 9 La Palmita massacre, prompting Chispas to make his way over the central Andes and out of Tolima.[113] Mariachi responded by launching denunciations against other former Liberal commanders across Tolima, accusing them of conspiring to return to war.[114] The move suggests equal parts cunning and anxiety—Mariachi's exploitation of an unforeseen circumstance to make a move against rivals, but also an insecurity about the viability of his own position.

If Mariachi could not make himself a regional player through Chispas, the 1960 elections presented another option. Therein lay the second circumstance, Mariachi's place in an evolving political milieu. Though not as sharp as historic rifts within the Conservative Party, incipient Liberal disunion over high politics (namely the notion that parity and alternation violated the party's majority rights) and the distribution of patronage began to map onto Gran Tolima's diverse Liberal constituencies. Mariachi signed on with the campaign of the party's traditionalist wing against the new dissident group, which called itself the Liberal Recovery Movement (MRL; Movimiento de Recuperación Liberal).[115] The prospect of election spoils and cemented standing within Tolima Liberalism whetted existing tensions within the region.

The third and final context, the curtailment of rehabilitation, offered Mariachi precious little advantage—and substantial risk. By the start of 1960, recipients of Rehabilitación loans began to exhaust their funds. Some former fighters opted for cattle rustling as an alternative—an obvious choice, given that the goods moved themselves, they could be sold for cash, and, as an added bonus, adversaries could be made to take the blame for their disappearance.[116]

Property crime was an especially vexing issue for officials on Gran Tolima's southwestern edge, where the web of trails encircling the Nevado del Huila volcano made a mockery of cartographically precise administrative boundaries. Life on the frontier here was also life in a border region; jurisdictional hurdles magnified the limited physical presence of the state. The triumph of market and social realities over prescriptive political rationality became intensely apparent in early January 1960, when Huila governor Andrade Manrique telegraphed leaders in southern Tolima, requesting their assistance in tracking down eighty cattle stolen from a ranch in Cauca. Once more, the Conservative Andrade Manrique proved himself willing to engage with the Communists, enlisting them alongside Liberals in the search.[117] Though not all officials were as accommodating toward marginal political groups as Andrade, the creole peace enabled a measure of civil political exchange.

The pressures of the previous months were coming to a head. Andrade's summons presented Mariachi with a useful pretext to disprove his men's involvement in the theft and, at a minimum, to show off some muscle against the Communists of Marquetalia (some of whom had indeed taken the cattle). Right after New Year's, Mariachi had journeyed to Bogotá to repeat to the press his accusation that Liberal fighters were preparing to join with Chispas and restart violence.[118] To curry favor with the government, Mariachi sent a commission from Planadas up to Gaitania (figure 4). As a local chronicler later pointed out, no matter the stresses on *convivencia,* it still existed in sufficient measure that Mariachi's men were able to walk straight into the village plaza without difficulty.[119] His Liberals had made threats against Fermín Charry in the past, but Marulanda confirmed in the mid-1980s that "no one suspected" anything in the dawn hours of that Monday. After a heated argument with Charry about the stolen cattle—which the Communist leadership had already ordered returned—Mariachi's men pulled out their revolvers and shot Charry and his two bodyguards dead. The bullets passed all the way through Charry, leaving holes in the wooden door of the village pharmacy that would be left there, a monument to what Marulanda, twenty-five years later, would still consider "the most painful [blow]."[120]

Like the rationale for Mariachi's foray into Gaitania, both the prosecution of the incursion and the aftershocks from Charro's death point to a contingent, postrehabilitation conjuncture. Even if Mariachi had planned Charry's death, as many would eventually claim, he was caught flat-footed by what followed. Overwhelmed by the Communists' instantaneous mobilization against his men in Gaitania, Mariachi was compelled to make overtures to some of the same Liberals he had implicated in the plot against peace. "Mariachi has tried to divide [us]," Germán Dussán, alias General Santander (figure 3), told a government intelligence agent, "but [we] won't get involved in anything so long as they don't bother [us] in [our] region."[121] Subsequent developments—discussed in chapter 5—would indicate that this was not merely a tactical decision by another Liberal commander. Communities were diverging from the shared regional experience of sustained warfare, with some opting to repudiate the exercise of force in favor of outwardly civil forms of internal sociability and relations with the state.

In the immediate term, such refusals helped to ensure that the post-assassination chaos resulted not in Mariachi's domination of southern Tolima, but in the army's reentry into the region. Importantly, this was an outcome that the Marquetalia Communists themselves favored. Mariachi descended toward total disrepute, his forces soon implicated in the robbery and murder of a National Coffee Federation agent—the product of their own search for resources amidst the scarcity of the post-Rehabilitación environment.[122] In the course of a handful of months, the existing balance between forces in southern Tolima fractured.[123]

The aftermath of rehabilitation in southern Tolima thus witnessed fresh conflicts between local factions, as well as the reworking of the state's presence in the area. Slighted by the Conservative critiques of 1959, the Lleras administration assumed a more activist posture in response to this and other localized clusters of homicides in Tolima.[124] The shifting political climate prompted the national and departmental states to modify their local partnerships, dropping a reliance on figures such as Mariachi while increasing the participation of the army. That local groups, including the Communists, initially welcomed the arrival of troops bespoke a popular faith in the state, born of generalized *convivencia* and the specific application of rehabilitation.[125]

At the same time, however, increased exposure to the state generated an accretion of resentments. By July 1960, these feelings boiled over, as the Marquetalia Communists renounced *convivencia* in its current form. In backcountry Spanish, Manuel Marulanda sent to Bogotá a long list of troubling encounters with Gran Tolima departmental and military officials. In cases dating back to 1959, departmental governors had refused to take action against men fingered by the Communists as responsible for cattle thefts. Most recently, officials had refused to lift a finger when civilians from Huila raided the farm where Marulanda pastured his livestock, destroying the livelihood he had assembled.[126] All this came in spite of what Marulanda called the Communists' "exemplary backing of civil and military officials."

The collective weight of the central and departmental governments' failures was too much for the Communists. In his declaration, Marulanda and his comrades—still presenting themselves as "ex-combatants," as they had in 1958—repeated their adhesion to peace and the government's policies. They wrote that before Charry's assassination, "the armed struggle had been terminated, and [it appeared] that we were in a new era, and that the struggles of the moment were pacific . . . policy fights [luchas políticas] without discrimination against any party." Repeated betrayals of their trust now "obligated us to change our position" and resume armed resistance.[127] This declaration of exit was not, however, irrevocable: Marulanda concluded that "we are willing to return anew to peaceful work, if the Government gives us every type of guarantees."[128] Manuel Marulanda Vélez might yet avoid shedding his skin to once more resume the persona of Tirofijo.

The layering of experiences onto acts of force was what instilled memory with meaning. The fact of Charry's death—realized by a former comrade whose hostility had long been known—was made worse by the government's inability or incapacity to achieve what Marulanda held to be right. The wounds of pilfered cattle and Charry's murder could scar over, but the scars were themselves an uncomfortable reminder, both of that which had been and that which might have been. The state was not directly involved in Charry's death, as it had been in the disruption of Marulanda's life in the 1950s. Yet neither was it living up to its ideal as arbiter. The search for new equilibriums—within the countryside and between state and countryside—would remain inconclusive in the aftermath of rehabilitation.

The texture of Colombian politics in 1959–60 gives lie to the fashionable notion that the National Front neutered struggle between the parties.[129] Debates over the shape of peace, charged through with assumptions about property and Colombia's past, remolded the National Front's reformist direction. At the local level, these disputes often assumed violent proportions, as families and movements vied to defend or reestablish their relation to land and authority. Such confrontations sapped the meaning of convivencia locally, while contributing to national contests about how the state should relate to the countryside. Lleras's commitment to institutional democracy moreover set the geographic, and ultimately temporal, bounds of rehabilitation. Rehabilitation's effects would continue to resonate in Colombians' political imaginations and lived realities, indeed defining patterns of reform and conflict well into the 1960s. These political struggles would, however, unfold against a very different national and international backdrop. Whatever consensus had existed early in the Second Republic was gone by 1960, replaced by divisions within the parties and rising popular disillusionment toward the state. With rehabilitation politically compromised from without and within, reform—and with it, the politics of expectation—would pass into new arenas.

5

Reformist Paths, 1960–1964

Rodrigo Méndez Lemaitre and Víctor González could scarcely contain their bewilderment. The two regional notables had driven four hours down the Caribbean coast from Cartagena to investigate what stacked up as one of Colombia's most complex agrarian conflicts. The affair had begun when workers displeased by the terms of their labor contract occupied portions of the extensive four-hundred-hectare San Silvestre ranch in Tolú. By its thirteenth month, the dispute had drawn attention from departmental officials, the national minister of agriculture, and—owing to the nationality of San Silvestre's imperious seventy-five-year old owner, Hans-Joachim von Mellenthin—the German Embassy in Bogotá.

Within hours of their appearance in Tolú, Méndez and González had identified near-complete failures in responsibility. The county executive demonstrated zero interest in acceding to von Mellenthin's demands that the laborers be kicked out, while the former U-boat commander, who had gone outside of Tolú to obtain police protection for his ranch, revealed his lack of respect for local authority. The impending 1962 elections added an additional, unpleasant political sheen to Méndez and González's interactions with the locals. And to top it all off, in the midst of this sweltering day out on Tolú's grasslands, three "gentlemen" claiming to be from "the Bogotá Office of Agrarian Reform" showed up unannounced in a jeep emblazoned with the insignia of a neighboring department. That one of the men spoke with a foreign accent (von Mellenthin would identify him as a fellow German) only injected further confusion into the jumble of jurisdictions and claims at play in Tolú.[1]

In their short but strange road trip, Méndez and González happened upon five essential features of Colombia's postrehabilitation experience with reform. The first concerned the trio of functionaries from the "Bogotá Office of Agrarian Reform."

During Alberto Lleras Camargo's final years in office, the Colombian state mounted a juridically and administratively ambitious program to tackle the problem of underdevelopment. Through new institutions dedicated to land reform and community development, government energies extended over the entire national landscape like never before under the National Front. Gran Tolima retained a privileged position within government programs, but the ambit of reform pulled officials farther away from Bogotá.

The second outstanding detail at Tolú was the foreign-sounding interloper, a geographer named Ernesto Guhl. Social scientists like Guhl designed and staffed Colombia's bevy of young developmentalist agencies; over the first half of the 1960s in particular, these intellectuals fanned out across Colombia's rural and urban peripheries, in search of knowledge which could be translated into meaningful social change. Though not entirely novel on the Colombian scene (Guhl had done government work since 1938, the year after his arrival to Colombia), these intellectuals comprised a growing breed within the *país letrado*—lettered men and, increasingly, lettered women associated with the policies of an increasingly autonomous state, rather than with partisan politics.[2]

Colombia's political scene nonetheless represented, as Méndez and González in some ways sensed, the third dimension surrounding reform. The internal party fragmentation that commenced in 1960 intensified after the 1962 election, clouding the national mood and complicating state efforts at reform. "A political observer ... must often feel he is [in] Alice-in-Wonderland's croquet game," the U.S. Embassy reported in 1963. "Just as the game is proceeding well and everything is understood, the wickets get up and walk away."[3] The presidential succession of 1962 was a crucial element in the confusion, as Lleras gave way to a pure creature of the *país político*, a Conservative whose questionable grasp of national affairs compounded the country's centrifugal political tendencies. The politics of the transition had yielded Lleras as Colombia's last option in 1958. Four years later, they defaulted to Guillermo León Valencia, a selection that few in the countries of letters and politics appreciated.

The fourth variable influencing reform, reformers, and politics is suggested by Méndez and González's observation about Guhl's accent. International influences seemed ever more prevalent in Colombian life after 1960, for ill and for good. Méndez and González's apparent discomfiture paled in comparison to other anxieties at San Silvestre: in 1960, von Mellenthin had warned a senior government lawyer, "There is not doubt that this [occupation] is the first step toward the Cuban system."[4] Fears over Communism's Latin American advent would be mobilized to encourage remediation of Colombia's inequalities, or, as in von Mellenthin's case, to vilify challenges to the distribution of property and power.

Colombia's reformist intellectuals possessed their own ambivalent relationship to internationalization. Educated in the United States and Europe, inspired by transnational movements in favor of reform, and in some instances funded by foreign foundations, the new *letrados* aspired to fuse the universalism of science with Colombia's particular realities.[5] However, as Guhl and his two associates perhaps discovered on their own dusty jeep ride to Tolú, the act of finding those realities could well strip away the lessons and benefits of their transnational lives. Though people such as von Mellenthin might perceive their every interaction through the lens of the foreign, for others the process of encountering Colombia's regions and localities showed that separate logics exercised a decisive role in the politics of development. In other words, while some Colombians might perceive their personal dramas as part of a global Cold War, the tempo and outcome of their interactions bore a distinctly homegrown dimension.

All of these elements of must be narrated at a quickened pace relative to the first years of the National Front because that was how so many Colombians lived the country's post-1960 history. A sense, even conviction, that "the revolution was around the corner" animated countless Colombians to action.[6] The urgent necessity of change pulled social scientists in a dozen directions at once. The early 1960s flew by in the hurry of conducting fieldwork, writing books, running government agencies, and training students who were even keener to transform Colombia. However, in that last pursuit the *letrados* and their pupils diverged. Social scientists and their state patrons advocated for measured modifications based in law and science.[7] The "revolution" lay in the end result. By contrast, to many university students "revolution" implied not only a goal but also a specific set of means inspired by the bearded youths who had swept to power in Cuba early in 1959. The friction between these two projects contributed to both Colombia's political mood and the decisions ultimately taken by some of the new *letrados* to divorce themselves from state-led reform.[8]

Méndez and González's day in Tolú contained a fifth and final attribute of midcentury reform. The families that had taken up residence on the grounds of San Silvestre made clear to Méndez and González that they expected a fair shake from the government when it came to the acquisition of land and secure transit to local markets. However, the families' presence at San Silvestre provided dramatic evidence of their willingness to employ direct action. "The Government doesn't give [us] lands to cultivate, so [we] have to search for them on [our] own," locals had reportedly said a year earlier.[9] This balance between hope and patience, and the state's capacity to manage it, represented the preeminent test of Colombia's democracy in the 1960s.[10] As President John F. Kennedy proclaimed from Bogotá in December 1961, "The great fight of the last decade in this Hemisphere was against tyranny and dictatorships. The great fight in the next decade—the decade in which we are now upon—is to prove that freedom and abundance go hand in hand."[11]

The question of patience applied to reformist intellectuals as well: what happened if the anticipated revolution were not around the corner, or the next one, or even the one after that? Through their encounters with provincial communities, the new *letrados* contributed to a body of knowledge about what their North American colleagues termed "the revolution of rising expectations." The danger with reform, policymakers and politicians came to realize, was that it generated a concomitant set of popular expectations, and thus the potential for frustration toward the state. Social scientists gradually came to recognize this disillusionment, but in the act of discovery they unearthed another disenchantment: their own. Given their expanded role in national intellectual and political life, those sentiments would mold their accounts of what happened to *convivencia* after the creole peace. The question of how development projects fared on the ground—a topic at the center of current historical studies of development—therefore has far broader implications.[12] The pursuit of development in Latin America nurtured social science scholarship, which in turn produced not just academic knowledge but also influential memories of the midcentury period.

THE ORIGINS OF REFORM

By 1960, numerous Colombians sensed that they were moving out of the conjuncture that their country had found itself in during the late 1950s. The midterm congressional elections signaled a shift in the democratic transition. Coalition politics might grow ever feistier, but the basic fact of the National Front was settled. In economic affairs, 1958 and 1959 had been years of "readjustment" and "stabilization"; 1960 would see ground broken on a less defensive and more forward-looking venture: "development" (*desarrollo*).[13] With the political and economic underpinnings in place, Colombia could turn toward the fuller enactment of *convivencia* in the social and economic realms, a step which promised to shore up civil political life.

The "new Colombia" laid out by Lleras Camargo demanded a new kind of Colombian state. In place of the "individualist State," with its emphasis on individual liberties,[14] Colombians would build what advocates termed a "solidarity" or "manager State" (*Estado solidarista* or *gerente*).[15] "The State," asserted a 1962 government training document, "should intervene, to stimulate or regulate the economy, with the goal of accelerating development, the only means to ensure a better standard of living for its members."[16] According to this view, the individualism of classic liberalism had unintentionally generated economic disparities. Now it would yield to "personal liberty [founded on] equality and social guarantees."[17]

This plan to modernize Colombia's state, and through it society, incorporated diverse origins. When he convened a group of national political and religious leaders to draw up the agrarian reform law that would become his administration's most famous legislative achievement, President Lleras announced that "all theses, from those of the Church to those of very radical ideological groups, will come together here."[18] Much the same could have been said of the entire reformist project. Colombians' assemblage of legal instruments and philosophical justifications pieced together older domestic ideas and novel foreign forms.

For administration Liberals, the Revolution on the March remained reform's polestar. The accomplishments of the 1930s seemed more consequential with the benefit of hindsight. One review concluded that the constitutional amendments of 1936, which established the "social obligations" of state and citizens, "anticipated the 1948 Universal Declaration of Human Rights."[19] The full potential of the Liberals' earlier project awaited culmination now that Alfonso López Pumarejo's adherents and their political progeny were back in power.

A central conceit of the Lleras administration's approach was what one key player termed *"mística"*—casting a mystique around reform that would inspire Colombians to participate in the process and thus secure the success of public policy as well as the political viability of the National Front. As the months ticked by, prospects for reform received two serious shots of mystique from abroad. The Vatican's May 1961 pronouncement of a papal encyclical, "Christianity and social progress," invigorated advocates of change inside the Catholic Church and out.[20] Father Lebret's 1958 report had diagnosed the scope of Colombia's development challenge and indicated various steps toward remediation. Pope John XXIII's 1961 moral endorsement turned social action into an imperative, all the more so after he issued a complementary doctrinal statement twenty-three months later.[21] Priestly circles in Bogotá rapidly turned to study the lessons of the pope's teachings, while civil bureaucrats disseminated word of church policy as evidence of the commitments that government and population owed one another.[22] Word from Rome potently reaffirmed the link between natural rights and modern citizenship rights.

The combination of practical guidelines and ideological substantiation offered by the Catholic Church through Lebret and John XXIII had its parallel in another foreign source. The November 1960 election of John Kennedy as president of the United States instantly grabbed Colombian imaginations. In the consideration of one Liberal Bogotá newspaper, Kennedy was nothing short of "president of half the world."[23] Pronouncements from Washington early in 1961 only deepened this effusive optimism. Kennedy's announcement of "a new alliance for progress" with Latin America, introduced in his January State of the Union speech and elaborated upon in a March address, seemed to fulfill hemispheric aspirations deferred since 1945 by Washington's coolness. Kennedy's pledge of dollars for development signified "a definite policy toward Latin America," *El Tiempo* wrote. "An authentic 'New Deal.' A restoration of the 'Good Neighbor' but this time based on more concrete plans and of joint and creative action. . . . This happy beginning allows us to entertain all hopes."[24] The renewed spirit of the 1930s would not proceed alone: Colombians might also enjoy the revivification of the Revolution on the March's international partnership with a Good Neighbor in Washington.

Separated by a matter of mere weeks, the "alliance for progress" and the pope's encyclical sparkled as a Catholic front for social advancement. Admiration and excitement around the pronouncements stretched well outside of Bogotá. Not long after, in a provincial town just over the central Andes from Gran Tolima, a female volunteer in Kennedy's Peace Corps found that "everybody had a picture, torn from *Life* magazine or something, of John Kennedy and Pope John XXIII. . . . It was *los dos Juans* [*sic*]."[25]

Alongside the positive influence of *los dos Juans* there loomed the negative counterexample of another foreign player: Fidel Castro's Cuba. Colombians had responded with substantial goodwill to the triumph of Castro's forces in January 1959; the fall of another Latin American dictatorship seemed a confirmation of the hemisphere's democratic trajectory.[26] Early reforms on the island attracted sympathy from Gran Tolima's urban Liberals. During the agitated middle months of 1959, as regional attentions fixated on the agrarian question, the Ibagué daily *Tribuna* published the verbatim text of Cuba's May 1959 Agrarian Reform Law, the Cuban revolution's first transformative measure.[27] Only those on the fringe right would have applied the "Communist" label to Havana's (or *Tribuna*'s) actions. As was transpiring in Colombia's own postauthoritarian transition, Cubans' quest to restructure their nation involved an array of still malleable options.

The picture would be substantially different a year later. Castro's consolidation of power in Cuba reminded nervous Colombians about shared authoritarian pasts. Castro's intensifying ties with the Soviet Union—which some Colombians recognized as being driven in no small part by Washington's intransigence—suggested too that Cuba was no longer an American affair. By July 1960, talk of "Muscovite imperialism" began to circulate in the major Liberal and Conservative newspapers. Commentators concurrently began to address agrarian reform in more urgent terms.[28]

Fears that the Cuban model would reach Colombia undoubtedly sped along the debate over agrarian reform. But the conspicuousness of Castro, Kennedy, and John XXIII can too easily overshadow the rhythms of Colombia's internal political process. The Lleras administration's provisions to manage the displacement crisis were always intended as precursors to a wider rural policy. Only in 1960, with political *convivencia* holding, and incremental measures tried, could such a step be contemplated.

To shepherd the National Front's key gambit against underdevelopment and violence through the legislative process, Alberto Lleras tapped his younger cousin, Carlos Lleras Restrepo. Chosen for his lengthy record of contributions to Colombian politics, economic policy, diplomacy, and intellectual life, the brainy, rotund Carlos so impressed one foreign expert that the latter dedicated his 1963 book on Latin American reform to Lleras Restrepo, the National Front's "master reformmonger."[29] Carlos's major role directing land reform came in the drafting process, where delegates from the Liberal and Conservative parties, along with the Catholic Church, committed to a program that mixed the two approaches to agrarian reform seen in earlier measures: a new legal regime for frontier colonization and stricter rules for existing properties, including expanded powers that allowed the state to carry out the paid expropriation of idle estates. The U.S. Embassy lauded the proposal as "a serious and far-seeing attempt to obtain land for small farmers with minimum adverse effects on [productive] large landownings."[30] The legislation found an exacting audience in Congress, where Liberal and Conservative opposition factions made passage somewhat harrowing. Still, by December 1961, Law 135 was ready for President Lleras's signature. Colombia, the economist Albert O. Hirschman wrote approvingly, was "living what is surely one of its finest hours."[31]

Alberto Lleras took special satisfaction from Law 135's birth, which came sandwiched between two other momentous occasions. Days before the signing, Castro had angrily denounced Colombia's role in spearheading Organization of American States action against Cuba. The move granted Lleras leeway to sever diplomatic relations with the island. He thus defused, on his own terms, a year and a half of domestic political pressure to break with Havana.[32] Days later, President Kennedy arrived in Bogotá to celebrate Lleras's Colombia as a partner in the Alliance for Progress. Lleras beamed throughout the entire state visit. At no other time in his career had international and domestic successes clustered so closely together. In Lleras's eyes, Washington was aligning with Colombia's positions on development and multilateral diplomacy, while at home his countrymen had committed to "this great task of justice, of production, of equilibrium, of peace for the Colombian countryside."[33] With nine months left before he would depart the presidency, Lleras's two proudest creations, the OAS and the National Front, seemed poised to carry his legacy deep into the young decade.

DEVELOPING THE COUNTRYSIDE

Justice, equilibrium, and peace were Bogotá's foremost concerns as the government launched Law 135's implementation. Colombia's reformist mystique downplayed the primacy of production. This was to be "a *social* agrarian reform," the law's backers explained. And as such, it would need to consist of something grander than granting small plots to the people of Tolú or ensuring that José Dolores received formal possession of his plot on the frontier. "The ... Agrarian Reform is not based simply on a legal and economic reorganization of territorial property, but on the comprehensive restoration of rural life [*vida campesina*]," a leading developmentalist bureaucrat told his peers in 1963. The reform would be "a process of rationalization of agrarian life and labor, with the goal of preparing the *campesino* for his own redemption, through his own efforts."[34]

To this end, and as a complement to Law 135, the Lleras administration began to activate a dull but hugely consequential earlier piece of administrative law. Indeed, outside of Law 135, Law 19 of 1958 represented the most wide-ranging piece of legislation passed under Lleras Camargo or his successor. Its major contribution to Colombia's developmentalist and citizenship regimes involved the devolution of some public services from the government to local Community Action Councils (Juntas de Acción Comunal). Thus, even as officials put forth a maximalist interpretation of the state's legal powers under Law 135, Law 19 marked a frank acknowledgment of the practical limitations to government action. Lleras admitted as much in his February 1959 speech to Popular Cultural Action: given its lack of revenues, the state could not improve the well-being of most of Colombia's population. "For that reason," Lleras rationalized, "we must search for additional means—more rapid, more direct, more energetic, less costly—that will proceed parallel to the State's effort." [35]

Law 19 sought to convert this shortcoming into virtue, through the creation of active political and social citizenship. Neighbors would come together in elected Community Action Councils that could contribute funds and labor to local infrastructure priorities, such as roads or schools. The councils and their projects would simultaneously provide forums for *convivencia,* improve basic material conditions, and lower the state's burden in the enterprise of development. [36] Publicity for Communal Action, as this community development agency was known, celebrated the program as both top-down and bottom-up, "a double current of correlation, which fundamentally makes the action of the State more democratic." [37] Community action, boosters believed, would allow the *país nacional* to put into daily practice the National Front's promise of civil interaction and greater equity.

Community development, like agrarian reform, only emerged as a fully fledged national initiative after 1960. A mere eighty-three councils were created in the first two years of Law 19, but growth exploded with the 1960 transfer of Communal Action from the Education Ministry to the muscular Interior Ministry: around three thousand councils sprang up in rural villages and urban neighborhoods during 1961 and 1962 on account of Communal Action's expanded budget and the addition of professional promoters trained to facilitate council formation. [38] In contrast to later years, when most expansion transpired in major cities, the initial boom was a provincial—even rural—phenomenon. [39] Central and southwestern departments hosted the highest number of councils per county. Huila, for instance, had nearly seven times as many councils per county as the 1962 national average. [40] At the county and departmental levels, then, councils became a widespread means for Colombians to respond to impoverishment and exclusion, through a new bond with the state. [41]

The scale of Colombian Communal Action could not help but attract the attention of scholars looking to crack the mystery of international development.

Agrarian reform, the crown jewel of the National Front, drew the well-established Hirschman, whose research endures as our best source on Law 135. Community development became the bailiwick of U.S. graduate students, including a talented twenty-something economist named Matthew Edel.[42] Edel became an incomparable observer of Communal Action, embedding himself in Bogotá's bureaucratic scene and scouring the country to determine how "experiments with popular responsibility" mattered for the development process.[43]

Fieldwork showed Edel how Community Action Councils spanned backward and forward, connecting communities still healing from violence and linking them to other reform initiatives. Though infrastructure projects were valuable in and of themselves (especially in the aggregate; Edel calculated a twofold return on Communal Action's spending), Edel was especially impressed by councils' local political meanings. In Calarcá (Caldas), the first county one came to on the hairpin trans-Andean road westward out of central Tolima, Edel learned of areas where the accumulated weight of partisan animosity was so great that villages had gone fifteen years "without greeting one another." The basic act of conversation resumed by the mid-1960s, thanks to a meet-up between separate councils coordinated by Communal Action promoters, that allowed onetime childhood acquaintances to come face to face anew.[44] It was a small step, but community action was premised on incrementalism, the remaking of Colombia one village and county at a time.

The benefits of community action, in other words, were seen to accumulate with scale. Edel came across instances where individual village councils federated within their county, forming collectivities that demonstrated a higher capacity to advocate for local needs. Edel found several such confederations pressing the government to implement an "intensification of agrarian reform." That kind of intangible, unquantifiable power stuck with Edel. The fact that it was materializing in sections of Colombia which had experienced particularly sharp violence—Chaparral, parts of the Sumapaz zone—was not lost on him either. When it came time to write his dissertation, Edel bookended his analysis with these stories from Tolima.[45]

Colombian officials themselves looked upon Gran Tolima as privileged terrain for reform. On its face, Communal Action's aim of locating and burnishing local leaders meshed seamlessly with the types of authority that the National Investigatory Commission had stumbled across in 1958—that class of "natural chiefs" fashioned by armed struggle. José Gómez Pinzón sounded the government's position on the possibility of this transition from rehabilitation to development. With "a democratic government" ensuring the security they had previously provided themselves, he said in January 1960, "ex-fighters . . . can devote all their authority and prestige to an eminently social project, such as community action."[46]

Gómez Pinzón's expectant note about the institutionalization of rural power for pacific ends seems to have found frequent fulfillment. Communal Action's high level of decentralization makes the task of reconstructing its operations difficult, but there are scattered, tantalizing hints of how onetime fighters turned to community action in the way that Gómez Pinzón hoped. In early 1963, Germán Dussán/General Santander (figure 3), won election as president of Rioblanco's freshly constituted Community Action Council.[47] Santander had been among the National Liberal Revolutionary Movement of Southern Tolima commanders to refuse Mariachi's overtures amidst the local breakdown of the postrehabilitation order in early 1960. That earlier decision may well have indicated the direction that Dussán would take in 1963, away from out-and-out coercion and toward substitute means of authority. Importantly, Dussán was not alone in his choice; the implications of this branching within Gran Tolima's communities would come to matter profoundly for the fate of rural peoples—and even national politics—later in the 1960s.

Lines of consanguinity ran from rehabilitation to both Communal Action and agrarian reform. The Carlos Lleras–led committee that created Law 135 called on the expertise of Tolima's Conciliation and Equity Tribunals "to shed valuable light on" a problem facing frontier land titling. Law 135, in turn, established a new class of officials to replace the tribunals.[48] Communal Action meanwhile owed a pair of debts to Father Lebret. First, the priest's focus on the county as Colombia's "base community" informed Communal Action's fundamental approach. Second, the All-Purpose Teams, which Lebret had proposed to "invigorate" counties, and which Rehabilitación administered, engaged in some of the earliest promotion efforts for Communal Action.[49]

Community action demonstrated the two sorts of changes that observers felt would be necessary for Colombia's development. The first consisted of reform's outward manifestations, those gestures toward a more equitable distribution of land and an improved standard of living. The second was to be found in the members of the Community Action Councils themselves: an awakening, the mobilization of the spirits for communal progress rather than violence. It was that second process that came to be seen by the early 1960s as the more constructive of the two, and as even a necessary precursor to meaningful material transformation.[50]

To depict the *país nacional*'s consciousness, speed along its appearance, and channel it toward productive ends, the Colombian state counted on a growing set of scholars who claimed objective knowledge of social change. The making of reform and the emergence of these contemporary men of letters were mutually constitutive. Unlike the traditional *país letrado*, the new intellectuals possessed no connection to high politics. Their realm was instead the state, through which they hoped to make ideas operative in the world, renovating the latter through the application of modern social science. In this, they made perfect allies and interpreters of the National Front's reformist mission.

THE NEW *LETRADOS*

Gregorio Hernández de Alba's life had come full circle. The 1940s and '50s had not been kind to the gentleman anthropologist who had put Colombia's pre-Hispanic civilizations on the map. First nudged out of academic circles by the arrival of his exiled French mentor in 1941, Hernández faced perilous expulsion from Colombian public life with the onset of radical Conservative rule in 1949. His protests against the National Police's massacre of a hundred indigenous inhabitants of Tierradentro (the incident that forced the Valencia Dussán brothers to flee their farms) were rewarded by the bombing of the Hernández family home in Popayán.[51]

Only the formation of the National Front put an end to Gregorio's wanderings through professional purgatory. From his newly acquired government post, Hernández impressed on his childhood companion Alberto Lleras the need to alter the state's policies toward indigenous lands. The president obliged, partially reversing the stance that had dominated Colombia's 140-year existence as an independent state. While the government retained a paternalistic stance, no longer would it push the unthinking dissolution of communal landholdings, which Hernández and other indigenists saw as deleterious to the physical and psychological well-being of Colombia's native populations. Instead, trained experts employed by the state would preserve certain indigenous political and social forms while "seek[ing] in a gradual and permanent manner the integration of [indigenous] groups ... to such levels of economy, sanitation, sociability, technology, and culture that they will be comparable to advanced *campesinos*."[52]

Lleras's implementation of Hernández's proposals was more than a favor to a lifelong friend. The remaking of indigenous policy matched well with Lleras's grand formula for *convivencia*, for it acknowledged and reinforced the local authority of indigenous institutions even as it prescribed a particular state-defined vision of citizenship.[53] In rhetoric and execution, the Indigenous Affairs Division that Hernández eventually headed became an integral, if specialized, component of the post-1960 boom in state development programs. Communal Action and Indigenous Affairs, Hernández wrote, "represent the direct application of the Colombian State's social policy."[54]

Hernández de Alba's redemption under the early National Front also portended the triumph of applied social science in Colombia.[55] Strategies for economic growth and social improvement were nothing novel, but practitioners held great faith that they possessed superior means informed by modern scientific knowledge. Colombia needed "social ... pacifistic ... humanist technical expertise [*técnica*]," the publisher of an ephemeral Bogotá magazine called *El Tecnócrata* (the *Technocrat*) wrote in 1962. "These three forms of *técnica* mean peace, progress, and fraternity ... [to use them] would be to better the motherland [*hacer patria*]."[56]

FIGURE 10. Orlando Fals Borda (left) and Father Camilo Torres
Restrepo (seated). Fondo Documental Orlando Fals Borda, Archivo
Central e Histórico, Universidad Nacional de Colombia, Bogotá.

However, though Hernández de Alba and his generation of social scientists experienced a renaissance in the early 1960s, the hour really belonged to a different discipline and its younger practitioners. The alluring option was sociology, as one aspiring graduate student made clear in her 1963 scholarship application. She deemed the study of statistics "indispensable," cultural anthropology "useful . . . with [its] knowledge of man's customs and ways of living." Yet of all scholarly approaches, sociology was the most expansive. "Sociologists can carry out a great service," she wrote in her application essay, "[by] making public [Colombia's] social reality, showing how the groups that people plan to study and improve are structured, studying human interrelations, real or felt necessities, popular attitudes, etc."[57] Anthropology was more a science for distant places and peoples. Sociology, on the other hand, was the urgent science of Colombia's entire society.

The nascent discipline's undisputed intellectual leader was Orlando Fals Borda (figure 10). By his twenty-seventh birthday the Barranquilla native had completed two degrees in the United States and was on his way to a third. His research on rural sociology, grounded in his observations of the Andean village of Saucío (Cundinamarca), had caught the attention of powerful institutional patrons, and so Fals completed his doctorate at the University of Florida on a Guggenheim Fellowship.[58] Though he would dabble in projects with domestic state agencies upon his return to General Rojas's Colombia in 1955, the fact that he was a Liberal—and a Presbyterian to boot!—made a job with an international organization the smart choice. When Albert Hirschman ventured back to Colombia himself shortly after the fall of the dictatorship, he noted with substantial approval the work that Fals Borda was conducting for a developmental arm of the Organization of American States based at the National University in Bogotá.[59] Fals was earnestly proud of his efforts, too. "Applied sociology . . . is much needed in view of the rapid growth of this country," he told a Florida professor in 1956, "and perhaps I could aid in smoothing somewhat the transitional stage." "After six years of contact with an agricultural community [i.e., Saucío]," he wrote to other contacts in the United States, "I am at last succeeding in channeling social change toward what I feel are progressive outlets." "It may be difficult, uncomfortable, and perhaps dangerous, but I must keep on pushing."[60]

Fortune struck Fals Borda in 1958. The "progressive outlets" he had sought to cultivate in Saucío were taking shape; locals were adopting scientific farming practices and harnessing their collective energies. "This is like discovering a gold mine under the dirt, discovering the great potentialities of our people," he giddily explained to his former advisor. The timing was ideal, for the democratic transition could ease Fals' self-professed "mission," as it also did Gregorio Hernández's.[61] Fals seized on the possibility of rapprochement with the state, composing a memorandum on "community action" to the minister of education. The minister obliged Fals by arriving in Saucío in late August 1958 to hear the sociologist speak on the village's experience building itself a school.[62] The prospect of a thousand Saucíos all across Colombia subsequently entered the institutional consciousness of the Education Ministry, such that the following year, the latest minister invited Fals and his colleagues at the National University (where Fals had been affiliated since 1956) to formulate a national plan for community development. Fals's stimulus was thus instrumental to the initial expansion of Communal Action, which commenced soon after.[63] The lessons of applied sociology were being translated into state policy, and by no less than the social scientists themselves.

Even as he bridged between the *país letrado* and the state, Fals Borda was also busy tending to the internal organization of his discipline. The institutionalization of Colombian sociology proceeded in lockstep with the scaling up of state-run development programs. Fals and his National University collaborators established a sociology program in 1959—one of Latin America's first, and one of the three to come into being at Colombian universities that year. In 1960, the field's profile growing, sociology spun off from its original home within the Faculty of Economics to become a self-standing faculty.[64]

All the while, Fals intensified his relationship to the state. He proved himself indispensable in the number two post at the Agriculture Ministry, a steady administrative hand amidst the political turmoil of the 1960 election season. Fals had already attracted the attention of Alberto Lleras, who saw in Fals the professional expertise that he thought the Colombian state and nation needed to advance. A word from the president ensured that Fals remained at the Agriculture Ministry long enough to help introduce Law 135 in Congress in mid-1960.[65]

Though Fals grumbled at the slowness of his exit from the government, his experience set a model for the infant Faculty of Sociology. "I have managed to demonstrate something of the sociologist's possible contribution to the *res pública*," Fals explained in his resignation letter to the Agriculture Ministry. As the faculty's inaugural dean, Fals moved to carry on with this lesson. Among the faculty's first acts was a contract with Communal Action to train the latter's promoters. The initial batch of students included old hands from Rehabilitación, meaning that the transition from postconflict reconstruction to developmentalism passed, in part, through the white halls of the National University.[66]

For those involved in the making of the Faculty of Sociology, the department marked a meeting point for what had previously been—through exile and happenstance—a cohort of would-be reformers dispersed around the globe. Fals Borda's "closest collaborator" turned out to be a man of the cloth, a sociologist trained in the mold of Father Lebret at Europe's preeminent center for Catholic learning. A foreign visitor who met him in late 1959 found Father Camilo Torres Restrepo (figure 10) to be "a very intelligent, attractive and candid though bewildering young man."[67] Fals himself later recalled Torres as a "pioneer of tolerance"—no mean feat in a hidebound Catholic Church hierarchy and deeply conservative society. "We accepted each other as we were," Fals once said. "We both felt that we were working for the same cause, which was greater than [those] other human or social characteristics."[68] For a time, anyway, *convivencia* would rule the Faculty of Sociology.

How to bring that dream to the rest of Colombia? The hunt for a formula was exhilarating. Intellectually, the odd pairing of Orlando Fals and Camilo Torres proved fruitful. Together, they delved into Marx. They each also taught the other's nominal specialty—Fals, the master of fieldwork, taught theory, while Torres, product of the high-minded Catholic University of the Louvain, instructed students on methodology.[69] Outside of the classroom, the sociologists moved at a breakneck pace. A 1962 record from the Faculty of Sociology shows Torres as dedicating sixteen hours a week to teaching, ten to research, and fifteen to conducting training on community action. On top of these forty-one hours, Torres had his duties as National University chaplain, as well as seats on the board of directors and technical studies committee (the latter of which was chaired by Fals) of the Colombian Institute of Agrarian Reform (INCORA; Instituto Colombiano de Reforma Agraria), the state's instrument for implementing Law 135. Lastly, Torres held—for a period—the deanship of the state's technocratic training center (another creation of Law 19). He was a fixture in seemingly every lettered corner of Bogotá.[70]

All this running around paid off, garnering international renown for the National University's Faculty of Sociology. Fals proclaimed before the faculty's first graduates in 1962 that "a true *mística* for science and for service to Colombia has been created [here]." Others were inclined to agree. Colombians became a fixture on the emergent hemispheric sociology scene, wowing audiences at international conferences and assembling—with the financial backing of the OAS and U.S. foundations—an academic infrastructure that was the envy of the region. Colleagues from other countries "cited [the] Faculty as an example to follow" as early as 1962. They also loftily referred to Fals's outfit as "'*el grito de Ipiranga*' for the hemisphere's sociologists"—a reference to Brazil's 1822 declaration of independence.[71] Latin America was striking out toward unbroken intellectual ground.

Herein lies another question of visibility. U.S. historians have portrayed the early 1960s as the maximum period of academia's linkages to government, above all the reigning influence of modernization theory. Kennedy's Alliance for Progress attempted to make real modernization theory's ideas about the progression of world societies toward the apogee of industrial, political, and social achievement, the United States.[72] Yet for all the attention that modernization theory and its institutional expressions have received since the start of the twenty-first century, underappreciated is the extent to which Latin Americans grappled with the problem of change in proprietary fashions. Modernization theory certainly pervaded the design of the Alliance for Progress, but in Colombia developmentalism and its related social sciences were already moving toward alternate models. Not long after President Kennedy's December 1961 visit to Bogotá, Fals and Torres found themselves abandoning the imported functionalist sociological theories that also formed a core component of the modernization paradigm. For Colombians, distinctive features of Colombia's process of social change were not pathologies, as functionalist theory held. To overcome this reigning framework, Fals wrote in mid-1962, National University sociologists commenced an effort "to create a sociological thought sown in Colombian realities, through the methodical observation and cataloguing of local social occurrences."[73] Fieldwork, in other words, demanded a questioning of theory.

Through the process of observing and cataloguing, academic *letrados* began to grasp a truly national conception of their country. Reconfigured ideas about space accompanied Colombian social science's erasure of the distinction between ideas and practice. Research and reform, city and countryside seemed to be compressing into a single stream. Investigators could remain in Bogotá and still gain insights into conditions in the provinces; amidst one of the highest rates of urban growth anywhere in Latin America, Colombia's countryside had come to the capital.[74] During the early months of the Faculty of Sociology's existence, a small group of students made contact with the expanding southern Bogotá neighborhood of Tunjelito, home to migrants hailing mainly from the eastern Andean highlands. Camilo Torres organized the enterprise, which quickly became the centerpiece of the National University's local developmentalist efforts. Dissatisfied by students' petty acts of vandalism during a 1959 protest against internal university policies, Torres hoped to locate "some unworked fields into which the students could channel their dissatisfactions." He was not disappointed, for Tunjelito became a formative living laboratory for the enactment of Christian fraternity and applied knowledge.[75]

Feeling along the raw edge where rural and urban Colombia joined also entailed exposure to the reverberations of rural violence, a first for most of the urban *letrados*. Moving house to house with pencils and survey forms in hand, Torres's students ticked off the number of Tunjelito neighbors who had come to Bogotá on account of "study," "work," "marriage," or "violence." The largest proportion of respondents—a third—answered "work," but more than one in five said that it had been "violence."[76] Out in the provinces, other social scientists recorded substantially higher levels of rural-to-urban flight. In El Líbano, Father Guzmán's home parish, a Guggenheim-funded, Berkeley-educated geographer found that almost 60 percent of people living in the county seat cited violence as responsible for their migration.[77] Here was a set of attitudes and social relations with serious national import. Gradually, violence and its legacies came to occupy a greater place in the Faculty of Sociology's research agenda.

A trip to Tolima taken by Orlando Fals Borda in 1962 illustrated sociology's shift from functionalism to observation, as well as the role that getaways from central Bogotá could play in the personal and intellectual evolution of the *letrados*. Fals had previously dealt with violence in his work, though from a markedly abstract, theoretical point of view.[78] The Colombian Institute of Agrarian Reform provided him with an opportunity to ground himself in a relevant rural ambit. Officials in Bogotá were keen to launch the first subdivision of coffee estates under Law 135 in a symbolically rich location: Cunday, one of the Sumapaz frontier counties wrecked by partisan fighting and government repression. INCORA asked the National University to help prepare and deliver questionnaires to the first batch of potential land recipients. Fals, together with ten students and an intermediary from the Catholic Church, spent the Holy Week vacation of 1962 surveying the county and its people.[79] Fals's field notes show how the journey put him back in his element. On almost thirty small notebook pages, most filled front and back, Fals diligently took down the names of local officials, calculated the income and expenses of the average day laborer family, and recorded how armed conflict had altered Cunday's social patterns.

For the most part, Fals found that Cunday's residents had moved past violence. Liberals and Conservatives had cast aside "the old hatreds," he wrote. "People are tired of violence. Now [they] have unified to demand that which interests all of them: land." "Driven by necessity," eighty-five people had started to farm the hills belonging to one of Cunday's declining estates. The collective effort had yielded *convivencia* (though, Fals learned, locals still identified strongly with their original partisan identities). Cunday's rural folk were also actively cultivating larger forms of associative life: Fals observed a Community Action Council composed of the estate's occupiers; locals additionally credited the national Catholic labor federation's local branch with the maintenance of tranquility.[80]

Cunday thus showed Fals where Colombia's rural society might be heading in terms of both attitudes and social systems. However, despite whatever sense of satisfaction that this produced for the sociologist-reformer, Fals scrawled down an admonition. "People . . . are reaching (have reached?) the saturation point" and were moving toward action. "In any case," Fals concluded, "the [implementation of reform] must be rapid. If it takes a while, the people will continue invading [the estates] and exploiting what has already been invaded. The problem is hunger . . . Hope must be fulfilled and numerous disappointments [consequently] averted."[81]

Similar sentiments about the onrushing possibilities and dangers of Colombia's future resounded throughout Colombian (and U.S.) thought in the 1960s. A particular pressure nonetheless fell on intellectuals like Fals Borda. Their scientific knowledge gave them claim to best comprehend and cope with social change, but as historian A. Ricardo López has argued, it also produced in them commensurate anxieties.[82] *Letrados'* excursions to Bogotá's slums and Tolima's mountains, and their roles inside the state's reformist apparatus, simultaneously introduced them to unknown pockets of Colombia and exposed the limits of their activist zeal. "It is sad to see how the judgments of the world are so different from the judgments of God," Camilo Torres marveled when he left his university chaplaincy for the deanship of the Advanced School of Public Administration (Escuela Superior de Administración Pública) in 1962.[83] Other reformist *letrados* would have agreed. In particular, the country of politics that lay outside the country of letters was increasingly crowding out their utopias.

THE *PAÍS POLÍTICO* AGAINST THE *PAÍS LETRADO*, 1960–1963

Apprehension and self-doubt plagued the *país político* itself as the Lleras administration neared an end. Where uncertainty about Colombia's prospects had surrounded Lleras's 1958 inauguration, a different sense of the unknown dominated political gossip four years later. One therapeutic—embraced especially by political figures just a few years older than Fals and Torres—was to create a counterpart genre to the National University's sociology series. Readers in Bogotá gobbled up books with titles like *The Colombian Dilemma* and *Colombia Pains Us*, expressions of pessimism that echoed press coverage and personal conversations. "The clearest characteristic of the current Colombian crisis," an intellectual with deep ties to the political class wrote in 1961, "is its total cast, its universality, its presence in each sector, in each hierarchy, in each manifestation of national life. This omnipresence of malady . . . in each corner of the motherland, in the citizen's every word and gesture, is the cause of that perplexity, of that confusion, that anguish and that pessimism which casts a shadow over our faith in the future." [84]

The easy heroism of the 1957 anti-Rojas struggle seemed distant amidst a politics whose content and tenor were shifting. Features of the National Front pact meant to ensure stability now complicated the work of legislators and bureaucrats. The relative consensus of the early Second Republic likewise evaporated, with the breakdown of internal party discipline (a trend which further impeded the legislative process) and the widespread deployment of divisive political rhetoric, above all the language of anti-Communism. For the new *letrados* and the communities they hoped to assist, the slowdown in government action fed disappointment, while the threat of being labeled a subversive chilled both the national and local enactment of reform.

The public face of Colombia's disorientation was Guillermo León Valencia, a product of the rigid ruling caste of Popayán (Cauca), southwestern Colombia's colonial center. Blocked from the presidency by Laureano Gómez's objections in 1957, Valencia proved the least objectionable candidate the second time around. Virtually no one was pleased. The U.S. Embassy discerned "widespread doubts that [Valencia] would be even a fair president." [85] When it came time to vote, Colombians still backed the National Front, albeit in smaller numbers and lower percentages than Lleras had attracted. [86]

Valencia rarely deviated from the low expectations that surrounded his election. "He was purely a gut politician, and a sometime poet, and [a] hunter of animals and women, and a lover of alcohol," Kennedy's ambassador to Bogotá recounted in 1969. "He was a very interesting, personable mediocrity. It's a wonder that he survived four years as President. He was . . . totally incapable of taking over such a high office as President of Colombia." [87] Shortly before his inauguration, Valencia announced—without a hint of sarcasm—that "my patriotism and my loyalty permit me to overcome my ignorance." [88] The eldest son of a nationally beloved poet, Valencia had all of his father's verbosity but none of his talents.

Colombia's revamped "manager State" thus fell into the lap of a politician with precious little aptitude for management. The results were not long in coming, for the economic conjuncture that had encouraged Colombia's democratic opening

lived on. The "decade of development," in other words, was not especially condu-
cive to development. Into the 1960s Latin America remained locked in an environment of low world commodity prices, to the extent that Colombia's economy lost
an estimated $500 million in revenue over the four years of Lleras's presidency.
Paradoxically, international development programs further squeezed government
coffers, both by introducing sizeable budgetary commitments and by promoting
fiscal reforms that failed to raise revenue.[89] The ensuing deficits introduced inflationary pressure within the economy, which Valencia worsened with policy decisions that undercut his own advisors. "It seems," the U.S. Embassy told Washington, "that everything this modern-day Midas touches turns to lead."[90]

The changeover from Lleras to Valencia reverberated down the bureaucratic
ladder, hamstringing developmentalist goals as well as macroeconomic policy. The
head of the Institute of Agrarian Reform later claimed that "I noted from the start
that in . . . Valencia we were not going to have the best of allies. Curiously, although
I oversaw one of the largest budgets in the country, I was unsuccessful in getting to
talk with [Valencia] even once."[91] Valencia was hardly more reassuring to the
lower-ranking professionals who staffed the "manager State," especially as Conservatives hungry for patronage posts turned their sights on well-funded development agencies. The subsequent controversy rolled on for months, leading Bogotá's
Liberal press to criticize the application of parity to such a specialized sector of the
bureaucracy on the grounds that "politicians and technicians are basic enemies
because a man cannot be a good administrator and a good party member at the
same time."[92] Such calls to modify the institutional architecture of the original
transition failed to move Valencia.

Democratic politics seemed all the more sclerotic against the backdrop of "revolution," a style and desideratum with tremendous mystique. Attraction to "revolution" fed changing political idioms and practices. Most prominently, the MRL,
the dissident wing of the Liberal Party, opted in mid-1960 to change its name from
the Liberal Recovery Movement to the Liberal Revolutionary Movement (Movimiento Revolucionario Liberal). The switch conjured both international and
domestic politics, the Cuban revolution and the Revolution on the March, for the
MRL's founder was Alfonso López Michelsen, son of Alfonso López Pumarejo. The
junior López, the U.S. Embassy reported, "conceives of his movement as represent-
ing something new in terms of social-economic factors, as a protest against bos-
sism and the old party structure, and as a vehicle for social and economic progress.
As such he tends to paint it as part of a new wave of aspirations that involves the
whole continent and hence something of the 'wave of the future.'"[93]

The future quickly shot past López Michelsen. In its initial electoral foray in
1960, the MRL drew over a fifth of the national Liberal vote, largely on the strength
of support from provincial Liberals fed up with the government's inability or
unwillingness to advance local priorities. López Michelsen built on this success in

1962, garnering half a million protest votes in a distant second-place finish to Guillermo Valencia, the constitutionally guaranteed winner. ("Liberals won't vote for a Conservative, even if that Conservative were the Holy Spirit," sniffed one regional MRL leader.)[94] It would be the MRL's high-water mark. The movement would never manage to overcome the implication of its 1960 shift from anti-alternation faction to self-proclaimed paladin of revolution; the tension between those within the MRL who remained more Liberal than revolutionary, and those who identified as more revolutionary than Liberal, fissured the movement nationally and regionally.[95] As occurred in southern Tolima ahead of the 1960 election, existing distinctions within the Liberal Party transferred onto the Liberal-MRL split, and then again onto intra-MRL divisions. López meanwhile proved too moderate, too close to the *país político*, for many regional MRL politicians, as well as many urban Colombians coming of political age. Though they might maintain the MRL label and participate in formal political institutions such as Congress, radical Liberals pursued a more openly oppositional stance in legislatures and on university campuses.

Fatal pressure on the MRL came as much from outside as within. Uneasy internal alliances among different regional blocks and competing programmatic agendas cracked in the face of determined assaults from critics who looked at the movement and saw only red. Scattered local Communist Party support for the MRL in the 1960 elections first raised the hackles of Liberal and Conservative leaders. López Michelsen's subsequent calls for the enfranchisement of the Communist Party—a measure he claimed would force the Communists out into the open—confirmed to these detractors that López was but a useful idiot for dark forces within Colombia. The MRL's vocal public defense of the Cuban revolution months later, soon after its rebranding as the Liberal Revolutionary Movement, hiked concerns still higher.[96] From there, it was a short step to connect the MRL and international Communism with Colombia's remaining pockets of rural violence. It was a clever reading of *convivencia:* with the creole peace having stabilized the countryside and the National Front pact having eliminated the basis for any future partisan conflict, the logic went, any remaining unrest must have a foreign connection. Presented in newspapers, on the radio, and in speeches, this narrative became a potent force in Colombia's public sphere from 1961 forward.[97]

The advent of anti-Communism as an obstacle to pluralism and reform marked a departure from the first years of the National Front. What had seemed a hemispheric certainty in 1958—the Americas' "unalterable course ... [toward] liberty and the juridical-constitutional order"—had since given way to peril. Many Colombians believed that international politics threatened to reignite violence and demolish democracy, paving the way for the installation of an authoritarian state. Whether it resulted from conviction or convenience, the capacity to conceive of Colombian politics on this scale gave inter- and intrapartisan feuds a sharper quality. Though the promulgation of the papal encyclicals and programs such as the Alliance for Progress could invigorate dialogue and action, enhancing Colombians' sense of the possible, internationalization on the whole constrained the kind of expansive politics seen early in the Second Republic. Previously plausible forms of political expression and collective action diminished under the specter of intimidation and retaliation.

Anti-Communism could suffuse Colombian provincial life even where people lacked a substantial sense of the international. Fals's conversations with Cunday's *campesinos* revealed little understanding of the United States, other than the fact that it was Colombia's largest trading partner, and still less comprehension of Cuba or the Soviet Union. Anti-Communism nevertheless mattered vitally for the exercise of political and social citizenship. If agricultural workers merely presented a petition for loans or better salaries (a key consideration given the context of falling coffee prices and rising inflation), they invited accusations of Communism from local coffee consortiums. This cast a pall over most forms of organizing—and, by extension, elevated the significance of the common Liberal-Conservative *campesino* front that Fals found.[98] Interparty *convivencia* could serve as an antidote to the violence of the past and the political intolerance of the present.

The diffusion of anti-Communism handed regional notables another tool with which to resist reformist imperatives coming from Bogotá. The agrarian reform law provides an illustrative example. Though Conservatives in Congress had been able to extract pro-landowner concessions during the legislative process, Law 135 promised to strike sufficiently at landed rural power that provincial elites were moved to initiate a three-pronged campaign against the measure's implementation.[99] Private legal maneuvers first commenced ahead of Law 135's final passage, as families with properties over the two-hundred-hectare threshold for potential expropriation used an old legal trick and divided their lands among various relatives.[100] Second, as it became clear that INCORA meant business, landowner interests sought to block supplementary decrees that would give Law 135 teeth. Fals Borda, for one, took this as proof that INCORA was doing worthwhile work.[101]

The final and crudest method was to equate reformism to Communism. This familiar chorus grew louder as the developmentalist state gained momentum. Some antagonists took to calling Communal Action "Communist Action." Other anti-Communist invective extended as far as the Catholic Church. Not even the pope's directives were immune: upon their arrival in the field in mid-1961, Communal Action's fifty inaugural promoters encountered flak from regional representatives of the National Coffee Federation. The promoters were blocked from taking their posts throughout the country because of an "outcry" that they had been "corrupted by Communist philosophy" during their training. The offending materials turned out to be Catholic social encyclicals, including John XXIII's latest offering.[102] The international influences informing and obstructing Colombian reformism could turn directly against one another.

Though conceived under Alberto Lleras, Colombia's developmentalist state only began to arrive at institutional and programmatic maturity under the uncertain regime of his successor.[103] Reformism thus faced a political environment characterized by internal fragmentation and external gravitational pull. As challenging as it is today to gain a clear picture of that era, it was infinitely more difficult for the supposed "natural chiefs" of the *país político* to control the country pulling apart in front of their very eyes. For the social scientist reformers of the *país letrado*, dysfunctional politics served as a backdrop for intensified exposure to what Alberto Lleras once termed "that other country"—that provincial Colombia, which was simultaneously separate from and subordinate to the worlds of politics and letters.[104] The frustrations of that country would bleed into the reformers' disillusionment during the Valencia presidency, reproducing for the *letrados* a version of provincial communities' alienation from the central state.

THE DISENCHANTMENT OF REFORM

Reformism posed a paradox to Colombian democracy in the early 1960s. While provincial Colombians were frequently exposed to democratic, participatory decision making through their Communal Action Councils, regional and national governments showed themselves to be unresponsive to popular demands. Reform could thus enhance Colombians' appreciation of their limited condition even as it held out the prospect of improved objective and subjective station. Development was simultaneously a primary goal and a central challenge for Colombia's transition.

Crucially, the absence of state action was not the sole determinant of such dissatisfaction; the state could lose legitimacy even where people had broad exposure to government programs. Reform could well reinforce or generate inequalities at the local level. That was the experience of the Zuñigas, a family of well-off Conservative farmers in Toribío (Cauca). Like Belalcázar, its neighbor to the southeast, Toribío's strategic position astride routes between the Magdalena and Cauca valleys, as well as the ethnic otherness of its extensive indigenous population, made it sharply contested ground. Raids by southern Tolima's Liberal fighters into Toribío seem to have peaked in the year and a half between the fall of Rojas and the creole peace, the period in which David and Sara Zuñiga fled the area along with their nine children. Though distant in space, the Zuñigas remained tied to their lands. Thus commenced at least four years' worth of efforts to divest themselves from Toribío, so that the family could assemble a more certain future elsewhere.

Sara's letters to officials in Bogotá suggest the unintended consequences of peace, namely how the privatized forms of authority which emerged during the creole peace subsequently solidified both in spite of and because of developmentalist initiatives. The outcome was macro stability at the cost of equity. Sara claimed in 1962 that "the bandits ... have turned into political bosses to maintain [our] exile and not let any Conservative [landowner] enter." Partisan identity thus meant that David Zuñiga would not be José Dolores. Moreover, Conservatives who wished to sell their properties had to obtain the permission of the preeminent power on the regional scene, General Peligro, who also demanded a quarter of the value of any sale. Faced with such constraints, David Zuñiga took the 6,000-peso Rehabilitación loan that he received in early 1959 and invested it in the family's refuge in Cali. The Zuñigas subsequently turned to the Conciliation and Equity Tribunals. Their literacy and relative wealth (which had also enabled David's size-able loan) made them likelier than most to bring their complaints before this new state instrument; their appeal was one of the first cases received by the Cauca tribunal. It took some eighteen months, but by the end of 1961 the tribunal succeeded in reaching an accord through which one of the men exploiting the Zuñigas' farm would pay them 4,000 pesos—a fraction of the 30,000 pesos the family claimed the property was worth, but money they needed to pay the Agrarian Bank for David's loan. The deal ultimately collapsed, Sara explained, when another de facto local authority threatened the Zuñigas: "We [the Zuñigas] would never return there and if we did they would kill us." By early 1962 Sara found herself pleading with Lleras's Conservative interior minister to assist her family and dozens of others by having the government extend their repayment periods. The ministry responded favorably to Sara's request, though it is unclear whether the Agrarian Bank heeded its suggestion of relief.[105]

The Zuñigas' complaint became a common one in areas of Gran Tolima where the National Liberal Revolutionary Movement of Southern Tolima—Sara's "bandits"—held sway. Around the time of the Zuñigas' tribunal-brokered conciliation deal, military intelligence reported "persistent" rumors that the remaining *limpio* commanders—Peligro, Gerardo Loaiza, and General Santander among them—were "materially losing prestige [because] their sympathizers come to see them as crooks and [as] leaders incapable of helping them to solve their problems without personal interests getting in the way." [106] Seen in this light, Santander's eventual leadership of Rioblanco's Community Action Council potentially marked the consolidation of local hierarchies rather than a triumph of rural democracy.

The implications of these processes for the Colombian state are not altogether clear. The *limpios'* renewed association with the state through its developmentalist initiatives, a measure to prop up the former's eroded authority, may have implicated the state in the regional crisis of legitimacy. In sections of Gran Tolima that had experienced intense periods of collective violence, *convivencia* involved, in part, the delegation of authority from government officials to local power brokers. Such imbrication of party and state in Colombia stretched back to the nineteenth century, meaning that this was an established and familiar phenomenon.[107] However, by 1961 the limits of the model's particular contemporary manifestations were becoming apparent. Memories of Lleras's final year in office point away from the difficulties of the Colombian state, so shaped are they by the legacy of John Kennedy's triumphal Bogotá appearance, the high-water mark of optimism around the Alliance for Progress.[108] Testimonies from the provinces speak to a different set of attitudes. "The morale of the peasants has hit rock bottom because of the Government's lack of attention to this County," an official in eastern Huila explained to his governor in 1964. "The *campesino* can no longer believe in official promises, because these have been many and he has always been deceived, from 1961 forward especially."[109] Statements from Communal Action's directors confirm this as a wider trend taking shape by 1962. Officials warned that year that if the government did not follow through on requests stimulated by its own programs, "the only thing obtained will be an intense Community resentment."[110] Such popular sentiments coincided with rejection of the state's local partners. The *país nacional*, as much as the *país político*, could question the meaning of politics and the value of the state's promises. To Kennedy's point about whether "freedom and abundance go hand in hand," many Colombians would have responded with ambivalence or doubt.

Yet the reforms of the early 1960s simultaneously presented communities with meaningful alternatives. The *país político*'s paralysis was matched by innovation from the *país nacional*, thanks in large measure to the state's community development outreach. The kind of civic organizing that Orlando Fals Borda had approvingly observed on his 1962 Cunday trip was taking root in other areas of Colombia. This current in social and political life was sufficiently pronounced by late 1965 for the U.S. Embassy to take note. "[Community Action] local councils [are] just now beginning realize they [are a] potentially important pressure group," the embassy explained in a cable on rural affairs. "In [a] number localities [they] have replaced officially recognized civil administrations as spokesmen for [the] community and have taken [the] lead in asking [the] central government for [a] redress [of] grievances."[111]

Colombian officials had been quicker to realize community development's capacity to foster these activities, such that the enthusiasm that had surrounded Communal Action's post-1960 expansion had ceded to hesitancy or outright rejection. Debates over the potential political consequences of community development had in fact circulated within the government as officials contemplated throwing the state's resources behind Communal Action.[112] Of particular concern was the prospect that unfulfilled expectations stemming from too rapid an expansion "would serve as an invitation to communism."[113] Such Cold War–era apprehensions must, however, be divorced from the base element: a cognizance that specific policy choices would bring about a politics of expectation which would in turn complicate, not ease, the task of governance. Though the anti-Communism of the 1960s imparted a particular set of concerns onto the matter, the political ramifications of development transcended the Cold War setting.

Confronted by Community Action Councils agitating for the realization of social citizenship, ancillaries of the state pursued various means to limit the repercussions. Jealous of Communal Action's access to potential voters, and eager to snatch up its funds, various politicians worked through Congress and regional political networks to impose their will on community development.[114] Among those spooked by this pressure from on high were executive branch functionaries, who responded by scaling back state-led community development. In 1963, for instance, Interior Ministry administrators ordered a review of Communal Action's collaboration with the Peace Corps, whose nearly three hundred volunteers had represented a modest if visible contribution to community development. The volunteers, officials wrote, were obliged to give "technical help to 'communal activities,' that is specific projects that require some technical help. . . . This means that *the Volunteers should not realize an . . . 'opening' or 'motivation' of communities,* but a . . . technical assessment and [assessment] of organization that involves efficiency in the technological and organizational realm." Objecting that "this orientation has not been observed in recent times," the Interior Ministry threatened to remove from service any volunteer who did not pass a government review.[115] Similar justifications helped to end Communal Action's practice of bringing community leaders to Bogotá for "social leadership development" (*capitación social*).[116]

The task of modernizing Colombia's society thus proved to be more politically fraught than any in the "manager State" expected. The supposedly apolitical, technical nature of developmentalist reform ran afoul of government appointees and their political patrons, who pushed back against the reformers on multiple sides. Like community development itself, the response was decentralized. It therefore represented, rather than a wholesale overturning of the National Front's programmatic commitments, a set of smaller political battles that added up to national significance. Every diversion of funds in exchange for votes, every government bulldozer which failed to arrive as promised to assist a village in finishing a new road cut, every school left unfinished due to insufficient resources—each disjunction between popular interest and government fulfillment dissolved bonds of affinity between citizen and state.[117] After 1960 virtually no Colombian spoke of the "Second Republic," that triumphal phrase of 1957–58. Disenchantment with reform helped breed this disenchantment with democracy because the possibilities present at the end of the prior decade had devolved into what one observer termed the lesser options "of petty politics, of inefficiency, of frustration."[118]

Orlando Fals Borda observed this process from up close. Midway through 1964, the now-famous sociologist returned to the village which had launched his career, to find that the shine had come off the "gold mine" he had uncovered and fostered in the late 1950s. The joint undertakings of Saucío's inhabitants, which had helped to inaugurate a national movement, were stagnating. "The decadence of communal action," Fals recorded in his notes. And none of the locals he interviewed had much of an explanation. "Perhaps the residents are tired," one ventured. Others remarked that people were simply interested in their own business. Fals posited that the dynamism of community development's heyday had been concentrated in Saucío's "most efficient and practical" leaders—a group in which he placed himself.[119]

The *letrados'* continued journeys through provincial Colombia left them with something of those communities' dissatisfaction toward the state and its process of reform. The *letrados'* work was challenging, to be sure, but their budding discontent ran deeper. "The young men who run Colombia's land reform must deal with vast rural agony and wordless rebelliousness," a visiting reporter wrote in 1963. "In bad moments, in frustration over their lack of progress, they half hope it will fail."[120] Even as the "manager State" expanded, hiring new social science graduates and opening new fronts in the national campaign for agrarian reform, the old mystique was draining out of its practitioners.

Two trips far afield from Bogotá defined Father Camilo Torres's trajectory. The first, taken on behalf of the Agrarian Reform Institute, brought him to the mouth of the Sinú River, a short hop from where his INCORA colleague Ernesto Guhl had previously visited the land dispute in Tolú. The labors of the poor Afro-Colombians who sought to eke out a living on the edges of the Sinú, against the wishes of the area's large landowners, captivated Torres. Seizing the most from this latest opportunity for Christian fraternity, Torres joined his hosts in tending rice shoots and drinking moonshine. Fals, who met Torres on the coast for a few days, explained thirty years later that "it was there, I think, where he began to become interested in active politics. . . . This contact with the agrarian question, the problem of land tenancy, that INCORA set up, was fundamental to his reorientation."[121] Fals was speaking as much about himself as about Torres.

Torres's horizons had already undergone a significant shift back in Bogotá. Students at the National University (and elsewhere in Colombia) had moved from voicing criticisms of Colombia's political, social, and economic "structures" to seeking exit from these entirely. Students rejected the terms of the National Front pact as restrictive, the pace of reform as too slow, the practice of community-focused sociology as insufficiently comprehensive.[122] The example of Cuba showed them that revolution was right around the corner.

Their stance would eventually cause them to break with many of their mentors, but Torres was certainly moving toward similar positions. Talk of modifying Colombia's "structures"—which was everywhere in reformist circles in those days—acquired a special meaning amidst the ferment of the National University. Contact with his students, and his growing familiarity with the country as a whole, drew Torres to start trying to reconcile Christianity with precepts of socialism. This stance won Torres the adulation of his students and censure from the "structures" he served: when a 1962 student strike shuttered the university and triggered retaliation from the administration, Torres went beyond the Faculty of Sociology's statement of support for the strikers by delivering a sermon that granted moral sanction to the protestors and anyone who "fights for a cause and dies for that cause." [123] It was altogether too much for the cardinal of Bogotá, who ordered Torres—already perceived to be a loose cannon—to leave the university. [124] Torres had suffered his first rupture with the church.

The "manager State" still held a place for Father Camilo. He transitioned from the National University to the Advanced School for Public Administration, from whence he undertook a second trip that opened his eyes to the realities of both rural Colombia and the *país político*. Early in 1963, one of the legendary leaders of the Liberal resistance of the Eastern Plains—a period and place far removed from anything that Torres had learned about violence from Bogotá's *desplazados*—asked the priest to open a training center in distant Yopal (Casanare). During his two weeks there, the priest charmed, listened, and drank his way into the confidence of the rough cowboys who came to hear him speak about cooperativism. Torres flew back to Bogotá eager to create a full-time offering for the betterment of the plainsmen. [125]

Partisan politics present and past would frustrate Torres's goals. When the priest debuted his proposal to the rest of the Colombian Institute of Agrarian Reform's board, Conservatives balked at handing such a project to Torres's Liberal boss. The board's second discussion of Camilo's proposal fared even worse. Álvaro Gómez, The Monster's son and political successor, attacked the Yopal school for daring to serve the Liberal fighters who had combatted his father's administration. [126] Torres would get his training center for Yopal, but in that showdown with Gómez, Torres realized that the reformist state could not function with the *país político* and its vices in the way. His alienation from the establishment advanced apace.

Peripheral Colombian communities were not alone in their growing disillusionment as the National Front period progressed. The techniques and commitments of applied social science intertwined the destinies of neighborhoods and villages with those of the reformist intellectuals who claimed to work on their behalf—a mixing of identity and experience that the National University's *letrados* would later deposit in the term "La Violencia." Historians speak today of the revolution of rising expectations in reference to the *reformados*—the reformed—but it applied too to the *reformistas*—the reformers. Both believed in the promise of Lleras's Colombia, the amplification of *convivencia* to all aspects of national life. The velocity of their expectations nonetheless outstripped the possibilities for reform.

This point was not lost on contemporaries. In the consideration of one of the agrarian reform's chief architects, the matter boiled down to national character. "No one wants to wait years," he argued in 1962:

> We Colombians put great faith in the magic power of words, in the capacity that they have, on their own, to convert themselves into reality. We have been raised with the conviction that, just as God made the world in six days, it is sufficient that a law or decree is issued, that the word is uttered, for everything to be left completed. Between

the idea and the reality we do not place a single obstacle, and if we catch sight of a void we fill it with imagination, closing our eyes to the limitations placed by available resources, incapable of concurrently satisfying everything that we are missing, and ignoring the inescapable restraint of time on every material project.[127]

That belief in the capacity of words was particularly true of the new breed of *letrados*, at least until their contacts with provincial Colombia provoked a crisis of faith. The first outcome of those encounters was a transformation of method, as theory gave way to observation. The very object of scholarly attention then shifted, plunging the *letrados* into still another political question, one separate from the politics of expectation surrounding reform, but still part of Colombia's transition. During the Lleras years, Colombians' memories of violence had occupied a significant place in social scientists' work. Yet, as Torres's exchange with Álvaro Gómez demonstrated, the politics of the past became an even more inescapable part of public life with the advent of the Conservative-led administration in 1962. Foreign scholars' comparison of Fals's Faculty of Sociology to Brazil's famously bloodless declaration of independence was ill-founded. Colombia's sociologists could not help but come across blood.

When he left the National University, Camilo Torres recognized this distinct challenge facing his generation of reformers. After remarking that "it is sad to see how the judgments of the world are so different from the judgments of God," the priest added that "in Christian work there are no failures, there are no '*aplancha-das*' as we say in Colombia."[128] Torres's reference spoke to its historical moment. The Colombian countryside was filled with "*aplanchadas*," people humiliated, even killed, with beatings from the broad side of a machete. By turning to chronicle these stories, the sociologists of the National University would learn the ultimate limits of their own relationship to politics and the state. The memories generated in the process would deeply, if subtly, inform their subsequent scholarship and notions of nationhood.

6

Books and Bandits, 1962–1964

Word could travel especially fast between city and countryside when a beauty queen sat at one end of the chain. Given that she had received her first crown at Ibagué's Folkloric Festival two years prior, it was fitting that the reigning national Queen of Queens gestured toward *convivencia* in September 1962. As Colombians throughout the country agonized over a spate of attacks levied by what they had taken to calling "bandits," the queen offered to visit the backwoods of her native Tolima to try to convince these misguided young men to turn to a life without arms. For foreign observers, at least, it was a preposterous notion. Ever since political leaders had committed to put an end to violence in the late 1950s, Colombians had tended to see women as a domesticating corrective to the excesses of political passions.[1] But the Queen of Queens' invitation, the U.S. Embassy commented, "probably had the opposite effect of inducting new recruits into banditry."[2]

The long process of invention behind "La Violencia" reached a crucial phase in 1962. At the same time that Orlando Fals Borda and his *letrado* colleagues' intellectual and personal undertakings intersected with high politics in the capital, nonpartisan, "bandit" assaults on Colombia's roadways spread fears about violence-as-practice. Within the ensuing debate over violence past and present, Colombians worked to grasp how the latest manifestations of violence were connected but not continuous with what they had confronted in the 1940s and '50s. The ideas and proposals that swirled through the public realm in the form of petitions, speeches, and academic monographs laid down the basic features of an enduring national narrative, as existing ideas of violence commenced their transformation into the concept of La Violencia.

We must therefore return to the question of what Colombians meant when they spoke of "violence." The 1962 publication of *La violencia en Colombia* by Fals and his collaborators expanded on the spirit of enquiry into violence that had characterized the early democratic transition. By disclosing the Peace Commission's findings, *La violencia en Colombia* opened anew the matter of responsibility for partisan violence in previous decades. The question of memory thus acquired unprecedented stature in Colombia's transition.

This new politics of the past would also inform the politics of the present. Beginning in 1962, varying forms of collective partisan and generational memory molded possible discussions of Colombians' common experience. This enactment of a revised elite *convivencia*, premised on the inadvisability of speaking about the past, has become a principal coordinate in accounts of the National Front period.[3] Yet the silence decreed by the *país político* was not as expansive or efficacious as has been supposed. Moreover, it paradoxically opened space for two alternate, oppositional versions of the past to enter widespread public consciousness.

Social science was the vehicle for the first of these. Scholarly approaches to violence-as-idea did not halt following the fierce debates of of 1962, though scholars found themselves retuning their approaches and conclusions in light of political opposition, as well as their own evolution as thinkers. Changes in violence-as-practice occasioned additional reconsideration. This latest round of interchange between the idea and practice of violence induced social scientists into an intellectually productive yet personally unsettling search for fresh frameworks through which to explain violence. Articulating his role as a bridge between the study of violence in the late 1950s and the scholarly wave of the 1960s, Germán Guzmán Campos recorded in the 1962 volume of *La violencia en Colombia* that "[we should] write up . . . the immense effort realized [against violence] since May 10, 1957 . . . as a second volume that could well be called 'How Peace Was Made.'" Two years later, chastened by the political fallout from his earlier work and troubled by the apparent direction of provincial security, Guzmán would not write so confidently of peace, and would instead cast violence as pervasive. The shift built toward one of those alternate accounts of the past—La Violencia, an expression of *letrado* experience.

As Guzmán's words suggest, the Lleras administration's rehabilitation programs stood at the heart of debates in 1962 and beyond. The new politics of the past accompanied a rejection of the Liberal president's approach, with its political pardon, funds for provincial reconstruction, and collaborative relationship between state and rural citizens. "Those measures are exhausted and cannot be employed again," *El Tiempo* said in August 1962, paraphrasing Colombia's recently installed minister of justice. "To do so would signify an excess of magnanimity toward those who did not want to rehabilitate themselves, but preferred instead to defy the State and declare war on the nation."[4] The beauty queen's appeal to persuasion as a means to peace thus reflected a style that was on the wane. The larger struggle between the countries of politics and letters to define Colombia's past bloodshed accordingly carried profound implications for the ways in which Colombians thought of and acted against contemporary forms of violence.

Joining intellectuals and politicians in these latest encounters with violence as idea and practice came a group of military *letrados*. This cohort of high-ranking young officers approximated the intellectuals' approach to violence as an object of scientific study, yet advocated a response premised on force that closely resembled the position of leaders from the Liberal and especially Conservative parties. As the language of peace gave way to an emphasis on top-down pacification, the Colombian military, armed with a new strategy and a new capacity, stormed to an unprecedented role in Gran Tolima.

Colombia's national political debates between 1962 and 1964 are essential to comprehending both the origins of Colombian social science and the post-1960 rise of a new Colombian military establishment—ideas and practices lauded by contemporaries throughout the hemisphere. Developmentalism served as a second shared context for social scientists and the military. As part of the expansion of the Colombian Armed Forces' portfolio, military thinkers took as an article of faith the positive association between military programs and socioeconomic development. The provincial experience of the early and mid-1960s suggested there was indeed an interconnection between the two, though not of the kind that military *letrados* anticipated—both could yield disillusionment. In other words, though Colombians gained a novel sense of the nation between 1962 and 1964, with studies of violence continuing to bridge the gap of understanding between cities and the countryside, and the army's campaigns bringing the Colombian state into previously isolated sections of the provinces, the expectant optimism of the early democratic transition and the creole peace had diminished. For rural communities and the reformist intellectuals of the National University alike, memories of this period began to displace recollections of the more distant past, granting a particular inflection to the vision of nation then coming into being.

THE MAKING OF *LA VIOLENCIA EN COLOMBIA*, 1960–1962

For all that Colombians wrote and talked about violence in 1957–58, the public never fully metabolized the findings of those enquiries. The vast corpus of memory and documentation compiled by the National Investigatory Commission never achieved wide dissemination, instead influencing policymaking from within the government. Absent a synthetic, national narrative about the recent past, partisan, regional, and local understandings of violence remained unreconciled.

It would take a meeting of minds, the collected experience of the National Investigatory Commission merged with the intellectual vibrancy of Colombia's new breed of social scientists, to begin to structure public consciousness around a single, shared referent. In their own ways, each camp in this endeavor embodied the lingering influence of the inquisitive ethos that characterized the early democratic transition. Indeed, Alberto Lleras Camargo—the symbol of that feeling—was the first to put the pieces in motion. During an impromptu stopover in El Líbano in January 1960, Lleras mentioned to the municipal council that Father Guzmán was "behind on writing a book about violence, given the knowledge that he has of the problem." The statement was the perfect expression of Lleras's penchants for *convivencia* and the written word, though the priest had apparently given no thought to the idea of a book. Since the Peace Commission had wound down its work a year earlier, Guzmán had returned to parish life, with the commission's archive in tow. The Catholic Church would soon reward him with the honorific title of monsignor (*monseñor*), in recognition of his service to the faith and to Colombia. Yet, like so many other witnesses to and stories about violence, Guzmán and his archive sat disconnected from any potential national conversation on the subject.[5]

Another year would go by before Guzmán commenced the writing process, and even then only at Lleras's renewed prodding. Amidst the National University *letrados*' turn to the subject of violence, Camilo Torres indicated offhand to his colleagues that they ought to examine Guzmán's archive. This innocuous proposal would prove to be a decisive moment for both the direction of Colombian social science and the futures of *letrados* old and new. On the sociologists' ensuing pilgrimage to see Guzmán in Líbano, talk of the archive and the Faculty of Sociology's commitment to studying the "Colombian problematic" soon arrived at a proposition for Guzmán to write about violence. The priest initially demurred, but at the academics' request, Lleras intervened to convince Guzmán of the venture's worth. The president also arranged for Guzmán's superiors to grant him leave to join his new interlocutors in Bogotá.[6] Lleras's fingerprints thus marked Colombia's second wave of investigation into violence, much as they had the first.

The groundwork for a seminal transformation in Colombians' idea of violence would be laid during the first half of 1962. Guzmán and his hosts commenced work with an intensity characteristic of the time, a feat aided by Guzmán's easy integration into the lettered city. The priest was no stranger to the discipline of sociology, as the National Investigatory Commission's contemplation of such enquiry attested, but now he had the luxury of reading alongside the country's best practitioners. He was particularly struck by Torres's personal and intellectual magnetism, above all his young counterpart's commitment to living the Gospel through a selfless sense of service bolstered by an educator's rigor.[7] In exchange, Guzmán offered not only the insights contained in his collection of interviews and documents, but also firsthand exposure to the rural Colombia once dominated by violence-as-practice, a world which the university's *letrados* had just begun to access. It was accordingly Guzmán who facilitated and accompanied Fals's formative 1962 field trip to the Sumapaz.[8]

As the book dreamt up by Lleras Camargo and the sociologists started to take form, the Peace Commission's example informed the *letrados*' undertaking in other ways. Seeking to reproduce something of the commission's structure, and to incorporate more of the diversity of contemporary social science, the Faculty of Sociology reached out to a military officer and a psychologist to contribute chapters to the forthcoming volume. Though these propositions were unsuccessful, Fals and Guzmán did eventually enlist Fals and Torres's contemporary (and Torres's first cousin) Eduardo Umaña Luna, a contrarian lawyer who had served in the state bureaucracy that helped to implement the creole peace.[9] And while this trio of the Catholic priest, the Protestant professor, and the freethinking jurist elaborated their pieces, Father Torres labored behind the scenes, obtaining funds from a prominent Liberal family's private endowment, the Peace Foundation (Fundación de la Paz), which enabled Guzmán's stay and the book's publication.[10]

That book—published in July 1962, a mere matter of months after its initiation—would become an instant classic. The most famous nonfiction work in Colombia's history, the first volume of *La violencia en Colombia* was certainly the most controversial. However, the full extent of the book's effect on intellectual and political life has never been fully appreciated, in part because the terms of the controversy that accompanied the first volume's release were later read back onto the early democratic transition, becoming unquestioned features of Colombians' accounts of National Front politics. By design, *La violencia en Colombia*'s more explicitly social scientific discussions introduced novel formulations about violence to Colombian public opinion. But by accident, the book's historical content triggered a reworking of politics, which eventually became an inescapable part of the idea of violence.

Thanks to this two-part analysis, the book managed to be, all at once, less and more than the sum of its parts. The longest volume in the Faculty of Sociology's ongoing monograph series, *La violencia en Colombia* was in part an exercise in intellectual pluralism, with each author receiving license to address topics as he saw fit.[11] To be certain, concepts from structuralist sociology tethered—albeit to varying degrees—each contributor's production to a common thematic. (It was no mistake that the book's original subtitle—dropped in the most recent edition—read *Study of a Social Process* [*Estudio de un proceso social*].) *La violencia en Colombia* guaranteed sociology's viability at the National University and confirmed the possibility of a proprietary national social science. The book's diversity of voices additionally spoke to a variety of audiences. Nevertheless, these strengths also had their downsides. "It is still possible," historian Carlos Miguel Ortiz wrote in the mid-1990s, "to make out the lack of integration between the rich material drawn from oral and written sources and the conceptualizations inspired by sociological theories, [a feature] which becomes more glaring as the discussion passes from one author to another."[12] *La violencia en Colombia*'s two volumes (the second from 1964) remain a difficult and even disorienting read, full of cryptic references to events, as well as an esoteric disciplinary terminology that even Fals began to turn away from as he completed the book.[13]

For all this, *La violencia en Colombia* is also full of unnoticed complexities. Consider first the book's long-term influences as a work of sociology. Unsurprisingly, the language of structuralism—how violence shaped "institutions" such as the family, or (in Umaña's extended chapter) how Colombia's judicial institutions failed to align with its "economic-social situation"—predominates.[14] However, when viewed against the backdrop of these *letrados'* longer engagement with the idea of violence, it becomes apparent that such analysis contributed to a gradual redefinition that ultimately culminated in the elevation of "violence" to "La Violencia." For instance, despite Guzmán's explicit description of the post-1957 period as one of peace, the structuralist lens opened the way to consider violence as a system unto itself, one which endured in spite of its apparent absence. "Violence is something more than a brutal massacre, than fires, than misery," Guzmán wrote with Fals, in a chapter on "consequences of violence." Entering into a line of argumentation that they would return to in their follow-up volume, Guzmán and Fals proposed that "violence is a problematic that has not passed . . . It lives on in its deepest implications, steeping factors that will hasten a radical change in the country's structures."[15] It was an opaque piece of reasoning, tied to the idea that Colombia's revolution was right around the corner. But it contained the seeds of a view that took violence as a defining feature of Colombian history.

Guzmán and Fals' evaluation additionally makes clear the ambiguous midcentury meanings of "*la violencia*." Where today there is an instant reflex to render the term as "La Violencia"—a historically specific instance of violence—at the time it could mean simply "violence."[16] There are indications that by the 1950s and '60s Colombians indeed employed the expression to delineate a block of time, rather than the general "technique of violence," as Fals defined it.[17] However, any such usage remained far from standardized or common; well into the mid-1960s, older notions of "political and economic violence," which lacked chronological specificity, still circulated widely.[18]

At the same time that he projected it as a broader problematic, Fals also subtly moved to fix a particular meaning to the term "violence." His personal papers indicate that he had for years privately toyed with alternative ways of writing the word.[19] He committed this to a public medium in *La violencia en Colombia* by placing the term in quotation marks, stating on the book's second page the importance which "Colombian society" afforded "the problem of 'violence'" (*el problema de "la violencia"*).[20] Guzmán emulated Fals's practice elsewhere in the book,

to describe not violence generally but Colombia's recent past; others would replicate it in the years to come. Beginning with the first volume of *La violencia en
Colombia,* the idea of violence took on new guises, becoming simultaneously more
expansive and more narrow.

As Fals used *La violencia en Colombia* as a proving ground for new ideas, Guzmán took the opportunity to return to the memory-work that had been left incom-
plete in 1958. His engagement with the academic literature on social change seems
to have only strengthened his conviction, initially expressed in 1958, about the
redemptive self-realization of Colombia's rural folk. Such systematization indeed
characterized Guzmán's entire effort in *La violencia en Colombia,* the second inter-
pretive cut he made at "violence." Over the first volume's opening two-thirds, Guzmán transmuted the drama laid down in eyewitness testimonies and his diary into
a structured exploration of midcentury violence's geographical and social permea-
tion. *La violencia en Colombia* accordingly wielded a bifurcated conclusion. The
book as a whole portrayed Colombia's experience with violence as the totalizing
crisis of national society.[21] "We can all be culpable, by commission or omission, for
the violent acts that have gone on," Fals wrote in the prologue.[22] At the same time,
however, Guzmán's writings also took a more specific bent, blaming the Conservative Party's "planned official violence" as the origin of Colombia's post-1946
national "catastrophe."[23] This indictment set off what Fals would later call "one of
the most agitated and intense debates in the country's history," which transfigured
Colombians' conversations about violence and inaugurated a crucible for the
National University's *letrados.*[24] These political, intellectual, and personal contexts
would all be essential for the gradual creation of "La Violencia."

VIOLENCE PRESENT, VIOLENCE PAST

Guzmán's chapters struck the *país letrado* as revelation. *La violencia en Colombia*'s
July 1962 appearance introduced to wide consumption unifying theories linking
violence to politics, economics, society, and culture (violence-as-idea), as well as
horrifying details about the agonies of massacre and mutilation (an imprint of
violence-as-practice).[25] The book left early reviewers stunned. Guzmán's "work is
the most serious, useful, objective, just, and patriotic investigation of the social
roots of violence, carried out with ... the human comprehension of an integral
disciple of Christ, and the scientific grasp of a rigorous sociologist," the Liberal
Fabio Lozano Simonelli, Lleras's former private secretary, wrote in mid-July.[26]

Crucially, this initial round of intellectual response transcended party. Even
Gonzalo Canal Ramírez, who had in many ways pioneered discussion of rural
violence after the fall of the dictatorship, admitted that he had difficulty sleeping
after he finished reading *La violencia en Colombia.* Guzmán and company had
realized the inquest that Canal Ramírez himself had left unconcluded in 1958, and

in epic style. *La violencia en Colombia,* Canal Ramírez stated in his late July review for *El Tiempo,* was "perhaps the most important of all the books I have read by a Colombian author." This provincial Conservative with deep ties to the military attributed much of the volume's success to Guzmán, explaining that virtually no Colombian could match the priest's clarity of mind about "this atrocious calamity," knowledge reinforced by the unimpeachable documentary evidence of the Peace Commission. "One cannot doubt" Guzmán's conclusion that "violence commenced as *campesino* self-defense against the abuse, avarice, and persecution of certain authorities," Canal Ramírez said.[27]

Such arguments about the violence of the past rapidly became bound up in arguments about violence in the present. In particular, two developing forms of violence-as-practice conditioned the political response to *La violencia en Colombia.* The first was a rare incursion of violence into the middle, provincial echelon of the *país político:* during what normally would have been the quiet midyear lead-up to the presidential inauguration on August 7, a congressman from each party's minority bloc fell victim to assassination.[28] Having come out just days earlier, *La violencia en Colombia* became grist for the ensuing congressional row. A Liberal congressman jumped on the fact that the murdered pro-Laureano Conservative happened to appear in the book, because of his apparent connections to Conservative guns-for-hire (*pájaros*) in his native Valle del Cauca.[29]

The second form of violence was more far-reaching. Violence was once more on Colombians' lips in mid-1962, and not solely because of the eponymous book. Whereas many Colombians had the previous year continued to speak of peace or the passing of an era of violence, during the period of *La violencia en Colombia*'s preparation various regions of the country saw the return of that scourge of 1958: roadway assaults in which even partisan identity was no guarantee of survival.[30] Though the attacks accounted for a small portion of homicides between January and July, their distribution across the national territory created a concern that transcended region (map 9). What was more, by interrupting normal transit across the Andes, most especially between Tolima and Caldas, the attacks apparently threatened to disarticulate Colombia as a nation. The chorus of Conservative opposition in Congress modulated in sync with assaults later in the year: with Huila smarting from a November incident that left more than two dozen people dead, including a prominent Conservative rancher, now-senator Felio Andrade Manrique—who as governor had made vital contributions to the creole peace in Gran Tolima—questioned how fewer than three thousand bandits could be "winning the war."[31]

The shift in the practice of violence was sufficiently marked to alter the way that Colombians spoke of violence. "Violence is no longer exercised from the state," the former editor of *Semana* wrote in April 1962; "political violence" had instead ceded to "a bandit violence."[32] Record-keepers inside the National Police concurred.

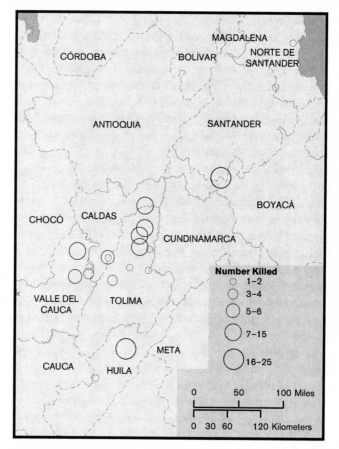

MAP 9. Roadway attacks, 1962. An interactive version of this map can be viewed at rakarl.com/research/forgotten-peace.

Around the time of the editor's declaration, the government's internal tallies of victims killed for partisan and related reasons gave way to the more focused but hardly less vague category "killed by bandit action."[33]

Who were these "bandits"? A top minister later estimated that "80 percent . . . are adolescents with ages ranging from 15 and 20 years."[34] However exaggerated the claim, the point was widely accepted: "the children of the backcountry," that generation of rural boys orphaned by the conflict of the 1940s and '50s, had come of age, with catastrophic results. In the minds of many, only a state of total separation from societal institutions could explain the "moral decomposition" and sadism characteristic of this latest breed of delinquent.[35] The exemplar remained Teófilo Rojas, alias Chispas, who at age twenty-seven was something of a graybeard among his fellow "bandits." Hounded incessantly by the military, Chispas had long since left the farm that the government had helped him buy under Rehabilitación, to once again rule the peaks that separated Gran Tolima from the western coffee heartland. Conventional wisdom pinned on Chispas and his gang (*cuadrilla*) one of the largest of early 1962's growing list of raids against buses and other vehicles. Central Colombia's great bogeyman had reawakened.

The appearance of such a reviled form of violence in 1962 brought with it serious implications for how sectors of the *país político* and *país nacional* judged the gains of the Lleras years, as well as Colombia's future course. First, the fact that one of the major beneficiaries of Rehabilitación loans was partaking in this new round of violence substantially revitalized previous Conservative opposition to Lleras's signature policy. Second, the demographic profile of Chispas's heirs apparent denoted an evident defeat for Lleras's attention to both generations and education. For this latest generation, a vocal sector of Colombian opinion maintained, there existed no possibility of rehabilitation.

Making this argument necessitated autobiographical revision for some. Committed though Laureano's followers claimed to be to the original intention of the National Front pacts, their place outside the governing coalition ensured that no specific policy of Lleras's was safe from censure. By late July, Senator Álvaro Gómez had resurrected a key contention from the heated debates of 1959, asserting that "monstrous bandits" like Chispas had received government aid, which made "the task of rehabilitation carried out by this government [seem more like] a program aimed at facilitating the crimes of violent gangs." This position was quite the turnaround for Gómez, as Liberal senators were quick to point out, a repudiation of Álvaro's own impassioned defense of Rehabilitación three years earlier.[36]

Such Conservative critiques of Liberal administration policy merged seamlessly with attacks on *La violencia en Colombia*. Álvaro Gómez, for instance, mixed his review of Rehabilitación with condemnation of the book, on the grounds that the latter was "underpinned by secret documents" and even "possibly financed with public monies."[37] When *El Siglo,* the Gómez family newspaper, eventually reprinted Álvaro's suggestion, it also dismissed *La violencia en Colombia*'s private, Liberal funder as "an institution that rushes to sponsor the recrudescence of hatreds."[38] This preliminary Conservative counterthrust foreshadowed a longer party strategy of impugning Guzmán and his coauthors' means.

Two features of midcentury Colombian intellectual life elucidate how the campaign against *La violencia en Colombia*'s intellectual merits proceeded. First, Colombians conceived of memory and history as separate modes of narrating the past, in a fashion that calls to mind Pierre Nora's distinction between the two.[39] Every Colombian to reach secondary school since the 1910s had received instruction emphasizing history as "the master of truth," objective and unimpeachable, a realm of knowledge beyond human control.[40] Memory, by contrast, was considered subject to whim and partiality. Subsections of Colombian society could therefore lay claim to "history" in order to deny alternative representations of the past legitimacy in the public realm. This strategy was reinforced by a structural quirk of the *país letrado*: during the decade prior to the National Front, the Conservative stranglehold on the state bureaucracy forced Liberals such as Fals to go abroad for advanced training.[41] As a result, by the 1960s the Conservative Party counted with fewer practicioners of contemporary social science. The Conservative response to *La violencia en Colombia* consequently relied, for the most part, on generic invocations of scientific truth that mirrored broad appeals to "history."

There was one important exception: the Conservative camp's answer to Camilo Torres, a Jesuit economics professor just off a stint studying sociology in Europe.[42] Miguel Angel González's lengthy September 1962 review of *La violencia en Colombia* is itself an underappreciated minor masterwork, as careful and thorough an examination of the book as has ever been produced. In a wide-ranging intellectual and moral survey, González pointed out Guzmán's uneven narrative, purported insufficient regional coverage in an ostensibly national study, and needled Guzmán and Fals's crude calculation of a decade's worth of homicides.[43]

The Jesuit's review catalyzed "the climax of reaction" to *La violencia en Colombia* in the Conservative press.[44] Initially published in early September by Bogotá's Jesuit university, the text was picked up within the month by the Conservatives' two national newspapers.[45] *El Siglo* then helped to land the heaviest blow on Guzmán. Following on González's insider recognition that Monsignor Guzmán had not obtained ecclesiastical permission to publish the book (a matter distinct from his authorized transfer from Tolima to Bogotá), *El Siglo* ventured that *La violencia en Colombia*'s positive coverage of a "child bandit" (figure 2) and related personages likely precluded it from ever receiving the Catholic Church's sanction. The next day, as if on cue, the cardinal archbishop of Bogotá reprimanded Guzmán for violating the relevant statute of canon law and disavowed the church's responsibility for the book's arguments.[46] Bogotá's Conservative press had shown itself to be more Catholic than Guzmán. Chastened by his superior's ruling, the priest departed, first for Europe and then for Mexico, prompting rumors that he been forced from the country. But Guzmán's sole surviving letter to Camilo Torres seems to indicate that the political climate had been the reason. Referring to himself as "this unhappy, humble, downcast, feeble son of democracy," Guzmán wrote to Camilo Torres to inquire, "Is it opportune for me to come back?" The ecclesiastical punishment he feared was not exile from Colombia, but, upon his expected return, a forced departure from the country of letters in Bogotá back to some parish in Tolima.[47]

Conservatives laid claim to history in much the same way that they presented themselves as the defenders of faith and morality. As Camilo Torres was to experience again the following year during the dustup over the Eastern Plains training center, Álvaro Gómez brooked no challenges to his father's legacy: even before the Jesuit's review, Álvaro denied the implication that his party bore blame for Colombia's descent into disorder. Any implication to the contrary was an anathema—a "deformation of history," in Álvaro's words.[48] The condemnations piled on. Sociology, *El Siglo* said, was but a façade "in the shadow of which [sociologists] concoct a plot of anti-Conservative history." *La violencia en Colombia*, the paper's editors and contributors stated again and again, exhibited "raw partisan flavor in 'technical' packaging," "four hundred pages of concentrated sectarianism, purified as much as possible through a 'sociological' filter."[49] In the Conservative telling, the past was found in the objective truth of history. To state otherwise would be an act of violence against the past itself.[50]

To this end, Conservative critics went after the evidentiary basis of Guzmán's writings. González's analysis spearheaded the effort: "In doing the 'history' of the conflict," that review read, "[Guzmán] did not consult many opinions, documents, or persons who played an eminent role in that historical period . . . The testimony of one criminal [Chispas] alone occupies at least twenty times as much space as all of the Most Reverend Archbishops."[51] *Letrados* and politicians rallied to the notion. One opinion piece agreed that *La violencia en Colombia*'s "pages lack intellectual honesty, for the simple reason that they evince neither scientific grounding nor documental gravitas."[52] According to this line of reasoning, the book's alleged partisan slant made a mockery of scientific objectivity, while its reliance on Guzmán's Peace Commission archive—which González referred to as "an *ad infinitum* system of self-citations"—was to be dismissed out of hand.[53] The memories of provincial Colombians, be they victims or victimizers, were increasingly portrayed as an illegitimate representation of the past.

Conservative politicians instead presented a forceful counternarrative of the twentieth century. The hinge was the Liberal Republic of the 1930s, which Conservatives painted as the true initiation of political violence. The leader of the Liberal opposition observed with relish at the start of the debate over *La violencia en Colombia* that Álvaro Gómez "surely must not have liked" that Guzmán and company "were hard-pressed to dedicate ten pages to . . . violence [under] Liberal governments, [compared to] over 300 to analyze the problem [under] Conservative governments."[54] Liberals objected little to the suggestion that clashes had transpired following the Liberal electoral victory of 1930; as one ranking Conservative indicated, this fact was not at issue.[55]

What was subject to dispute were questions of regional and national responsibility, as well as proportionality—the difference between violence and "violence," the use of coercion in politics versus the systematic repression of one party. The parties' positions were mirror images of one another: Liberals maintained that Conservative resistance, not government action, had led to disorder in the early 1930s, while Conservatives held that the reverse rule applied to the late 1940s.[56] Conservatives pointed to the Liberals' onetime use of the phrase "undeclared civil war" as evidence of equivalency, though the term predated urban Colombia's discoveries about violence.[57] Moreover, by October 1962, Conservatives had hardened the positions taken in previous years. For instance, Laureano's former vice president—a minister in the Liberal government of 1930—had described in 1960 how "triumphant Liberals had let loose persecution on the defeated Conservatives, especially in the departments of Boyacá and the Santanders." He nonetheless lauded the Liberal government for carrying out "every imaginable effort to halt the bloodletting," even if those efforts ultimately had only partial effect.[58] By contrast, in 1962 Laureano's camp pushed a narrative of complete victimization. Repression against Conservatives in 1930, an *El Siglo* editorial thundered, had been "ordered by Liberal authorities. And with the complicity of the government [in Bogotá] . . . And lasted throughout the Liberal administration."[59]

The past was becoming interchangeable with the present. The appearance of *La violencia en Colombia* coincided precisely with the National Front's first presidential transition, and made keener political conversations about how the new government should tackle the upswing in rural violence. The book's implicit endorsement of Alberto Lleras's approach to *convivencia* served as a counterpoint to the zero-conciliation discourse emanating from the administration. The perceived need for national unity in support of the latter led in turn to a concerted push to quash the debate around partisan responsibility stemming from the book. The book therefore fed directly into hugely consequential responses to ongoing questions of violence-as-idea and violence-as-practice. Denial of the Peace Commission's memory-work intersected with a broader repudiation of its peace-work.

Guillermo León Valencia diverged from his predecessor in terms of more than personal style. Valencia shared few of Lleras's sensitivities around the authoritarian legacies of the 1940s and '50s. Though Lleras seemed increasingly willing late in his presidency to embrace a more militaristic approach to the problematic of violence, he could not bring himself to commit. "There are political difficulties inhibiting the Government in taking a stronger line," a British police consultant advised London in June 1962. "I feel that they are a little frightened of public opinion. They believe that stronger measures might lead the public to think that the Government was acting undemocratically or working back towards some form of dictatorship."[60] Moreover, Lleras and his advisors were "strongly identified, rightly or wrongly, with an appeasement policy towards the bandits." Free of such constraints, and imbued with an understanding of violence that delegitimized most forms as "banditry," Valencia could be "entirely committed to the *elimination* of violence."[61] The order of the day would be pacification by force of arms, rather than "persuasion and systems of conciliation," as during Lleras's time.

Once more, events in the provinces would help to condition political receptiveness. A week after Valencia's August 7 inaugural called for an uncompromising national campaign against violence, an armed Conservative band massacred more than two dozen people on a highway in a northern region long spared such collec-

FIGURE 11. "The Decisive Match": "The 'National' Team [President Valencia (kicking ball), Justice Minister Charry Samper (at left), War Minister General Ruiz Novoa (behind Valencia), and other ministers] against 'Los Violentos,'" *El Tiempo,* August 26, 1962, 4.

tive bloodshed (map 9). A disgusted Canal Ramírez summed up the national mood when he termed the episode "a typical case of current violence . . . Cruel, ghoulishly cruel, merciless, exterminatory . . . Terrorist."[62] From labor unions, professional associations, and business groups, as well as from individual citizens, came a months-long flood of correspondence and pronouncements. These beauty queens, engineers, women's activists, merchants, students, large landowners, and lawyers broadcast to the administration and the nation their refutation of any popular or political support for those exercising violence. They also proposed prescriptions for combating the problem, a gamut of ideas that ran from the application of developmental "technical expertise" to the establishment of the death penalty.[63] Not since the "days of May" that brought down the dictatorship had urban Colombia engaged in such a loud and simultaneous expression of voice.

The administration publicized its own strategy in a series of dramatic speeches before Congress on August 21 and 22 (figure 11), a moment where the influence of *La violencia en Colombia* began to manifest itself. Summoned by eager legislators in both chambers, Valencia's "young, energetic" ministers enumerated both the scope of the issue and potential solutions. Minister of War General Alberto Ruiz Novoa delivered the best-known intervention—"the most complete treatise ever heard" in Congress on midcentury violence, in the assessment of Gonzálo Sánchez G. and Donny Meertens.[64]

More consequential to reformers within the countries of letters and politics were the other addresses. Previewing the administration's policy decisions, the interior minister declared that "the definitive battle" against the "criminals [who] have declared war on the Republic" would demand "all [of Colombia's] resources, require though this will reduction in the rhythm of other national activities." In addition to requesting from Congress sweeping special powers to reform the judiciary, Valencia would soon seek a 20 percent "peace quota" supplanting an earlier tax earmarked for socioeconomic development.[65] High-level officials within the government and the Liberal Party griped to U.S. diplomats about the potential damage done to the country's reform prospects and overall economic health.[66] While numerous Liberal notables shared Valencia's prioritization of the anti-violence program, Conservatives tended to push harder to make it a reality.

The controversy around Guzmán, Fals, and Umaña's book was pulled deeper into this conversation by the last of Valencia's ministerial vanguard, the "owlish" thirty-two-year-old minister of justice Héctor Charry Samper (figure 11). The evolution of his personal thinking highlighted changes within the Liberal Party on the question of violence, while his stances on Rehabilitación and on discussions of the past anticipated the *país político*'s encounter with *La violencia en Colombia* writ large. In 1959, wunderkind and then-congressman Charry Samper told fellow legislators that "the Colombian State is directly responsible for [the fact that] Colombian *campesinos* were injured. On that basis, the State has the responsibility to rehabilitate them, as they were injured by the State's weapons." This Liberal idea of violence drew surprisingly little critique from opposition Conservatives, though Charry Samper was careful to add that "those who persist in crime ought to be punished."[67]

At the onset of Valencia's administration, Charry's preferences for law and order, previously secondary, now defined his position. As Charry and his colleagues lined up to deliver their remarks, congressmen filled the chamber with substantial talk of the Lleras years. Tolima's pro-Laureano senator said, for example, that Lleras's "amnesty" was directly responsible for current bandit depredations. To this, Charry Samper ventured a halfhearted defense of Lleras's policies, "affirming that in their epoch they were good and produced positive results. He nonetheless clarified that those measures were outworn, and that they could not be employed again because that would signify an excess of magnanimity for those who did not want to rehabilitate themselves, but rather preferred to defy the State and declare war on the nation." Colombia was no longer engaged in "a war between Liberals and Conservatives," but one between bandits and the state.[68]

Discussing the past consequently seemed senseless to Charry. Declaring himself part of a chronological—and, one presumes, spatial—generation "that did not participate in [Colombia's undeclared civil war], that did not receive wounds at the hands of the enemy, that does not have a personal or generational grievance to bring in a putative judgment of responsibility," Charry explained to the overflowing congressional galleries that "I feel free of hatred, I feel free of rancor." Responding to the Liberal and Conservative legislators assembled before him, and to the National University *letrados* a few miles to the northwest, Charry laid out what would soon coalesce into the gospel of the National Front. "The greatest service that we can provide to the country is to simply abstain from continuing to make recriminatory judgments. Not only that, but also to abstain from continuing to conjure up theories about violence." Charry therefore pledged that "belligerent politician though I may have been, I will never again in the public plaza nor in parliament partake in a recriminatory debate . . . I will never again utter a single word aimed at offending Conservatism." [69] The vow brought the gallery to its feet.

The notion of rehabilitating Colombia was not entirely dead at the start of the Valencia administration. Cabinet members spoke of education efforts and programs for urban *desplazados* as "a true work of rehabilitation," one untainted by the ills of Lleras's Rehabilitación. [70] In the words of Charry Samper, "Those who are at peace, those who have met their obligations to the Colombian State have nothing to fear." [71] Those who fell outside of these categories had lost their chance. It was an understandable sentiment for Colombians traumatized by violence, though one that would come to have drastic repercussions for provincial Colombia and Gran Tolima in particular.

As the administration's proposals for judicial reorganization and special taxation worked their way through Congress in late September, *La violencia en Colombia* interjected itself anew into the political scene, threatening to upend any move toward consensus within the countries of politics and letters. The timing was accidental, a result of the book's publication schedule. The initial run of one thousand copies sponsored by the Peace Foundation rushed so rapidly into the hands of the *país político* and state bureaucracy that whispers of government censorship were not far behind. Scarcity made the experience of encountering the book an unusually social one, as copies passed among those who knew someone with access to this rare item. [72]

A second, five-thousand-copy edition of *La violencia en Colombia* landed in bookstores days after the splashy appearance of the Jesuit priest's critique. (Indeed, in a twist, a pamphlet version of the latter was bundled and sold with the book, a commodification of the controversy that boosted sales.) The climactic phase of the book's reception immediately hit its peak. The U.S. Embassy commented that the "hue and cry [was] sufficient to justify a sequel entitled *Violence Caused by 'Violence.'*" [73] The power of the past shook the government, as The Monster roused from the infirmity of his old age. The fledgling Bogotá publishing house which had picked up *La violencia en Colombia*'s second edition—and previously released titles expressing the *país político*'s melancholia—happened to count among its bipartisan owners Valencia's pro-Laureano minister of labor. "Reportedly . . . livid with rage over the book," Laureano confronted his adherent over its publication. Sufficiently shaken, the minister offered to resign, a maneuver that triggered a wider cabinet crisis.[74]

The incident nonetheless paled compared to ill will between the parties. Conservative spirits were already primed by *El Tiempo*'s response to the Jesuit review, a column by a venerable Liberal *letrado* that, among other perceived offenses, equated Conservatism's "doctrinaire" commitment to "precept" with that of Hitler, the Soviets, and "religious fanatics." In the face of these successive outrages, *El Siglo* saw a concerted conspiracy at work. The paper thereafter moved into overdrive; by early October, *La violencia en Colombia* dominated the editorial page, receiving coverage in up to three columns per day. "We had not wanted to touch on these historic points, less so when we journalists are pledged to a campaign against violence," read *El Siglo*'s October 1 editorial. However, the newspaper continued, the column by that Liberal *letrado*—a self-described sociologist of the old stripe—"cannot go unnoticed. . . . Until this campaign of anti-Conservative defamation is called off, the debate cannot be closed. All signs indicate that the offensive against violence should also orient itself against the 'sociologists' of yesterday and today, who have shown themselves to be better snipers than the so-called combatants."[75] To the Conservative mind, sociology was more and more showing itself to be a danger to the future and to the past: a medium for the perpetuation of violence and an end run around the objectivity of history.

With the Liberal Party reopening the door to the past, some Conservatives in Congress opted to celebrate rather than minimize their party's contribution to partisan conflict. Their comments reflected regional identities rather than the generational one expressed by Charry Samper. A Huila congressman who belittled Guzmán and his coauthors as "mak[ing] their living in a more shameful way than a bunch of courtesans" jumped to the defense of his recently murdered colleague from Valle del Cauca, a department where violence was most associated with bands of gunmen whose fluid formations had lent them the name "birds." That term, "*pájaro*," the Huila representative proudly explained, "has been applied 'to Conservative greats,' and is, as such, honorable." At the height of the controversy months later, the wife of former president Mariano Ospina Pérez invoked a reference typical of her husband's era, telling a Conservative gathering that "I have no other doctrine than that of the Conservative Party's *chulavita*." The president of the Senate, who hailed from the *chulavitas*' home department, took a milder stance, admitting that "there might have been [normal] human excesses and perhaps very explainable exceptions" during the government's mobilization of such semi-official forces in decades past. He nonetheless lauded the *chulavitas'* "glorious sacrifice of defending the Republic" during the dark days following Gaitán's 1948 assassination.[76]

Never under the National Front had the major currents of the two parties traded such pointed language. The deterioration in political discourse raised a pair of profoundly uncomfortable scenarios. The first sprang from the old belief that debates in Congress would cause the countryside to combust. As Canal Ramírez and others feared, "Recrimination about past dead will not resurrect any of them, but rather bring more dead."[77] As a form of violence-as-idea, the new politics of the past might provoke violence-as-practice.

It seemed also that partisan charges and countercharges might escalate sufficiently to undo *convivencia* within the *país político.* The politics of the past were threatening the politics of the present. National political figures therefore rushed to prevent contagion, causing the *La violencia en Colombia* controversy to metamorphosize almost overnight from climax to what Fals later called anticlimax. In order to deescalate the political fight, the editors of *El Tiempo* and Ospina's *La República* asked publishers from "almost every daily newspaper in Colombia" to come to Bogotá. The gathering showed the deep interpenetration of the country of politics and that sector of the country of letters that lay in its orbit. Together, these groups would lay out rules for a new *convivencia* in the public sphere.[78]

The administration rolled out the red carpet for the event. In a room at the national capitol named for President Valencia's famed poet father, nearly forty editors listened to Justice Minister Charry Samper and his colleagues from the interior and war ministries recap their August speeches before Congress. Their message was entirely in line with the reigning hemispheric model of social change: modify attitudes and behaviors would follow. Both the ministers and the meeting's conveners spoke of violence as a particular problem of knowledge, specifically that Colombians' low understanding had taken the form of apathy toward the rise of banditry. Charry concluded that "the press' contribution [would be] . . . decisive" in the quest to correct this through the creation of "a national consciousness."[79]

The country of letters intended to help the country of politics to police itself, while also disciplining the rest of the nation. Even before the ministers' remarks, the editors had approved—with one dissension—a seventeen-point declaration of principles. The covenant's centerpiece was "advoca[cy] for democratic virtues: justice, tolerance, and concord." To this end, the declaration included several statements against antidemocratic governments, at home and throughout Latin America. The real heart of the declaration nonetheless remained the question of violence in Colombia. By adhering to the agreement, newspapers committed to strip out any and all partisan labels from their coverage. Perpetrators of violence would heretofore appear as "simply criminals and killers"; victims would similarly lack any partisan labels. Violence would receive "total condemnation . . . whatever its motive or origin," state institutions the newspapers' unwavering support.

The declaration of principles also established a means to deal with the past. Decades later, this would be the declaration's most-cited provision: that journalists would "avoid all polemic about the responsibilities that the parties have had in violence, leaving the necessary historical judgment to a generation less preoccupied and involved."[80] Charry Samper's personal vow to forget the past thus won, in theory, extension to vast swaths of Colombia's public sphere.

The editors' meeting remade the National Front, distilling into exaggerated form some of the political impulses that had gone into the pact's creation. Subsequent Colombian scholars would confuse the timing, arguing that the postponement of judgment to an undefined future—the establishment of a "pact of forgetting"—furthered an abdication of accountability that the *país político* also advanced by stating that "we are all responsible [for violence]."[81] Although it is possible to locate invocations of "the forgetting of mutual wounds" in public discourse from the first years of the National Front, it took the release of *La violencia en Colombia* for the idea of forgetting to move from a "unwritten covenant" to an explicit and far more frequent expression.[82] That much was clear to the promoters of the editors' meeting, who themselves had to collapse time in order to connect the necessities of 1962 to the democratic spirit of 1957–58. "This meeting," *La República* said in its write-up, "is an index of the new climate that the plebiscite and the constitutional acts which complement it have created."[83] More than four years on, *convivencia* had been redesigned.

Both the backers of the editors' meeting and later critics of the National Front shared the country of letters' faith in the sway of the written word. Concerns about "words as explosive as a Mauser [rifle], poisonous and suffocating adjectives" animated the editors' gathering.[84] The intellectual successors of Fals's generation would, for their part, later grant the "gentlemen" behind the National Front the mythic authority of word as fiat. Such attribution was overly generous. The stipulations of the editors' declaration of principles held for a matter of hours. "A few days passed from the [meeting] and it turned out that the pile of earth [that they intended to throw over the book] didn't amount to anything," the Communist Party's review of *La violencia en Colombia* remarked later in 1962. Even *El Tiempo* could not resist publishing details of bandit exploits.[85]

What of the *país político*'s capacity to deny the past? In a way, the editors' meeting established a national consensus on violence that surpassed even that of *La violencia en Colombia*. By bringing a transregional sampling of notables to the capital, the meeting introduced a scale that at least partially escaped Colombia's centrifugal tendencies. (The meeting's Conservative organizer was especially proud of the participation of editors from the Atlantic coast, a region that had not witnessed the bloodshed experienced in the Andean region.)[86] However, given that the meeting's intellectual project was one of negation, the best that this national conceptualization could hope to do was to hold distinctive partisan, regional, and generational understandings in an unresolved state of suspension. In seeking to block discussion of the past, political and press elites opened the way for alternative representations to fill the void.

Two examples highlight this incompleteness. One was apparent at the precise moment in which the majority of editors approved their declaration of principles. The sole holdout was the Liberal editor of Ibagué's *Tribuna*. The champion of Tolima's displaced Liberals, and an unceasing auditor of Bogotá's shortcomings toward the provinces, the newspaper refused to go along with what it saw as continued metropolitan condescension and neglect. "*Tribuna* does not need to approve any declaration for its readers and the government to know that it condemns violence," the editor stated, in a virtual duplication of what residents of Gran Tolima had said when the National Investigatory Commission got under way in 1958. "Outside of . . . the columns, the newspapers, the halls of government and [elite] clubs, the reality is well known and nothing is done to transform the life of the Colombian man." [87] Understandings of violence, and of the state, could retain their regional feel.

The second affront to prohibitions on discussing the past was the ongoing project of the National University's *letrados*. Guzmán, Fals, and Umaña had come to *La violencia en Colombia* with the *letrados'* characteristic faith in the transformative capacity of words. Privately, they might joke about the aftermath of the book's publication. "Why haven't you answered the letter I sent you?" Guzmán asked Torres from Rome some eight months after the publication of *La violencia en Colombia*. "Could it be that they stole it from you for the *counter-book to the book* about that little conflagration of violence?" [88] The damage had nonetheless been done. The *letrados* silently endured personal attacks, even death threats, throughout what Umaña would eventually call "tremendous confusion and chaos." [89] In an important difference from how debates over Rehabilitación had unfolded in 1959, the Conservatives' bitterly divided factions were unified in 1962. Lleras and his approach to *convivencia* would have few high-profile defenders once the Conservative-led government took the reins of political discussion away from Congress. Indeed, Lleras's own voice was silent; claiming to have "completed my task physically knackered, unable to make a single intellectual or physical effort," Lleras could finally realize his long-desired departure from public life. [90]

The isolation experienced by Fals and his colleagues did not sap their will to continue, but it did slowly whittle away at their original sense of engagement. In his prologue to the 2005 edition of *La violencia en Colombia*, Fals still conveyed a perceptible bitterness. [91] His band of intellectuals had expected ideas to sway minds and move the *país político* to action. Instead, seemingly an entire half of the political class had moved against them. Fals the Protestant and Torres the Catholic priest had succeeded in establishing the Faculty of Sociology as a space of *convivencia*, but they now found that such tolerance did not extend as deeply into public life as they had hoped. Yet *La violencia en Colombia* was but the first volume in a larger work, the continued influence of which would augment challenges to the politics of the past laid down in October 1962.

IDEAS AND PRACTICES OF VIOLENCE, 1963

Despite the political hubbub in the capital, *La violencia en Colombia* continued to modify the terms with which Colombians talked about violence. For instance, Communist Party intellectuals—already familiar with Fals's earlier works of social science—found *La violencia en Colombia*'s first volume an unusually satisfying read. One of the party's leading theorists delighted in what he portrayed as the *país político*'s hysteria toward the book, telling other party members that it would be "difficult to find in history [a similar] case where the dominant class publicly renounces out of pure fear its right to direct the debate over the national crisis."[92] Additionally, the *letrados*' structuralist take on violence hewed closely to the Communists' conviction that violence was an inevitable outgrowth of the "current political and economic regime"; unlike most contemporary explanations of violence, *La violencia en Colombia* avoided assigning much if any blame to the Communist Party.[93]

Above all, Fals's innovative move to put the term "violence" in quotation marks heralded a wider intellectual shift within the country of letters. Describing the recent conflict as "*la violencia*" allowed for Communist Party intellectuals to distinguish it from "other eras of violence," namely the civil wars of the nineteenth century. *La violencia en Colombia* gave Communist *letrados* an enduring vocabulary through which to write about violence.[94]

Violence remained at the center of intellectual life in the year after *La violencia en Colombia*'s publication, in no small part because the real-world practice of violence continued in the same molds as 1962. Two days shy of Colombia's 1963 independence day celebration, half a dozen uniformed men halted a line of vehicles at a spot called La Italia, a mile deep into northeastern Caldas on a stretch of road parallel to the Tolima line. Despite the fact that the army had finally caught up to Chispas seven months prior, these slopes of the central Andes had gained little respite due to stepped-up depredations by what must have seemed the remaining horsemen of the apocalypse: Sangrenegra (Blackblood), Desquite (Revenge), and Tarzán.

The trio shared similar origins. Desquite had been an army veteran and small-time thief who swore retribution on the world for the lynching of his best friend (or for the death of his father at the hands of Conservatives; the stories varied). The Three Horsemen often acted in concert, but at La Italia Desquite had a smaller complement at his side. Their relatively narrow mandate to eliminate Conservatives went out the window when the forty-plus men ordered from their vehicles tried to fib about their partisan affiliations. At close quarters, Desquite's little band killed and dismembered nearly the lot of them. The scope and brutality of the episode vaulted Desquite to uncharted heights of notoriety, entrenching in the region's memory an already familiar modality of violence-as-practice.[95]

Building upon the intellectual work of 1962, Bogotá's *letrados* formulated a second round of ideas out of these atrocities. Their insights oftentimes remained buried in well-trodden arguments. One of Fabio Lozano Simonelli's columns, for instance, dedicated considerable attention to the question of foreign Communist support for Colombia's upheavals. Yet his opening line signaled a potentially broader interpretation. "Across the country," he wrote, "the sense is spreading that 'a second violence' has commenced."[96]

This feeling of distinctiveness, that the violence of 1962–63 and the violence of 1948 or 1958 represented "two violences," as Lozano Simonelli further suggested, guided other theses. Only now, with the partisan violence of the 1940s and '50s passed, and a separate form of violence at hand to focus attentions, could that earlier period be envisioned in a new light. Other *letrados* therefore began to consistently follow Fals's practice: some fifteen months after the appearance of *La violencia en Colombia*'s first volume, a National University historian concluded that the exercise of "violence" as a political tool had been generalized in the country since independence. Even so, to describe what had taken place from 1948 to 1958, the historian—perhaps independently, perhaps following his colleague Fals's lead—set the term apart with quotation marks. "*La violencia*" was to be handled as a discrete period.[97]

This initial reconceptualization of "violence" would be one of two steps that would lead to the creole peace becoming a forgotten peace. Much as had occurred in 1959–60, the eruption of localized violence in 1962 had raised doubts locally and regionally about the success, if not the very existence, of peace. Discussion of "the two violences" helped to elevate such considerations to a national plane, a process which merged with the Conservative political discourse emanating from Bogotá to obscure the accomplishments of the late 1950s.

However, the ideas of "the two violences" and "*la violencia*" both left unresolved the precise relationship between the 1940s and '50s on the one hand, and the 1960s on the other. That second step, which involved transforming "*la violencia*" into a continuous block, would prove over the long run a vital ingredient in the consolidation of "La Violencia." "Violence" would first need to go through an additional redefinition, an intermediate stage that once more emanated from Orlando Fals and the intellectual world of the National University's reformist *letrados*.

THE *LETRADOS* REVISIT VIOLENCE, 1963–1964

As other men of letters applied and refined their ideas, the authors of *La violencia en Colombia* went about their preexisting habits. Umaña hopped between posts at the Justice Ministry, while Fals returned to teaching and researching. Guzmán remained in Bogotá as well, joining Fals and Camilo Torres within the developmentalist state and expanding his archive on violence. The subject required additional attention, and so over the course of roughly eighteen months, the three *letrados* dedicated what time they could to a follow-up study.

La violencia en Colombia's second volume, published in 1964, never lived up to its more famous predecessor. However, scholars' subsequent marginalization of the book has meant a missed opportunity to comprehend post-1962 trends in violence and intellectual life—that is, trends within the *país nacional* and the *país letrado,* and in particular how the latter portrayed the former. Though the second volume did not shape a decisive historical shift, as the first volume did, it still attests to the moment.

The concerns of 1962–63 translated into a heavy dose of unease about "[the] children of violence," "the generation of the backcountry"—that rural cohort which furnished "the new antisocial," "*el neocriminal.*"[98] Umaña in particular sounded a near panic. "We must wage a 'holy war' for children," he pleaded in a long chapter dedicated entirely to the "social problem" of "abandoned children." His government service equipped him with not only ample statistics to chart the paucity of the state's protective services, but also firsthand contact with the ills that apparently gripped a generation and consequently threatened Colombia's future. The vital heart of Umaña's chapter thus proved to be the reprint of a report he had prepared the previous year, in which he summarized his inspection of an overcrowded, parasite-infested, and—to his eyes—morally vacuous Bogotá orphanage.[99] Umaña's account was fundamentally an urban one, but he clearly intended it to speak to the entire national predicament.

While Umaña's warning about the dire state of Colombia's youth fit well with the overall tenor of the volume, the fact that he only contributed one chapter to the book gave his words a coherence that Guzmán's lacked. The torrid pace of *letrado* life in 1963 apparently held Fals back from writing much other than the second volume's introduction, and prevented Guzmán from either fully fleshing out promising insights or ironing out inconsistencies in tone. So, for instance, Guzmán made explicit—as Umaña did not—the link between the city and the provinces. It was, in part, a familiar argument about rural incitement by urban agitators, though Guzmán skipped the common trappings of anti-Communism. More compellingly, he also put a twist on his interpretation, dubbing the persistence of violence after 1958 as "Urban Violence." It was the first published appearance of the term "Violencia"—with a capital letter—in a work of Colombian social science. However, Guzmán had not achieved a conceptual breakthrough: the derivation of the idea remains unclear (though, as will be seen, it almost certainly originated with Orlando Fals), and in any case Guzmán scarcely pursued it more than a page past its initial appearance.[100]

In total, *La violencia en Colombia*'s second volume reads as even less of a coherent whole than its predecessor. Its hurried assembly perhaps made this inevitable. Laboring in a scholarly genre still in formation in Colombia, and further pressured by a different set of political conditions than had existed during preparation of the first volume, Fals, Guzmán, and Umaña confronted a moving target. Beyond Guzmán's previous suggestion that "a second volume that could well be called 'How Peace Was Made,'" there survives no indication of how the collaborators initially envisioned this project. Perhaps the only piece to survive intact from 1962 was what became the opening fifth of the book: unused material from the Peace Commission, namely annotated versions of the legal codes drawn up by the Liberal resistance of the Eastern Plains in the early 1950s, as well as the organic law adopted by the National Liberal Revolutionary Movement of Southern Tolima in 1957.

On this question of what to include in the book—and how, more generally, to treat the question of violence—Germán Guzmán wrestled to reconcile political demands with his moral obligations and intellectual propensities. Chastened by the ecclesiastical sanction his previous effort had garnered, Guzmán took care to clarify that this present contribution was his and his alone. The fundaments of his philosophy otherwise remained unshaken. Defying the calls of the new *convivencia* to keep violence out of public discussion, Guzmán professed once more his faith in the power of conversation as the basis for a different *convivencia*. "To converse is to persist toward the solution," he proclaimed toward the end of the second volume, reasoning that interruptions to public dialogue had compromised the consistent application of anti-violence policies.[101] He had a specific approach in mind: Rehabilitación, which he ultimately returned to defend. Indeed, over the course of the second volume's final half, Guzmán adopts a more upbeat perspective. The violence of 1962–63 occupied his mind early on in the drafting, but as he neared completion, it was as if he could not help but recognize the advances of the post-1957 era. There was no time to square these contrasting positions, a reality which ensured that the second volume still retains the feel of a molten intellectual creation that barely had a chance to cool.

The second volume's unresolved tensions appear as well in the book's treatment of theory. Coming as it did after the sociologists' abandonment of functionalism, the 1964 volume contains less theorical rumination than had its 1962 predecessor. The old ways of thinking were not totally neglected: primary source material derived from the Peace Commission offered a brilliant illustration of armed groups' self-generated "norms and attitudes," while Fals's summation of the first-volume controversy culminated in a rather forced analysis of "attitudes," "roles," and "structures."[102] Yet cut free from their original intellectual moorings, Fals and Guzmán had greater possibilities for experimentation.

The result would have important implications for how Colombian scholars understood "violence." Fals and Guzmán plugged into a nascent global exchange on the idea of violence during the preparation of the second volume. Absent a firm disciplinary grounding of their own, the sociologists—Guzmán more than Fals— gravitated toward the latest findings from behavioral sciences in the United States. Arguments about the biological bases of aggression, culled from the latest international publications, consequently seeped into *La violencia en Colombia*.[103] "The problem [of violence] cannot be circumscribed to this or that bandit or that massacre . . . or a certain geographical zone," Guzmán concluded, employing this new conceptual toolkit for an argument that he and Fals had made in the first volume. "Violence is not . . . Chispas, Tarzán, Desquite, or Sangrenegra, nor the massacre of La Italia. Violence is an antisocial state, a latency which intensifies or wanes but that conceals itself in the deep recesses of human groups." Violence was, in other words, "latent [*larvado*]" across humankind, "almost always passive and imperceptible."[104]

The idea of "violence" thus underwent a marked enlargement. Even as he dutifully compiled lengthy lists of mass homicides, Guzmán decoupled violence from any specificity of time or place. The price of escaping the jargon of Fals and Guzmán's first volume was a naturalization of violence. In contrast to conceptualizations of state violence in later Latin American cases, there was little space here for reconciliation or justice. Though Guzmán in particular could come back to the reassuring lessons of the creole peace, which his commission had helped build in 1958, the stage was set for a further intellectual and popular suppression of memories from that period. If violence existed everywhere, it was also temporally omnipresent. The differences between violence of the decade after 1946 and the bloodshed of the early 1960s could theoretically be bridged; the "two violences" could be made one, obliterating the creole peace.

The transformation of "violence" into "La Violencia" entailed multiple steps. Substantial pieces of the first two steps were in place by 1964, with the publication of *La violencia en Colombia*'s final volume. First, violence had to acquire a certain fixity, a winnowing process that could be either discursive ("the problem of 'violence,'" "Urban Violence") or conceptual (the eternally "latent violence"). Second, the disparate patterns of partisan, economic, state, collective, and individual violence that existed in 1946, 1948, 1952, 1955, 1958, and 1962 had to be merged into an unbroken block.[105] This had not fully transpired by 1964, but certain threads of connection had been identified. Moreover, the view of violence as ever-present in Colombia would facilitate the eventual privileging of temporal continuity and the disappearance of ideas about transition.

Structurally similar ideas about violence could derive from diverse sources. Though the intellectual eminence of *La violencia en Colombia*'s authors gave its arguments heft, and its influence can be traced through various works of the period, the book was not necessarily the sole progenitor of opinions around violence as an innate trait or an unbroken, decades-long thread. The Colombian military was, for obvious reasons, predisposed to view the past two decades as a period of nonstop conflict. The theories that military thinkers developed about violence exercised a less direct role in shaping national ideas of violence over the long term. They did, however, serve as the cornerstone of Bogotá's policies toward the provinces during the first half of the Valencia presidency.

THE COLOMBIAN MILITARY'S IDEAS
AND PRACTICES OF VIOLENCE

Colombia's 1962 violence controversy pitted the *convivencia* of Guzmán and the Lleras years against not only a Conservative worldview with burgeoning geographic, social, and political reach. The presidential succession also opened space for the assertion of groundbreaking counterviolence strategies by the Colombian military. The two were, in fact, necessary complements: the hue and cry against "banditry" required concrete means to achieve its goal, and the armed forces required a hospitable political environment in order for its plans to rise to the top of the state's agenda.[106]

Violence had proven an intellectual problem for the Colombian military as much as for politicians and *letrados*. The fighting that had gathered steam from the mid-1940s was primarily a civilian affair, evident confirmation of an early twentieth-century adage that "Colombia is a country of peculiar things / Civilians make war / And the military peace."[107] In the relatively rare instances when the army was charged with combat, its capacities seemed at odds with the mission at hand. Tanks, for instance, were hardly a formula for success in the abrupt topography of eastern Tolima coffee country, as the Villarrica stalemate of 1955 indicated.[108] A group of U.S. military and intelligence officers who toured Colombia four years later ascertained a pronounced "lack of 'know how' in the techniques of anti-guerrilla operations." The military, they judged, had "met very limited success" in what Washington increasingly saw as an crucial area. Part of this stemmed from the fact that numerous Colombian officers doubted the value of the enterprise, feeling instead that the armed forces should concentrate on ensuring security from external threats.[109] On the other side of the ledger, the military played a minor part in the making of the creole peace. The military's most consequential role was perhaps that of spoiler, but such actions lacked coherence. Scattered officers out in the provinces objected to the terms of Rehabilitación, and opted—against the dictates of national command and civilian authority—to continue their pursuit of now-demobilized fighters.[110] By splitting men like Chispas off from the option of peace, army units helped to give rise to the bands that would comprise the "second violence."

That renewed challenge of early 1960s' "banditry" would gradually be met by a military establishment with an overhauled assessment and composure. Having moved clear of the venality and worst political intrigues of the Rojas era, the senior officer corps evinced a greater confidence and unity. The passage of time also allowed these men to reflect on the lessons of the creole peace. Thus, on the one hand, top commanders maintained a faith in the potential of civilian-led reform, including Lleras Camargo's specific approach. One high-level internal 1962 report contended that the armed forces "would have to do nothing or practically nothing if political-social-economic and moral programs had [previously] been put into practice . . . and if the rehabilitation programs that the National Government is currently carrying out had been intensified." [111] On the other hand, those same commanders exhibited a marked pessimism about "the duration or sincerity" of rural Colombians' commitment to *convivencia*. Appearances could be deceiving, some military men felt, which could lead both authorities and *campesinos* of genuine good-will toward a false sense of security. [112] Though military officers would not go so far as to theorize about their own role in fostering the "second violence," by 1961 they already believed that it was time to take a greater role in solving Colombia's problems. If the political parties could be only partially trusted to undertake the necessary work of reform, it fell to the military to engage Colombian society directly. [113]

The rationale for this reorientation drew also on interpretations of Latin America's agitated political environment. As occurred with the reformist *letrados,* military thinkers increasingly thought about the nation through international referents. Their particular evaluation was shared by others throughout the hemisphere: from Bogotá to Washington, civilian and military figures reckoned that Colombia occupied a unique and dangerous place in a global struggle against Communism. "There exist in Colombia thousands of peasants who have efficiently fought the Armed Forces over the course of more than ten years, which makes the situation in this country more dangerous," the Ministry of Foreign Relations reasoned in 1961. [114] The military concurrently judged the potential merger of "social-syndical agitation" with the legacies of rural violence (what Guzmán would later term "Urban Violence") to be "the gravest part of our problem." [115]

The prospect that urban radicals or foreign agents would link up with seasoned provincial ex-combatants was not entirely imagined. But would-be revolutionaries rapidly learned that the violence they advocated was not the violence practiced by the men up in the mountains. A young Communist sent by the party to confer with Chispas walked away from a week on the Caldas-Tolima border "bowled over [by Chispas's] brutishness." "It was impossible to indoctrinate them; they were too deformed," the Communist concluded, arriving at his own version of *La violencia en Colombia*'s lost-generation thesis. [116] He was lucky to depart from the encounter with his life. The generation of the state of siege's de facto advance guard had been a student organizer from Cali who journeyed to the other side of the Iron Curtain and then to Cuba in the early months of the island's revolution before making his way to eastern Cauca in early 1961. This eager emulator of Fidel Castro lasted just weeks in the mountains, until he ran afoul of the local armed band and provoked a gruesome death at the hands of precisely the kind of men he had hoped to turn to the revolutionary cause.[117]

If there were lessons to be learned from these urban-to-rural revolutionary pilgrimages, they benefited the Colombian Armed Forces. Tracking even handfuls of urban radicals deep into the provinces provided a testing ground to refine specific tactics. When followers of the slain Cali student leader popped up near the Venezuelan frontier in the company of demobilized fighters from the Liberal resistance of the 1950s, Bogotá dispatched as its point man Colonel Álvaro Valencia Tovar. Valencia Tovar had shown his mettle disarming the spirits in Caldas during the late 1950s, and now gained a national reputation as the man with the magic formula for quieting potential trouble.[118] From the Venezuelan border operation of late 1961 nearly through the birth of the FARC in 1966, Valencia Tovar would be a key fulcrum for both internal military deliberations about the "second violence" and state relations with constituencies that comprised the creole peace.

Valencia Tovar's success in the field was but one current feeding into the formation of military doctrine. The armed forces took their own lettered turn, mirroring in form and content the developmentalism of the early '60s. Military officers of Fals and Torres's generation compiled their thinking in new theoretical publications and brought in social science experts like the National University geographer Ernesto Guhl to illuminate the interplay of the environment, culture, and reform on Colombia's national problems.[119] The process of systematizing knowledge about violence and reform received additional impetus from a U.S. foreign policy establishment itself coming to terms with the question of rural warfare.[120]

U.S. diplomatic and military personnel, and their intellectual backers from the modernization theory camp, were especially drawn to the promise of what they termed civic or civic-military action—the involvement of Latin American soldiers in the delivery of services, from health care to infrastructure construction, to civilian populations. Within the Colombian context, the U.S. Embassy explained in 1964, civic action could "win the support of the populace and gain a measure of political stability and socio-economic improvement, thereby reducing or eliminating conditions which would contribute to further outbreaks of banditry." As an added benefit, it was thought that soldiers would be able to carry out public works at lower cost than civilian contractors, and that such tasks would help to infuse the armed forces with a new sense of purpose, keeping them out of the political arena.[121]

U.S. ideas about the intersection of development and anti-violence policy dovetailed perfectly with Colombian officers' diagnosis about the necessity of a more direct role for the military in national policy. With consultation from U.S. advisers, in early 1962 Ruiz Novoa, then serving as commander of the army, packaged knowledge from officers such as Valencia Tovar into a tactical master plan he dubbed "Plan Lazo" (Snare). A military establishment previously content to "simply maintain ... the status quo" in the countryside became primed for "the destruction or capture of known bandits." Specialized mobile intelligence detachments would take the fight directly to the bandit gangs, while regular units would assist through combat operations and civic action. Lazo anticipated that the last of these approaches would eliminate the underlying causes of violence, and in the short run produce additional intelligence, as local populations came to trust the military and, by proxy, the state.[122]

"Like 'the day of creation'" was reportedly how President Valencia felt about Plan Lazo's unveiling at a cabinet meeting three weeks after he assumed office. Not only had Ruiz Novoa "opened [Valencia's] eyes to the real magnitude of the problem" of violence, but the general had a solution in hand. Behind the scene, dissenting voices within Bogotá's political class questioned the wisdom of the plan. Still smarting from the 1953 coup against his father, Álvaro Gómez expressed reservations about ceding so much authority to the military, while developmentalist Liberals recoiled at the administration's spare-no-expense support for Lazo and the anti-violence campaign.[123] The course was nonetheless set, the national government armed with a putatively technical strategy to match the rhetoric flowing from Congress and the press (figure 11).

Of course, military *letrados'* capabilities for observation and action far exceeded those of their civilian counterparts. Where Camilo Torres's sociology students enumerated population counts with pencils and clipboards, army units began to accumulate data on local inhabitants' "[political] tendency and grade of trustworthiness" and to treat Tolima adults caught without an official identification card (*cédula*) or a military-issued safe-conduct pass (*salvoconducto*) as "suspect individual[s]."[124] Where Fals applied the lessons of community organizing learned at Saucío in the early 1950s, colonels commanding 1963's northern Tolima operations revived practices employed eight years earlier at Villarrica: while entire villages in counties like El Líbano fled military sweeps, two thousand more people—"suspected [bandit] accomplices, declarants, witnesses, and those [detained] for purposes of identification"—spent days behind barbed wire on farms repurposed as detention facilities. The acquisition of intelligence from these populations, a congressional fact-finding mission would later determine, relied in no small part on torture.[125] The army's coercive capacities, coupled with enhanced detention powers passed as part of the Valencia administration's judicial reform package, thus dislocated individual bodies and collective life in pockets across central Colombia. The subregional extent of this process, together with the virtual national consensus against banditry, meant that such state violence did not attract anywhere near the partisan denunciations that had met the far broader Conservatization campaigns of the 1940s and '50s.

Through measures both administrative and technological, Plan Lazo also remade Gran Tolima's geography. The Quindío coffee belt, which spread across Caldas and Valle del Cauca, and included some of Chispas's favored turf, was unified under a single military command. No longer would traditional departmental boundaries confine the army's freedom of movement.[126] In a tangible sense, too, soldiers came to enjoy greater mobility than ever before. A handful of helicopters received under U.S. military assistance permitted Army teams to jump at fresh intelligence. However mobile the small (and dwindling) bandit bands might be, the military possessed a decisive technological advantage.[127] Even topography, it seemed, could be bested.

Once sprung, the snare closed swiftly. Intelligence sources postulated that death and capture had reduced the bandits' ranks from over three thousand at the start of 1963 to around twenty-five hundred by May. Press reports similarly put the number of major, "organized" bandit gangs at just four, two of them operated by the Horsemen on the Tolima-Caldas border. Colombia was face-to-face with an "unparalleled opportunity," Valencia told the U.S. ambassador in April, adding that "now was the time if ever to strike final telling blows." Within six months, the government's "definitive battle" against banditry crossed a decisive threshold: October's death toll dropped below one hundred, the first time such a level had been seen since the armed forces began recording deaths at the start of the democratic transition (figure 12).[128]

Statistics did not capture the entire story. For one, government accounting methods switched under Valencia, such that military casualties became included in monthly tallies. The accelerating downward trend in homicides was therefore even more pronounced than it appeared, especially as the armed forces stepped up its operations and incurred more losses.[129]

More significantly, the very meanings of peace had changed. Indexes of violence were below the highs of the creole peace, yet the texture of these latest gains had a discrete quality, as relations between the state and provinces morphed from their Lleras-era incarnation. Martial metaphors abounded, as officials in particular spoke less of "peace" than of "the battle of the peace," "a . . . crusade for peace," or, simply, "pacification."[130] The provincial population was seen now as a source of intelligence to be tapped, and less of a partner with whom *convivencia* would be built. Even as the practice of violence waned on the national scene, the practice of peace lacked the sense of optimism and participation that had accompanied it entering the democratic transition.

Civic-military action epitomized the government's assumption of this paramount role for itself in the anti-violence campaign. The apparent extent of military contributions to development drew praise from abroad as multiple observers "commended" Colombian programs "as being among the most successful in Latin America."[131] Opinion within Colombia was, by contrast, decidedly mixed. In the pages of *La violencia en Colombia*'s second volume, Monsignor Guzmán expressed his doubt about the efficacy of civic action as a policy tool. "Civic-military campaigns," he wrote, were at best "transitory," a poor substitute for a regular state

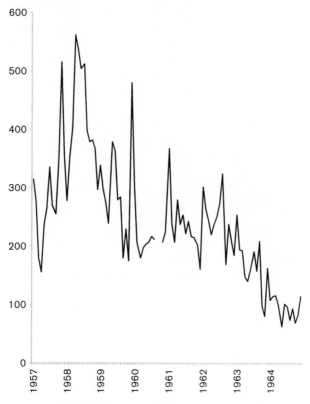

FIGURE 12. Monthly homicides attributed to partisan violence and banditry, January 1957–December 1964.

presence.[132] Though he did not draw the connection outright, the tone of the book registered the disparity between civic action and the engagement that had typified the creole peace.

Out in the provinces, civic action brought the past into focus. Though civic action was celebrated as a means to improve the public image of the army and the state more generally, the U.S. consul in Cali discovered that communities' contact with civic-action units did not "in the slightest" overcome local memories of Conservative- and dictatorship-era police and military repression.[133] In the geographic heart of Gran Tolima, military contractors served to remind residents of an increasingly circumscribed set of possibilities. The planned twelve-mile road through the Tolima-Huila borderlands, to connect the villages of Gaitania and El Carmen (map 3), had employed Marquetalia's Communists during the creole peace. Completion of the road now fell instead to army engineers as part of a larger highway project that its designers hoped would bind southern Tolima together and, finally, bestow the region with its own access through the central Andes to the Cauca River valley.[134] The road network also bore unmistakable political symbolism. Even in the construction phase, the Tolima highway would allow the state to project itself as never before into territory that—however divided among Communists, Liberals, and Conservatives—had long determined its own affairs. The latitude permitted to frontier communities, and supported for a time by Rehabilitación, was shrinking.

THE FINAL TELLING BLOWS, 1964

Massacre by massacre, military raid by military raid, Vipradel (the professional acronym used by Víctor Eduardo Prado Delgado) lived the Valencia administration's "definitive battle" from up close. Barely sixteen years old when chance threw him his first assignment—photographing the death of forty *campesinos* murdered on their way to vote for Alberto Lleras in August 1958—the Alvarado (Tolima) native entered manhood as Gran Tolima's unofficial chronicler. Befriending the police and army allowed Vipradel to bring extraordinary details of the region's defining events to readers in Ibagué and Bogotá. He often followed a few hours behind the Three Horsemen, as occurred at the La Italia massacre, when, first through the entryway of the little house which stood near the site, Vipradel was knocked on the shoulder by the decapitated head that Desquite had left atop the door as a macabre prank. At other moments, however, Vipradel brushed right up against the day's great villains. Enjoying a beer and taking in a local fair with the county executive one afternoon, Vipradel and his host were briefly joined by a man who turned out to be none other than Desquite himself. Though politics was not his beat, Vipradel grasped better that day the linkages that sustained banditry in his home department.[135]

Whatever combination of influence, fear, and vote-mongering led that county executive to collaborate with Desquite, such relationships were coming to an end. Cries to deny partisan support to those who would commit violence, as old as the National Front, gained fresh relevance from 1962. The discourse around the evils of "banditry" allowed political stances to change, leading regional and local politicians to back away from armed partisans. The process was still slow: angling to protect their "electoral base[s]," two Tolima politicians, including Valencia's eventual appointee as governor, alternately blocked and sought a negotiated disarmament for Desquite. But as Gonzalo Sánchez and Donny Meertens explain, the disappearance of this "quasi-institutional support" forced the Three Horsemen onto far less certain social and physical terrain.[136]

Denied political backing, and the logistical support that often went along with it, gangs turned to a self-defeating cycle of extraction and retaliation against communities that had previously lent support. Sangrenegra or Desquite's claims to be acting for the greater good of Tolima, credible among some pockets of opinion, evaporated in the face of reprisal killings against suspected government collaborators and multiple rapes. Hounded from every side, the Three Horsemen fell in quick sequence in early 1964: Desquite on March 17; Sangrenegra, the "most feared bandit operating in Colombia," five weeks later, miles away from Tolima; and Tarzán by mid-May. (Vipradel was soon on the scene.)[137] Intelligence officers sent word to Bogotá that "the state of anxiety that reigned" from northern Tolima through Caldas was dissipating.[138] Nationally, May's banditry-related homicides totaled sixty-two—an 80 percent reduction from Valencia's first month in office. Relieved communities started to hold peace festivals, an expansion of the practice pioneered by Jorge Villamil Cordovez at the start of the creole peace.[139]

The triumphs of Plan Lazo in early 1964 called into question many rural ideas about violence. Renowned bandits had transcended simple fame, achieving the level of myth; their improbable capacity to survive, to dodge army patrols and to evade death, bred talk of the supernatural—an ability to become part of the landscape by transforming into a tree when danger approached.[140] The same technologies that collapsed space, allowing the government to catch up to the Three Horsemen, now carried the bodies of the vanquished out of the backcountry, to be seen by publics by turns grateful and questioning. Vipradel's camera captured *campesinos* in Líbano racing to glimpse Desquite's corpse, as well as some of the twenty thousand people in Ibagué who congregated for the same spectacle. A new future seemed possible. Nevertheless, and despite the fact that such practices would never merit inclusion in the analyses of the military *letrados*, the burial party that lay Sangrenegra's body into the earth placed a two-ton stone over the site. A memorial of sorts to the bandit's victims, the act was meant to ensure as well that he would not become myth once more and somehow return to the mountains of Tolima.[141]

The apparent anticlimax of *La violencia en Colombia* unexpectedly veered toward danger in November 1962. At the behest of General Ruiz Novoa, Colonel Valencia Tovar had "devoured and studied" the brand-new book during his July vacation, producing by the second week of August a secret report for the army's internal consumption. When a copy of the report leaked to an opposition Conservative senator three months later, the U.S. Embassy's earlier wisecrack about "*Violence Caused by 'Violence'*" nearly came to pass. Laureano's followers in Congress howled at Valencia Tovar's endorsement of the book's worth, alleging Liberal favoritism within the military. The minister of war stepped in to defuse the situation with his own denunciation of the book, but not before putting tanks onto the streets of Bogotá on a Saturday night to dissuade a rumored Conservative coup plot. "Of course . . . we had to go into hiding for two weeks," Orlando Fals Borda explained decades afterward. "That shows, doesn't it, what the environment was like, the intolerance, politics in the worst sense, no?"[142]

La Violencia's final component was a set of political commitments, born of a sense of generational disenchantment. The seeds of this, too, were evident by 1964. The reformist *letrados'* developmentalist vocations gave them more or less constant exposure to the vices and failings of Colombia's political class, an experience that fed a gradual, burgeoning separation from the *país político* and the state it commanded. In contrast, the political ramifications of the *letrados'* work on rural violence was characterized by moments of intense punctuation. A series of these, culminating with the coup talk of November 1962, came with the inaugural release of *La violencia en Colombia*.

Momentum toward another was building as the book's concluding volume arrived in early 1964. Rehabilitación figured prominently once more in this debate between the *país político,* the *país letrado,* and the *país nacional.* However, the stakes were far higher than two years earlier. Politicians and the army seemed on a collision course with the rural groups who had openly shared in the creole peace. The specter of outright confrontation between the two camps put the reformist intellectuals on a path to Marquetalia and the southern Tolima frontier. The story of *La violencia en Colombia* did not stop with the coining of "La Violencia." The biography of the book, and of its authors' subsequent pursuits, is in myriad ways the biography of the FARC.

7

Confrontation, 1963–1966

The cameras have projected their glances and words across a half-century, out of the deepest mountains of southern Colombia and into the present day. Intended to connect distant audiences with the suffering and resistance of frontier Colombians, the footage shot by two French filmmakers still imparts the immediacy of their September 1965 encounter with Gran Tolima's creole Communists. Pedro Antonio Marín/Manuel Marulanda Vélez/Tirofijo and Ciro Castaño Trujillo strike a defiant tone on the eve of a possible assault against Riochiquito by the Colombian military. After a nod to the faces behind the camera that beckon them on, each man speaks, with practice and simplicity, of past battles. "We have an . . . an experience of more than 15 years of struggle," Ciro advertises. "And those 15 years have allowed us to make the *guerrilla* movement a strong, capable, and dynamic [one]." Marulanda possessed special reason to insist that military action only caused "the movement to spread, to become even stronger."[1] News reports had for months offered speculation that Tirofijo had been killed or wounded in combat—early chapters in the tale of a man who would die countless deaths in the press over the years that followed.[2] Marulanda took advantage of the Frenchmen's presence to issue a rejoinder. "The spoken and written press," he explains, "is an instrument of propaganda to distort the reality of the . . . struggle, of [we] men who are facing up to the government."

The scenes recorded by the Frenchmen are not themselves unmediated portrayals of rural life. In the film's final cut, two other figures, men recently arrived from the city, receive greater screen time than Marulanda and Ciro. These urban Communists depict themselves as being one with the indigenous majority that comprised Ciro's forces. Riochiquito is "our" region, the younger Communist lectures to the silent crowd that has gathered around him. The older Communist goes further; reading off a sheet of paper that conveys lettered authority, his voice reaches prophetic ecstasy as he exclaims that "the Central Committee of our party is accompanying us and will not only accompany us, but will direct the heroic action of the resistance fighters!"

With over a year of backcountry warfare under their belts, these men were well able to claim belonging and mutual affinity. Their presentation of a fundamental unity between themselves and their rural comrades is nonetheless belied by pronounced differences in their respective takes on politics and violence. The outward messaging of the urban Communists who had relocated to Gran Tolima indicated a unity of revolutionary purpose, directed at the achievement of national power. The rural Communists' interactions with the wider world, by contrast, revealed understandings of rights and obligations rooted in the provinces. Such differences in scale had become readily evident over the prior two years, as the escalating crisis facing Gran Tolima's frontier communities compelled Communists and their critics to appeal to local, regional, and national partners with ever-greater urgency.

The eventual predominance of the urban Communists' discourse, with its emphasis on national and international scales, indicates both the state of memory in the mid-1960s and how understandings of the past would evolve in later years. The *país político*'s desire to limit discussion of past violence opened the way for two arguments on that very subject, each grounded in a specific set of memories. The first was that of reformist *letrados* like Orlando Fals Borda, the second that of the Communists. In the long run, the Communist viewpoint, as well as the *país político*'s dissociation from the political alignments of the early creole peace, infused Colombia's post-1962 history with an air of inevitability. In other words, scholarly and popular reflections tend toward a particular idea of violence, in which confrontation between the state and rural peoples, above all the Communists of Gran Tolima's frontiers, was preordained.[3]

Yet urban and rural Colombians did engage in serious attempts to forestall confrontation between Bogotá and Gran Tolima. More importantly, it was the precise shape of these efforts' breakdown that gave rise to chronicles of inevitability. From April 1964 through September 1965, the countries of politics and letters, as well as lettered military men, tussled publicly over the question of whether Marulanda and his fellow frontier Communists deserved the fate of Colombia's worst "bandits." In so doing, urban Colombians looped back to Rehabilitación and the creole peace. For Conservatives atop the administration, Rehabilitación remained eminently refutable. For others, the approaches of the late 1950s—dialogue, consensual expressions of *convivencia*—glimmered as guides by which to grasp the nature of rural grievances with the state and the response that urban Colombians ought to take.

Bogotá's politicians and intellectuals were not alone in this final bout over Rehabilitación. On opposite sides of Gran Tolima, rivalries arose over how communities should relate to the state. Should alliances approximating those of the late 1950s be built or rebuilt in order to ensure communal progress? Or should the state's moves be interpreted as aggressions and responded to in kind? These questions were most evident at Riochiquito and El Pato, the last sites where the Rehabilitación story unraveled. However, even the inhabitants of Marquetalia, whose purported martial belligerence made them Bogotá's initial target, invoked alternate referents as confrontation loomed in early 1964. The final chapter in the creation of the FARC thus reveals how categories such as "revolution," so seemingly natural to the 1960s, in fact emerged from limited contexts, their meanings moreover changing as they contended with countervailing ideas and practices.

REHABILITATION REVISITED: EL PATO, 1958–1963

The elimination of the Three Horseman, Colombia's most feared bandits, brought about an instantaneous pivot in Colombians' discussions on the problem of violence. The broad class of "banditry" incorporated two categories: men like Sangrenegra and Desquite, whose origin stories and criminal pasts reached back into the 1950s, but whose profiles skyrocketed in the 1960s; and those Communist fighters who opted for peace in 1957–58, only to have their forms of collective life branded as "banditry" by local opponents and the regional and national state. With the former category vanquished, attentions turned to the latter.

Gran Tolima's Communist settlements (map 5) had by the mid-1960s become the stuff of minor legend in their own right. Marquetalia most especially presented a beacon of possibility to Colombia's political left, the manifest realization of authentic popular desires and popular achievements.[4] To critics, Marquetalia and its counterparts transcended basic concerns about crime and lawlessness. By such accounts, these spaces were gashes in the nation's sovereignty, "independent republics" that might soon become Colombia's Sierra Maestra, Andean facsimiles of the Cuban revolution's birthplace.[5] The regions' aura of apartness was encouraged by an absence of firsthand knowledge. For much of the early 1960s, the only information to flow out of the independent republics seemed to be denunciations of the government and vague statements of revolutionary intent.[6]

Nonetheless, as the eventual entry of the two French filmmakers into Riochiquito would make clear, gaining access to the independent republics was not so complicated for those with the right connections or a certain level of initiative.[7] However cautious or fleeting, these instances of contact demonstrated how interdependent the supposedly independent republics were with the larger world.[8] The channels opened by Rehabilitación remained essential in this regard. So learned the government's head indigenist advocate, Gregorio Hernández de Alba, when he broached the idea of reestablishing indigenous control over what had been the upper reservations of Tierradentro. When the two sat down in the town of Belalcázar to discuss the Riochiquito movement's relinquishment of its members' lands, Ciro Castaño's second-in-command scoffed at Hernández's proposal. His comment sounded less that of a man out for revolution and more the complaint of a pressed frontier farmer who pined for easier days. "If they want to kick us out," Hernández de Alba was told, "let them come search for us, because we will be waiting for them. Or [they should] give us five million pesos and cancel our debts with the Agrarian Bank."[9] A newly appointed public works inspector received more than an earful the following year, when Ciro's men chased him from the area.[10] The material enticements of the creole peace—farming loans and infrastructure jobs—continued to hold powerful meanings for local populations.

The quest to replace resources lost since the 1950s, and, with it, the matter of how to relate to outside groups, dominated frontier Communist life in the first half of the 1960s. This drive to practice *convivencia* in the immediate term, as well as to ensure propitious material conditions for its sustainment, brought together, albeit in sometimes radically different combinations, familiar players from Colombia's earlier experiments with peace and reformism. The resulting network of institutions and individuals spanned the creole peace and the ensuing developmentalist turn: Rehabilitación and community action, Monsignor Germán Guzmán Campos and the Communist combatants he had met at the fringes of Gran Tolima in 1958, the reformist military *letrado* Colonel Álvaro Valencia Tovar and the regional planter class of the surgeon-turned-songwriter Jorge Villamil Cordovez. The density of their connections and the durability of their exertions varied between the independent republics, as did the draw of violence-as-practice, that substitute means of social and political interaction.

The locus of the earliest political outreach arose in the Pato River basin, Gran Tolima's rainiest and most isolated Communist frontier. The project rested on the shoulders of Martín Camargo, long the Communist Party's master provincial operator (figure 13). Camargo had for decades worked at the edge of the party's inner circle, as other leaders strained to chart a course through a political environment far out of their control. Frustrated by ranking comrades' myopic focus on fund-raising, and seeking perhaps to replicate the tales of Liberal heroism he had grown up hearing in Santander (his father had been a bodyguard for Liberal champion Rafael Uribe Uribe during the War of a Thousand Days), Camargo won a victory of sorts in 1952 when the party transferred him to the coffee districts between Bogotá and Gran Tolima. There, Camargo could both direct the party's new cadre school and build closer ties with the armed movement in southern Tolima, which he considered the party's foremost rural hope.

By 1953, as the schism between Communists and "clean" Liberals grew irreversible, Camargo had permanently cemented his move to this rural scene. His political

FIGURE 13. Martín Camargo (second from left), among *desplazados* from El Pato, 1964. Prado Delgado, *Sur del Tolima*, 32.

guidance would mold passages big and small. On the one hand, Camargo participated in the mass peregrinations of the mid- and late 1950s, from southern to eastern Tolima, and then from eastern Tolima down into the frontier piedmont along
the Pato (map 5). On the other, Camargo played the part of political godfather to
the young Pedro Antonio Marín, rebaptising him as Manuel Marulanda Vélez.[11] So
much of what the founders of Marquetalia, Riochiquito, and El Pato learned about
the joining of armed self-defense with political organization, of an organic practice
of violence with ideas to ensure its propagation, came from Camargo. It was no
accident that the only library the Peace Commission observed was at El Pato.

Yet during the creole peace, the value of this military-political coupling came
undone in Martín Camargo's mind. El Pato entered a new phase after the fall of the
dictatorship. Fighters reporting to Camargo's military counterpart, alias Richard,
committed to the pardon offered by the Lleras government, while small numbers
of Liberal Party combatants and Conservatives moved from other regions to El
Pato, drawn by the promise of open lands and peace. "We declare with pride that
we practice the authentic National Front, as we Liberals and Conservatives live
alongside one another [*convivimos*] in complete harmony," a group of colonists
from the upper Pato wrote to Bogotá. In time, *convivencia* would take institutional
form, through the establishment of several Community Action Councils, one of
them headed by Camargo.[12] Though El Pato's location astride the borders of Huila,
Caquetá, and Meta complicated the task of obtaining government assistance, the
area's push for collective betterment kept receiving official sanction and public
funds even after Rehabilitación wound down.

Martín Camargo nevertheless remained unsatisfied. The problem with Rehabilitación was not that "it loaned money to ex-combatants," he explained in a 1964 letter to President Guillermo León Valencia. Instead, Bogotá had not permitted El Pato "to *DIRECT from within* the policy of regional progress." Camargo's determination to realize that goal spiked in early 1960, when a spat with the Communist Party's regional leadership—the first of many—led him to decamp for Neiva. To compensate for this knock to his authority, Camargo erected what he revealingly referred to as a "self-rehabilitation" operation. He would sit at the center of this web of outside backers, fulfilling his vision of himself as the irreplaceable intermediary.[13]

Branches of state served as the starting point. Some figured into the long view of Camargo's plan. Government titling teams and teachers arrived along the Pato to formalize the settlers' homesteads and to educate their children. Camargo also pursued government aid to ensure a diverse and viable regional economy. Extension agents from the Ministry of Agriculture, for instance, assisted El Pato's farmers in planting cacao, a crop whose high value-to-weight ratio made it an especially worthwhile commodity on such a distant frontier. To overcome the gap until such products began yielding dividends, Camargo arranged for his Community Action Council to receive emergency food aid, sent from the United States to Colombia under the Alliance for Progress.[14]

Other Camargo collaborators were rather less conventional. El Pato's colonists often cycled out of the area between harvests, heading upland on the paths back toward Huila, to the territory's vastest estate, where they could augment their irregular income through day labor.[15] Oliverio Lara Borrero was master of those twenty thousand hectares, a tract nearly twice as large as all of the privately held lands redistributed under the first two years of the 1961 agrarian reform. His vast holdings in southern Colombia made Lara—the don of a major Bogotá commercial firm and childhood classmate of Alberto Lleras Camargo and Gregorio Hernández de Alba—a formidable player within the country's rancher class and, for some colonists and the left, a hated symbol of inequality.[16]

From Neiva, Martín Camargo could look past Lara's poor reputation. Unimaginable wealth lay right on El Pato's doorstep, and what was more, the baron of Caquetá showed himself amenable to an arrangement. Lara's vision of regional advancement may have operated on a plane higher than Camargo's, but they proved complementary. Lara the businessman, cognizant of the environmental limitations of this waterlogged corner of the Andes, also appreciated how a partnership with El Pato lowered his expenses and risks. As a result, when El Pato colonists returned home from Lara's ranch early in 1964, they led with them three hundred world-class beef cattle. Lara's total commitment of a thousand head stood to double the bovine population that Camargo's followers had purchased with their Rehabilitación loans. The gift brought Lara goodwill from the Communists down the mountain, as well as the promise of his own herd's expansion once the

Pato-bound livestock reproduced.[17] Camargo and Lara each had their critiques of Rehabilitación as a means to foster *convivencia*. However, they both perceived a chance to take into their own hands the development of the frontier and its people. Whatever self-serving ends their actions advanced, it seemed that they could simultaneously move toward a common good and thus achieve a particular form of *convivencia*.

Martín Camargo's comrades within the Communist Party took the opposite stance on alliance with the state and with a leading class enemy. Camargo never clearly identified who was behind his gradual separation from the party. At times, he placed blame on regional cadres, who, unchecked by the party bureaucrats in Bogotá, enacted policies that rejected rapprochement with other political currents in Gran Tolima. When Camargo thought it better to appeal to anti-Communist sentiments, he implicated Richard, claiming that El Pato's military chief had returned from a trip to the Soviet Union in 1962.

No matter the explanation, the results were clear: beginning in 1962, Communist commanders in El Pato compelled the region's rearmament. The directive went out for every man to sell his cattle or other goods in order to purchase a rifle. This sea change, Camargo fretfully observed from Neiva, distracted from agricultural work and portended a resumption of hostilities with the government and the traditional parties. Trotting out an old Communist epithet, Camargo decried his rivals as "adventurist," amateurs whose willful lack of political foresight would run *campesino* interests into the ground.[18]

Camargo now sought out a new round of backers. If Huila's planter class had helped to make the region's creole peace, venturing out to El Pato early in the democratic transition, perhaps it could now save *convivencia*. At the beginning of 1963, Martín Camargo rode back to El Pato in the company of Jorge Villamil, "in search of an entente with the region's Communist Chiefs [*sic*] to advance improved works for regional progress." Camargo planned it to be the first in a renewed series of visits with outside sponsors, including the cacao promotion campaigners.[19]

Instead, once back in Neiva, Camargo received word that Richard and his party assessors had ordered Camargo's detention were he to attempt again to return. Out of conviction or convenience, the Communists depicted Camargo's entire portfolio—the teachers, the cacao plantings, the food aid—as part of Plan Lazo, the U.S.-backed anti-violence plan. Denounced as "an international agent . . . plant and spy of imperialism and the government," Camargo was suddenly proscribed within the community.[20] El Pato was rent in two.

It was not yet the end of the road for Camargo. A multitude of avenues remained to be explored; the deal with Lara, for instance, was still months away from consummation. With a hefty political price already paid, Camargo could also become less selective about which sectors of the state he interacted with. Beginning in 1963, Camargo felt free to meet and correspond with military commanders in Neiva.[21] It was both cathartic and productive: increasingly desperate to regain his lost standing, and feeling that he could shape what was turning into a national debate on the independent republics, Camargo typed out page after page to anyone who might carry influence. From 1964 to 1965, more than fifty of his letters traveled out from Neiva to the president, cabinet ministers, top generals and battalion commanders, newspaper editors, and regional notables ranging from Villamil to party directors. The onetime Communist cadre and veteran of the heaviest fighting of the 1950s had become the most prolific petitioner in all Colombia.

Camargo was right when he observed in one of his first letters that the involvement of men like Lara and Villamil distinguished El Pato from the other independent republics.[22] *Convivencia* as political compromise and developmental agenda also owed much to Camargo's own energies and preoccupations. Nonetheless, talk around and policy toward the three independent republics was converging. In the letters that followed, Camargo's evolving portrayals of the past, and the identities of his would-be interlocutors, indicated a declining role for local concerns. Events at Riochiquito and Marquetalia would set the regional and even national atmosphere that ultimately altered the balance between peace and violence.

THE FUTURE OF PEACE: RIOCHIQUITO, 1962–1963

Across the Magdalena Valley in Tierradentro, contestation over the present and future viability of peace was truly a regional affair. Tensions sprang not from within the Communist movement at Riochiquito, as occurred at El Pato, but from the sheer density of political and social actors involved: Cauca politicians angered at their Huila colleagues' apparent tolerance toward the Communists; residents displaced to Riochiquito's peripheries by the violence of the 1950s; Gregorio Hernández de Alba and other bureaucrats interested in the defense of Tierradentro's indigenous population; and military commanders interested in containing large-scale conflict. These groups split along two ideas of violence. Regional critics of Riochiquito argued that the existence of the Communist movement represented an ongoing outrage, the violation of law and rights through coercion. The opposing perspective, that the true resumption of violence would only come with a violation of the creole peace status quo, brought Communists and military officers together in an unlikely partnership—one that formed the crux of Bogotá's policy toward Riochiquito.

Odious though they might have found the Communists, in the early 1960s even Riochiquito's opponents acknowledged that the state of affairs in eastern Cauca differed from that of previous epochs. The central local complaint from the creole peace's later stages matched that of its early days—Tierradentro remained a land neglected in spite of government pledges. Riochiquito began to climb the regional and national agenda only around the 1962 election, when Cauca's Liberal notables from the *país político* took notice of Tierradentro's plight. Warnings that Ciro had a scheme to scare eastern Cauca's Liberal voters away from the polls, and thus swing the departmental election in favor of the dissident Liberal Revolutionary Movement, propagated a new level of regional concern that gradually expanded to include Bogotá.[23]

An October 1963 missive from Cauca's Liberal congressional delegation to the ministers of interior and war illuminates how such cases of regional discord could merge into the national discussion around the "second violence" of banditry. Identifying themselves as one-time participants in the creole peace, the congressmen averred that "the well-meant intentions of the National Front Government failed to win the Riochiquito intruders' readjustment to collective life. All efforts in this sense have been in vain . . . [Belalcázar's] indigenous live under a state of most absolute neglect by the authorities, subject to the regimen the bandits wish to impose on them." In the congressmen's mind, the "inexplicable sympathy, or at the very least, unjustified tolerance" demonstrated by Huila officials helped to clarify how such a situation had maintained itself.

"What is left to do?" the legislators asked rhetorically. "Simply that the Government decide to exercise its authority, without any hesitation, in the region of Riochiquito." Here the politicians pointed to the larger problematic that involved all of the independent republics. "The laws offer various paths for [the government] to make use of the systems it judges most suitable: those of the 'hard line' and those of the 'gentle line.'" The three congressmen specified potentially applicable legislation on indigenous and agrarian affairs, as well as sections of the extraordinary governmental powers then being exercised by the Valencia administration. "But the most important thing," they concluded, "is to act before it is too late."[24]

Bogotá had, in fact, taken to lumping Riochiquito into the phenomenon of banditry well prior to this concerted regional pressure. Ciro Castaño's forces were said to number five hundred, the largest concentration of bandits in the country. Yet even the National Police's dry quantitative tables reflected a belief that Riochiquito was different, "in recess" rather than "active."[25] The gentle line, not the hard line, could be applied. Nonetheless, and unlike at El Pato, the military would take the lead in the state's dealings with Riochiquito.

Publicly, the initiation of military-led development programs around Riochiquito raised expectations of an impending invasion. Communist and *campesino* organizations across Colombia decried the arrival of the first army civic-military action teams near the region in mid-1963.[26] However, Ciro had other ideas entirely. Be it through ministering to their spirits as the officiant at their wedding or ministering to their material needs, Ciro held deep concern for the people he had helped to shelter and organize under the shadow of the Nevado del Huila. And their needs were tremendous. "I have never seen a more miserable group of Indians than those I viewed at Riochiquito . . . that was an atrocious [level of] destitution, out there the Indians weren't so much indigenous as indigent," a Communist Party adviser from Ciro's era told an interviewer decades later. Ciro observed the army's increasing presence in Huila as an opening "to get [Riochiquito] out of this misery" while also preserving the peace he had built.[27]

The means to make contact were readily at hand. Riochiquito's residents frequently passed by an army post on the way to the weekly market in Pacarní, a village across the Huila border (map 3). Ciro quietly sent word up the command chain that Riochiquito would welcome a small number of government-provisioned schoolteachers. Through different channels, he also arranged for a priest to come deliver the sacraments.[28] In small but meaningful ways, the independent republic of Riochiquito was on its way to greater interdependence.

As 1964 approached, Riochiquito's peace was not an entirely convincing proposition. The mutual overtures between Ciro and the army advanced against a backdrop of mistrust between the Communists and sundry state agencies. Flyers attributed to Riochiquito deplored the anti-bandit campaign and the collateral climate of anti-Communism, which it dubbed "official violence . . . the new wave of *chulavita* barbarism that the Conservative Government . . . is unleashing on our country."[29] In Bogotá, the National Police made a case for armed intervention against Ciro, but recognized "that the government will abstain from adopting steps against him so as not to violate the provisions" of the 1958 pardon.[30] For all sides, the state violence of the 1940s and '50s and the creole peace seemed simultaneously immediate and distant. Whether violence would return on a large scale, and what this would mean for memories of the period since 1957–58, became an increasingly imperative subject as the nation concentrated on the third independent republic.

PATHS TO MARQUETALIA

Marquetalia was from the start the outlier of its fellow independent republics, beset by frictions with rivalrous neighbors. Riochiquito had its share of enemies, but none so organized and militarily capable as the forces of southern Tolima's former Liberal resistance, Marquetalia's arch-enemies. The list of contending parties arrayed around Marquetalia had grown to include the army, which returned to southern Tolima in 1960 to defuse passions resulting from the assassination of Marquetalia's Charro Negro. In time, however, the presence of the state's coercive arm enhanced rather than lessened the chances of confrontation. Marquetalia's Communists, their old *limpio* adversaries in Tolima, and newly antagonized Conservative villages across the Huila border all engaged in livestock rustling to scare up resources and score retaliation for past offenses. What might have passed in other contexts as rural peccadillos was instead magnified by the area's deep memories of betrayal and by the expanding footprint of the army.[31]

By 1963, the Communists on the one side and the countries of letters and politics on the other spoke of each another in different dialects. Marquetalia's residents wrote to Bogotá time and time again, complaining of expected "guarantees" from the government that never arrived, and the consequent need to act in self-defense.[32] In turn, newspapers, army officers, and politicians placed Marulanda with Desquite and Sangrenegra among the country's four greatest bandit leaders. Experience, including a failed January 1962 operation to capture him, moreover demonstrated that Tirofijo was not a foe easily bested by force.[33]

The government's 1964 decision to move definitively against Marquetalia therefore took many by surprise. "Had it not been for the success enjoyed in [northern Tolima and] other violence areas . . . after the beginning of the year," the U.S. Embassy explained in a July summary, "it seems doubtful that the [Colombian] military would have considered itself capable of a campaign against Marquetalia at this time, but elation at progress made and irritation at the insolence, as well as the criminal deeds emanating from Marquetalia, stimulated a decision to attack this region." The embassy—generally a savvy and seasoned diplomatic team—admitted to Washington that it was "quite startl[ed]" by the pace of events.[34]

Outside of government, other Colombians scrambled to stay ahead of the situation. The counterexamples of Riochiquito and El Pato held out some hope that an alternative to outright military force might exist. "Riochiquito, Pato, and Guayabero [a satellite area of El Pato] . . . have remained inactive and have expressed interest in reincorporating themselves and in respecting the Government," stated a March 1964 intelligence estimate. "The pacific reintegration of [these] groups through political, economic, and social action will be sought." Civic-military action and the precepts of the Plan Lazo would facilitate good state relations with the countryside and thus defuse the potential for further violence on the part of the Communists.[35]

Perhaps this model could also be extended to Marquetalia, if only rural and urban peoples could be made to talk, and the reality of the countryside comprehended. This had been the dual ideal behind the publication of *La violencia en Colombia,* and before it the Peace Commission. The times seemed to demand that the model be called into being once more. Significantly, the initiative came from other lettered corners: in mid-April, a trio of lawyers from the radical faction of the Liberal Revolutionary Movement—including one of Colombia's foremost socialist thinkers and a congressman who had gotten his start working as a defense attorney for imprisoned Liberal and Communist fighters from Tolima in the 1950s—approached the War Ministry to propose "a commission of socio-economic study" for Marquetalia. Not only did the top general offer to facilitate the commission's travel to Marquetalia (and no less on the eve of what everyone guessed to be an impending military campaign), but the lower-ranking military *letrados* present also suggested the composition of the commission.[36] Colombia's most famous social scientists would get a crack at averting a massive application of violence.

Monsignor Guzmán, Orlando Fals Borda, Eduardo Umaña Luna, and Father Camilo Torres were thus thrust back into the public eye. Their assent to the nomination was a marked shift from their reclusion during the controversies of 1962. Yet the *letrados* felt little choice. The thought of a major military campaign was bad enough, but this one threatened to shatter whatever was left of a once and future *convivencia* in southern Tolima. Marquetalia additionally exemplified the social change that so occupied these reformist intellectuals. If such change were not able to express itself, their fear went, unpredictable revolution might ensue.

Guzmán and his colleagues therefore accepted the mantle of the new commission. Together with the commission's MRL members, they explained in a public communiqué their aspiration to "initiate a dialogue with the *campesinos* . . . learn their real situation and their needs . . . [and inform] the *campesinos* of the government's intentions in relation to the economic and social development of these communities." As befitted a group of *letrados,* they indicated that the effort would close with a written report.[37]

Though they did not yet realize the implications of their move, Guzmán and company had arrived at an intellectual and political crossroads. Their partnership with MRL politicians hinted that a leftward drift was under way, a political evolution already evident in the case of Torres. However, the commission's informal charter simultaneously evinced the *letrados'* continued faith in the state as an agent for change. The resolution of the tension between these two positions would ultimately entail a rejection of the *letrados'* embedded position within the state. In April 1964, that outcome was still around the next corner.

The *letrados* went into the turn hard and fast. While their work had always possessed a sense of urgency, their public lives up to this point had moved with the quickening flow of time. Now, time seemed to sweep against them. The *letrados* also reflected a general anxiety around them. In addition to the question of Marquetalia, concerns about the economy and doubts about Valencia's leadership further weighed down the national mood.

The denouement came for the *letrados* scarcely a week after the idea of the commission had first been floated. The initial signs had been auspicious enough, with the acting minister of war reluctantly giving the commission a green light. A foe familiar to Guzmán and Torres then threw up a fatal roadblock. Expressing "fear that the priests would be kidnapped," Bogotá's cardinal denied permission to travel to any priest not serving in the military. It was "senile reasoning lacking the merest justification," Guzmán would write four years after the fact, his retrospective anger speaking volumes about the effect that the prelate's refusal had on the *letrados.* Viewing the priests as indispensible for "the cause of peace and *convivencia,*" the commission's secular members called off the entire project.[38]

All that was left to do for the moment was to issue a final statement. The "spirit of dialogue" and search for knowledge had been restrained, but words still might sway a few attitudes and sooth the *letrados'* sense of duty. Fals, Umaña, and their last remaining MRL partner consequently

> put on the record our best intention to assist in the task of national reconstruction, of which Marquetalia was but one part . . . Of course, it is our hope that such problems will be resolved without painful trauma. May it be that there is no resumption to the holocaust of lives and goods that accompanies violence. Violence whose causes are not found . . . in factors like the propaganda of any ideology, but in the misery and neglect in which a great part of the Colombian population remains. Whatever type of action that is put forth to reincorporate these areas into the normal life of the country, far from being repressive, should flow from the elemental defense of Human Rights, giving preference to that plan which gets at the economic and social root of the phenomenon.[39]

Only in eulogizing the promise of the creole peace could Fals and Umaña seamlessly combine their voices in a way they never had in *La violencia en Colombia*'s two volumes. Denied the chance to return to the countryside at its hour of maximum need, alienated by the actions of the state in which they were still embedded, the *letrados* stretched toward uncharted forms of expression and analysis, which would reach culmination in the concept of "La Violencia."

As the door slammed shut on a reconstituted Peace Commission and the idea of violence which it embodied, an episode in Bogotá highlighted the alternative paradigm espoused by the administration. The last ill word uttered against Rehabilitación in the capital, it took the form of high political theater. The setting was a banquet thrown at Bogotá's most exclusive hotel by the nation's powerful rural lobby, to honor the armed forces for "the recuperation of the countryside from banditry." The room was charged with a gossipy nervousness, for over the prior weeks minister of war General Alberto Ruiz Novoa had become increasingly outspoken about what he saw as the country's need for structural change. Addressing the senior civil and military leaders now in attendance, the general hit on well-trodden topics from his public discourse. Peppering his speech with by-now familiar citations to Father Lebret's 1958 development study and, obliquely, *La violencia en Colombia* (onto which he cast aspersions), Ruiz expounded on the connection between violence and "social and economic injustices," namely the agrarian question. Resolution of these knotty issues necessitated a "national purpose," which, to his mind, self-serving civilian interest groups were incapable of providing.[40]

Conservative leaders had already cried foul at Ruiz's apparent campaign to present himself as a solution to Colombia's malaise. However, at the banquet Ruiz had the temerity to convey his message in front of President Valencia, who spent the evening seated two spots over from the minister of war. When he rose to speak after Ruiz, Valencia overcame his fame as a politician who had words but no thoughts, to deliver a devastating retort.[41] He led by repeating the Conservative charge of mid-1962: that Rehabilitación, while launched by the "patriotic" Alberto Lleras, had done nothing more than "finance atrocious criminals." Valencia then, by turns mocking and serious, picked apart Ruiz's points one by one. Central to his reasoning was a refutation of Ruiz's claim to scientific knowledge about violence. What Colombia had witnessed, Valencia stated matter-of-factly, was "a banditry that does not correspond to economic necessities, but to a criminal and reproachable instinct."[42] It was a bravura performance.

There remained no question after Valencia's speech that there could be zero redemption for those it labeled "bandits," that his government was committed to meet violence with violence. And as chance would have it, that same afternoon, after ten days reconnoitering Marquetalia, the army made its first contact with Tirofijo's men.[43]

THE BATTLE FOR MARQUETALIA, 1964

Marquetalia was an otherworldly realm. The high-altitude cold made the area seem as if it were in some other country. The journalist Vipradel, who would spend nearly a year covering the army in southern Tolima, also recorded sights that for him called to mind previous epochs of history. For one, there were the region's concentration of five hundred indigenous Nasa, who seemed to Vipradel to step right out of the era of the Conquest (he did not know that some of their Cauca kin had met President Lleras at ACPO's headquarters in 1959). There were vestiges too of even older worlds: despite being recently felled, the remnant of an ancient tree—taller still than two men, wide enough to perhaps land a helicopter on—still lorded over the "small plateau" where Marulanda had made his home (figure 14).[44] From that same vantage point in mid-June, during their first night in the heart of Marquetalia, soldiers would hear muffled explosions from this direction or from that slope of the next hill. It gradually dawned on them that the Communists had laid booby traps along the footpaths that snaked through these mountains, traps that were being set off instead by the fauna of this "millenarian forest."[45]

Having traversed this land for years, and having had long combat experience on top of that, the Communists were masters of Marquetalia's terrain (to a point; the army's helicopters cut down on the advantage). However, to ensure the survival of their movement, Marulanda and his comrades also had to reach out to the Colombia that lay beyond. Their proclamations over the course of 1964 reveal a crucial shift in the tactics of claims-making, from a position grounded in provincial understandings of rights and obligations to the language of violent revolution for which Marquetalia would be remembered. In much the same way that the collapse of the reborn Peace Commission moved the *letrados* in new intellectual

FIGURE 14. Ceremony marking the government occupation of Marquetalia, June 1964. Prado Delgado, *Sur del Tolima*, 124.

directions, the schism between Bogotá and Gran Tolima's Communists permitted, and in many ways demanded, updated biographical narratives and ideas of violence. It was only through the battle for Marquetalia that Marulanda's defensive, frontier violence could become linked to the global politics of revolutionary warfare.

Had a reconstituted Peace Commission entered Marquetalia, the urban reformers would have encountered, as later envoys did, the men who made this link possible. The prospect of Marquetalia's elimination moved the Communist Party leadership in Bogotá to dispatch to each of the three independent republics a pair of commissars, one from the party and one from the Colombian Communist Youth (Juventud Comunista Colombiana). Ties between the party and its rural brethren had never been particularly strong; even after the fall of the dictatorship allowed the party space to rebuild its networks, contacts remained tenuous, with a still-small party apparatus often having to pester the independent republics to keep up on their dues.[46] Nonetheless, discipline was what had attracted men like Pedro Antonio Marín/Tirofijo to the party, and it was discipline that now drew the party's praise. Party thinkers opined that the political orientation instilled by the party had allowed the independent republics to preserve the "symbols and promises of peace" that arose in 1957–58, and thus to avoid the descent into banditry that afflicted other rural areas. Government aggression against Marquetalia might herald the return of generalized conditions of violence, so the party saw it as incumbent to guide the independent republics through the coming crisis.[47]

The Communist Party's natural choice to send to Marquetalia was a seasoned cadre who operated under the pseudonym Jacobo Arenas. Arenas's life bore a striking resemblance to Martín Camargo's: both came out of a radical tradition within the northeastern Liberal stronghold of Santander, a politics that acquired national import during the Revolution on the March.[48] Furthermore, like Camargo, Arenas, a practiced union organizer, was "sent by the [Central Committee] to many spots where there were nuclei of armed fighters . . . that did not have a clear idea of what they should be doing." As a consequence, Arenas consistently appeared on the ground in key spots around Gran Tolima, including Villarrica during the army's 1955 offensive. Yet here the similarities ended, for Arenas's role in these missions never equaled Camargo's. Nor did Arenas's activities quite match up with his personal self-regard. The footage of him shot by the French filmmakers in 1965 shows every sort of preening, a mustachioed man given to rhetorical grandiosity and obsession with his appearance.[49]

In Marquetalia Arenas finally had his great stage, a forum to match his ambitions. Students, urban workers, and provincial folk from all parts of Colombia—in addition to like-minded people from around the world—had already rallied to the cause of the area's defense, spray-painting slogans on city walls and issuing denunciations of the Colombian state and its subservience to "Yankee imperialism."[50] To maximize this outpouring of solidarity, and to fulfill the party's mandate, Arenas and his Communist Youth companion typed out a declaration with their rural hosts. Not strictly an expression of violence-as-idea, the statement explained to the broader world the rationale behind Marquetalia's position. It was to become the public face of frontier Communism for decades to come.

Issued on Colombia's July 20 independence day, amidst ongoing combat around Marquetalia, the Guerrilla Fighters' Agrarian Program (Programa Agrario de los Guerrilleros) opened with an invocation of the past: "We are the spirit of a revolutionary movement building since 1948." In this vision of history, the National Front blended with its authoritarian predecessors by means of the "four wars" (1948, 1954, 1962, and 1964) which "they have unleashed against [Marquetalia]." The "oligarchy" had accordingly denied Marquetalia's inhabitants the options of "the pacific path, the path of the democratic mass struggle, the legal paths that the Colombian Constitution designates."

As a result, the program reasoned, "and as we are revolutionaries who by one means or another will play the historic role assigned to us . . . we had to search for another path: the path of armed revolution in the struggle for power." The program invited other progressive and left groups to join "a great revolutionary and patriotic struggle . . . for a democratic government of national liberation" that would have as its centerpiece "an effective Revolutionary Agrarian Reform that changes the core of the Colombian countryside's social structure." The seizure of both large and U.S.-owned landholdings, and the subsequent redistribution of free property to *campesinos,* would surpass "the Agrarian Reform of bourgeois lies" to attain "a Colombia for Colombians," free of the violence of class exploitation.[51]

In its own way, the Guerrilla Fighters' Agrarian Program achieved a synthesis of the intellectual currents of post-1962 national discourse: discussion of the need for structural change, focused on the countryside; and a conceptualization of a persistent or recurrent violence. Yet the provenance of the program's language and concerns bespeaks an underlying tension born of the fraught 1964 conjuncture. Though Jacobo Arenas's name appears nowhere in the program (it instead displays the signatures of Manuel Marulanda, his lieutenants, and, it claims, "more than a thousand *campesino*[s]"), he exercised an unmistakable influence on its creation. The blame placed on the government for propelling Marquetalia toward the armed path certainly fit with the worldview and experience of the frontier Communists themselves, but the program's particular framing closely echoes earlier Communist Party Central Committee assessments.[52] The program's pronounced emphasis on imperialism and its call for an all-encompassing, national agrarian reform further reflect a layering of ideas conveyed from the city by the party's urban cadres.[53]

Arenas's imprint on the program comes into focus when considered alongside lesser-known communiqués that filtered out of Marquetalia in the months before and after May 1964. A week prior to their first skirmish with the army, Marulanda and more than three hundred other "settlers and *campesinos* of Marquetalia" turned to custom for one final attempt to forestall the invasion. In a typed four-and-half-page letter—their longest-ever petition to Bogotá—Marquetalia's inhabitants presented President Valencia with a full accounting of their grievances. With painstaking detail, they itemized the unfairness of market relations on the frontier, where the absence of quality roads put their investments at risk and forced up the price of imported goods. They outlined as well each outrage, each stolen chicken and act of human violence, suffered at the hands of their local rivals and the army since the January 1960 assassination of Charro Negro.[54] They thus gave a resentful twist to a rural tradition of claims-making grounded in tropes of regional productivity.

The letter additionally employed a second device common to provincial petitions, one that showed Marulanda and his comrades to be legalists to the last. "The government and the armed forces [are] outside of the law," the letter explained, for they were in violation of Article 16 of the constitution, which pledged protection to citizens' lives and goods. The letter wryly noted that the "special treatment to which we are to be subjected" did not live up to the government's obligation under Article 16. Having adopted a jeering tone toward President Valencia's intelligence since the start, the letter's authors put their charge in terms they thought he might better understand. When the constitution is violated, the letter continued, "it is up to the people to restore [it] and overthrow the government . . . as the honorable President will recall from his own experience in May 1957, when at the initiative of the grand capitalists and landlords . . . the military dictatorship [was] over-thrown."[55] Even as the order of the previous seven years was being unmade in southern Tolima, and other notions of political struggle were entering the picture, Colombians grasped for fragments of the Second Republic's initial promise.

Arenas's departure for Gran Tolima unspooled a line meant to tether the provinces to the metropolis. What followed was far from an imposition. A shared lexicon aided the Marquetalia Communists' acceptance of Arenas's message; when they wrote in the classic veins of the frontier, as they did in that final screed to Valencia, Marulanda and company already spoke of "oligarchs." Transmission also ran the other way, with rural ideals working their way into Arenas's proclamations, as occurred with the agrarian program's references to the abolition of existing debts and the expansion of state-provisioned credit in the countryside. Yet this encounter between urban and rural Colombia yielded a fluid layering, rather than an easy fusion, of ideas and priorities. At a time when the Marquetalia movement's stature was on the rise, its outward-facing image would be degrees removed from the inner workings of its *campesino* base.[56]

Could Arenas's thread also bind Marquetalia more closely to the other independent republics, and indeed to the country as a whole? The agrarian program of July 1964 aimed at a national universalism of this sort, a transcendence of the specific contexts of the Tolima frontier. This political aspiration would soon meld with military imperative. Communist Party instructions handed down during the dark days of 1947 had encouraged villages to form *autodefensas* (self-defense forces) that could fend off Conservative aggressions. When, in 1957, "it was thought that arms were unnecessary . . . [and] words sufficed," Marquetalia's Communists had demobilized their *autodefensa*. "The most painful [blow]"—Charro Negro's murder—prompted them to reactivate a small self-defense unit under Tirofijo's command in 1960.[57] However, over the second half of 1964, as Marquetalia's larger complement of men-at-arms dwindled against unrelenting pressure from an army fresh off its victories against bandits in the north, and as the region asphyxiated from an economic blockade, it became clear that the defense of Marquetalia was unsustainable (figure 15).[58] Already pushed onto the armed path, the movement would have to march its way clear of destruction.

The fertile, distant Andean slopes that became Marquetalia had first been a refuge for an entire community—men, women, and children—fleeing war with the government, the Conservatives, and the *limpios*. Tirofijo's decision to gather forty-odd of the region's remaining fighters to strike out for other territories therefore amounted to the adoption of displacement as a profession by a small core of the movement. Long before the Cuban revolution, the party had a theory for this

FIGURE 15. Army troops with residents of Marquetalia, 1964. Prado Delgado, *Sur del Tolima*, 110.

progression, what thinkers termed the transition from self-defense to the *guerrilla,* a higher stage of struggle involving mobile formations. A few Communists from other corners of Tolima—the great coffee town of Chaparral, the frontiers of the Sumapaz—sent word that they would join their Marquetalia comrades in the attempt.[59] The sinews between previously dispersed Communist pockets began to draw tighter.

And yet Marquetalia would come to overshadow all the others. It is easy to lose sight of this fact today, thirty-odd years after Tirofijo and Arenas stepped out of the forest and back into the direct sight of urban Colombia. In 1964, however, Marquetalia was one of three nodes of a regional diaspora with a shared history. To be certain, it already stood as the most famous and—in the eyes of some—most menacing of the group. There was still no guarantee that its leaders would direct the future, that Marquetalia would one day be celebrated as "a place that marks a beginning."[60] The possibilities for *convivencia* on the frontier had to be foreclosed upon first.

OTHER REPUBLICS, 1964–1965

The months leading up to the invasion of Marquetalia introduced a frightening imperative to those seeking to preserve *convivencia* at El Pato and Riochiquito. The strain took a heavy toll on Martín Camargo; an *El Tiempo* reporter who met him in Neiva weeks prior to the invasion found him with a "grave face and . . . wary look."[61] The "self-rehabilitation" of El Pato had taken a dramatic turn for the worse in February, when a Communist commander blocked two Agrarian Bank inspectors from interviewing colonists indebted to the institution. The possibility of expanded credit, and the favorable renegotiation of terms for those with outstanding Rehabilitación-era loans, melted away. What was more, the El Pato *autodefensa* opted to clamp down on any whiff of outside interference. While the Pato fighters kicked the teachers and agronomists invited by Camargo out of the zone, urban Communists expelled Camargo from the party for his collaboration with the government. Most dramatically, the *autodefensa* started to confiscate settlers' property, obliging them to leave El Pato as well. In May, as the army marched into the valleys of Marquetalia, fifteen families had made their way from El Pato to Neiva. A human tide emptied out of El Pato over the following months, as the number of displaced families climbed to 72, then to 136, and finally, by the end of 1964, 164—nearly 850 people. Fewer than half that number remained.[62] What had commenced as a split in the leadership over the direction of El Pato had transformed into a profound social crisis. The area of El Pato itself seemed to be unraveling alongside the gains of peace.

It was altogether too much for Camargo. His letters to Bogotá, beforehand very much focused on development, underwent what he termed "a total change." "I preferred following the path of the . . . National Front, which is the policy of citizen understanding without discrimination [to party]," he explained. But he now felt that the events of February 1964 had revealed that stance to be misguided. The situation at El Pato instead demanded the entrance of the army. Camargo dismissed disgustedly any other option for handling Gran Tolima's Communists, asking Jorge Villamil to pass along word to Monsignor Guzmán and Father Camilo that their efforts to visit Marquetalia were pointless.[63]

The sudden appearance of a Pato *desplazado* diaspora around Camargo (figure 13) did finally grant him political traction in Neiva. The influx of so many hundreds of destitute settlers could hardly have come at a worse time for Huila officials. Expenditures to secure the creole peace and to combat banditry over the past half-decade had left the department with an enormous budget deficit that meant it could, among other consequences, cover only two-thirds of Huila's teacher salaries at a time when peace should have allowed more schools to operate. Unable to divert funds to assist the Pato *desplazados*, in February 1965 the governor convened officials from Communal Action and the military, along with Camargo's representative and other displaced presidents of El Pato's Community Action Councils, to petition Bogotá for assistance with the displacement crisis. Camargo's arguments in favor of a prompt military incursion against El Pato, before the March rains began, also gained more of a hearing among Liberal circles in Neiva and Bogotá.[64]

It was ultimately the defense of El Pato's displaced that made the definitive case for military action, and military action that made for El Pato's final undoing. Word that Pato's Richard had died in an explosives accident while preparing to join the defense of Marquetalia helped to give officials the confidence to encourage settlers to return to the region. However, the twenty-eight who did make the journey back into the valley to harvest their crops found themselves staring down the Communists' gun barrels. Stripped of their belongings, and displaced once more, the settlers returned to Neiva carrying the Communists' demand that army posts be withdrawn from El Pato's borders. With this, army commanders decided that the gentle line had failed. It was instead time "to break up the militant hard-core Communist bands in these areas so that military civic actions programs can be instituted." [65]

The army's mid-March 1965 occupation of El Pato precipitated one of the most arduous and today little remembered strands of the state's confrontation with Gran Tolima's Communists. The army missed Martín Camargo's recommended window of time, leaving both targeted Communists and fleeing settlers to trudge through downpours that lasted upwards of a week. Intense though Tirofijo's famed combat in the valleys of Marquetalia was, conditions at El Pato shattered those trying to leave it: three months into its pursuit of the Pato *autodefensa*, the army came across a trio of fighters who had starved to death out in the jungle. Civilians fared little better. Hundreds of additional families left El Pato as the army arrived, in what became known as the Black March, or the March of Death. By one account, two hundred people succumbed to hunger and exposure on the trek to Neiva and other Huila towns. [66] When the army announced at the end of 1965 that "peace has returned to El Pato," it was a peace empty of nearly all human content. [67] Martín Camargo had never taken this eventuality into consideration. His idea of violence, based on personal experience and personal grudge, centered on the Communist heads of the independent republics. In his haste to return himself to what seemed his natural leadership, he overlooked the capacity of the state's armed forces to enact violence on a quantitatively greater scale.

As people departed El Pato, others drew to Riochiquito. Though they varied in their political allegiances, contacts came from Bogotá in hopes of bridging between the national and the local, and thus keeping the state's confrontation with Marquetalia from becoming a full-fledged regional affair that enveloped Riochiquito. That encounter between urban *letrados* and their Communist counterparts which never transpired at Marquetalia thus materialized instead in Riochiquito. And, initially, it was no Cold War clash, no collision of Communists and the state. Entrusted by President Valencia to follow up on Ciro Castaño's overtures, in March 1964 Colonel Álvaro Valencia Tovar helicoptered from Neiva into the forested vastness of Tierradentro, where he found himself face to face with Riochiquito's newly arrived Communist Party cadre. The mood was more festive than anything else, with Ciro's sister breaking out a bottle of cane brandy for a "toast to peace and to understanding between the Army and the people of Riochiquito." Standing side by side, this first gathering—the cadre from the Caribbean coast; the Bogotá-born counterinsurgent and his army colleagues; Ciro's sister, who had come to Cauca as a *desplazada;* and onlookers from Tierradentro's indigenous Nasa community— suggested something of how the possibility of peace could bring together the nation's disparate regions.[68]

Yet such a political project ran enormous risks for Ciro Castaño himself. Alongside the effort to articulate the linkage between Riochiquito and Bogotá, there existed the pull of a substitute regional venture that might overthrow Riochiquito's relative tranquility. Word got to the Communist Party's metropolitan bureaucrats that Ciro found nothing "more terrifying ... than the possible migration of the comrades from Marquetalia, because Riochiquito was at peace and [he] did not wish for that territory to be disturbed by war."[69] Against this fear, Ciro had to weigh party discipline, a consideration reinforced by the presence of the party cadre and likely by tales of Martín Camargo's estrangement. Nor could Ciro tear himself away entirely from his personal bonds with Marulanda and his men. His loyalties were impossibly divided.

A multi-sided game accordingly ensued, with no individual or group fully aware of what the others knew. Ciro thought he had the better of Valencia Tovar, pitching proposals for collaboration that, at a minimum, might win material benefits for his people. Alternatively, the fighters of southern Tolima hoped, Ciro's entrees with Valencia Tovar would allow the Communists to capture the colonel and thus gain a bargaining chip to relieve Marquetalia. However, what neither group of Communists grasped was that the army quickly gained full knowledge of the plot, intelligence that allowed Valencia Tovar to push on in his collaboration with Ciro.[70]

But in turn, Valencia Tovar never learned that Ciro allowed his territory to serve as a rearguard for the combatants from across the Tolima border. In September 1964, just after Ciro concluded a school construction contract with the army, Tirofijo, Arenas, and others realized in Riochiquito what they called the First Guerrilla Conference of the Southern Bloc (Primera Conferencia Guerrillera del Bloque Sur)—a formalization of regional adherence to July's agrarian program and a new plan to spread their practice of violence to frontier regions throughout southern Colombia. It would be months more before the Southern Bloc's strategy became known. In the interim, the early months of 1965 filled with ideas of violence from Tierradentro's *desplazados,* who tried desperately to convince the government that Ciro's men were one and the same as Tirofijo's. However, work as they might, government intelligence agents on Tirofijo's trail could find no such proof. Government policy primarily followed the lead of its insurgency expert; putting the kidnapping scheme aside, Valencia Tovar remained committed to maintaining the national-local linkage with Ciro.[71]

It took a rather accidental act of violence to bring an apparent clarity to the situation in eastern Cauca and western Huila. Marulanda/Tirofijo framed the original operation in spatial terms as well, calling it "the return to the world"—a message to urban Colombia that he had survived ten months of warfare laying ambushes and avoiding counterambushes out on Tolima's farthest frontier. With support from Ciro, who provisioned reconnaissance and dozens of indigenous porters, Marulanda and five dozen fighters struck out from Riochiquito in mid-March 1965 to seize the town of Inzá, a long day's march distant (map 3). To shave time off the final approach, the Communists tried to commandeer the regular early-morning, intercounty bus on its way toward the town center. However, they did not count on the presence of several policemen on board. When the smoke of the resulting gun battle cleared, sixteen people on the bus, including two nuns, lay dead.[72] In an instant, local, regional, national, and even international scales collapsed in on one another.

Tirofijo's gambit to call attention to Marquetalia by widening the conflict reverberated beyond his vision of the regional. State development projects and everyday life came to an immediate stop throughout eastern Cauca; a Peace Corps volunteer living a three-hour drive to the west of Inzá stated that "in our village, when the dimensions of what had happened [became apparent], everybody was terrified."[73] Policymakers in Bogotá fixated on the kinds of violence practiced, seeing a Cuban hand at work. "There were three [public officials] shot. That already indicates who inspired the assault," President Valencia told a group of journalists with whom he happened to be meeting when the minister of war telephoned with the news. Inzá residents distinguished what seemed to be additional proof of Cuban involvement, observations that they shared with the metropolitan press. For these people from the last corner of Gran Tolima, the Caribbean accent of the Communist Youth's cadre betrayed not a fellow countryman, but an extranational threat.[74] Amidst all of this scalar switching between the local, regional, national, and international, one issue now appeared resolved: the regional critics had been right all along about Riochiquito and Marquetalia.[75]

Some of those critics, and new local partners, took the initiative following Inzá. Cauca and Huila politicians' competing ideas of violence regarding Riochiquito acquired greater import as they intersected with and exacerbated frictions within Tierradentro. Tensions had been on the rise there ever since the calamitous massacres of the early 1950s; for locals displaced to the area's peripheries, Ciro's resulting presence meant that the wounds of the past could never be closed. After entering Tierradentro in early 1961, the magistrates of the Conciliation and Equity Tribunal emerged with a palpable sense of this strain. These lawyers could tally the *desplazados,* hear their stories, but no more—even had the independent republic of Riochiquito seemed within reach, the magistrates held no jurisdiction over the once-communal indigenous lands that lay there. It was a moment of profound disquiet for these legal *letrados,* who embodied the state and at the same time its limits. "Something must be done," the magistrates wrote to Bogotá, as if dreaming of some higher power to come in and fix what they could not. "Because who can guarantee that Riochiquito's *desplazados,* who today wander about almost without faith or hope in justice, will not tomorrow come together to move toward the reconquest of their lands?" Such "a bloody second act," the tribunal admonished, "would be fatal to the peace that Cauca has recovered with so many sacrifices, and that Colombia needs so urgently to consolidate."[76]

For one local, Miguel Valencia, the previous decade had brought sacrifices but no inner peace. The way to a desired future entailed additional violence. He was among the *desplazados* counted by the tribunal's magistrates, one of the dozens of members of his extended family to have been forced in 1954 from the indigenous reservation that would comprise the upper section of the independent republic. Miguel Valencia's hatred of Ciro thereafter ran deep—separation from his people's lands also meant the depletion of the political and social authority he had enjoyed as a leader of his community.[77] But as the national state came closer to Riochiquito, and Cauca officials ramped up their denunciations, Valencia gained a means to reassert that lost clout. Guided by their conviction that Riochiquito represented an intolerable threat, in 1964 Cauca officials tendered Miguel Valencia's *desplazado* comrades shotguns for their collective defense. The nearby army post—newly reestablished in Belalcázar's southern tip, as part of the government's encirclement of Riochiquito—thought it appropriate to contribute the requisite shells. So armed, Riochiquito's *desplazados* presented themselves as an *autodefensa*—a not accidental borrowing from the Communist nomenclature and practice of a people at arms.[78] Miguel Valencia proved a bane to Ciro, as well as a headache for regional and national officials, both during the final stage of Riochiquito's contested peace and after.

Whether through good planning or dumb luck, Miguel Valencia's first strike against Ciro went far in equaling the score of personal pain. Weeks after the Inzá raid, four dozen men under Valencia laid an ambush along Riochiquito's lifeline, the road that ran along serrated ridgelines east to Pacarní. The government-issued shotguns helped make the affair a messy one, but that was the *autodefensa*'s intent. Caught unawares, their market-bound mule-train blasted at close quarters, fourteen of Ciro's followers perished—including two of his teenage sons. Ciro personally came down through the mountains to bring the mutilated bodies back home.[79]

Reactions to the massacre captured the full gamut of ideas about violence along the border. Huila bureaucrats, with their favorable inclination toward Riochiquito, immediately denounced the attackers as "bandits."[80] The Communists took a bifurcated stance, each half reflecting the divergent approaches of urban and rural Communists. Even as Riochiquito's mimeograph machines pumped out flysheets denouncing military commanders as the *autodefensa*'s "pimps," Ciro made sure that local authorities were notified of the assault. He also looked to the national, writing once more to Álvaro Valencia Tovar. The colonel then made what would turn out to be his final flight to Ciro's independent republic.[81]

The backdrop of Riochiquito's looming confrontation with the outside made the military man's gesture all the more meaningful. Ciro had always admired Valencia Tovar's courage, but under the circumstances, the colonel's manly fortitude was something to behold.[82] As the two ambulated through Riochiquito's tiny urban core, noting the recently completed school and stopping for people to shake their visitor's hand, Valencia Tovar made his personal pitch for Riochiquito to be spared. "For me this is not just deep-felt sorrow, but also the loss of an opportunity to make peace," Valencia Tovar explained. The army, he reiterated to Ciro, "couldn't give a damn about" Ciro's Communist affiliation. What mattered instead was for Ciro to keep his independence before his party, to remember that he was "not the leader of a combat force [but of a whole zone]."[83] Through this personal appeal, the representative of Colombia's political core shrugged off the international and its obsession with ideological conflict, to focus on the local while keeping the greater region at bay.

Momentum toward confrontation, building from all scales, had nonetheless become unstoppable, notwithstanding a handful of additional, last-ditch attempts in the months that followed Valencia Tovar's trip.[84] In early September, accompanied by a small cohort of Colombian Communist Party contacts, the two French filmmakers headed into Riochiquito along the road from Pacarní.[85] Their cameras would record the aerial bombardment that followed less than a week later; the little collection of homes and shops where Valencia Tovar had previously landed soon filled with waves of troops ferried in by helicopter. The timing was no coincidence. Having refined its practice of violence since the battle for Marquetalia, the army commenced the assault ahead of the harvest, to deny Ciro and Tirofijo the means to prolong any defense. But the creole Communists had already tucked themselves higher in the mountains, and with the bombardment they began the vertical trek out of Riochiquito, with families, pack horses, and cattle in tow.[86] In order to cancel out the government's rolling military advantage, the Communists would need to hatch fresh ideas and practices of violence, and in the process redefine their relationship to space and scale.

The fall of Riochiquito allowed other Colombians to promote their own conceptions of region and nation. From just outside Riochiquito's borders, Tierradentro's Liberal and Conservative leaders telegraphed to the presidential palace that "in these moments the citizenry, irrespective of race, religion, or politics, feels deeply excited before so desired a goal. [The] Armed Forces' occupation [of] Riochiquito signifies a step forward not only for us, but for the entire country."[87] The same local notables who had criticized the state for not expelling Ciro, and who had before that taken the Lleras government to task for failing in its obligations under rehabilitation, finally found reason to cheer.

For officials in Bogotá, the occupation of Riochiquito completed the first phase of a project to reunify Colombia. The mission to capture Marquetalia had been given the name "Operation Sovereignty," and with the fall of the last great independent Communist republic in September 1965, the state could be said to assert its rightful authority over previously unconnected sections of national territory. Nonetheless, a profound issue of governance remained, for the Valencia government had not so much recaptured lost zones as it had inserted the state into peripheries where formal institutions had rarely been seen. In order for its claim on the national to endure, the state would need to ensure its presence in the regions. Counterinsurgency theorists termed this process "consolidation," but the imperative was broader, one wrapped up in the same politics of expectation that marked community development and Rehabilitación.[88] Therefore, the state's successes and failures after the end of formal campaigning determined the shape of *convivencia* as political compromise and developmentalist goal.

REGION, NATION, AND THE BIRTH OF THE FARC, 1965–1966

The cultural manifestations of the creole peace blossomed anew as the "second violence" came to a conclusion. As national homicide levels remained at the lowest levels of the National Front (figure 12), communities across Gran Tolima convoked "pro-peace festivals" to celebrate the triumph over banditry and to mobilize funds for civic betterment.[89] Yet the invocation of regional pride and desires for peace could also transpire in unexpected places. During those tense middle months of 1965, between the ill-fated raid on Inzá and the army's arrival in Riochiquito, men and women from both Ciro's and Marulanda's ranks joined in a celebration of peace. Replete with a beauty pageant, the night gathered funds for the common defense.[90] On still another level, it also served as a lived prayer to ward off violence, a play to reconnect with a recent past of peace that appeared ever more distant.

The progenitor of Gran Tolima's celebratory folkloric jubilees found himself pondering the meanings of peace as the fight against the independent republics entered its final stage. Since his humble musical debut in his father's home not quite a decade earlier, Jorge Villamil had become a sensation, fame broadening his world from the capitals of Gran Tolima all the way to Europe. By late 1965 he was back in Bogotá, and able to take stock of news from back home. Displacement once more served as the theme, though now the directionality ran in reverse. From one of his sisters, who represented the family within Huila's planter class, as well as from the Pato *desplazados* themselves, Villamil learned of the travails of the hundreds of displaced settlers who were creating a stir in Neiva.[91] Having grown up among such frontier folk, served them as a doctor under Rehabilitación, and very nearly assisted them alongside Martín Camargo, Villamil could not help but be moved. This fresh wave of José Dolores would have to find their way home.

The problem, Villamil surmised, was that El Pato could not exist without settlers, and those settlers could not return without more effective action from the state. The trail back to the Pato River might still have been open six months after the army's invasion, but the *desplazados* were in no condition to make the journey. Villamil explained to the Interior Ministry that even though they had lost everything in their exodus, the Agrarian Bank refused to extend them credit, for so many had never repaid the bank for loans made under Rehabilitación. Nor had the Institute of Agrarian Reform or other state lending agencies committed to the reconstruction of El Pato. Two and a half years after Villamil had ridden into the valley with Martín Camargo, and even with Communist fighters routed from the area, government institutions refused to resume their engagement with the community.

Were the indebted Pato settlers among those provincial Colombians who skipped their loan payments out of a belief that the money stood in for reparations owed them by the state? If so, Villamil made no mention of it in his letter to the government. Instead, the grievance he described belonged more to the present than the past. "The colonists find themselves very disheartened by what they consider the State's INDIFFERENCE," Villamil warned. The Communists responsible for much of the violence and displacement experienced at El Pato had largely been pushed out, but the valley lacked the basic material requisites of *convivencia*. Villamil therefore put forward a short list of measures—small loans to each displaced family, El Pato's definitive jurisdictional transfer from Caquetá to Huila—that would put the zone back on the way to progress. Such enlightened steps, Villamil hoped, would establish "a solution not solely for the human dimension, but as a precedent suited for any regions threatened with attack by the Reds." [92] The suggestion was a political complement to Villamil's musical career, a means to consolidate a regional project while also contributing to the nation as a whole.

Yet Villamil's vision of regional action was already a dead letter. However vaunted as a model for the Americas, the Colombian military's developmentalist turn could not substitute for civilian authorities' neglect of the frontier. The army's development plan for El Pato received authorization but no funding from the Valencia administration; and the dearth of roads and other infrastructure to entice colonists meant that the military "arrived at a dead spot in the reestablishment of public order," no matter its success in "[taking] away the bandits' dominion of the zone." [93] Moreover, though the government had initially handled the independent republics in sequence, by late 1965 Marquetalia consumed attentions and budgets. When the Interior Ministry, perhaps acting on Villamil's encouragement, proposed a new military command that would straddle Huila and Caquetá, the War Ministry rejected the notion as unfeasible. The military, top generals admitted, was "not in [a] condition" to engage El Pato "until it finalized Public Order operations under way against ... Tirofijo ... and Ciro Castaño."[94] Officials in Bogotá similarly rejected the governor's proposal for a "recuperation fund" for Huila as financially impossible.[95] Absent the government support cultivated by Martín Camargo or urged by Jorge Villamil, and with the military heading the state's partial presence, El Pato would remain largely uninhabited for more than ten years.[96] Denied access to the national, this locality could not reincorporate itself.

Displacement would also influence local developments in Riochiquito and, along with them, regional and national scales. To be certain, most of Tierradentro's population remained in place in spite of the violence of the invasion. Valencia Tovar's last visit had not been entirely fruitless. His appearance in Riochiquito, and the decision of departmental authorities to investigate the Pacarní massacre, convinced Ciro to refrain from retaliating against Miguel Valencia's *autodefensa* and generating more displacement. More significantly, Riochiquito's inhabitants did not elect to abandon the region en masse at any point in the long lead-up to confrontation. Valencia Tovar took solace in this, ranking the prevention of an "exodus [of] biblical proportions" as the greatest achievement of his negotiations with Riochiquito.[97] If peace could not be preserved, the effects of violence-as-practice could at least be bounded.

Civil and military authorities started the consolidation of Tierradentro with vigor. Armed conflict brought greater urgency to Gregorio Hernández de Alba's established interest in seeking the "incorporation and development" of Riochiquito's five thousand indigenous inhabitants. To sever whatever link existed between creole Communists and locals, the army rapidly coordinated an intensive visit by developmental agencies national and transnational, to show the Nasa "a sign of sympathy and bring them closer to the State's programs."[98] The visit was to be the first phase in a massive outlay of state resources, coordinated by a special military command that could transcend the usual jurisdictional limits of the Cauca-Huila borderlands (the model behind the later proposal for El Pato). Authorized by President Valencia on the recommendation of consolidation's lead architect, Valencia Tovar, the Tierradentro command extended Plan Lazo's revision of administrative geography into Gran Tolima.[99] In exchange, the existing state indigenist project imparted to the military's strategy an even more pronounced developmentalist flavor.

Violence-as-idea would nonetheless manage to supplant vital elements of Riochiquito's postinvasion story in written accounts of Colombian history. The army's arrival marked an inflection point in history-making: when Tirofijo's and Ciro's fighters hiked up and out of Riochiquito, shedding the pack animals and then the people who could not keep up with the terrain, they did not so much step out of history as transport history with them. Much of our knowledge of Colombia after September 1965 comes precisely from these men, who accentuated the legend of Marquetalia by portraying a small band of Communists from southern Tolima as far more suited to the rigors of guerrilla warfare than their comrades from

Riochiquito.[100] This literal and figurative separation from the bulk of the population has left out of history those not at arms. In so doing, it has also privileged narratives of violence in retellings of Colombia's past.

What of those other *desplazados* from Riochiquito? Their fate reveals an ongoing influence for ideas about violence. In late 1966, a year after the Communists' ouster, regional politicians and military officers struggled to reassemble the pieces of a border zone which had never been orderly. A heated point of debate was the status of nearly 350 *desplazados* who had either been forced out by the army's operations or rounded up over assumed ties to the Communists, and whom the army still held at a camp not far from where Miguel Valencia's *autodefensa* had ambushed Ciro's kin. Huila's government had already resolved the status of hundreds more displaced Tierradentro residents, accepting them back to its territory.[101] Cauca officials, by contrast, stood firm in their opinion that Riochiquito demanded a hardline approach. Cauca's governor made every possible argument that the *desplazados* should not be allowed to return, for instance claiming that Riochiquito's displaced "had suffered brain-washing, [that they] were infected with the Marxist thesis of the Moscow or Peking line, and as such . . . cannot be left alone because they have been indoctrinated by Communist cells." The antipathy of Cauca's *país político* toward Huila's was likewise undiminished: one of the Cauca governor's subordinates berated an army major for deigning to suggest that all of Tierradentro's police posts pass to Neiva's control in order to ensure cross-border coordination and thus speed along resolution of the *desplazado* issue.[102] The density of state institutions at Tierradentro theoretically gave officials more capability to address displacement than had ever occurred during the early creole peace. Despite this, uneven political will, grounded at its core in violence-as-idea, limited the state's effective reach into Gran Tolima's southwestern borderlands.

Violence-as-idea also structured remembrance of the creole peace within the government. While Cauca's delegation debated the *desplazados'* future, a senior departmental administrator produced the incriminating documents that regional politicians had pursued for years: evidence of Tirofijo, Ciro, and Charro Negro's conviction by a 1957 military court-martial, and records of the Lleras-era clemency boards that upheld the decision.[103] However, absent from this presentation was any reference to the 1959 decision of Huila's Conservative governor, Felio Andrade Manrique, to suspend the sentences as part of the creole peace. Though the oversight likely resulted from the disjunction of national and regional archives, it reflected other logics as well. Adhesion to widespread conceptions about "banditry"—ideas which gathered additional force thanks to talk around the "second violence"—blurred what had come between 1957 and 1966. Their vehement sentiments against Riochiquito—a mixture of talk of banditry, assumptions about Tierrandentro's ethnic otherness, and anxiety about a wayward border zone—made Cauca politicians more likely to forget the creole peace.

The row over Riochiquito's *desplazados* signaled how Gran Tolima, and Colombia as a whole, had reached the end of the process of experimentation with democracy and reform begun in 1957. The breakdown of coalition rule's high politics had commenced with the 1960 and 1962 elections, a trend now confirmed in 1966. With no legal or financial solutions forthcoming from capitals caught up in the latest election season, and already lacking any statutory authority to keep the 350 *desplazados* in detention, the local brigade was forced to release them for financial reasons, just days after its commanders conferenced with Cauca's governor on their fate.[104] In spite of the previous year's massive outlay of resources to Tierradentro, officials had exhausted their options. At the same time, developmental priorities were shifting. Opting to abandon Gregorio Hernández de Alba's program of reconstituting indigenous reservations, the Institute of Agrarian Reform eventually ordered an end to legal protections for communal landholdings. The move diminished the prerogatives of Tierradentro's indigenous councils, which, for a brief moment in 1966, had been entrusted to resolve the land disputes underlying the zone's displacement crisis.[105] Colombia's transition would thus close with the central state assuming greater authority over local and regional affairs.

However, Colombia's transition had always been about more than formal democratic politics or policy choices. The human relationships that grew out of urban and rural Colombians' encounters had been equally integral, and it was these that determined how the transition would be represented. For the country's most famous *letrados,* the consequences of violence-as-practice broke the link that had bound them and their young social science disciplines to the state. When confrontation between Bogotá and Gran Tolima's creole Communists arrived, in spite of the *letrados'* best efforts, years' worth of ties between city and countryside, constructed in the quest to understand violence, yielded a common if differentiated disillusionment. Both urban men of letters and rural Communists were forced to modify their conceptions of violence, and the latter their practice. The campaign against the independent republics was thus a decisive moment in national understanding of violence.

The memories of that process of disenchantment would crystallize in subsequent years into a pair of reinforcing narratives which would alter the meaning of the creole peace as well as raise the prominence of violence-as-idea in Colombia's public consciousness. For the *letrados,* above all those sociologists from the National University, Colombia's national experience came to be described in an apparently simple term: "La Violencia."

For those Communists who survived the confrontations of 1964–65, the moment had arrived to merge violence-as-practice and violence-as-idea as never before, to elevate on a political and spatial plane their conflict with a state that had refused to treat them on equitable terms. As they exited the last of the independent republics, Marulanda/Tirofijo and Jacobo Arenas came to the realization that their existing vision of violence would not be sufficient for the struggle ahead. Following the plan laid down with the creation of the Southern Bloc, the combined ranks of Marquetalia and Riochiquito—several hundred people in total—divided into seven detachments in order to survive and spread the Marquetalia model of the mobile guerrilla—not simply a force that engaged in hit-and-run tactics on a day-to-day basis, but one that could operate on a grand spatial scale. The army nevertheless made those first months "very difficult," Jaime Guaraca later recalled; while the Communists' approach to warfare was evolving, the army's matured farther and faster. If the increasingly far-flung frontier Communists were to hang on, violence-as-practice would need to be better coordinated, violence-as-idea scaled up to match mobility's larger new ambit and to project an image of strength.[106]

This latter task of building a political and ideological superstructure placed Arenas back in the spotlight. As the Southern Bloc's roving groupings made plans to reassemble for a second conference, Arenas and a handful of other provincial representatives snuck across the Magdalena Valley to a party safe haven then hosting the Tenth Communist Party Congress. Arenas made the most of the encounter with his urban brethren, successfully challenging them to prepare a doctrine supportive of armed rural struggle, even as the party line concentrated on peaceable political organizing.[107] Lettered legitimation in hand, a triumphal Arenas gradually continued on across the eastern Andes, down to where Southern Bloc delegates were assembling in the piedmont north of El Pato—just a short ways from where he would die a full quarter-century later, an old man still in the fight.

The Second Guerrilla Conference of the Southern Bloc resolved one set of internal tensions within the combined ranks of Gran Tolima's frontier Communists. Though Ciro would be elected second-in-command behind Tirofijo, the Marquetalia guerrilla had definitively eclipsed the Communist force from Riochiquito. By the end of their three weeks together in April and May 1966, conference attendees had reorganized the Southern Bloc's disparate forces under internal statutes aimed at guaranteeing a capacity for constant mobility. This emphasis on a particular style of violence-as-practice confirmed what the flight from Riochiquito had already accomplished, once combat and hardship whittled down an itinerant population of hundreds, leaving a set of eighty or a hundred fighters that had Marquetalia veterans at their core.[108]

However, another internal contradiction manifested itself anew among the Marquetalia survivors themselves. The second conference's most visible accomplishment was the adoption of a new public face for the movement: this loose alliance of combatants would now call itself the Revolutionary Armed Forces of Colombia, or FARC. With this, the supraregional aspirations of the Southern Bloc became national, even international. These scales also found their way into the gathering's closing statement. Deeply influenced by the latest news of goings-on abroad that he learned at the Tenth Party Congress, Arenas dedicated the conference's official declaration almost entirely to denunciations of U.S. imperialism around the globe, from the Dominican Republic to Vietnam. Unlike the agrarian program of nearly two years prior, there was no mention of land. The FARC's end goal was "popular insurrection and the seizure of power for the people." [109]

To erase the discrepancy between the FARC's internal governance and its outward image, those present at the founding needed to imagine the FARC as a novel innovation. The Second Guerrilla Conference of the Southern Bloc therefore had to be portrayed as a rupture with the past. "The history of the southern Tolima guerrilla in the 1950s is another story, which has nothing to do with the history of the FARC," Arenas repeatedly insisted to an interviewer two decades afterward. [110] Guaraca claimed that the conference marked "the first time a guerrilla movement in Colombia arose with precise political documents and with rules to regulate the internal life of the combatant." [111] The contention elided a well-established tradition of legal and political invention by armed groups on the frontier, epitomized by the Liberal resistance's famous 1952–53 Laws of the Plains and the organic statutes of Marquetalia's arch-rivals, the National Liberal Revolutionary Movement of Southern Tolima.

Yet in a subordination of memory to politics, Guaraca also played down pieces of the Communists' own experience. The second conference's decision to eschew formal ranks reproduced the choice the frontier Communists had taken in a very different moment at the end of 1957, when the possibilities of peace led them to demobilize the *autodefensas* and put all combatants on equal status. Indeed, this imperative toward selective depictions of the past proved so strong that when an account purporting to be Marulanda's field journals appeared in 1973, it skipped over the period between the mid-1950s campaigns of the military dictatorship and the climactic 1964 battle at Marquetalia. [112] This suppression of memory had nothing to do with the decision made by the *país político* that created the National Front. Instead, the Communists' vision of the past now had no place for the creole peace.

"From the mountains of Colombia" became a shibboleth in FARC communiqués over the following years. On one level, the statement's vagueness was a device meant to hide the precise locations of FARC fighters. But on a political level, the phrase reinforced what the designation FARC had already introduced. By transcending the regional identity of the Southern Bloc and claiming a presence throughout the Andes, Communist *letrados* helped to make a set of *campesinos* from the southern Colombian frontier speak for all Colombia's rural peoples, those *campesinos'* distinctive experience with violence stand in for the history of the entire nation.

Epilogue

The Making of "La Violencia"

Five years on from the publication of *La violencia en Colombia*'s first volume, Germán Guzmán Campos and Orlando Fals Borda returned to the question of violence. The joint ventures of 1962 and 1964 would not be replicated this time, for each man worked at least in part from exile. However, both used their books to grapple with a shared dilemma, one that was moreover responsible for their withdrawal from Colombia. Through this process of reflection, Guzmán and Fals comprised part of a global intellectual turn that, beginning in the middle of the decade, questioned the assumptions of the early 1960s. In the United States, young anthropologists began to contest the relationship between their discipline and state power.[1] The political scientist Samuel Huntington meanwhile critiqued the modernization theory of the U.S. academe from the opposite end of the political spectrum, insisting on the primacy of political stability over unmediated political change.[2] But the turn was evident elsewhere too: in Africa, for instance, novelists cast doubt on the developmentalist course set by still-young national governments.[3]

The experience of Colombian developmentalism had an important place in Fals's disillusionment, but violence was the central issue. His group had spent years thinking about violence, witnessing the scars it left on the countryside, and sorting through its political ramifications, but only later did violence-as-practice—immediate, visceral, brute force—touch the National University *letrados'* own ranks. Their failed play to halt the invasion of Marquetalia served as a fatal blow to whatever remained of their sense of social-scientific objectivity. They had previously tried to answer pressure from the country of politics with more ideas, more studies, but for Camilo Torres Restrepo especially, the *letrados'* conventional tactics no longer appeared sufficient. "We progressives are very intelligent. We speak very well. We enjoy popularity," the priest wrote to a confidant. "But the reaction moves one of its powerful fingers, and we stop dead in our tracks. We cannot continue without organization and without weapons [that are] at least equal." Over the months that followed, Torres "moved from a reformist and strictly academic role to political activity," setting the stage for what would become Guzmán's and Fals's own exits from their established lettered modes.[4]

Revolution became the order of the day—"the 'obligation' to the world" of "today's Christian," Torres insisted.[5] How that structural change was to come about remained an open question. Initially, Torres aspired to introduce *convivencia* to Colombia's left with the "Platform for a Movement of Popular Unity." His timing was exquisite: a worsening national economic crisis, and concurrent displays of political debility from the National Front coalition, rocketed his public profile to new heights at the start of 1965. However, the Catholic hierarchy countered each step. By May 1965, a year after Marquetalia, Torres appeared to be on his way out, given license to return to Europe to complete his doctorate in sociology. He nevertheless remained at the last moment, slamming shut this door to the *letrado* world and setting up a final confrontation with his superiors, who declared his political statements contrary to Catholic Church teachings. Within weeks, Father Torres was simply Camilo. Freed to tour the country to drum up support for what he was now calling the "United Front of the Colombian People," he "filled the plazas and mobilized the masses as no one had seen since Gaitán's time."[6]

Camilo simultaneously drew closer to other strategies. Violent revolution remained a possibility, he told the United Front, because Colombia's "ruling class" controlled the terms of the nation's transformation. Camilo therefore reached out by mid-1965 to what struck him as "the future": the Army of National Liberation (ELN; Ejército de Liberación Nacional), a new armed movement, created in the mold of the Cuban revolution, that had begun operations in northern Colombia at the start of the year. When it became clear by October that the United Front could not satisfy the fractured left, and that the army had learned of his communications with the ELN, Camilo left behind the lettered city for the life of the rural combatant.[7]

Camilo's decision to adopt violence was not altogether unexpected. In 1963, he had presented a paper that Fals and others judged to be his finest sociological work, a consideration of the role "*la violencia*" exercised over "socio-cultural change in rural areas."[8] The assessment of how violence had remade rural consciousness and catalyzed a class of authentic popular leaders mirrored the impressions that Guzmán had recorded, first in his notebooks and then in *La violencia en Colombia*. The distinction lay in the context. Witnessing the military campaigns against Marquetalia and El Pato brought Camilo's analysis into the realm of politics; as his critique of the country's most important "structures" became more pointed, he came to envision violence in Colombia as a response to "state violence financed by the oligarchy." The forms of collective mobilization that violence engendered would thus provide the germ of Colombia's needed revolution.[9] The Colombian left had for years espoused similar ideas about the countryside, but Camilo thought himself and the national situation sufficiently unique to avoid the deadly fate of those who had previously attempted the leap from violence-as-idea to violence-as-practice.

It was not to be so. Camilo's death in February 1966, during his first armed action as a guerrilla fighter, devastated the National University's *letrados*. Sociology would bear the stigma of subversion for years to come.[10] On an individual level, Camilo's colleagues struggled with the loss of this exemplary man and all it entailed. The process turned out to be costliest for Guzmán, who had been especially drawn to his fellow priest's intellectual and personal vivacity. Part of the United Front team even after Camilo's death, Guzmán soon went into temporary exile in Mexico, as the military went about jailing anyone with a potential association with the ELN. He had made a analogous move during the *La violencia en Colombia* controversy in 1962, but that had been by choice; this time there was no possibility of containing the damage. Back teaching at a Bogotá university by early 1968, Guzmán returned from a conference to find himself out of a job and disowned by his friends—"harassed from all sides, with long days without work," he later confided to Fals.[11]

"Almost hopeless," Guzmán turned to his one standby: *La violencia en Colombia*. Without first obtaining permission from Fals or Eduardo Umaña Luna—a move calculated to spare them further pain, but one that greatly strained their relationships—Guzmán republished his sections of book's first volume alongside three new chapters on "the current moment." This third and final cut at violence-as-idea— which covered the failure of the Marquetalia mission and the campaign against the independent republics, the rise of the United Front and the effort to reconcile Christianity with revolution—allowed Guzmán an opportunity to process Camilo's death and his own parallel transition away from the position the *letrados* had held in the early 1960s. The creole peace seemed equally distant to Guzmán.[12]

Guzmán's 1968 reissue of *La violencia en Colombia* made none of its progenitors' splash on the national scene. The book undermined the long-term place of the original volumes in Colombian public life, inasmuch as it comprised part of Guzmán's protracted withdrawal from his previous beliefs and collaborations. After publication, Guzmán definitively departed Colombia (and the church, thus following Camilo's example one more step). He took with him to Mexico the archive of the National Investigatory Commission, giving rise to rumors that he had sold or handed off the collection.[13] Some of the old vitriol against *La violencia en Colombia*'s documentary base was consequently rekindled, and the original record of the commission's memory- and peace-work lost to future researchers.

While rather less dramatic and personally catastrophic, Fals's experience after Camilo's death ultimately altered the terms by which Colombians thought about both violence and the mid-twentieth century. His exile came about for different reasons: where *convivencia* had once energized the Faculty of Sociology, discord now reigned. Fals and his ties to foreign institutions and foreign ideas came increasingly under fire from the same students who had helped inspire Camilo to embrace revolutionary politics and also facilitated his contact with the ELN.[14] However, those same foreign ties offered Fals a temporary way out. From his temporary haven in the United States, he started to ponder the twists and turns his intellectual project, his discipline, and Colombia's politics had taken since 1962.

The resulting book, which Fals finished early in 1967, had many intended purposes: a critique of the "objective" sociology of Fals's past and a call to action for a more engaged social-scientific practice, it also sought to contemplate Camilo's legacy against the larger backdrop of Colombian social change.[15] Though Fals did not consider it sufficiently noteworthy to reflect on at any length, his treatment of the latter goal proved to be his major intellectual intervention. Fals dedicated *Subversion in Colombia: Social Change in History* (*La subversión en Colombia: Visión del cambio social en la historia*) to two essential figures from 1960s reformism: Otto Morales Benítez, leader of the National Investigatory Commission and champion of agrarian reform; and Camilo Torres, whom Fals introduced later as the "symbol of our 'generation of La Violencia.'"[16] This simple statement marked a watershed in the country of letters: it was the first appearance of the term "La Violencia" in a major work of Colombian social science.

The idea of La Violencia had long been with Fals. At the inauguration of the Faculty of Sociology in 1959, Fals's dean had explicated on the state of the social sciences, prompting Fals to scribble, "He requests research on La Violencia" on the back of his copy of the speech.[17] The concept made it into *La violencia en Colombia* simply as "*la violencia,*" but even that was enough to occasion a preliminary shift in how *letrados* described Colombia's national experience. By 1965, Fals felt on firmer intellectual ground, and published his first essay invoking La Violencia.[18] His international renown presented him other opportunities to debut the idea. By the end of the year that same essay appeared in English translation, as part of an influential volume on Latin American politics by social scientists from across the hemisphere.[19]

But La Violencia required Camilo's death to come fully into being. The idea offered Fals a means to reflect on the personal and collective commitments of his cohort of reformers.[20] It also represented an expression of what historian Leslie Jo Frazier has termed "empathetic memory," an attempt to connect with the rural Colombians whom the *letrados* had encountered throughout the early 1960s.[21] The term followed a tradition of references to "generation," but blended these together to forge an undifferentiated, national conception of experience. During the democratic transition of 1957–58, some Colombians had spoken of those countrymen born since the 1920s as the "generation of the state of siege"—a decidedly urban reference, one that acknowledged the lack of information about rural violence. In *La violencia en Colombia*'s second volume, Guzmán had portrayed the rise of banditry as an outgrowth of "the generation of the backcountry." Fals's "generation of La Violencia" took the former term's preoccupation with coming of age and placed it in a guise drawn from the latter. As he defined it, the generation of La Violencia— a group he identified even more closely with himself than with Camilo—"grew up in [La Violencia's] atmosphere of terror, observing it in its bloody deformities, suffering its intolerances and injustices, and participating in its miseries."[22]

As the rest of Fals's book made apparent, this arresting version of violence-as-idea also contained the frustrations toward the established order that urban *letrados* had accumulated during the process of studying and transforming Colombia. Provincial Colombians possessed no shortage of reasons to feel distrustful and resentful toward the state and its political drivers, but they did not necessarily share these with their urban countrymen. Fals thus appropriated provincial Colombians' experience with violence, layering onto it the memories of his group of reformist intellectuals. In the process, he formalized a representation of Colombia as a nation, one united despite differences in space and scale.

La Violencia came into being as Colombia was witnessing far less violence.[23] The period beginning in the late 1960s was dissimilar to the peace that had come a decade earlier, lacking the trust or optimism of 1958. The fight against banditry and the independent republics between 1962 and 1965 had left Gran Tolima and other regions of central and southern Colombia traumatized and militarized. Nonetheless, the particular forms of state, partisan, and bandit violence seen in the 1940s, '50s, and '60s came to an end, as the overall incidence of homicide also fell. Recourse to the technique of violence in public life, though not banished, had been greatly reduced from midcentury.

With violence no longer dominating national attentions, these shifted in the late 1960s and into the 1970s to sectors of the *país nacional* that were adopting alternative means of political and social mobilization in regions apart from Gran Tolima. One focal point became the Caribbean coast, where *campesino* leagues— initially sponsored by the post-1966 National Front administration in the hopes of reviving the flagging agrarian reform—took on an independent line, eventually engaging in mass occupations of large landholdings.[24] Fals figured among those attracted to the spectacle of hundreds of thousands of organized rural folk. Upon his return to Colombia, he landed back in his native Caribbean, observing and encouraging this new expression of communal self-realization while simultaneously advancing his pioneering practice of participatory social science.[25]

Back in Gran Tolima, the FARC meanwhile remained marginal geographically and politically, a force of a few hundred men.[26] For the aspiring revolutionaries who departed Colombia's universities to join the FARC in the late 1960s, the misalignment between the idea and practice of violence came as a hard realization. It took upward of twenty-five days on foot for volunteers to arrive at mythical sites like El Pato, where they thought an authentic Colombia, a Colombia steeped in "a tradition of violence," awaited. However, these urban youths had not anticipated sitting out in the jungle under incessantly rainy skies, awaiting little more than their next meal and experiencing what struck them as hardship for its own sake—"the guerrilla . . . as a way of life," as one arrival from the city commented. Concerned about losing what they envisioned as a strategic reserve, to be deployed to its fullest when national conditions were ripe for the revolution, Communist Party leaders resisted temptation to push the FARC toward battle. "We observed that we did not advance because we were part of a soporific strategy," that same urban activist later explained, "a political strategy full of vagueness and gaps that made the revolution a distant, unreachable dream." The fault was not entirely on party theorists back in Bogotá; as much as they admired Tirofijo and Jacobo Arenas's natural leadership, urban cadres thought them hopelessly secluded in the mountains.[27]

Their expectations dashed, a small collection of schismatics reengineered their idea of violence, with an eye toward immediately bringing it into the world of practice. As one of these warrior-theorists detailed, "[We] conceived of the struggle as the clash of two forces' backbones, one of which destroys the morale of the other and annihilates the enemy." Their theater would not be the countryside, but the city, where they could maximize the influence of spectacle on popular consciousness. "The people like to see, touch, feel, verify," reasoned another Communist disillusioned by the FARC and the Communist Party.[28] His group's early practice of violence in the mid-1970s therefore tended toward the symbolic, a reclaiming of the nation's emblems and spaces from an undemocratic *país político*—one that had gone so far as to steal the 1970 presidential election from an opposition that had gained significant urban support over the second half of the 1960s. The resulting alliance between young opposition activists and breakaway elements of the FARC would take its name—the 19th of April Movement (M-19; Movimiento 19 de Abril)—from that defining political event.

This pairing of armed action with a specific expression of anti-elite politics would have profound implications for the ways in which Colombians thought about the violence of the past. Alongside the formation of the M-19, important figures from the country of letters—among them Gabriel García Márquez and Fals—agreed to open an independent journalistic forum, free of both the sectarianism that crippled the left and the subservience to moneyed political interests that tainted the "great press." With the end of sixteen years of National Front rule mere months away, Colombians in search of political alternatives snapped up the *letrados'* upstart magazine by the tens of thousands.[29] Fals's regular "Forbidden History" column thus reached a far larger audience than his academic work, providing many readers with what was likely their first exposure to the idea of La Violencia.[30] Moreover, the magazine's association with the M-19 reinforced the anti-oligarchical tenor of the term. The logic of M-19 violence accordingly became the logic attributed to the violence of the past. As Daniel Pécaut has suggested, the M-19's disproportionate influence in Colombia's public sphere generalized its portrayals of an exclusionary National Front.[31]

However much this perspective on the past validated the arguments that Jacobo Arenas had made since 1964, the M-19's dexterity with symbolic and, increasingly, physical space represented a challenge to the FARC. By the early 1980s, the M-19 had taken its war to the provinces, spreading throughout the mountains and capturing the southernmost frontier capital. Refusing to be bested, the FARC's leadership repositioned the organization onto a national footing.[32] The ever-present friction between urban cadres, with their national and international vision, and the local and regional priorities of the FARC's *campesino* base was decided in favor of the former. Rather than vegetate in the jungles, from 1982 onward the guerrilla would seek to project itself nationally. To this end, delegates to the Seventh Guerrilla Conference appended the label Popular Army (Ejército Popular) onto the FARC's name.[33] The time had finally come for the FARC to break out of the mountains and other pockets where it had survived for decades, and to begin the march toward the cities and the seizure of power.

The ability of this idea of violence to successfully take shape in practice depended on a contingency of unprecedented import. Beginning in the 1970s, Colombia's strategic position atop the continent guaranteed its integration into emerging drug-trafficking circuits. Though the country's niche lay in the processing and transshipment of cocaine, frontier farmers—the creole Communists' historic social base—found coca, the raw stuff of the drug, a reliable commodity. Local FARC commanders could, as a result, tax the production and movement of cocaine through their territory. The results of this new means of frontier development were twofold. For the FARC, it yielded revenue to more than double the Popular Army's footprint in barely half a decade, part of a broader expansion of armed groups around the country.[34] Even in Colombia's cities, which had been spared the bloodshed of midcentury, the rivalries and reprisals inherent in the illegal trade caused indicators of violence to explode. By the mid-1980s, the national homicide rate, which had already begun to pull away from those of several other Latin American countries late in the previous decade, hit levels not seen since the start of the National Front.[35] Colombia was becoming synonymous with violence once more.

As Colombia again confronted violence-as-practice, national interest in violence-as-idea surged, prompting a new generation of *letrados* to redouble their efforts. "'Are we a violent country?' comes the question from the social sciences," noted a writer in late 1980.[36] Five years later, those same social scientists could observe that "the topic [of violence] has not only come out of the ghetto, but . . . has become a daily subject of conversation for Colombians: it has become open to everyone."[37] Journalists rode at the front of this wave, simultaneously meeting and feeding public interest. They first won interviews with the more readily accessible and willing founders of the M-19, but soon gained access to Colombia's oldest guerrilla. A cease-fire between the FARC and the government occasioned a second wave of interviews in 1985 and 1986, granting urban Colombians—and the world—a window onto a rural world perhaps even more mythical than Marquetalia had been to Colombians in the early 1960s. The multitude of testimonials that resulted inaugurated the modern study of the FARC.[38]

In this moment, scholars turned to the history of Colombian social science for tools to comprehend violence-as-practice. Gonzalo Sánchez G., a childhood *desplazado* from northern Tolima and a National University graduate of the restless 1960s, headed the endeavor.[39] While his colleagues would later christen him "dean of Violencia researchers,"[40] Sánchez in fact carried out far more foundational work, which placed La Violencia at the center of lettered and popular interpretation. In the mid-1980s, just shy of his fortieth birthday, Sánchez co-organized two collaborative volumes that became touchstones of violence-as-idea. One grew out of the First International Symposium on La Violencia, a gathering of scholars that included Germán Guzmán Campos, who shared what remains an indispensable account of the making of La violencia en Colombia.[41]

Sánchez's second production made clear the influence of Guzmán and the former priest's *letrado* partners. The similarities stretched from content to form; the urgency of research into violence and the pace of academic output recalled the Faculty of Sociology's trajectory in the 1960s. Hoping to stimulate new avenues of research, Sánchez packaged together recent scholarly interventions and the urtexts of Colombian social scientific research on violence. Colombians in the mid-1980s therefore had close at hand Camilo Torres's 1963 interpretation of violence and sociocultural change, and the 1965 essay where Fals originally introduced "La Violencia."[42] Born of the same process of disenchantment in the mid-1960s, the FARC and La Violencia reemerged alongside one another as they approached their twentieth anniversaries.

Crucially, this appropriation of the concept of La Violencia reinscribed its meaning. Together with his Dutch wife, Donny Meertens, Sánchez had spent the late 1970s gathering court records from provincial courthouses, reviewing congressional debates over Rehabilitación, and tracing the war against banditry through the regional press. The resulting work, published in 1983 and soon a classic, made obvious from the opening sentence its authors' intellectual debt to Fals:[43] "This book is aimed, first of all, at an entire generation, the 'generation of la Violencia,' which lived during the twenty years stretching from 1945 to 1965."[44] In borrowing this generational identity, Sánchez altered its temporal referents. Fals's dating of the "generation of la Violencia" to 1925 had made the epoch of La Violencia coterminous with his early life as a *letrado*. In turn, by moving the generation's starting point forward two decades, to the year of *his* own birth, Sánchez converted La Violencia into a childhood crucible. His definition moreover established a temporal coherence to violence that would have been foreign to the *letrados* of 1962.[45]

More importantly, Sánchez and Meertens's 1983 book transformed a term with which to describe the past into the past itself. "La Violencia" held so much explanatory power as a scholarly concept and personal signifier that the book superimposed it onto the historical record. Sources that had originally described "*violencia*" were now made to refer to "la Violencia."[46] This helped to construct a chronology that emphasized violence over peace.

Sánchez would take the analysis further in subsequent works, arguing to Colombian and U.S. audiences that "Colombia has been a country of *permanent and endemic warfare*."[47] The worsening of the current war—a disastrous urban 1985 action by the M-19; the end of the cease-fire with the FARC; unceasing attacks on the left by a combination of landed interests, drug gangs, and state security forces—only deepened Sánchez and the *letrados*' quest to uncover the causes of violence. Even as their attentions increasingly turned to the latest manifestations of violence-as-practice, however, the past and present blended together. "The new cycle of la Violencia, barely discernible in 1984–85, has regrettably turned into an occurrence whose dimensions have gone far beyond what was previously foreseeable," Sánchez reflected in 1992.[48] In light of the violence-as-practice of the 1980s, *letrados* invested new authority in a specific expression of violence-as-idea, a Violencia that had now never ended. *Letrados* promoted La Violencia into the dominant framework for understanding the past, but at the cost of distinguishing between continuities and discontinuities.

The exigencies of Colombia's late twentieth-century violence-as-practice eventually drew the *violentólogos* (violence-ologists)—as Sánchez and the academics surrounding him became known—away from the study of the 1940s and '50s.[49] In contrast with their *letrado* forbearers, the top figures of Sánchez's generation never underwent a complete falling-out with the state. The group reached a peak in its influence in the late 1980s, a moment that called to mind the National Investigatory Commission of 1958.[50] Their 1987 government-commissioned report called for an expansion of democracy as a means to overcome Colombia's multiple varieties of violence. The recommendations indirectly contributed four years later to the creation of a decentralized, pluralist constitution—Colombia's first new national charter in over a century. However, as historian Jefferson Jaramillo Marín has written, the report's ideas about violence also inadvertently contributed to a sense that violence was ingrained in the Colombian character. The *violentólogos*' notion of a "culture of violence," intended to signal violence's recurrent place in Colombia's history, was instead read in ways that seem to have impeded public engagement on behalf of peace.[51] The blurry boundaries between past and present, evident in the *letrados*' conceptualizations of La Violencia from a few years earlier, complicated the politics of present violence.

Public responses to the *violentólogos'* 1987 report underscored how violence-as-idea remained the subject of interpretration from nonlettered sections of Colombian society. Likewise, the enthronement of La Violencia in the 1980s had varied origins. To the extent that anyone within the *país político* cared to erase the events of the 1940s and '50s from the public sphere, La Violencia offered a partial solution, by elevating what occurred to—as Sánchez put it—the level of "Great Historical Process, which was extrinsic to, and transcended, those who participated in it."[52] The term also proved attractive in the provinces, helping people to make sense of their experiences by connecting it to a larger national story. Though Sánchez rightly suggests that La Violencia could never serve as a positive unifying myth, as the Mexican Revolution did for much of Mexico's twentieth century,[53] it nevertheless derived power from its integrative function, its capacity to bring socially and spatially diverse actors together—however ephemerally—around a single referent.[54] Even if it established a black legend for Colombia, La Violencia still succeeded in binding the local and regional into a national narrative.

At the same time, however, this adaptability obscured the means by which La Violencia represented the past. Beginning with Orlando Fals and continuing through Gonzalo Sánchez, intellectuals embedded in La Violencia representation of their personal pasts—their memories of the 1960s, of an alienation from the political establishment. While, as Pierre Nora has written, the creation of a new "generation" marks the exercise of memory in a "pure" form, the formulation of La Violencia yielded a distinct outcome. Rather than denying history outright through an assertion of generational memory—an inversion of Colombians' 1962 debates over *La violencia en Colombia*—the *letrados'* social scientific authority invested their depictions with the weight of history, presenting them as a true accounting of Colombia's past.[55] At worst, this mode of narrating the past risks suppressing alternative expressions of memory from the provinces and countryside, which cannot count on the influence that lettered interventions possess in public life. At a minimum, later intellectuals' assuredness about the overlap between personal and national experience has made La Violencia an overly convenient form of violence-as-idea. In the three decades that have ensued since the rise of the *violentólogos*, scholars of Colombia have scarcely renewed investigation into the linkages between midcentury politics, memory, and violence.

In the opening decades of the new millennium, the state beckoned the *violentólogos* again, placing them at the head of efforts to catalog the scope and texture of the conflict that had inaugurated their career in the first place. This process would be unlike the Latin American truth commissions of the 1980s and later, and unlike Colombia's own experience in the late 1950s; this time, the campaign to resolve the violence of the recent past would take place outside a democratic transition. The experiences of other countries nevertheless provided models that were not present in the 1950s. Colombians can now craft comprehensive ideas about violence using sophisticated mechanisms for theorizing the role of memory, as well as for collecting individual and communal memories in the hopes of creating "a unifying and inclusive narrative." "Far from trying to promote . . . a collection of settled truths," Sánchez writes, contemporary memory-work seeks "to add to an open social and political debate."[56]

Simultaneously, however, the *violentólogos* have remained bound to older perspectives. Although a 2011 law treats 1985 as the opening of the conflict, the final report of the government's memory commission, issued in 2013, emphasizes the start of the National Front in 1958 as the "origin [of] the contemporary armed conflict in Colombia." The report indirectly refers to the creole peace by delimiting La Violencia to the period 1946–58.[57] Yet it treats the early years of the National Front with little of the plasticity and plurality afforded to the post-1985 period, presenting the 1950s and '60s instead as a settled truth, rather than as a potential example of Colombians' "capacity for resistance" against violence.[58]

In contemporary Colombia, then, memory-work is a project for the recent past. The mid-twentieth century, by contrast, continues to appear in Colombia's public sphere as a matter of historical record. Though the country of letters often feels ignored or excluded by the country of politics, social scientists have effected a greater influence on Colombia's image of itself than even they have realized. In a process initiated with the invention of La Violencia, *letrados'* conviction about the supremacy of forgetting in midcentury national life has obscured the formative role that their memories, along with those of their predecessors and of the FARC, play in shaping the nation's understanding of its past.

The moments of collective bewilderment that have taken shape since Colombians' talk of violence has recently turned to talk of peace underscore the need to revisit the forgotten experience of the 1950s and '60s. The founding generation of Jacobo Arenas and Tirofijo gone because of old age, the succeeding generation of leaders hunted down by the state, and their ranks thinned since the start of the millennium, the FARC had moved to the negotiating table by 2012. It was not their first encounter with the state over the prospect of peace, but it quickly became the most promising. Commentators expressed surprise upon learning that expanded political participation and economic and social development—not the establishment of a socialist economy or a handover of power—comprised the heart of the upcoming agenda. "Good news," declared one National University economist. "The FARC are no longer Communists."[59]

Unasked was the question of whether they had ever been. That the FARC not only persisted but reached their peak a decade after the end of the Cold War suggests that something else had been at stake. The disconnect between the discourse of urban cadres and the priorities of the FARC's rural base, indiscernible for decades, came to the surface when urban Colombians penetrated the mountains and mythology surrounding the FARC.[60] Thanks to the start of the peace process, local and regional representations of the FARC have achieved a national stage as well. Other sectors of the *país nacional* have likewise gained a voice in defining how Colombians think about their country's recent past of violence.

The future of peace in Colombia is far from assured. Three decades of atrocities have left trust a scarce good in the public realm; political negotiation will also neither unravel Colombia's convoluted system of land ownership nor put an end to the drug trade. Critics of the government's dealings with the FARC lambast the process as a surrender to international forces out to subvert Colombia's sovereignty. By late 2016, the opposition's ideas about violence in Colombia had exercised a decisive role over the trajectory of peace with the FARC.

But more than a half-century ago, Colombians faced many of these same issues around violence and peace, and opted to labor, collectively if not cooperatively, to resolve them. The memories of that process left Colombia with many of the intellectual frameworks that have been applied to the conflict of the early twenty-first century. Peace may indeed be a more difficult proposition in Colombia today, but the origins of contemporary democracy's challenges are not located solely in a past of violence. By examining the local, regional, and even national meanings of belonging and prosperity, present as well as past, the causes of violence, and potential practices to counter it, can be brought into our ongoing global conversations about peace and violence.

A NOTE ON CITATIONS, INSTITUTIONAL ABBREVIATIONS, AND ARCHIVES

Citations generally include the archive name, collection, subcollection (where applicable), box or volume number, folder number or name (where applicable), and folio number (where applicable). For instance, a citation for Archivo General de la Nación, Ministerio de Gobierno, Despacho Ministro, Caja 9, Carpeta 74, Folio 100, appears as AGN.MinGob. DM.9.74.100. Citations from the Archivo Histórico de Ibagué cite the shelf, file, and folio numbers. Citations from the Archivo de la Presidencia include the year rather than the subcollection. Citations from the Archivo Alberto Lleras Camargo cite the box, folder, and document numbers. Citations from the U.K. National Archives cite only the folder accession number.

Citations with no specific page number cite documents that are only one page in length. In most archives, the reverse side of documents are not separately marked. Therefore, when a citation references the reverse side, the folio number is followed by "+."

Citations to undated documents include a bracketed date in those cases where an approximate date can be deduced from the document's location in the archive and a bracketed date with a question mark in those cases where an approximate date is difficult to determine.

In accordance with the formatting of the document titles themselves, accent marks are generally not employed. Unless otherwise noted, English-language documents are between the U.S. Embassy, Bogotá, and the Department of State.

Documents from the 1960s that were housed at the Archivo de la Presidencia at the time of my research in 2006–7 have since been moved to the Archivo General de la Nación. The archive's organization remains largely the same, though some material was lost during the transfer. I hold digitized copies of the majority of documents cited in this book.

INSTITUTIONAL ABBREVIATIONS

306	Record Group 306: United States Information Agency
59	Record Group 59: Department of State
AC	Abogado Consultor
AGN	Archivo General de la Nación, Bogotá, D.C.
AHI	Archivo Histórico de Ibagué, Tolima
AHM	Archivo Histórico de Medellín, Antioquia
AI	Asuntos Indígenas
ALC	Archivo Alberto Lleras Camargo
AOH	Albert O. Hirschman Papers
AParl	Asuntos Parliamentarios
APR	Archivo de la Presidencia de la República, Bogotá, D.C.
BLAA	Sala de Libros Raros y Manuscritos, Biblioteca Luis Ángel Arango, Bogotá, D.C.
Bohannan	Charles T. R. Bohannan Papers
CDF 1955–1959	Central Decimal File
CdI	Concejo Municipal de Ibagué, Actas
CDP	Colombia Documentation Project
Clarín	*Radioperiódico El Clarín* transcripts
CLR	Archivo Carlos Lleras Restrepo
CM	Consejo de Ministros
CMil	Casa Militar
CP	Cargos Públicos
CTR	Colección Camilo Torres Restrepo
CUA	Catholic University of America, American Catholic History Research Center and University Archives, Washington, D.C.
DCA	Digital Collections and Archives, Tisch Library, Tufts University, Medford, Mass.
DIP	Dirección de Información y Prensa
DM	Despacho Ministro
DNP	Departamento Nacional de Planeación
DSP	Despacho Señor Presidente (in APR); Despacho Sr. Presidente (in PR)
EG	Fondo Documental Ernesto Guhl
ES	Archivo Eduardo Santos
FO	Foreign Office
GHdA	Archivo Gregorio Hernández de Alba
HIA	Hoover Institution Archives, Stanford University, Stanford, Calif.
JFKL	John Fitzgerald Kennedy Library, Boston, Mass.
JMCP	John Moors Cabot Papers
JMG	Junta Militar de Gobierno
LBJL	Lyndon Baines Johnson Library, Austin, Tex.
MinGob	Ministerio de Gobierno
MRL	Archivo Movimiento Revolucionario Liberal
NARA	National Archives and Record Administration II, College Park, Md.
NAUK	National Archives, Kew, Surrey

NSArchive	National Security Archive, Washington, D.C.
NSF	National Security Files (in JFKL), National Security File (in LBJL)
OC	Oficina del Consejero
OFB	Fondo Documental Orlando Fals Borda
OHI	Oral History Interviews
OJ	Oficina Jurídica
OR	Office of Research
OPS	Office of Public Safety
OR	Oficina de Rehabilitación
PDRR	Production Division Research Reports, 1956–1959
PL	Partido Liberal
POF	President's Office Files
PR	Presidencia de la República
PUL	Public Policy Papers, Department of Rare Books and Special Collections, Princeton University Library, Princeton, N.J.
RAC	Rockefeller Archive Center, Sleepy Hollow, N.Y.
RG 1–2	Record Group 1.2 : Rockefeller Foundation Projects
RPCV	Returned Peace Corps Volunteer Collection
S 311	Series 311 : Colombia
SG	Secretaría General
SIC	Servicio de Inteligencia Colombiana
SJ	Sección Judicial
SNF 1963	Subject-Numeric File 1963
SNF 1964–1966	Subject-Numeric File 1964–1966
SP	Secretaría Privada
SS 311-R	Subseries 311.R : Colombia—Social Sciences
TG	Archivo Programa Radial Tolima Grande
UdA	Colección Patrimonial, Universidad de Antioquia, Medellín, Antioquia
UN	Archivo Central e Histórico, Universidad Nacional, Bogotá, D.C.
USCCB.OGS	United States Conference of Catholic Bishops, Office of the General Secretary

ARCHIVES

Colombian Archives

Archivo General de la Nación (AGN), Bogotá, D.C.
  Colección Camilo Torres Restrepo (CTR)
  Departamento Nacional de Planeación (DNP)
  Ministerio de Gobierno (MinGob)
    Asuntos Indígenas (AI)
    Despacho Ministro (DM)
    Oficina Jurídica (OJ)
    Secretaría General (SG)
  Presidencia de la República (PR)
    Abogado Consultor (AC)

Asuntos Parliamentarios (AParl)
Casa Militar (CMil)
Consejo de Ministros (CM)
Despacho Sr. Presidente (DSP)
Dirección de Información y Prensa (DIP)
Junta Militar de Gobierno (JMG)
Oficina de Rehabilitación (OR)
Oficina del Consejero (OC)
Secretaría General (SG)
Secretaría Privada (SP)
Servicio de Inteligencia Colombiana (SIC)
Archivo Histórico de Ibagué (AHI), Tolima
Sección Judicial (SJ)
Concejo Municipal de Ibagué (CdI), Actas
Archivo Histórico de Medellín (AHM), Antioquia
Radioperiódico El Clarín transcripts (Clarín)
Archivo de la Presidencia de la República (APR), Bogotá, D.C.
Consejo de Ministros (CM), Actas
Despacho Señor Presidente (DSP)
Secretaría General (SG)
Colección Patrimonial, Universidad de Antioquia (UdA), Medellín, Antioquia
Archivo Movimiento Revolucionario Liberal (MRL)
Sala de Libros Raros y Manuscritos, Biblioteca Luis Ángel Arango (BLAA), Bogotá, D.C.
Archivo Alberto Lleras Camargo (ALC)
Archivo Carlos Lleras Restrepo (CLR)
Cargos Públicos (CP)
Archivo Eduardo Santos (ES)
Correspondencia
Partido Liberal (PL)
Archivo Gregorio Hernández de Alba (GHdA)
Archivo Programa Radial Tolima Grande (TG)
Archivo Central e Histórico, Universidad Nacional (UN), Bogotá, D.C.
Fondo Documental Orlando Fals Borda (OFB)
Fondo Documental Ernesto Guhl (EG)

U.K. Archives

National Archives (NAUK), Kew, Surrey
Foreign Office (FO)

U.S. Archives

Catholic University of America (CUA), American Catholic History Research Center and University Archives, Washington, D.C.

United States Conference of Catholic Bishops, Office of the General
Secretary (USCCB.OGS)
Digital Collections and Archives (DCA), Tisch Library, Tufts University,
Medford, Mass.
John Moors Cabot Papers (JMCP)
Hoover Institution Archives (HIA), Stanford University, Stanford, Calif.
Charles T. R. Bohannan Papers (Bohannan)
John Fitzgerald Kennedy Library (JFKL), Boston, Mass.
National Security Files (NSF)
Oral History Interviews (OHI)
President's Office Files (POF)
Returned Peace Corps Volunteer Collection (RPCV)
Oral History Interviews (OHI)
Lyndon Baines Johnson Library (LBJL), Austin, Tex.
National Security File (NSF)
National Archives and Record Administration II (NARA), College Park, Md.
Record Group 59 (59): Department of State
Central Decimal File (CDF) 1955–1959
Subject-Numeric File 1963 (SNF 1963)
Subject-Numeric File 1964–1966 (SNF 1964–1966)
Record Group 306 (306): United States Information Agency
Office of Research (OR)
Production Division Research Reports, 1956–1959 (PDRR)
National Security Archive (NSArchive), Washington, D.C.
Colombia Documentation Project (CDP)
Office of Public Safety (OPS)
Public Policy Papers, Department of Rare Books and Special Collections,
Princeton University Library (PUL), Princeton, N.J.
Albert O. Hirschman Papers (AOH)
Rockefeller Archive Center (RAC), Sleepy Hollow, N.Y.
Record Group 1.2 (RG 1–2): Rockefeller Foundation Projects
Series 311 (S 311): Colombia
Subseries 311.R (SS 311-R): Colombia—Social Sciences

MICROFILM COLLECTIONS

Records of the U.S. Department of State Relating to Internal Affairs of Colombia
1960–1963, Scholarly Resources

ONLINE RESOURCES

CIA Freedom of Information Act Electronic Reading Room (CIA FOIA)
http://www.foia.cia.gov/

NOTES

EPIGRAPH

Alberto Lleras Camargo, "La crisis institucional," *El Espectador,* December 7, 1955.

INTRODUCTION

1. Darío Betancourt E. and Martha L. García B., *Matones y cuadrilleros: Origen y evolución de la violencia en el occidente colombiano, 1946–1965* (Bogotá: Tercer Mundo Editores, 1990); and Grupo de Memoria Histórica, *¡Basta ya! Colombia: Memorias de guerra y dignidad* (Bogotá: Imprenta Nacional, 2013), treat violence as a continuous phenomenon since the 1940s. The most famous declaration of violence as a constant in Colombia's postindependence history is Gonzalo Sánchez G., "Raíces históricas de la amnistía o las etapas de la guerra en Colombia," in *Ensayos de historia social y política del siglo XX* (Bogotá: El Áncora Editores, 1984), portions of which appeared in English in Sánchez G., "La Violencia in Colombia: New Research, New Questions," trans. Peter Bakewell, *Hispanic American Historical Review* 65, no. 5 (November 1985): 789–807.

2. Government-FARC concordance on their conflict's historical and more recent roots is discussed in Juan Gabriel Tokatlián, "El acuerdo sobre drogas en La Habana: Un moderado paso radical," *Razón Pública,* June 8, 2014, http://www.razonpublica.com/index.php /conflicto-drogas-y-paz-temas-30/7676-el-acuerdo-sobre-drogas-en-la-habana-un-moderado-paso-radical.html.

3. For the violence-democracy paradox, see James A. Robinson, "Colombia: Another 100 Years of Solitude?," *Current History* 112, no. 751 (February 2013): 43–48. On reform, see letter, President John F. Kennedy to President Alberto Lleras Camargo, September 7, 1961, JFK.POF.114.Colombia General 1961.

4. Germán Guzmán Campos, "Palabras finales," in Germán Guzmán Campos, Orlando Fals Borda, and Eduardo Umaña Luna, *La violencia en Colombia,* vol. 1 (Bogotá: Taurus,

2005 [1962]), 458. Each chapter of *La violencia en Colombia* is cited separately here to disambiguate authorship. All translations are my own.

5. Marc Chernick observes that Colombia was "one of the few [global] examples of a negotiated accord" during the Cold War era. Marc W. Chernick, *Acuerdo posible: Solución negociada al conflicto armado colombiano*, trans. Juan Fernando Esguerra (Bogotá: Ediciones Aurora, 2008), 20, 20n3.

6. E.J. Hobsbawm, "The Revolutionary Situation in Colombia," *World Today* 19, no. 6 (June 1963): 248.

7. Albert O. Hirschman, *Journeys toward Progress: Studies of Economic Policy-Making in Latin America* (Garden City, N.Y.: Anchor Books, 1965), 325, for quote. See also memorandum, Roberto Piñeda Castillo, Presidente, Tribunal de Gracia, to Comisión Especial de Rehabilitación (hereafter CER), March 31, 1960, 4, AGN.MinGob.DM.60 .462.111.

8. Paige Arthur, "How 'Transitions' Reshaped Human Rights: A Conceptual History of Transitional Justice," *Human Rights Quarterly* 31, no. 2 (2009): 334.

9. Samuel Moyn, *The Last Utopia: Human Rights in History* (Cambridge: Belknap Press, 2010), especially chapter 1.

10. See, among other works, Moyn, *The Last Utopia*; Emilio A. Crenzel, *Memory of the Argentina Disappearances: The Political History of "Nunca Más"* (New York: Routledge, 2012).

11. "1958 [alocución de año nuevo]," speech by Lleras Camargo, December 31, 1958, in *El primer gobierno del Frente Nacional*, vol. 1, *Mayo de 1958–agosto fal de 1959* (Bogotá: Imprenta Nacional, 1960), 222.

12. Matthew Connelly, "Taking Off the Cold War Lens: Visions of North-South Conflict during the Algerian War for Independence," *American Historical Review* 105, no. 3 (June 2000): 739–69.

13. Robert A. Karl, "The Politics of Colombian Development in Latin America's Long 1950s" (unpublished paper).

14. This book treats "the state" as a discrete set of institutions and practices. While influenced by earlier historiography on the role the popular classes played in shaping the state, it subsumes that literature's related assertion of the state as "claim" under the rubric of politics, rather than "state formation." See especially Gilbert M. Joseph and Daniel Nugent, eds., *Everyday Forms of State Formation: Revolution and the Negotiation of Rule in Modern Mexico* (Durham and London: Duke University Press, 1994).

15. Petition, Luis Eduardo Hernández et al. [San Bernardo (Cundinamarca)] to Lleras Camargo, January 12, 1959, 2, 5, AGN.PR.DSP.117.51.2, 5. I have approximated the orthographical style of the original.

16. Herbert Braun, *The Assassination of Gaitán: Public Life and Urban Violence in Colombia* (Madison: University of Wisconsin Press, 1985), 20, for quote. The term's broader meanings appear in *Anales del Congreso* (hereafter *Anales*) 2, no. 136 (July 21, 1959): 1706; Guillermo Amaya Ramírez, *Memoria del Ministro de Gobierno al Congreso de 1959* (Bogotá: Imprenta Nacional, 1959), 43.

17. "Lleras habla sobre la violencia en el Tolima: 'Es indispensable reeducar para la convivencia a miles de compatriotas,'" *El Tiempo*, November 2, 1957, 1.

18. Sánchez G., "La Violencia in Colombia," 792.

19. Lleras Camargo, "La crisis institucional," *El Espectador,* December 7, 1955 ("an undeclared"); Luis López de Mesa, "Un historial de la violencia," *El Tiempo,* September 30, 1962, 18 ("confused").

20. Orlando Fals Borda, "El conflicto, la violencia y la estructura social colombiana," in *La violencia en Colombia,* 1:432, 436, 441 (for quote).

21. Herbert Braun offers a penetrating examination of the cultural divide between urban and rural Colombia in "'¡Que Haiga Paz!' The Cultural Contexts of Conflict in Colombia," in *Peace, Democracy, and Human Rights in Colombia,* ed. Christopher Welna and Gustavo Gallón (Notre Dame, Ind.: University of Notre Dame Press, 2007).

22. Frederick Cooper, "Conflict and Connection: Rethinking Colonial African History," *American Historical Review* 99, no. 5 (December 1994): 1539; Sebouh David Aslanian et al., "How Size Matters: The Question of Scale in History," *American Historical Review* 118, no. 5 (December 2013): 1431–72.

23. Odd Arne Westad, *The Global Cold War: Third World Interventions and the Making of Our Times* (Cambridge and New York: Cambridge University Press, 2005); Hal Brands, *Latin America's Cold War* (Cambridge: Harvard University Press, 2010).

24. Aslanian et al., "How Size Matters," 1459 (for quote), 1461, 1463.

25. Carlos Arango Z., *FARC, veinte años: De Marquetalia a La Uribe,* 3rd ed. (Bogotá: Ediciones Aurora, 1985), 23–26; Alma Guillermoprieto, *Looking for History: Dispatches from Latin America* (New York: Vintage Books, 2001), 19–39.

26. Outstanding examples of this regional literature include Jaime Arocha, *La violencia en el Quindío: Determinantes ecológicos y económicos del homicidio en un municipio caficultor* (Bogotá: Ediciones Tercer Mundo, 1979); Carlos Miguel Ortiz Sarmiento, *Estado y subversión en Colombia: La Violencia en el Quindío, años 50* (Bogotá: Fondo Editorial CEREC, 1985); Gonzalo Sánchez G. and Donny Meertens, *Bandits, Peasants, and Politics: The Case of "La Violencia" in Colombia,* trans. Alan Hynds (Austin: University of Texas Press, 2001); María Victoria Uribe, *Matar, rematar y contramatar: Las masacres de La Violencia en el Tolima, 1948–1964* (Bogotá: CINEP, 1990); Betancourt E. and García B., *Matones y cuadrilleros;* Mary Roldán, *Blood and Fire: La Violencia in Antioquia, Colombia, 1946–1953* (Durham and London: Duke University Press, 2002). For the emergence of the field, see the epilogue and Uribe, *Matar, rematar y contramatar,* 11.

27. See, for instance, Reunión de Orden Público, Acta, February 7, 1961, 4, AGN.Min-Gob.DM.22.205.34. Studies of Sumapaz zone grant a transborder perspective, but contribute less to our understanding of the state: José Jairo González Arias and Elsy Marulanda Alvarez, *Historias de frontera: Colonización y guerras en el Sumapaz* (Bogotá: CINEP, 1990); Elsy Marulanda Alvarez, *Colonización y conflicto: Las lecciones del Sumapaz* (Bogotá: Instituto de Estudios Políticos y Relaciones Internacionales, Universidad Nacional de Colombia, and Tercer Mundo Editores, 1991).

28. Definitions of Gran Tolima—also known as Tolima Grande—vary. Useful maps include "Regionalizacion y division politica," n.d., UN.EG.26.2.22; *Gran atlas y geografía de Colombia* (Bogotá: Intermedio Editores, 2004), 109.

29. Michael T. Taussig, *Law in a Lawless Land: Diary of a Limpieza in Colombia* (Chicago and London: University of Chicago Press, 2005), 191–92.

30. Herbert Braun, review of *Blood and Fire: La Violencia in Antioquia, Colombia, 1946–1953*, by Mary Roldán, *Hispanic American Historical Review* 83, no. 3 (August 2003): 596.

31. "Lleras habla sobre la violencia en el Tolima," 1.

32. For the connection between coffee and violence, consult Frank Safford and Marco Palacios, *Colombia: Fragmented Land, Divided Society* (New York: Oxford University Press, 2002), 353.

33. "Report on a Visit to the Department of Tolima," April 16, 1958, 1, enclosure to Despatch 29, British Embassy, Bogotá, to Foreign Office, April 16, 1958, NAUK.FO 371/132194.

34. I do not employ the common translation "peasant," which implies a limited set of economic and social relations. The term "*campesino,*" by contrast, encompasses not only peasants who controlled their own means of production but also rural wage and day laborers, and workers in tenancy and sharecropping arrangements.

35. Alexander W. Wilde, "Conversations among Gentlemen: Oligarchical Democracy in Colombia," in *The Breakdown of Democratic Regimes: Latin America*, ed. Juan J. Linz and Alfred Stepan (Baltimore and London: Johns Hopkins University Press, 1978).

36. Cooper, "Conflict and Connection," 1517–18, 1532–33; Daniel James, *Resistance and Integration: Peronism and the Argentine Working Class, 1946–1976* (Cambridge and New York: Cambridge University Press, 1988), 3.

37. Louise E. Walker, *Waking from the Dream: Mexico's Middle Classes after 1968* (Stanford: Stanford University Press, 2013), 225–26. A related critique is Connelly, "Taking Off the Cold War Lens," 739–40.

38. Marco Palacios, *Between Legitimacy and Violence: A History of Colombia, 1875–2002*, trans. Richard Stoller (Durham and London: Duke University Press, 2006), 174, for quote. Representative examples include Alfredo Molano, *Amnistía y violencia* (Bogotá: CINEP, 1980), 61. It is telling that one of this orthodox view's primary dissenters is a foreigner: Daniel Pécaut, *Guerra contra la sociedad* (Bogotá: Espasa, 2001), 27–30, 32–33.

39. "Programa agrario de los guerrilleros," July 20, 1964, in Jacobo Arenas, *Diario de la resistencia de Marquetalia* (Bogotá: Ediciones Abejón Mono, 1972), 128.

40. John L. Comaroff, "Reflections on the Colonial State, in South Africa and Elsewhere: Factions, Fragments, Facts and Fictions," *Social Identities: Journal for the Study of Race, Nation and Culture* 4, no. 3 (1998): 342–43, for quote.

41. On "dropping out" in Mexico, see Eric Zolov, *Refried Elvis: The Rise of the Mexican Counterculture* (Berkeley: University of California Press, 1999), 12, 134, 144.

42. Pablo Piccato makes suggestive comments about the Mexican case in "Comments: How to Build a Perspective on the Recent Past," *Journal of Iberian and Latin American Research* 19, no. 1 (2013): 92–94, 96.

43. Molano, *Amnistía y violencia*, 107; and more recently Sánchez G., *Guerras, memoria e historia*, 2nd ed. (Bogotá: La Carreta Editores, 2009), 29–30, 56.

44. Elizabeth Jelin, *State Repression and the Labors of Memory*, trans. Judy Rein and Marcial Godoy-Anativia (Minneapolis: University of Minnesota Press, 2003), xviii.

CHAPTER 1. MESSENGER OF A NEW COLOMBIA

1. "La clase campesina," speech by Alberto Lleras Camargo, February 22, 1959, in *El primer gobierno*, 1:260.

2. "La Iglesia: El problema no. 1," *Semana*, February 17, 1959, 8; "Hay que combatir la tremenda inercia que pesa sobre el pueblo colombiano," *El Tiempo*, February 22, 1959, 21; "Gran recepción al Presidente en Guateque," *El Tiempo*, February 23, 1959, 17, for quote.

3. *El Tiempo*, February 23, 1959, 17; *Semana*, February 24, 1959, Separata; *El Campesino*, March 1, 1959, 8–9, 16.

4. Petition, Alfonso Rey-Leal [Armenia] to Lleras Camargo, February 25, 1959, 1–2, AGN.PR.SP.29.11.1–2; "Conferencia pronunciada por el Dr. Mauricio Mackenzie, al tomar posesion de la Presidencia de la Academia Colombiana de Jurisprudencia," February 27, 1959, 12, AGN.MinGob.SG.224.2106.46, for quote. See also *Anales* 2, no. 101 (May 6, 1959): 1197. Mackenzie's biography can be found in *Quién es quién en Colombia*, 3rd ed. (Bogotá: Oliverio Perry Editores, 1961), 73–74.

5. "Gran recepción al Presidente en Guateque," 17; "Hay que combatir la tremenda inercia," 21.

6. Gaitán's political taxonomy is best described in Braun, *The Assassination of Gaitán*, 6, 77.

7. I draw here on Angel Rama, *The Lettered City*, trans. John Charles Chasteen (Durham and London: Duke University Press, 1996), especially 23.

8. Gabriel García Márquez, "Prólogo," in Lleras Camargo, *Memorias* (Bogotá: Taurus, 2006), 9.

9. Lleras Camargo, *Mi gente*, 3rd ed., vol. 1 (Bogotá: Banco de la República, 1976), 33 ("nomadic poverty"), 104, 110 ("literary," "would have drowned"), 111, 127, 130; Lleras Camargo, *Nuestra revolución industrial* (Bogotá: Aedita Editores, 1957), 21–22; Leopoldo Villar Borda, *Alberto Lleras: El último republicano* (Bogotá: Planeta, 1997), 51, 57.

10. Villar Borda, *Alberto Lleras*, 28–29; Lleras Camargo, *Mi gente*, 110, 33–87, 151–53.

11. Lleras Camargo, *Mi gente*, 127.

12. Carlos Caballero Argáez, "Nacimiento de un intelectual: Alberto Lleras Camargo en los años veinte del siglo XX," in *Alberto Lleras Camargo y la Universidad de los Andes* (Bogotá: Escuela de Gobierno Alberto Lleras Camargo, Universidad de los Andes, 2007), 54–58 (58, for quote).

13. Lleras Camargo, *Memorias*, 169–72; Richard Stoller, "Alfonso López Pumarejo and Liberal Radicalism in 1930s Colombia," *Journal of Latin American Studies* 27, no. 2 (May 1995): 381–84; Villar Borda, *Alberto Lleras*, 97–98; "Alberto Lleras," *El Tiempo*, June 19, 1929, 3 ("perhaps"), cited in Villar Borda, *Alberto Lleras*, 105.

14. Villar Borda, *Alberto Lleras*, 104–5; Lleras Camargo, "Hora de América," *Revista de América* (January 1945), in *Alberto Lleras: Antología*, vol. 5, *El diplomático*, ed. Benjamín Villegas (Bogotá: Villegas Editores, 2006), 48; Lleras Camargo, *Nuestra revolución industrial*, 21, 11; Lleras Camargo, *Mi gente*, 33–34.

15. Stoller, "Alfonso López Pumarejo and Liberal Radicalism," 385; Gabriel García Márquez, "Cuando el país era joven," *Acción Liberal* 1 (January 1960): 58 (for quote), 60–61.

16. Lleras Camargo, *Mi gente*, 142 ("the best part;" "Back then"); García Márquez, "Cuando el país era joven," 58 ("Liberalism").

17. "López Pumarejo: Vivió y murió en acre olor de tempestad," speech by Lleras Camargo, November 30, 1959, in Alberto Lleras Camargo, *Reflexiones sobre la historia, el poder y la vida internacional*, ed. Otto Morales Benítez (Bogotá: Tercer Mundo Editores and Ediciones Uniandes, 1994), 32.

18. Escuela Superior de Administración Pública (hereafter ESAP), "Memorando numero 5: Sobre capitacion y preparacion del personal en el campo de administracion social," June 30, 1961, 1, AGN.CTR.5.1.128.

19. The politics of the 1936 agrarian reform are discussed in Hirschman, *Journeys toward Progress*, 140–57; Stoller, "Alfonso López Pumarejo and Liberal Radicalism," 393. López's philosophy is summarized in Stoller, "Alfonso López Pumarejo and Liberal Radicalism," 372–75. Useful comments on the views of *los nuevos* and Lleras appear, respectively, in Gerardo Molina, *Las ideas liberales en Colombia: 1849–1914*, 12th ed., vol. 1 (Bogotá: Tercer Mundo Editores, 1988), 155–56, 250–52; and Villar Borda, *Alberto Lleras*, 98, 149, 153–54, 170–71.

20. "Lleras: Un inconformista," *Semana*, August 5, 1958, 15; Villar Borda, *Alberto Lleras*, 176, 179–80, 217; Caballero Argáez, "Nacimiento de un intelectual," 70–71; Lleras Camargo, *Mi gente*, 142–43.

21. The connection between Lleras's writing and speaking is discussed in Otto Morales Benítez, "Prólogo," in Lleras Camargo, *Reflexiones*, xi; and García Márquez, "Prólogo," 9; see also Lleras Camargo, *Memorias*, 234. For Lleras's early political career, see Villar Borda, *Alberto Lleras*, 173–74, 222; García Márquez, "Cuando el país era joven," 60.

22. Villar Borda, *Alberto Lleras*, 96–97, 237, 239–40, 242–43; Villar Borda, "Alberto Lleras y la edad de oro de la OEA," *Revista Credencial Historia* 100 (April 1998), http://www .banrepcultural.org/blaavirtual/revistas/credencial/abril1998/10001.htm; Álvaro Tirado Mejía, *Colombia en la OEA* (Bogotá: Banco de la República and El Áncora Editores, 1998), 16–20, 372–73.

23. Quoted in Brett Troyan, "Gregorio Hernández de Alba (1904–1973): The Legitimization of Indigenous Ethnic Politics in Colombia," *European Review of Latin American and Caribbean Studies* 82 (April 2007): 94.

24. Tirado Mejía, *Colombia en la OEA*, 52–53 ("problems"), 68–69 ("the universal"), 69–72 ("pacific settlement"); "Estamos obligados a ser audaces en nuestros experimentos," speech by Lleras Camargo, April 29, 1945, in *Alberto Lleras: Antología*, 5:69–77; "El sistema regional tiene que conordinarse con el universal," speech by Lleras Camargo, May 11, 1945, in *Alberto Lleras: Antología*, 5:80–83. The Colombian position was codified in Articles 51–54 of the U.N. Charter.

25. Lleras Camargo, "La conferencia de San Francisco y la cancillería colombiana," *Revista de las Indias* (July 1945), in *Alberto Lleras: Antología*, 5:90.

26. Stoller, "Alfonso López Pumarejo and Liberal Radicalism," 394–96; letter, Lleras Camargo to Eduardo Santos, March 14, 1946, 2–3, BLAA.ES.Correspondencia.9.7.525–26.

27. Lleras Camargo, *Memorias*, 233–35.

28. Álvaro Tirado Mejía, *Aspectos políticos del primer gobierno de Alfonso López Pumarejo, 1934–1938* (Bogotá: Procultura and Instituto Colombiano de Cultura, 1981), 294–97.

29. José A. Galvis Serrano, "El cuartelazo de Pasto," *Revista Credencial Historia* 193 (January 2006), http://www.banrepcultural.org/blaavirtual/revistas/credencial/enero2006 /cuartelazo.htm ("Civil war"); letter, López Pumarejo [New York] to Lleras Camargo, December 4, 1940, 1, BLAA.ALC.1.5.45 ("provoke").

30. Palacios, *Between Legitimacy and Violence*, 118–20; Galvis Serrano, "El cuartelazo de Pasto."

31. Telegram, López Pumarejo [New York] to Lleras Camargo, February 1, 1944, BLAA. ALC.1.5.49, for quote; Galvis Serrano, "El cuartelazo de Pasto."

32. "La rebelión quedo circunscrita a Pasto," *El Tiempo,* July 11, 1944, 8; García Márquez, "Prólogo," 9, for quote.

33. Letter, Lleras Camargo to Santos, March 14, 1946, 2, 3; Palacios, *Between Legitimacy and Violence,* 121.

34. Letter, Lleras Camargo to Santos, March 14, 1946, 4.

35. "Madurez de la democracia," speech by Lleras Camargo, May 8, 1946, in *Alberto Lleras: Antología,* vol. 4, *El gobernante,* ed. Benjamín Villegas (Bogotá: Villegas Editores, 2006), 250–59. For his writing style, see Lleras Camargo, *Mi gente,* 143.

36. Memorandum no. 236, British Embassy, Bogotá, to Foreign Office, October 29, 1946, 1–2, NAUK.FO 371/52042; Germán Guzmán Campos, "Antecedentes históricas de la violencia," in *La violencia en Colombia,* 1:42; Villar Borda, *Alberto Lleras,* 122–23, 231–32, 234; "Discurso ante el Congreso de los Estados Unidos," speech by Lleras Camargo, April 6, 1960, in *El primer gobierno del Frente Nacional,* Vol. 2, *Agosto de 1959–julio de 1960* (Bogotá: Imprenta Nacional, 1960), 286, for quote.

37. The best account of intra-Liberal politics is Braun, *The Assassination of Gaitán,* 104–18. See also Palacios, *Between Legitimacy and Violence,* 139. Lleras describes his information sources in letter, Lleras Camargo [Washington] to Santos, February 8, 1952, 2, BLAA.ES.Correspondencia.9.7.545. See also his 1947 comments as editor of *Semana,* in Guzmán Campos, "Antecedentes históricas de la violencia," 42–43.

38. For the 1930s, see Javier Guerrero, *Los años del olvido: Boyacá y los orígenes de la Violencia* (Bogotá: Institutional de Estudios Políticos y Relaciones Internacionales, Universidad Nacional de Colombia, and Tercer Mundo Editores, 1991). For the 1940s, see especially Roldán, *Blood and Fire*; Betancourt E. and García B., *Matones y cuadrilleros.*

39. Preparations for the conference are detailed in Braun, *The Assassination of Gaitán,* 129–31; conference business in Tirado Mejía, *Colombia en la OEA,* 84–98. For Gaitán's career, see Braun, *The Assassination of Gaitán,* chapters 1–5. Lleras mentions his link to Gaitán in *Memorias,* 149.

40. Events in Bogotá are dramatically narrated in Braun, *The Assassination of Gaitán,* chapters 6–7. Gonzalo Sánchez G., *Los días de la revolución: Gaitanismo y 9 de abril en provincia* (Bogotá: Centro Cultural Jorge Eliécer Gaitán, 1983), is the best study of the provincial uprisings. The political breakdown is detailed in Braun, *The Assassination of Gaitán,* 195–99; Palacios, *Between Legitimacy and Violence,* 142–46; Wilde, "Conversations among Gentlemen," 38–40, 46–58; César Augusto Ayala Diago, "El cierre del Congreso de 1949," *Revista Credencial Historia* 162 (June 2003), http://www.banrepcultural.org/blaavirtual /revistas/credencial/junio2003/raro.htm; Arturo Alape, *Las vidas de Pedro Antonio Marín, Manuel Marulanda Veléz, Tirofijo* (Bogotá: Editorial Planeta, 2004), 62–64.

41. Quoted in Villar Borda, *Alberto Lleras,* 271–72.

42. Palacios, *Between Legitimacy and Violence,* 145–46; memorandum no. 81, British Embassy to Foreign Office, September 11, 1959, 1, NAUK.FO 371/139524, for quote; Paul H. Oquist, *Violence, Conflict, and Politics in Colombia* (New York: Academic Press, 1980), 227. For the Liberal resistance, see also Roldán, *Blood and Fire,* 154–55, 257; Alape, *Las vidas,* 102–13.

43. E. J. Hobsbawm, "The Anatomy of Violence," *New Society* 28 (April 11, 1963): 16.

44. Letter, Lleras Camargo to Santos, February 8, 1952, 2.

45. Liberal Party National Directorate Circular No. 20, "La declaración de Benidorm," September 28, 1956, 2, BLAA.ES.Correspondencia.9.7.588+ ("exile"); letter, Lleras Camargo [Washington] to Santos, December 31, 1952, 2–4, BLAA.ES.Correspondencia.9.7.552–54 ("I have," "I am," "I feel," "democratic education"); letter, Lleras Camargo [Madrid] to Santos, March 26, 1929, 2, BLAA.ES.Correspondencia.9.7.490.

46. Lleras Camargo to Santos, December 31, 1952, 3; "Lleras: Un inconformista," 16 ("[thought]"); letter, Lleras Camargo to Santos [Paris], June 1, 1955, 2, BLAA.ES.Correspondencia.9.7.561 ("corner," "All this"); Villar Borda, *Alberto Lleras*, 305.

47. Palacios, *Between Legitimacy and Violence*, 150–51; Lleras Camargo, "Discurso ante la Comisión de Acción Política de Medellín," *El Independiente*, March 3, 1956. Copies of all of Lleras's published production from 1955–56 can be found in his personal archive, as well as in *Alberto Lleras: Antología*, vol. 3.

48. *El Tiempo*, September 12 and 15, 1953; Guzmán Campos, "La segunda ola de violencia," in *La violencia en Colombia*, 1:118. At least 18,700 people ultimately received amnesty, including the military officers behind the 1944 Pasto coup attempt. Germán Guzmán Campos and Orlando Fals Borda, "Algunas consecuencias de la violencia," in *La violencia en Colombia*, 1:313n5; Eduardo Umaña Luna, "El ambiente penal de la violencia o factores socio-jurídicos de la impunidad," in *La violencia en Colombia*, 1:377–82. See also Sánchez G., "Raíces históricas de la amnistía," 223–25.

49. Various dispatches, NARA.59.CDF.2995.721.00/1–1155; "Memorandum sobre orden publico en el pais," August 12, 1959, 4, AGN.MinGob.DM.7.51.27. See also Malcolm Deas, "Violent Exchanges: Reflections on Political Violence in Colombia," in *The Legitimization of Violence*, ed. David E. Apter (London: Macmillan, 1997), 384.

50. Despatch 93, "Censorship—Closing of *El Tiempo*," August 5, 1955, 721.00/8–555, NARA.59.CDF.2995.721.00/8–255; memorandum, "Tension Increasing in Colombia," Albert Gerberich to Dearborn and Lyon, August 17, 1955, 2, 721.00/8–1755, NARA.59.CDF.2995.721.00/8–255.

51. Lleras Camargo, "Discurso en el homenaje al Doctor Eduardo Santos," *El Espectador*, September 24, 1956; letter, Lleras Camargo to Santos [Paris], December 1, 1955, 1, BLAA.ES.Correspondencia.9.7.563; Despatch 195, "Interview with Alberto Lleras Camargo by Sam Pope Brewer, *New York Times* Correspondent," September 13, 1955, 1, 721.00/9–1355, NARA.59.CDF.2995.721.00/8–255.

52. Liberal Party National Directorate Circular No. 20, 3 ("incompatible"); Lleras Camargo, "Un país ocupado," *El Espectador*, January 5, 1956; Lleras Camargo, "Discurso ante la Comisión;" Lleras Camargo, "Carta a un conservador antioqueño," *El Espectador*, December 5, 1955.

53. Despatch 488, "The Third Political Party," January 26, 1955, 5, 721.00/1–2655, NARA.59.CDF.2995.721.00/1–1155; Despatch 100, August 20, 1955, 1, 721.00/8–2055, NARA.59.CDF.2995.721.00/8–255; Lleras Camargo, "La recriminación lustral," *El Espectador*, December 14, 1955, for quote.

54. Lleras Camargo, "La centralización liberticida," *El Espectador*, November 26, 1955. See also Lleras Camargo, "Paz sin condiciones," *El Espectador*, November 29, 1955.

55. Liberal Party National Directorate Circular No. 20, 1.

56. Ibid.; excerpt from diary of Camilo Vásquez Carrizosa [1957?], 1–2, BLAA. ALC.3.36.523.

57. Letter, Laureano Gómez [Benidorm] to Luis Ignacio Andrade et al., September 9, 1956, 1, BLAA.ALC.3.36.534. See also James D. Henderson, *Las ideas de Laureano Gómez* (Bogotá: Tercer Mundo, 1985), 64–66; Darío Acevedo Carmona, "El Pacto de Benidorm o el olvido como antídoto para conjurar los fantasmas del odio y de la sangre," in *Tiempos de paz: Acuerdos en Colombia, 1902–1994*, ed. Medófilo Medina and Efraín Sánchez (Bogotá: Alcaldía Mayor de Bogotá, Instituto Distrital de Cultura y Turismo, 2003), 230. For the photograph, see Caballero Argáez, "Nacimiento de un intelectual," 68.

58. "El Pacto de Benidorm," in *Tiempos de paz*, 257 ("repudiat[ing]," "the persistence"); letter, Gómez to Andrade et al., September 9, 1956, 2 ("violence," "a means," "impartial"); letter, Lleras Camargo to Gómez [Barcelona], October 27, 1956, 2, BLAA.ALC.3.36.540 ("a frenzied," "that time").

59. "El Pacto de Benidorm," 256, 257.

60. Letter, Lleras Camargo to Gómez, August 13, 1956, 2, BLAA.ALC.3.36.529.2; letter, Lleras Camargo to Gómez, October 27, 1956, 1–2.

61. Karl, "The Politics of Colombian Development"; "Prosperous President," *Time*, July 16, 1956, 32; memorandum, "Comments on Situation in Colombia," Gerberich to Davis, Belton, and Maurice Bernbaum, January 19, 1956, 721.00/1–1956, NARA.59.CDF.2996.721.00/1–356, for quote.

62. César Augusto Ayala Diago, "La explosión de Cali: Agosto 7 de 1956," *Revista Credencial Historia* 117 (September 1999): 11.

63. Letter, Lleras Camargo to Gómez, August 13, 1956, 2, for quotes; letter, Lleras Camargo to Guillermo León Valencia, September 4, 1956, 2, BLAA.ALC.3.36.533.2. See also memorandum, American Department, Foreign Office, "Recent Colombian Politics," January 4, 1957, 1+, NAUK.FO 371/126492.

64. "Chairman of the Board," *Time*, January 28, 1957, 43; Jonathan Hartlyn, "Military Governments and the Transition to Civilian Rule: The Colombian Experience of 1957–1958," *Journal of Interamerican Studies and World Affairs* 26, no. 2 (May 1984): 253; Robert A. Karl, "State Formation, Violence, and Cold War in Colombia, 1957–1966" (Ph.D. diss., Harvard University, 2009), 45–47; Despatch 536, "Assessment of President's Bid for Additional Term; Opposition Political Activity; Assessment of *Time* Article," February 8, 1957, 1–2, 721.00/2–857, NARA.59.CDF.2996.721.00/2–557; Despatch 659, March 28, 1957, 2, 721.00/3–2857, NARA.59.CDF.2996.721.00/2–557, for quote. On Rojas and Perón, see Telegram 199, September 24, 1955, 1+, 721.00/9–2455, NARA.59.CDF.2995.721.00/8–255.

65. "Manifiesto de los dos partidos," March 20, 1957, in *Alberto Lleras: Antología*, vol. 3, *El político*, ed. Benjamín Villegas (Bogotá: Villegas Editores, 2006), 229–45; "El acuerdo de los partidos políticos de marzo 20," March 20, 1957, in *Alberto Lleras: Antología*, 3:246–50; "Confirmación de la proclamación de la candidatura del Doctor Valencia en Bogotá," April 1957, in *Alberto Lleras: Antología*, 3:251–61; Karl, "State Formation," 52–55.

66. "'El estudiante de la mesa redonda': Dialoga con 'la generación del Estado de Sitio,'" *Semana*, June 28, 1957, 15.

67. Despatch 926, "Economic Weekly Review—No. 7," June 27, 1957, 3, 821.00/6–2757, NARA.59.CDF.4241.821.00/6–757; letter, Lleras Camargo [New York] to Santos [Paris], December 5, 1956, 2, BLAA.ES.Correspondencia.9.7.592, for quotes.

68. Alberto Bermúdez, *Del Bogotazo al Frente Nacional: Historia de la década en que cambió Colombia* (Bogotá: Tercer Mundo Editores, 1995), 204–11; Karl, "State Formation," 55–56; memorandum, British Embassy to American Department, Foreign Office, May 16, 1957, 1–13, NAUK.FO 371/126492; interview with José Gómez Pinzón, by Carlos Ronderos, in Carlos Ronderos, *Rebelión y amnistía: La historia colombiana del siglo XX contada por sus protagonistas* (Bogotá: Espasa, 2003), 114–18.

69. Karl, "State Formation," 52–57; Bermúdez, *Del Bogotazo al Frente Nacional*, 204–11; Despatch 751, May 8, 1957, 721.00/5–857, NARA.59.CDF.2996.721.00/5–157; memorandum, British Embassy to American Department, May 16, 1957, 1–13; memorandum, Attorney General Eduardo Piñeros y Piñeros to Director, Oficina de Información, Palacio Presidencial, May 29, 1957, 1, AGN.PR.DIP.10.30.2; Despatch 755, May 10, 1957, 721.00/5–1057, NARA.59.CDF.2996.721.00/5–157 ("delirious").

70. Lleras and Laureano had included it in the Benidorm agreement's final paragraph. "El Pacto de Benidorm," 257.

71. "Nada nos desviará en la meta que nos hemos trazado," speech by Lleras Camargo, June 1957, in *Alberto Lleras: Antología*, 3:286.

72. Karl, "State Formation," 63–64; Consejo de Ministros (hereafter CM), Acta No. 152, June 24, 1957, 9–10, 12, AGN.PR.CM.147.14.282–83, 285.

73. "Pacto de Sitges," in *Tiempos de paz*, 259–65; Despatch 116, "Sitges Pact," August 8, 1957, 2, 721.00/8–857, NARA.59.CDF.2997.721.00/7–157.

74. Despatch 223, "Projected Constitutional Amendment," September 11, 1957, Enclosure 1, 2, 721.00/9–1157, NARA.59.CDF.2997.721.00/9–157; *Alberto Lleras: Antología*, 3:206–7; Bermúdez, *Del Bogotazo al Frente Nacional*, 272 ("the problems"); Despatch 119, "Public and Private Reactions to Sitges Pact," August 9, 1957, 2, 721.00/8–957, NARA.59. CDF.2997.721.00/7–157 ("new Colombia"). The *junta* also added an article committing 10 percent of the annual national budget to education ("Projected Constitutional Amendment"; *Anales* 2, no. 177 [September 1, 1959]: 2262).

75. Karl, "State Formation," 67–69.

76. Despatch 500, "December 1 Plebiscite on Constitutional Reform," December 5, 1957, 4, 721.00/12–557, NARA.59.CDF.2997.721.00/12–157, for quote; Karl, "State Formation," 71.

77. Servicio de Inteligencia Colombiana (hereafter SIC), "Apartes algunos noticieros," January 24, 1958, 2, AGN.SIC.3.4(1/4).133, for quote. For additional examples, consult *radioperiódico* transcripts in AGN.PR.SIC.3.4(1/4), AGN.PR.SIC.5.6.

78. This point about the Civil Front's evolution is suggested by Ronderos, *Rebelión y amnistía*, 116.

79. Speech by Major General Gabriel París, October 18, 1957, 30, AGN.PR.JMG.2.38.20, for quote; Hartlyn, "Military Governments," 261. Seven of the plebiscite's fourteen articles dealt with parity.

80. Memorandum of conversation, October 23, 1957, 2, Enclosure 1 to Despatch 396, "Conversation with Liberal Leader Lleras Camargo," October 25, 1957, 721.00/10–2557, NARA.59.CDF.2997.721.00/9–157.

81. Karl, "State Formation," 72; SIC, "Apartes algunos noticieros," March 6, 1958, 2, AGN. PR.SIC.3.4(2/4).347, for quote.

82. Memorandum, "Observations on Colombian Election Returns," Gerberich to Wardlaw and Bernbaum, March 19, 1958, 1, 721.00/3–1958, NARA.59.CDF.2997.721.00/3–

458 ("king-maker"); Karl, "State Formation," 75; SIC, "Apartes algunos noticieros," March 5, 1958, 3, AGN.PR.SIC.3.4(2/4).335 ("we . . . face").

83. Estado Mayor General, Comando General de las Fuerzas Armadas, "Anexo de Inteligencia," April 15, 1958, 2-3, 7, AGN.PR.JMG.9.61.71-72, 77; various reports in AGN. PR.SIC.3.3; Despatch 514, March 18, 1958, 1, 721.00/3-1858, NARA.59.CDF.2997.721.00 /3-458, for quote.

84. Despatch 557, April 1, 1958, 1-2, 721.00/4-158, NARA.59.CDF.2997.721.00/3-458.

85. Despatch 562, April 2, 1958, 2, 721.00/4-258, NARA.59.CDF.2997.721.00/3-458; "La alternabilidad de los partidos es necesaria y civilizadora, dice el Dr. Lleras," *El Tiempo,* April 18, 1958, 1; Hartlyn, "Military Governments," 262-63; Despatch 633, April 25, 1958, 721.00/ 4-2558, NARA.59.CDF.2997.721.00/3-458, for quote.

86. "Joint WeekA No. 31," August 1, 1958, 1, 721.00(W)/8-158, NARA.59.CDF.2999.721 .00(W)/1-358.

87. Memorandum, "Post Mortem on the May 2 Revolt and the May 4 elections," Gerberich to Wardlaw and Sanders, May 12, 1958, 1, 721.00/5-1258, NARA.59.CDF.2997.721.00/ 3-458; Despatch 59, "Joint WeekA No. 29," July 18, 1958, 3, 721.00(W)/7-1858, NARA.59. CDF.2999.721.00(W)/1-358 ("Lleras"); "La credencial," speech by Lleras Camargo, June 16, 1958, in *El primer gobierno,* 1:46 ("overwhelm[ed]"); SIC, "Apartes de algunos radio-periodicos," February 3, 1959, 2, AGN.PR.SIC.5.6.27 ("the task").

88. Hartlyn, "Military Governments," 265-66; Despatch 893, "Joint WeekA No. 19," May 9, 1958, 3, 721.00(W)/5-958, NARA.59.CDF.2999.721.00(W)/1-358, for quote.

89. "Las Fuerzas Armadas," speech by Lleras Camargo, May 9, 1958, in *El primer gobierno,* 1:30, for quote; report, Armed Forces General Command to Minister of War Brigadier General Alfonso Saiz Montoya, December 2, 1958, 2, AGN.PR.SG.299.53.42. The speech's influence is discussed in Francisco Leal Buitrago, *El oficio de la guerra: La seguridad nacional en Colombia* (Bogotá: Tercer Mundo Editores and IEPRI, 1994), 70, 72.

90. "Palabras del Presidente de la Republica en la noche del 22 de abril de 1.959," 11-12, attached to Despatch 732, "President Lleras Analyzes Political and Economic Situation," May 5, 1959, 721.00/5-559, NARA.59.CDF.2998.721.00/1-659 ("simple application"); Hartlyn, "Military Governments," 268, 270; CM, Acta No. 1, August 28, 1958, APR.CM.41.4-10; Despatch 129, "First Year of the Lleras Administration," September 22, 1959, 6, 721.00/9-2259, NARA.59.CDF.2998.721.00/9-859 ("outstanding").

91. Despatch 119, "Joint WeekA No. 32," August 8, 1958, 1, 721.00(W)/8-858, NARA.59. CDF.2999.721.00(W)/1-358 ("on the whole"); "Civilian Takes Over," *Time,* August 18, 1958, 36 ("an example"). Representative radio transcripts can be found in AGN.PR.SIC.5.6.

92. Letter, Lleras Camargo to cabinet, March 18, 1959, 4, AGN.PR.DSP.117.52.44. Lleras deployed similar imagery in "Informe al Congreso," speech by Lleras Camargo, July 20, 1959, in *El primer gobierno,* 1:499.

93. CM, Acta No. 1, August 28, 1958, APR.CM.41.4 ("economic and social policy"), 5 ("facilitate").

94. "La credencial," 45 ("*Convivencia*"); "1958 [alocución de año nuevo]," speech by Lleras Camargo, December 31, 1958, in *El primer gobierno,* 1:233 ("a site"); "Discurso de posesión," speech by Lleras Camargo, August 7, 1958, in *El primer gobierno,* 1:64-65 ("the acclimatization").

95. "Tolima: 'Villarruina,'" *Semana,* March 3, 1959, 22.

96. "Nada nos desviará en la meta que nos hemos trazado," 288.

CHAPTER 2. ENCOUNTERS WITH VIOLENCE, 1957-1958

1. Germán Guzmán Campos, "Los grupos en conflicto," in *La violencia en Colombia*, 1:168, for quote; Guzmán Campos, "La quiebra de las instituciones fundamentales," in *La violencia en Colombia*, 1:305. Guzmán's notebook appears in Guzmán Campos, "Los grupos en conflicto," 168; and "Semblanza de jefes guerrilleros," in *La violencia en Colombia*, 1:197. The sole biographical treatment of Guzmán is "German Guzman Campos o la paz sin reposo," in *Protagonistas del Tolima siglo XX: Las más importantes personalidades del Tolima desde 1900 hasta 1995* (Bogotá: Pijao Editores, 1995), 302-9.

To the greatest extent possible, I have used *La violencia en Colombia* as a primary source to reconstruct Guzmán's knowledge of violence as of 1958. In most cases, I delineate quotes taken from his later writings.

2. CM, May 1958, APR.CM.40.

3. Petition, residents of Cabrera and Villarrica to *junta*, May 24, 1958, 1-2, AGN.PR. JMG.11.73.5-5+, for quote. See also "Boletin informativo de las Fuerzas de Policia no. 4: Comprendido del 25 de julio al 10. de agosto de 1.958" [August 1958], 2, AGN.PR.CMil.7.5.302.

4. Alberto Lleras Camargo, "Fiebre obsidional," *El Espectador*, November 17, 1955 ("the state of siege"); Lleras Camargo, "Discurso en el homenaje al Doctor Eduardo Santos," *El Espectador*, September 24, 1955 ("Colombians").

5. I draw here from "La empresa de rehabilitación," *El Tiempo*, October 8, 1958, 4.

6. Misión "Economía y Humanismo," *Estudio sobre las condiciones del desarrollo de Colombia*, 2 vols. (Bogotá: Aedita Editores, 1958), 1:3, 63, 369–74 (369 for quote); Cámara de Representantes, Comisión Quinta, Acta No. 13, September 4, 1958, 6, AGN.PR.SG.296.15 (1–5).167; memorandum, British Embassy, Bogotá, to Foreign Office, July 24, 1958, 3, NAUK. FO 371/132194. For other foreign economic advisers, see Jeremy Adelman, *Worldly Philosopher: The Odyssey of Albert O. Hirschman* (Princeton: Princeton University Press, 2013), 295–334. Lebret's life and work are outlined in Hugues Puel, "Catholicism and Politics in France in the 20th Century," *Oikonomia: Rivista di Etica e Scienze Sociali* (February 2000), http://www.oikonomia.it/index.php/en/2016/56–2001/febbraio-2001/181-catholicism-and-politics-in-france-in-the-20th-century.

7. "Primer informe del sindico-gerente del Servicio Nacional de Asistencia Social 'SAS' a la H. Junta Militar de Gobierno y a la H. Junta Directiva de la institucion correspondiente al periodo comprendido entre el 10 de agosto y el 31 de diciembre de 1.958" [1959], 20, AGN. PR.DSP.111.63.23; Gonzalo Canal Ramírez, "Balance de opinion: Semana 29 de septiembre— 5 de octubre de 1957" [October 1957], 1, AGN.PR.DIP.9.5.1, for quote; memorandum, British Embassy, Bogotá, to American Department, October 4, 1957, 3, NAUK.FO 371/126493.

8. A seminar examining Lebret's report in fact occasioned Lleras's February 1959 visit to ACPO (see chapter 1). References to the report include Departamento Administrativo de Planeación y Servicios Técnicos, Sección de Programación del Desarrollo Social, "Introduccion a los aspectos sociales del plan general de desarrollo economico y social de Colombia," July 1962, 5, AGN.CTR.8.1.63; *Anales 7*, no. 109 (November 12, 1964): 1814.

9. For a related discussion of social science and geographic scale, see Roger Chartier, "The Saint-Malo–Geneva Line," in *Conflicts and Divisions*, ed. Lawrence D. Kritzman, trans. Arthur Goldhammer, vol. 1, *Realms of Memory: Rethinking the French Past* (New York: Columbia University Press, 1996).

10. See also Adelman, *Worldly Philosopher*, 676.

11. This observation draws on the classic perspective of James Ferguson, *The Anti-Politics Machine: "Development," Depoliticization, and Bureaucratic Power in Lesotho* (Minneapolis: University of Minnesota Press, 1994).

12. Misión "Economía y Humanismo," *Estudio*, 1:249.

13. "Violencia: Datos inéditos," *Semana*, July 22, 1958, 19.

14. Ministerio de Educación Nacional, Instituto de Formación de Supervisores Escolares, "Seminario: Colombia ante un grave problema: La violencia y sus secuelas. Informe final," June 1958, 12, 15 ("there is"), 16 ("to realize"), 24 ("aboriginal"), 28 ("inherited," "warlike spirit," "extreme ambitions," "physical resistance"), 50 ("Anthropological factors"), AGN.PR.SG.298.50.78, 81, 82, 94, 118. The report also includes a particularly perceptive section on partisan conflict in the 1940s and '50s. The report was subsequently circulated to the Colombian press: "Violencia: Se mata porque sí," *Semana*, August 5, 1958, 10–11.

15. For "tragedy," see, among others, "Gobierno a la marcha," *Semana*, August 26, 1958, 12.

16. Gonzalo Canal Ramírez, "La macabra estadística," *El Tiempo*, February 8, 1958, 4 ("It is now time"); *Quién es quién en Colombia*, 204; Gonzalo Canal Ramírez, "Causas de la violencia," *El Tiempo*, June 5, 1958, 4; Despacho 962, "Joint WeekA No. 23," June 6, 1958, 4, 721.00(W)/6–658, NARA.59.CDF.2999.721.00(W)/1–358; Gonzalo Canal Ramírez, *Estampas y testimonios de violencia* (Bogotá: Canal Ramirez, 1966), 5, 8–9, 12–13 ("a peasant region"), *Esta fue mi vereda*, directed by Gonzalo Canal Ramírez (1958; Colombia).

17. Similar contemporary estimates include letter, Antonio García [Santiago, Chile] to Junta Militar de Gobierno, 1957, 5, AGN.PR.JMG.4.69.5; Maurico Amiot, United Nations Food and Agriculture Organization representative, "Necesidad de la promocion social de la agricultura en Colombia," January 1959, 1, AGN.PR.SG.306.55 (1–2).5. The first widely publicized calculations by Colombian academics are Guzmán Campos and Fals Borda, "Algunas consecuencias de la violencia," 312–17.

In the late 1970s, political scientist Paul Oquist provided a year-by-year breakdown of the roughly two hundred thousand deaths he said had occurred between 1947 and 1966; Oquist, *Violence, Conflict, and Politics in Colombia,* 227. Subsequent historiography has accepted these figures, though for a critique of Oquist's estimates, see Ortiz Sarmiento, *Estado y subversión*, 23n1.

18. Writings on this subject include Jaime Posada and Gonzalo Canal Ramírez, *La crisis moral colombiana* (Bogotá: Antares, 1955); "Examen a fondo de la situación del país hizo el jefe del liberalismo," *El Tiempo*, February 26, 1958, 14; Guillermo Bravo Villamil, untitled manifesto [1958], 8, 1, BLAA.ES.PL.12.2.410, 403.

19. Canal Ramírez, *Estampas y testimonios de violencia*, 32. See also Secretaría de Agricultura, Departamento del Tolima, *La violencia en el Tolima* (Ibagué: Imprenta Departmental, 1957), 11.

20. Canal Ramírez, "La macabra estadística"; Canal Ramírez, "Causas de la violencia"; "Preliminary Summary Report of the Colombia Survey Team," 2, "The Colombia Survey Team Preliminary Summary Report: Field Survey Nov.–Dec. 1959," February 1, 1960, HIA. Bohannan.12.The Colombia Survey Team/Preliminary Report/Field Survey/1959 November–December; Guzmán Campos and Fals Borda, "Algunas consecuencias de la violencia," 320; "471.718 desplazados en 128 municipios," *El Tiempo*, July 26, 1953, 18. Oquist claimed

that 2 million Colombians were displaced between 1947 and 1966 (Oquist, *Violence, Conflict, and Politics*, 227).

21. Lars Schoultz, "Urbanization and Changing Voting Patterns: Colombia, 1946–1970," *Political Science Quarterly* 87, no. 1 (March 1972): 30n22; Canal Ramírez, *Estampas y testimonios de violencia*, 32, for quote.

22. Secretaría de Agricultura, Departamento del Tolima, *La violencia en el Tolima*, 5 (for quote), 10–13, 15. The report's influence is suggested by Despatch 915, "Report on Violence in Tolima," May 22, 1958, 1, 721.00/5-2258, NARA.59.CDF.2997.721.00/3-458; see also Grupo de Memoria Histórica, *¡Basta ya!*, 113.

23. Despatch 101, "Joint WeekA No. 31," August 2, 1957, 6, 721.00(W)/8-257, NARA.59. CDF.2999.721.00(W)/1-357; Molano, *Amnistía y violencia*, 76.

24. "Carta al lector," *Semana*, January 20, 1959, 9.

25. See various articles, *El Tiempo*, February 10–14, 1958.

26. "Comisión investigadora de la violencia pidió Alberto Lleras," *El Tiempo*, February 26, 1958, 1; "Examen a fondo de la situación del país," 14, for quotes. Valencia's comment and its fallout are discussed in "Examen a fondo de la situación del país"; Despatch 623, "Joint WeekA No. 4," January 24, 1958, 1–2, NARA.59.CDF.2999.721.00(W)/1-358; "Un diálogo entre Gómez y Montalvo," *El Tiempo*, February 26, 1958, 1. Unless otherwise noted, homicide statistics and observations about patterns in violence are taken from a database in my possession.

27. See, for instance, "Indeclinable contra la violencia ha sido la política de *El Tiempo*," *El Tiempo*, October 18, 1957, 1, 7.

28. Decreto Legislativo No. 0165, May 21, 1958, *Diario Oficial* (June 28, 1958): 914–15. Because the decree was not released to the press at the time of its promulgation (see *El Tiempo*, various dates, May 1958), historians have never worked with its full text.

29. Ibid., 914.

30. Jefferson Jaramillo Marín, *Pasados y presentes de la violencia en Colombia: Estudios sobre las comisiones de investigación* (Bogotá: Pontificia Universidad Javeriana, 2014), 53–56.

31. I draw here in part on the critique of Miguel Angel González, S.J., *La violencia en Colombia: Análisis de un libro* (Bogotá: Centro de Estudios Colombianos, 1962), 3–4.

32. Morales Benítez's earlier peace-work is detailed in Despatch 312, "Views of Otto Morales Benítez on Violence," October 4, 1957, 2, 721.00/10-457, NARA.59.CDF.2997.721.00/7-157. See "Colombianos aquí y allá," *Semana*, November 4, 1958, 43, for quote.

33. "German Guzman Campos," 305–7. See also interview with Eduardo Umaña Luna, by Mauricio Galindo Caballero and Jorge Valencia Cuéllar, in Mauricio Galindo Caballero and Jorge Valencia Cuéllar, *En carne propia: Ocho violentólogos cuentan sus experiencias como víctimas de la violencia* (Bogotá: Intermedio, 1999), 140, 143.

34. "German Guzman Campos," 305–7; Germán Guzmán Campos, "Tensión popular y primera ola de violencia," in *La violencia en Colombia*, 1:69 ("epicenter"); Guzmán Campos, "Reflexión crítica sobre el libro 'La Violencia en Colombia,'" in *Pasado y presente de la violencia en Colombia*, ed. Gonzalo Sánchez G. and Ricardo Peñaranda (Bogotá: CEREC, 1986), 351 ("a moral"). Armando Moreno narrates the assassination of Armero's priest in his blog *Letrasenelojo*, http://letrasenelojo.blogspot.com.

The remaining commission members are entirely voiceless in the documentary record and subsequent studies. The best introduction is Jaramillo Marín, *Pasados y presentes de la violencia en Colombia*, 54–55.

35. Jaramillo Marín, *Pasados y presentes de la violencia en Colombia,* 57–58, provides a useful, though overstated, reconstruction of the commission's first weeks.

36. "Boletin informativo de las Fuerzas de Policia no. 4: Comprendido del 25 de julio al 10. de agosto de 1.958" [August 1958], 2, AGN.PR.CMil.7.5.302. See also petition, residents of Cabrera and Villarrica to *junta,* 1–2; letter, Hernán Valencia Echeverry [Calarcá (Caldas)] to Junta Militar de Gobierno, June 4, 1958, 1–2, AGN.PR.JMG.9.61.129–30. Unless otherwise noted, observations about displacement patterns are drawn from a database in my possession.

37. "Respaldo a la Comisión de la Violencia," *El Tiempo,* June 25, 1958, 16 ("to advance;" "to analyze"); Guzmán Campos, "Reflexión crítica," 351 ("we start"). See also interview with unnamed Peace Commission members, by Olga Behar, in Olga Behar, *Las guerras de la paz* (Bogotá: Planeta, 1985), 34–35.

38. "Discurso de posesión," speech by Lleras Camargo, August 7, 1958, in *El primer gobierno,* 1:55–56, 64 (for quote). The politics of pacification are, like the National Front pact itself, most often treated as a fait accompli: William J. Long and Peter Brecke, *War and Reconciliation: Reason and Emotion in Conflict Resolution* (Cambridge: MIT Press, 2003), 37; Acevedo Carmona, "El Pacto de Benidorm o el olvido como antídoto."

39. Despatch 460, "Violence Problem Increases," January 27, 1961, 9, 721.00/1–2761, Records of the U.S. Department of State Relating to Internal Affairs of Colombia 1960–1963 (hereafter Internal Affairs), reel 1. Similar descriptions include Guzmán Campos, "Tensión popular," 56; Álvaro Campo Posada, "Informe sobre la violencia en Caldas," February 1, 1961, 4, APR.DSP.1961.5.Orden Publico.

40. "Buscar urgentemente el origen de la violencia pide 'El Catolicismo,'" *El Tiempo,* February 8, 1958, 1, 19. See also "Informe al Congreso," 459.

41. Memorandum of conversation, August 8, 1957, 2, DCA.JMCP.1.3.Colombia: Declassified Documents from 1957, for quote; "Examen a fondo de la situación del país," 14; Despatch 1000, "Joint WeekA No. 25," June 20, 1958, 3, 721.00(W)/6–2058, NARA.59.CDF 1955–1959.2999.721.00(W)/1–358; *Anales* 1, no. 4 (July 24, 1958): 37.

42. Concejo Municipal de Ibagué (hereafter CdI), Acta No. 18, December 15, 1958, n.p., AHI.CdI.1958; CdI, Acta No. 40, May 29, 1959, 6, 8, 10, AHI.CdI.1959; Plutonio, "No estamos conformes," *Tribuna,* July 11, 1959, 4, for quote; Néstor Hernando Parra, "Víctimas de la barbarie," *Tribuna,* August 26, 1959. For Ibagué's architectural transformation, see Flora Morcate Labrada and Olimpia Niglio, "La restauración del club campestre de Obregón&Valenzuela en Ibagué: Una experiencia académica," *Arquitectura y Urbanismo* 33, no. 1 (2012): 137–43. Population data from Contraloría Seccional del Tolima, *Anuario estadístico histórico geográfico de los municipios del Tolima 1956* (Ibagué: Imprenta Departmental, 1957); and Contraloría Seccional del Tolima, *Anuario estadístico histórico-geográfico de los municipios del Tolima 1958* (Ibagué: Imprenta Departmental, 1960).

43. For displacement as a Liberal phenomenon, see among others Plutonio, "Derechos desamparados," *Tribuna,* July 7, 1959, 4; and the discussion below. Unless otherwise noted, voting patterns taken from a database in my possession and from *3'000.000 de colombianos cedulados: 1 plebiscito y 2 elecciones; Diciembre de 1958* (Bogotá: Registraduría Nacional del Estado Civil, 1958).

44. SIC, "Boletin subversivo nr. 10," January 27, 1958, 3, AGN.PR.SIC.3.3.25; "Paralizado Ibagué como protesta por la violencia política," *El Tiempo,* January 28, 1958, 1, 15.

45. "Paralizado Ibagué," 1 ("collective eruptions"), 15; "Termina el paro en Ibagué," *El Tiempo*, January 29, 1958, 1, 16 ("tense," "any [act]").

46. "Paralizado Ibagué," 15; "Termina el paro en Ibagué," 16, for quotes.

47. "12 muertos en Rovira, Tolima," *El Tiempo*, January 31, 1958, 1 ("war"), 21 ("the department's"); "El gobierno y los directorios estudian la situación del Tolima," *El Tiempo*, January 31, 1958, 1, 21.

48. "Paralizado Ibagué," 15; "Termina el paro en Ibagué," 16.

49. Letter, Valencia Echeverry to Junta, 2. See also petition, Leopoldo García P. [alias Peligro] et al. [Herrera (Rioblanco) (Tolima)] to Junta Militar de Gobierno, January 18, 1958, 1–4, AGN.PR.JMG.10.62.4–8; and various documents, AGN.PR.CMil.7.5.

50. For Lleras Camargo, see "Discurso de posesión," 64. For one of many other uses, see memorandum, "Transcripción oficio No. 037017-CE-EM-E2/206 procedente del Comando del Ejército," Brigadier General Alberto Gómez Arenas, Armed Forces Commander General, to Interior Minister Guillermo Amaya Ramírez, December 16, 1958, 2, AGN.MinGob.DM.4.30.335. For earlier instances from the 1940s, see Guzmán Campos, "Tensión popular," 50.

51. The term is generally attributed to Miguel Antonio Caro, the famed nineteenth-century scholar-president.

52. Arthur, "How 'Transitions' Reshaped Human Rights"; Crenzel, *Memory of the Argentina Disappearances*.

53. Interview with Germán Guzmán Campos, by Arturo Alape, in Arturo Alape, *La paz, la violencia: Testigos de excepción*, 3rd ed. (Bogotá: Planeta, 1993), 222, for quote.

54. Ibid.; interview with unnamed Peace Commission members, in Behar, *Las guerras de la paz*, 34–35; Guzmán Campos, "Reflexión crítica," 351–52 ("open interviews"); "El problema de los desplazados," *El Tiempo*, July 26, 1958, 6; "La Comisión de la Violencia irá a Cauca, Tolima y Huila," *El Tiempo*, July 22, 1958, 1; "La Investigadora irá a Tierradentro, el Huila y el Carare," *El Tiempo*, August 18, 1958, 8; "Recibida por el obispo de Ibagué la Comisión de Paz," *El Tiempo*, August 23, 1958, 8.

55. Ramiro Andrade, "Detalles ignorados del movimiento: Cinco de los comandantes narran sus actividades," *El Tiempo*, September 3, 1958, 8; Guzmán Campos, "Semblanza de jefes guerrilleros," 196–97. For an illustrative example from central Tolima, see statement of Abdón Guarnizo Céspedes, January 4, 1962, Sumario no. 3724, for homicide, initiated May 18, 1959 [Valle de San Juan], Tribuna Superior, Ibagué, AHI.SJ.1.13.3.32–32+.

56. This interpretation of movement is inspired by Yael A. Sternhell, *Routes of War: The World of Movement in the Confederate South* (Cambridge: Harvard University Press, 2012).

57. "471.718 desplazados en 128 municipios," 18. See also Guzmán Campos, "La quiebra de las instituciones fundamentales," 297.

58. "Lista general de deudores del almacen de Pedro Luis Duque en el municipio de Fresno" [1961/62], AGN.MinGob.OJ.138.1075.5. See also the comments in Roberto Pineda Giraldo, *El impacto de la violencia en el Tolima: El caso de El Líbano*, Monografías sociológicas, no. 6 (Bogotá: Facultad de Sociología, Universidad Nacional de Colombia, 1960), 34; Guzmán Campos, "La segunda ola de violencia," 128; Guzmán Campos, "La quiebra de las instituciones fundamentales," 304–5.

59. Guzmán Campos, "Tensión popular," 75; Guzmán Campos, "Los grupos en conflicto," 168.

60. Guzmán Campos, "Tensión popular," 116, for quotes. See also interview with unnamed Peace Commission members, in Behar, *Las guerras de la paz,* 37. The scope of the commission's work appears in "Es enorme la voluntad de paz en el país, dice Otto Morales," *El Tiempo,* July 30, 1958, 1; and Guzmán Campos, "La segunda ola de violencia," 130, which puts the total number of interviews at twenty thousand.

61. I draw here on the distinction between "selective" and "indiscriminate" violence, in Abbey Steele, "Seeking Safety: Avoiding Displacement and Choosing Destinations in Civil Wars," *Journal of Peace Research* 46, no. 3 (May 2009): 419.

62. Previous discussions of homogenization have explored local contexts, a level of analysis that obscures the predominance of Conservatization. Examples include Arocha, *La violencia en el Quindío,* 155; Ortiz Sarmiento, *Estado y subversión,* 217, 256.

63. See the numerous Liberal works Guzmán cites in *La violencia en Colombia.*

64. For the importance given to such direct exposure, see petition, residents of Cabrera and Villarrica to *junta,* 1–2; Guzmán Campos, "Tanatomanía en Colombia," in *La violencia en Colombia,* 1:254.

65. Decreto Legislativo No. 0165, 914; interview with Guzmán Campos, in Alape, *La paz, la violencia,* 221.

66. Guzmán Campos, "Semblanza de jefes guerrilleros," 202.

67. Guzmán Campos, "Tanatomanía en Colombia," 257, for quote; James D. Henderson, *When Colombia Bled: A History of the Violencia in Tolima* (University: University of Alabama Press, 1985), 179–80; Uribe, *Matar, rematar y contramatar,* 61, 61n37.

68. Guzmán Campos, "Semblanza de jefes guerrilleros," 197, for quotes; Andrade, "Detalles ignorados del movimiento," 8.

69. Roldán, *Blood and Fire,* chapter 1, explores the politics of Conservative mobilization.

70. Guzmán Campos, "Semblanza de jefes guerrilleros," 197, for quotes; Andrade, "Detalles ignorados del movimiento," 8; Andrade, "Cuál es la situación del 'Movimiento Revolucionario' del Suroeste del Tolima," *El Tiempo,* September 3, 1958, 8. Loaiza's economic standing is suggested by Uribe, *Matar, rematar y contramatar,* 55–56; David Gómez Rojas, *Semblanzas del conflicto colombiano: Esquema de consenso nacional de paz* (Bogotá: Produmedios, 2008), 40.

71. Interview with Olimpo Paéz, by Carlos Arango Z., in Arango Z., *FARC, veinte años,* 167–68 ("warrior"); Guzmán Campos, "Manifestaciones culturales de los grupos en conflicto," *La violencia en Colombia,* 1:237; Andrade, "Detalles ignorados del movimiento," 8; Guzmán Campos, "Semblanza de jefes guerrilleros," 198 ("they gave me").

72. Guzmán Campos, "Semblanza de jefes guerrilleros," 198 ("we were"). Details on Parra appear in Andrade, "Cuál es la situación," 8; interview with unnamed Peace Commission members, in Behar, *Las guerras de la paz,* 34–35.

73. Andrade, "Detalles ignorados del movimiento," 8, for quote. Though this article claims to be an exclusive, the discussion with Peligro is nearly identical to what Guzmán recorded in his notebook. See Guzmán Campos, "Semblanza de jefes guerrilleros," 197–98.

74. Andrade, "Detalles ignorados del movimiento," 8 ("they were"), 19 ("the big violence"); Uribe, *Matar, rematar y contramatar,* 64, 67, 144.

75. Andrade, "Detalles ignorados del movimiento," 8 ("Combat"); Guzmán Campos, "Semblanza de jefes guerrilleros," 197 ("a pure," "an incredible talent"). Local respect for

García's leadership is also raised in Homero Hernández Nariño, "Crónica de un pueblo olvidado de Colombia: Herrera—Sur del Tolima" [2010], [8], http://www.centrodememoria historica.gov.co/descargas/memorias_region/cronica_de_un_pueblo_olvidado_herrera_tolima.pdf.

76. Guzmán Campos, "La segunda ola de violencia," 130 ("new way"); Guzmán Campos, "Semblanza de jefes guerrilleros," 199; Guzmán Campos, "Palabras finales," 460. See also Guzmán Campos and Fals Borda, "Algunas consecuencias de la violencia," 321–24; Fals Borda, "Epílogo," in *La violencia en Colombia*, 1:456.

77. "El contacto con los campesinos, relatado por el Padre Guzmán," *El Tiempo*, November 26, 1958, sec. 2, 2; Andrade, "Cuál es la situación," 8.

78. This point draws on Jaramillo Marín's assumption that the priests' power to receive confession aided the commission's work. Jaramillo Marín, *Pasados y presentes de la violencia en Colombia*, 55.

79. Guzmán Campos, "Semblanza de jefes guerrilleros," 199–200.

80. Medófilo Medina, "La resistencia campesina en el sur del Tolima," in *Pasado y presente de la violencia en Colombia*, 237–44; Alape, *Las vidas*, 136–47.

81. José Jairo González Arias, *Espacios de exclusión: El estigma de las repúblicas independientes 1955-1965* (Bogotá: CINEP, 1992), 45–46; Guzmán Campos, "Los grupos en conflicto," 179, for quote; Guzmán Campos, "Semblanza de jefes guerrilleros," 198; Alape, *Las vidas*, 161. The term "orthodox" appears in Andrade, "Cuál es la situación," 8.

82. González Arias, *Espacios de exclusión*, 50–56; González Arias, "La Violencia en el Huila, 1946-1966," in *Historia general del Huila*, ed. Bernardo Tovar Zambrano and Reynal Salas Vargas, vol. 2 (Neiva: Academia Huilense de Historia, 1996), 358–62, 365; González Arias and Marulanda Alvarez, *Historias de frontera*, 18, 40; Alfredo Molano, "La colonización: Voces y caminos," in *Yo le digo una de las cosas . . . : La colonización de la Reserva la Macarena*, ed. Alfredo Molano, Darío Fajardo, and Julio Carrizosa ([Bogotá]: Fondo FEN Colombia, 1989), 56.

83. La Herrera, for instance, lay an oftentimes harrowing four-day ride from the town of Chaparral. Hernández Nariño, "Cronica de un pueblo olvidado de Colombia," [4]; Henderson, *When Colombia Bled*, 200. On the importance of air transport to the commission's tour, see *El Tiempo*, September 3, 1958, 8.

84. Guzmán Campos, "Los grupos en conflicto," 180–81.

85. This analysis is based on a comparison of various photographs in Germán Guzmán Campos, Orlando Fals Borda, and Eduardo Umaña Luna, *La violencia en Colombia: Estudio de un proceso social*, 2nd ed., vol. 1 (Bogotá: Ediciones Tercer Mundo, 1964). See as well *El Cronista*, October 1, 1964, 5; *Riochiquito*, directed by Jean-Pierre Sergent and Bruno Muel (1965; France).

86. Guzmán Campos, "Los grupos en conflicto," 172–73, for quote; Guzmán Campos, "Manifestaciones culturales," 234.

87. "El contacto con los campesinos," 2. See also "La cara de la violencia," *Semana*, December 9, 1958, 37.

88. "La Comisión de la Violencia visitará a Cauca, Tolima y Huila," *El Tiempo*, July 22, 1958, 13. See also Amaya Ramírez, *Memoria del Ministro de Gobierno al Congreso de 1959*, 63.

89. "Report of the Colombia Survey Team: Part I: Colombian Survey (Oct.–Dec. 1959)," April 1960, Chapter 1, Paragraph 72, HIA.Bohannan.13, for quote; Jaramillo Marín, *Pasados y presentes de la violencia en Colombia*, 62.

90. See, for instance, Palacios, *Between Legitimacy and Violence*, 135–36.

91. "Respaldo a la Comisión de la Violencia," 16; "La Comisión de la Violencia irá a Cauca, Tolima y Huila," 1; "Recibida por el obispo de Ibagué la Comisión de Paz," 8; and the discussion in Nicolás Buenaventura, *Historia PCC, Tomo II. Cuaderno II: El origen del Frente Nacional (1957–58)* (Bogotá: CEIS-INEDO, 1990), 49. Later usages of "Peace Commission" include Sánchez G., *Guerra y política en la sociedad colombiana* (Bogotá: El Áncora Editores, 1991), 78.

92. Hugo Vezzetti, *Sobre la violencia revolucionaria: Memorias y olvidos* (Buenos Aires: Siglo Veintiuno, 2009); John Dinges, *The Condor Years: How Pinochet and His Allies Brought Terrorism to Three Continents* (New York and London: Free Press, 2004).

93. Guzmán Campos, "Tensión popular," 116.

94. Jan Gross, *Revolution from Abroad: The Soviet Conquest of Poland's Western Ukraine and Western Belorussia*, expanded ed. (Princeton and Oxford: Princeton University Press, 2002), 116–17, for quote. I also draw here on Roldán, *Blood and Fire*.

95. Consult, for instance, Greg Grandin, "The Instruction of Great Catastrophe: Truth Commissions, National History, and State Formation in Argentina, Chile, and Guatemala," *American Historical Review* 110, no. 1 (February 2005): 46–67.

CHAPTER 3. THE MAKING OF THE CREOLE PEACE, 1958–1960

1. Vicente Silva Vargas, *Las huellas de Villamil* (Neiva: Fondo de Autores Huilenses, 2002), 71–74, 37–39. *Esta fue mi vereda* contains evocative portrayals of social relations on a large coffee farm.

2. Interview with Jorge Villamil Cordovez, by Vicente Silva Vargas, in Silva Vargas, *Las huellas de Villamil*, 482; Silva Vargas, *Las huellas de Villamil*, 306–7; SIC, "Boletín subversivo nr. 41," May 26, 1958, 2, AGN.PR.SIC.3.3.224.

3. Silva Vargas, *Las huellas de Villamil*, 23–29, 314–15.

4. The *tiple* is a small member of the guitar family. Along with the guitar, it serves as a main instrument in *bambuco* performances.

5. This version of the lyrics follows Silva Vargas, *Las huellas de Villamil*, 314. I have omitted the sixth verse, which is followed once more by the second, third, and fourth verses.

6. Most reports of displacement do not provide specific statistics. I have nonetheless been able to account for nearly 2,600 *desplazados* returning during the early Lleras administration, as compared to 335 returning between 1957 and 1958. The former figure does not include press reports of "thousands" of families returning. My sense is that twenty thousand returnees would be a conservative estimate. This would represent between 1.25 and 2.5 percent of the estimated displaced population (see chapter 2), but between 4.5 and 9 percent of those *desplazados* who actively wished to return home. For the latter calculation, see Robert A. Karl, "Century of the Exile: Colombia's Displacement and Land Restitution in Historical Perspective, 1940s-60s," *Canadian Journal of Latin American and Caribbean Studies* (forthcoming).

7. For "truce," see CER, Acta No. 4, September 18, 1958, 2, AGN.MinGob.DM.3.28.11.

8. I draw here on John Borneman, *Political Crime and the Memory of Loss* (Bloomington: Indiana University Press, 2011), 51.

9. "Third Force," *Time*, June 25, 1956, 35; "US Red Cross Sends Aid," *New York Times*, August 8, 1956, 9; "Violencia: Datos inéditos," 19–20.

10. Programa Tolima Grande, April 8, 1956, 2–3, BLAA.TG.4.2.148–49; "Colombia Paper Halts," *New York Times*, April 8, 1956, 10 ("subversive"); "Bogota Paper Resumes," *New York Times*, April 9, 1956, 9; letter, Eduardo Santos [Paris] to Lleras Camargo, May 1, 1956, 2, BLAA.ES.Correspondencia.9.7.578 ("I am exasperated").

11. Memorandum, British Embassy, Bogotá, to American Department, Foreign Office, May 3, 1957, NAUK.FO 371/126492.

12. Despatch 57, "Political Violence in Colombia: The Guerrilla Situation," July 18, 1957, 3, 721.00/7–1857, NARA.59.CDF.2997.721.00/7–157, for quote; memoranda, British Embassy to American Department, February 28, 1957, 1, April 16, 1957, 2, and May 3, 1957, NAUK.FO 371/126492; Despatch 761, "Joint WeekA No. 18," April 18, 1957, 4, 721.00(W)/4–1857, NARA.59.CDF.2999.721.00(W)/1–357; Henderson, *When Colombia Bled*, 200. Yet sectors of the state continued to undermine the talks: "El asesinato de De la Pava: Nieto Linares y Fortunato Gómez huyan de la justicia," *El Tiempo*, August 20, 1959, 3.

13. Henderson, *When Colombia Bled*, 200, 145; Andrade, "Detalles ignorados del movimiento," 8, for quote.

14. "Ayer en el Tolima," *El Tiempo*, December 1, 1963, 4.

15. I draw here on "Informe al Congreso," speech by Alberto Lleras Camargo, July 20, 1959, *El primer gobierno*, 1:459.

16. "Political Violence in Colombia," 2; memoranda, British Embassy, to American Department, June 14, 1957, 2, and July 12, 1957, 2, NAUK.FO 371/12649; CM, Acta No. 145, May 22, 1957, 12, AGN.PR.CM.147.14.151; memorandum, Comisión Seccional de Rehabilitación, Cundinamarca, to José Gómez Pinzón, Consejero de la Presidencia de la República, June 30, 1959, 6–7, AGN.PR.SG.303.16.6–7. On the withdrawal of outside military forces as a form of redress, see Borneman, *Political Crime and the Memory of Loss*, 30.

17. Andrade, "Detalles ignorados del movimiento," 8, for quotes; "La ley del Sur del Tolima," in *La violencia en Colombia*, by Germán Guzmán Campos, Orlando Fals Borda, and Eduardo Umaña Luna, vol. 2 (Bogotá: Taurus, 2005 [1964]), 173–81. See also "Exguerrillero que delinca será objeto de severa sanción," *El Tiempo*, September 3, 1958, 8; "Ley seca en toda la zona guerrillera," *El Tiempo*, September 3, 1958, 8; Andrade, "Cuál es la situación," 8.

18. Guzmán Campos, "Semblanza de jefes guerrilleros," 197, for quote; Guzmán Campos, "Los grupos en conflicto," 179.

19. For the important case of the Sumapaz, see "Fórmulas de paz prestaron los guerrilleros del Tolima," *El Tiempo*, July 11, 1957, 6; "Political Violence in Colombia," 4; Rocío Londoño and Medófilo Medina, "Eso también explica la muerte de Gaitán: Entrevista con José María Villarreal," *Análisis Político* 38 (December 1999): 69–70. For the Plains, see Germán Sánchez G., *Guerra y política*, 39; Karl, "State Formation," 115–16.

20. Petition, García P. [Peligro] et al. to Junta, 1–4. Just four of the petition's signers gave their identity card numbers, a detail suggesting the signers' eagerness to express another marker of their citizenship. That all of them did not list the number likely reflects the state's minimal presence in southern Tolima.

The petition's author was likely Revolución. See interview with unnamed members of the Peace Commission, in Behar, *Las guerras de la paz*, 35–36.

21. This point borrows from Daniel Pécaut, *Violencia y política en Colombia: Elementos de reflexión*, ed. and trans. Alberto Valencia Gutiérrez (Medellín: Hombre Nuevo Editores, 2003), 146–47.

22. I draw here on United States Information Agency, Office of Research and Intelligence, "Communist Propaganda Activities in Colombia, 1957," January 31, 1958, 1, NARA.306. OR.PDRR.4.P-1/1–58.

23. Buenaventura, *Historia PCC, Tomo II*, 72–74.

24. For negotiations at Marquetalia and Riochiquito, see Karl, "State Formation," 112; González Arias, "La Violencia en el Huila, 1946–1966," 369–70. For El Pato, see "Political Violence in Colombia," 3–4; "'Repúblicas independientes': Pato, otro objetivo," *El Tiempo*, June 20, 1964, 15. For Quintero Luna, see also José Chalarca, *La caficultura en el Huila: Historia y desarrollo* (Bogotá: Comité Departamental de Cafeteros del Huila, 2000), 12, 73. Luna sat on the National Coffee Federation's departmental committee alongside Jorge Villamil's sister Graciela, who inherited the seat upon the death of their father. See chapter 7.

25. The term is from Jaime Guaraca; see Alape, *Las vidas*, 234. The question of respect is suggested by Álvaro Valencia Tovar, *Testimonio de una época*, 2nd ed. (Bogotá: Planeta, 1992), 484.

26. Alape, *Las vidas*, 258–60; Eduardo Pizarro Leongómez, *Las FARC (1949–1966): De la autodefensa a la combinación de todas las formas de lucha* (Bogotá: Tercer Mundo Editores, 1991), 156–57; Luis Alberto Matta Aldana, *Colombia y las FARC-EP: Origen de la lucha guerrillera: Testimonio del comandante Jaime Guaraca*, 2nd ed. (Tafalla, Spain: Txalaparta, 2008), 113–15; interview with Jaime Guaraca, by Carlos Arango Z., in Arango Z., *FARC, veinte años*, 148.

27. Alape, *Las vidas*, 29, 129, 203–11; Alberto Vargas Meza, "Relato de la sangrieta pesadilla," *El Espectador*, March 19, 1965, 3.

28. Alape, *Las vidas*, 258–60; Matta Aldana, *Colombia y las FARC-EP*, 113–15; interview with Guaraca, in Arango Z., *FARC, veinte años*, 148. The population of Marquetalia likely ran in the high three figures; see Marulanda's 2008 comments in "Texto completo de la carta escrita por Manuel Marulanda y leída por el 'Mono Jojoy,'" *El Tiempo*, July 18, 2009.

29. Valencia Tovar, *Testimonio de una época*, 349.

30. *Esta fue mi vereda*.

31. Borneman, *Political Crime and the Memory of Loss*, 3, 7.

32. Apendice 2 [1957], AGN.PR.SG.294.59.59.

33. "Anexo de inteligencia no. 3," March 3, 1958, 1, AGN.MinGob.DM.4.31.208. On the seasonal connection between violence and coffee, see also Sánchez G., *Guerra y política*, 71.

34. "La antiviolencia, una política nacional," *El Tiempo*, June 25, 1958, 4, for quotes.

35. Observations about displacement patterns are drawn from a database in my possession.

36. Ortiz Sarmiento, *Estado y subversión*, 310. See also Pineda Giraldo, *El impacto de la violencia en el Tolima*.

37. Petition, Alvaro Varón et al. [Valle de San Juan] to Lleras Camargo, November 1958, 1, 3, AGN.PR.DSP.111.72.10.

38. Guzmán Campos, "Los grupos en conflicto," 162. Cf. Víctor A. Bedoya, "La copla y la tierra," *Tribuna*, August 20, 1959, 5.

39. The practice seems to have been particularly prevalent in Santander. See, for instance, "Pacto de paz firmaron liberales y conservadores de Piedecuesta," *El Tiempo*, July 29, 1958, 6.

40. Memorandum, Tolima Governor Darío Echandía to Interior Ministry, September 16, 1958, 1 ("proposal"), 3 ("Complete calm," "The insurgents"), AGN.MinGob.DM.7.52.114, 116; SIC, "Boletin informativo no. 165," September 5, 1958, 1, AGN.MinGob.DM.4.30.143 ("an agreement," "pledged"); "Firmado acuerdo de paz entre Planadas y Casaverde, Tolima," *El Tiempo*, September 4, 1958, 1, 15.

41. Various documents, AGN.PR.SIC.3.3; "10 millones de pesos en cosechas a punto de perderse en Natagaima," *El Tiempo*, June 11, 1958, 7.

42. SIC, "Boletin informativo no. 169," September 10, 1958, 1, AGN.PR.SIC.4.5.49.

43. SIC, "Boletin informativo no. 252," December 20, 1958, 2, AGN.MinGob.DM.4.30.315. See also "Orden publico: Doctrina de paz," *Semana*, November 18, 1958, 20.

44. "La dinámica del Frente Nacional," speech by Lleras Camargo, December 1, 1958, in *El primer gobierno*, 1:181.

45. "Calendario nacional," *Semana*, December 2, 1958, 38; Karl, "State Formation," 140.

46. Crenzel, *Memory of the Argentina Disappearances*.

47. "La Comisión de la Violencia irá a Cauca, Tolima y Huila," 1; "La Investigadora irá a Tierradentro, el Huila y el Carare," 8; "Recibida por el obispo de Ibagué la Comisión de Paz," 8.

48. Interview with Guzmán Campos, by Alape, in Alape, *La paz, la violencia*, 223.

49. "La situación nacional," speech by Lleras Camargo, September 29, 1958, in *El primer gobierno*, 1:119.

50. As is the case with so much of the commission's existence, the documentation is fragmentary, the most express evidence on this point coming in an interview with unnamed Peace Commission members (likely Guzmán and Morales), in Behar, *Las guerras de la paz*, 37.

51. CER, Acta No. 42, July 1, 1959, 8, AGN.MinGob.DM.3.28.246. The former view is also discussed in Gonzalo Canal Ramírez, "Balance de opinion: Semana 7 al 16 de octubre de 1.957" [October 1957], 3, AGN.PR.DIP.9.5.7.

52. See CER, Acta No. 1, September 8, 1958, 1, AGN.MinGob.DM.3.28.1.

53. *Anales* 2, no. 187 (September 7, 1959): 2440.

54. Despatch 170, "Joint WeekA No. 35," August 29, 1958, 1, 721.00(W)/8–2958, NARA.59. CDF.2999.2999.721.00(W)/1–358; Karl, "State Formation," 314, 316; "La conspiración," speech by Lleras Camargo, December 3, 1958, in *El primer gobierno*, 1:185, for quote. See also Amaya Ramírez, *Memoria del Ministro de Gobierno al Congreso de 1959*, 42. A useful chronology of the state of siege during the National Front period is Gustavo Gallón Giraldo, *Quince años de estado de sitio en Colombia, 1958–1978* (Bogotá: Librería y Editorial América Latina, 1979), 27.

55. CM, Acta No. 113, October 9, 1961, APR.CM.42.941.

56. Despatch 322, "Joint WeekA No. 47," November 25, 1960, 7, 721.00(W)/11–2560, Internal Affairs, reel 2.

57. The commission, comprised of the ministers of government, justice, war, public health, education, and public works, met weekly from September 1958 until the end of 1959. In 1960 it convened a smaller circle of ministers fortnightly.

58. "La rehabilitación," *Semana*, January 13, 1959, 21; "Un anti-inmovilista: Gómez Pinzón," *Semana*, January 20, 1959, 14.

59. Memorandum, Gómez Pinzón to Francisco Triana, Director Técnico de Obras de Rehabilitación, Ibagué, April 13, 1959, AGN.PR.OC.1.6.22; CER, Acta No. 42, July 1, 1959, 7.

60. Karl, "State Formation," 165; CER, Acta No. 42, July 1, 1959, 7, for quote. The 5 percent calculation is extrapolated from 1960 budget figures: "Proyecto de presupuesto de gastos para la vigencia fiscal de 1.960 por dependencias y conceptos economicos" [1959], AGN.PR. DSP.114.19[a].156. If related expenditures are included, the 1959 figure rises to 112 million pesos.

61. "La rehabilitación," 25.

62. CER, Acta No. 40, June 19, 1959, 4–5, AGN.MinGob.DM.3.28.230–31.

63. Molano, Amnistía y violencia, 65; Sánchez G., Guerra y política, 70.

64. "Informe que presentan los directores ejecutivos a la Comision de Rehabilitacion," July 1960, 11, AGN.MinGob.DM.11.85.11; "Gran impulso ha recibido la educación en el Tolima," El Tiempo, July 17, 1960, 6.

65. "Informe al Congreso," 459. See also "Un anti-inmovilista: Gómez Pinzón," 13; Germán Zea, Memorias del Ministro de Justicia al Congreso Nacional en sus sesiones ordinarias de 1959 (Bogotá: Imprenta Nacional, 1959), 21.

66. The teams are discussed in more detail in Karl, "State Formation," 186–97.

67. The literature on this subject includes Braun, The Assassination of Gaitán, 69–73.

68. Memorandum, Gómez Pinzón to Senate President, August 1, 1959, 3, AGN.PR. OC.1.6.44.

69. "Gómez Pinzón examina la rehabilitación," El Tiempo, January 29, 1960, 11; "La situación nacional," 120; CER, Acta No. 1, September 8, 1958, 2; CER, Acta No. 16, November 19, 1958, 3, AGN.MinGob.DM.3.28.98; interview with José Joaquín Matallana, by Alape, in Alape, La paz, la violencia, 216–17; Gómez Pinzón, "Plan tentativo de rehabilitacion del Departamento del Tolima," September 16, 1958, 2, AGN.PR.DSP.111.55.7, for quote.

70. "La rehabilitación," 22.

71. "La situación nacional," 121.

72. CM, Acta No. 10, October 30, 1958, APR.CM.41.92.

73. CER, Acta No. 14, November 5, 1958, 2–3, AGN.MinGob.DM.3.28.80–81. Lleras hoped that Congress would take up the issue in 1959 ("Programa del Congreso extraordinario," speech by Lleras Camargo, January 12, 1959, in El primer gobierno, 1:242).

74. Despatch 412, "Joint WeekA No. 50," December 12, 1958, 7, 721.00(W)/12–1258, NARA.59.CDF.3000.721.00(W)/10–158, for quote. The full text of Decree 0328 of 1958 can be found in Molano, Amnistía y violencia, 161–65. On the oft-confused distinction between pardon and amnesty, see Umaña Luna, "El ambiente penal," 374.

75. Zea, Memorias del Ministro de Justicia, 311.

76. Memorandum, Piñeda Castillo to CER, 3–4. See also the discussion in Karl, "State Formation," 147–49. Piñeda Castillo headed the civilian tribunals, which ultimately rejected roughly two-thirds of the 947 applications that they received. He testified in March 1960 that thanks to this individualized treatment, not a single pardon recipient had violated the terms of Decree 0328.

77. Memorandum, Lleras Camargo et al. to Attorney General, June 17, 1959, 2, AGN. PR.DSP.117.54.5.

78. Molano, Amnistía y violencia, 101.

79. "La restauración de la paz en el Tolima," speech by Darío Echandía, September 1958, in Darío Echandía, Humanismo y técnica (Bogotá: Editorial Kelly, 1969), 265–67, 269 (for

quote); Apolinar Díaz-Callejas, "Memorias actualizadas de un colombiano sentenciado a muerte," *Nueva Sociedad* 100 (April 1989): [12–13].

80. Memorandum, Caja de Crédito Agrario, Industrial y Minero, "Creditos de rehabilitacion con garantia del estado" [July 1959?], 1–2, AGN.PR.SG.303.9.14–15.

81. Ibid., 1–4; marconigrama, Tolima Governor Darío Echandía to Interior Minister Guillermo Amaya Ramírez, February 11, 1959, AGN.MinGob.SG.223.2087.112. The average valuation for rural properties in Rovira in 1958 was only 5,885 pesos. Contraloría Seccional del Tolima, *Anuario estadístico histórico-geográfico de los municipios del Tolima 1958*, 277. Chispas relates his life story in Guzmán Campos, "Semblanza de jefes guerrilleros," 200–210.

82. "Creditos de rehabilitacion," 3–4.

83. Memorandum, Gómez Pinzón to Senate President, 2.

84. CER, Acta No. 19, December 24, 1958, 2, AGN.MinGob.DM.3.28.115; memorandum, Gómez Pinzón to Senate President, 2, 7. Two other state lending agencies were also involved: the People's Bank (Banco Popular) extended credit to people living in provincial urban centers, and the Ranching Development Fund (Fondo Ganadero) made loans specifically for ranching. The term of the loans was five years at 6 percent annual interest. Gallón Giraldo, *Quince años de estado de sitio*, 156.

By comparison, the Rojas-era Office of Rehabilitation and Aid made 8,928 loans in twenty-six Eastern Plains counties. Averaging just over 1,000 pesos, the loans totaled 7.38 million pesos. Diana Andrade Melgarejo, "Guadalupe era de Tame pero Villavicencio se impuso: La rehabilitación de los Llanos Orientales, 1948–1957" (undergraduate thesis, Universidad de los Andes, 2009), 47.

85. "Creditos de rehabilitacion," 1.

86. This point is based on a comment of Peligro's in Andrade, "Detalles ignorados del movimiento," 8. Similar center-periphery relationships likely also explain the concentration of loans in Neiva and Ibagué, whose banks accounted for the second- and fourth-highest number of loans after Chaparral. Alfredo Molano Bravo, "Entrevista con Miguel Pascuas en La Habana," *El Espectador*, July 5, 2014, suggests the link between Ataco and Neiva.

87. "Ecos de la violencia en el Tolima: 3.500 fincas rurales son abandonadas en Rovira," *El Tiempo*, February 15, 1958, 9; "Memorandum sobre orden publico en el pais," 3; Guzmán Campos, "Semblanza de jefes guerrilleros," 200, for quotes.

88. *El Tiempo*, May 9, 1959, 4. Other accounts of Rehabilitación's achievements include Jorge Enrique Gutiérrez Anzola, *Violencia y justicia* (Bogotá: Ediciones Tercer Mundo, 1962), 58; Gómez Rojas, *Semblanzas del conflicto colombiano*, 132–33, 138–39, 143.

89. Memorandum, Eduardo Alvarez Gutiérrez, Interventor de Rehabilitación, to Justice Minister Germán Zea Hernández, October 9, 1959, AGN.PR.OC.1.3.15, for quote; Junín Battalion, Third Brigade, "Analisis de la violencia," November 18, 1959, 2, HIA.Bohannan.31. Item No. 13 Colombia/SA Oct 1959–Jan 1960.

90. In March 1960, officials estimated that Rehabilitación had resettled eight thousand families. A thousand Bogotá-based *desplazados* received direct payments for clothing and transport costs related to repatriation ("Lleras, el liquiador del caos nacional," *El Tiempo*, March 30, 1960, 15; "Informe que presentan los directores ejecutivos," 23). Rehabilitación-coordinated colonization is outlined in Karl, "State Formation," 167–77.

91. Most studies on displacement theorize the influence of ideas in the urban context and do not contemplate the possibility of return migration. See, for instance, Palacios,

Between Legitimacy and Violence, 167–68. Compare as well discussions of armed groups as builders of a "new consciousness": Guzmán Campos and Fals Borda, "Algunas consecuencias de la violencia," 323; and Camilo Torres, "La violencia y los cambios socio-culturales en las áreas rurales colombianas," in *Once ensayos sobre la violencia,* ed. Gonzalo Sánchez G. (Bogotá: Fondo Editorial CEREC and Centro Gaitán, 1985), 65.

92. SIC, "Boletin informativo nr. 167," September 8, 1958, 1–2, AGN.PR.SIC.4.5.44–45. The letter can also be found in Sánchez G., "Raíces históricas de la amnistía," 271–73.

93. "Orden publico: Guerrilleros cesantes," *Semana,* November 25, 1958, 15; "Los pactos han sido eficaces para la pacificación del país," *El Tiempo,* November 26, 1958, sec. 2, 2 ("propos[ed]"); "Colombianos aqui y alla," 43 ("multitudinous guffaws"). The facilitation offered by Tierradentro's apostolic prefect was all the more remarkable given his violent repression of peasant organizing over the prior decade. Pizarro Leongómez, *Las FARC,* 172.

94. Alape, *Las vidas,* 270.

95. Catherine LeGrand, "Labor Acquisition and Social Conflict on the Colombian Frontier, 1850–1936," *Journal of Latin American Studies* 16, no. 1 (May 1984): 31–32; Alfredo Molano, *Selva adentro: Una historia oral de la colonización del Guaviare,* 2nd ed. (Bogotá: El Áncora Editores, 2006), 49.

96. The Peace Commission witnessed this structure at El Pato. Guzmán Campos, "Los grupos en conflicto," 173.

97. Claudio Lomnitz-Adler, *The Return of Comrade Ricardo Flores Magón* (Brooklyn: Zone Books, 2014), chapter 14.

98. Alape, *Las vidas,* 278. See also *Riochiquito.*

99. Letter, Ciro Castaño et al. to Vicente Gómez Cajiao et al., March 15, 1961, 1–2, AGN. MinGob.DM.64.500.69–70 ("we have"); *Ciro: Páginas de su vida* (Bogotá: Ediciones Abejón Mono, 1974), 36, 38 ("within").

100. These paragraphs draw extensively on Alape, *Las vidas,* part 1, especially 77–8.

101. "Delicada situación en el sur del municipio del Ataco," *Tribuna,* April 23, 1960, 2; [ex-guerrilleros del] Sur del Tolima, "Peticiones que hacemos al Gobierno," July 1960, 2, APR.SG.1960.8.Orden Publico Correspondencia. See also Molano Bravo, "Entrevista con Miguel Pascuas." Malcolm Deas makes a similar observation about Marulanda in "Violent Exchanges," 375–76.

102. Michael F. Jiménez, "The Many Deaths of the Colombian Revolution: Region, Class and Agrarian Rebellion in Central Colombia," *Papers on Latin America,* no. 13 (Columbia University, Institute of Latin American and Iberian Studies, 1990): 23.

103. Pierre Gilhodès, "Agrarian Struggles in Colombia," in *Agrarian Problems and Peasant Movements in Latin America,* ed. Rodolfo Stavenhagen (Garden City, N.Y.: Anchor Books, 1970), 433.

104. Alape, *Las vidas,* 272–73, 279; Matta Aldana, *Colombia y las FARC-EP,* 116–17; [Rehabilitation public works spending for Tolima] [1959], 1–2, AGN.PR.DSP.111.55.48–49; SIC, "Boletin informativo nr. 235," November 28, 1958, 2, AGN.PR.SIC.4.5.173. Communists also worked on infrastructure projects at Riochiquito and El Pato. Memorandum, "Informe sobre obras in Belalcázar (Páez)," Hernán Salbarriaga Hernao, Director de Contratos Nacionales, Secretaría de Obras Públicas Departmentales, Cauca, to Cauca Governor Henry Simmonds Pardo, October 15, 1962, APR.SG.1963.14.Gobiernos Seccionales; Molano, "La colonización," 57.

Guaraca received a 1,500-peso rehabilitation loan—less than half the overall average, but a sum equal to the better part of what Guaraca would have earned from a year's wages on Marulanda's road crew. Matta Aldana, *Colombia y las FARC-EP*, 116; memorandum, "Fallas existentes en la Rehabilitacion del Huila" [1959], AGN.PR.SP.32.41.55.

105. For a typical invocation of "*haciendo patria*," see petition, Ernesto Ruiz White [Bogotá] to Interior Minister Eduardo Zuleta Angel, August 18, 1960, 1, AGN.MinGob.DM.13.106.5.

106. Quoted in Alape, *La paz, la violencia*, 245–46.

107. Pizarro Leongómez, *Las FARC*, 193; Molano, *Selva adentro*, 78. But, see also the qualification from William Ramírez Tobón, who originated the concept "armed colonization": "La guerrilla rural en Colombia: ¿Una vía hacia la colonización armada?," in *Estado, violencia y democracia: Ensayos* (Bogotá: Instituto de Estudios Políticos y Relaciones Internacionales and Tercer Mundo Editores, 1990), 70–71.

108. Petition, Misael Antonio Valencia Dussán and Rafael Valencia Dussán [Belalcázar], to Interior Minister, May 13, 1965, AGN.MinGob.DM.64.500.49. See also Comando Militar Tierradentro, "Aprobado el plan socio-economico del Comando Militar de Tierradentro, por el Ministerio de Guerra," October 22, 1965, 7, AGN.MinGob.AI.204.1823.92; confidential memorandum, Gregorio Hernández de Alba, Jefe de la División de Asuntos Indígenas, to Interior Minister Alberto Mendoza Hoyos, March 23, 1965, 2, AGN.MinGob. DM.64.500.64; Alape, *Las vidas*, 232; Movimiento Agrario de Riochiquito, "Asi se desarrolla la violencia en Colombia," December 1962, AGN.MinGob.DM.45.376.193; Joanne Rappaport, *The Politics of Memory: Native Historical Interpretation in the Colombian Andes* (Durham and London: Duke University Press, 1998), 146–48; memorandum, Gloria Triana de Wiesinger and Jaime Valencia Valencia, División de Asuntos Indígenas, to Pedro Javier Soto, Jefe del Departamento de Estudios Técnicos del INCORA, March 9, 1964, 2, AGN. MinGob.AI.197.1726.102; petition, Luis Palomino et al. [Páez (Belalcázar) (Cauca)] to Lleras Camargo, January 27, 1959, AGN.PR.SP.31.25.5; "Lista de las personas deplazadas por la violencia de Araujo y Riochiquito en el municipio de Paez (Tierradentro) Cauca" [1961], AGN. MinGob.DM.64.500.77.

109. Population data derived from "Resultados preliminares del censo ejecutado en 9 de mayo de 1.951," 1951, 1, BLAA.GHdA.1431.

110. Palomino et al. to Lleras Camargo. The signatories to this document largely correspond to people appearing in "Lista de las personas deplazadas por la violencia de Araujo y Riochiquito." See also Concejo Municipal de Paéz [Belalcázar], Resolucion No. 2, December 13, 1960, 2, APR.DSP.1960.3.Concejo M/pal.

111. Roldán, *Blood and Fire*; Karl, "State Formation," 7–12, 204–6.

112. Comando General de las Fuerzas Militares, "Informe complementario no. 8 del cuadro de violencia," February 21, 1961, 19, APR.SG.1961.3.Fuerzos Militares Informe.

113. Letter, Simón de la Pava Salazar to César Mendoza Morales et al. [1957?], 4, AGN. PR.SG.292.29.19. See also Karl, "State Formation," 205–6.

114. "Informe al Congreso," 499, for quote; Contraloría Seccional del Tolima, *Anuario estadistico historico geografico de los municipios del Tolima 1956*, 8; Henderson, *When Colombia Bled*, 203; CER, Acta No. 4, September 18, 1958, 1. Tolima placed below the national average in per capita departmental revenues and expenditures in the years for which data are available. "Ingresos publicos departamentales per capita 1957–1958" and "Gastos departmentales per capita, 1957–1958" [1957], AGN.PR.SG.294.59.86, 87.

115. Karl, "State Formation," 45.

116. Ibid., 217–19.

117. "Repúblicas independientes," 15; "Los departamentos en estado de sitio," *Semana*, January 20, 1959, 23.

118. "Joint WeekA No. 17," April 27, 1959, 5, 721.00(W)/4-2759, NARA.59. CDF.3000.721.00(W)/10-158; Molano, *Amnistía y violencia*, 130; Uribe, *Matar, rematar y contramatar*, 85; memorandum, Ramón Acevedo Blanco, Jefe, Departamento de Orden Público, Interior Ministry, to Solicitor General Rodrigo Noguera Laborde, June 3, 1959, AGN.MinGob.DM.7.56.77. See also *El Clarín* transcript, May 30, 1959, 12:15 P.M. broadcast, AHM.Clarín.6.

119. "Acta numero uno," October 8, 1966, 11–12, AGN.MinGob.AI.207.1888.145. Marulanda had been sentenced to fourteen years in prison, Charry to thirteen, and Ciro to two, on charges including homicide, theft, and arson. See also Dirección General de la Policía Nacional, "Información general de orden publico no. 180," November 16, 1962, 1, AGN. MinGob.DM.34.292.36; petition, Cenon Muñoz V. et al. [Belalcázar] to Huila Governor Jaime Afanador Tovar, April 29, 1965, 4, AGN.MinGob.DM.61.467.21. See also chapter 7.

120. CER, Acta No. 40, June 19, 1959, 5–6; Superintendencia Bancaria, "Informe de visita A: Fondo Ganadero del Huila S.A. de Neiva," July 27, 1959, 3, AGN.PR.SG.309.80.6.

121. I draw here on the classic formulation of David Bushnell, *The Making of Modern Colombia: A Nation in Spite of Itself* (Berkeley: University of California Press, 1993).

122. Silva Vargas, *Las huellas de Villamil*, 75–77; Liliana Martínez Polo, "Villamil, un joven de 79," *El Tiempo*, September 21, 2008.

123. Silva Vargas, *Las huellas de Villamil*, 315, references the song's Christian undertones.

124. "Ibague canta a Colombia," accessed June 20, 2013, http://ibaguecantaacolombia .mex.tl/frameset.php?url=/1384680_Ibague-Canta-a-Colombia.html; "El sanjuanero," *Alcaldía de Ibagué*, accessed June 19, 2013, http://www.alcaldiadeibague.gov.co/web2 /joomla/index.php?option=com_content&view=article&id=274:el-sanjuanero&catid=16: ibague-capital-musical&Itemid=67; "Adriano Tribin Piedrahita o el fundador del Festival Folclorico Colombiano," in *Protagonistas del Tolima*, 772, 774.

125. CdI, Acta No. 41, June 2, 1959, 2, AHI.CdI.1959 ("the city"); Adriano Tribín Piedrahita, "Pasión y vida de una apoteosis," n.d., http://www.festivalfolclorico.com/index.php /el-festival ("Work").

126. Events included Neiva's Bambuco Pageant as well as the Northern Festival, also called the Pro-Peace of Progress Carnival of Líbano, both established in 1960. Silva Vargas, *Las huellas de Villamil*, 90. See also chapter 7.

127. "'Laureano ganará,' es el nombre de bambuco compuesto en Espinal," *El Siglo*, March 12, 1960, 16.

128. "Murió el dirigente político conservador del Huila Felio Andrade," *Caracol*, October 14, 2010, http://www.caracol.com.co/noticias/actualidad/murio-el-dirigente-politico-conservador-del-huila-felio-andrade/20101014/nota/1371424.aspx; Silva Vargas, *Las huellas de Villamil*, 107–12.

129. Nelson Lombana Silva, "Militares sabotean 41 festival folclórico colombiano en Ibagué," *Partido Comunista de Colombia*, June 24, 2013, http://www.pacocol.org/index.php /comite-regional/tolima/4660-militares-sabotean-41-festival-folclorico-colombiano-en-ibague.

130. Rafael Arboleda, "La obra del compositor Villamil Cordovez," *El Cronista*, February 8, 1964, 14, 16.

131. CdI, Acta No. 41, 1, 2 (for quote), 3. See also Abel Ricardo López, "'A Beautiful Class. An Irresistible Democracy': The Formation of the Middle Class in Bogotá, Colombia, 1940–1960" (Ph.D. diss., University of Maryland, College Park, 2008), 120–21.

CHAPTER 4: PEACE AND VIOLENCE, 1959–1960

1. For the role of breezes in local life, see Contraloría Seccional del Tolima, *Anuario estadístico histórico geográfico de los municipios del Tolima 1956*, 350.

2. Differing versions of the episode exist. This account draws on "Siete, los muertos," *Tribuna*, July 26, 1960, 1, 6; "30 detenidos por la matanza en el Valle," *Tribuna*, July 27, 1960, 1, 2; memorandum, "Transcribir informe," Brigadier General Alberto Rueda Terán, Secretario General, War Ministry, to Interior Minister, September 21, 1960, 1, AGN.MinGob. SG.225.2116.92; memorandum, "Su oficio número 00363 de agosto 4," Tolima Governor Rafael Parga Cortés to Interior Minister Alberto Zuleta Angel, August 10, 1960, 2–3, AGN. MinGob.SG.225.2116.97–98.

3. Deas, "Violent Exchanges," 366.

4. Germán Guzmán Campos, "Tanatomanía en Colombia," 246–52.

5. I borrow here from Pierre Bourdieu, "The Force of Law: Toward a Sociology of the Juridical Field," *Hastings Law Journal* 38 (July 1987): 816; and Hendrik Hartog, "Pigs and Positivism," *Wisconsin Law Review* 4 (1985): 899, 932, 934.

6. "Los departamentos en estado de sitio," 23.

7. "1958," 211; "La comunicación con el pueblo," speech by Alberto Lleras Camargo, April 22, 1959, in *El primer gobierno* 1:316; *Anales* (September 7, 1959): 2442.

8. *El Clarín* transcript, March 20, 1959, 7 P.M. broadcast, AHM.Clarín.1.

9. *El Tiempo*, May 9, 1959, 4.

10. Uribe, *Matar, rematar y contramatar*, 84; CER, Acta No. 31, April 14, 1959, 2, AGN. MinGob.DM.3.28.182; telegram, Echandía to Nemesio Camacho, Jefe, Sección de Orden Público, Interior Ministry, April 8, 1959, AGN.MinGob.DM.7.52.232; memorandum, Sarmiento R., Jefe, SIC Tolima, to Jefe, SIC, May 21, 1959, 2, AGN.MinGob.DM.7.52.157.

11. "La comunicacion con el pueblo," 315–16.

12. Another eight people were wounded.

13. Calculations on homicides and massacres in this section are based on the tables in Uribe, *Matar, rematar y contramatar*, which were checked against a database in my possession.

14. Ruling, Tribunal Superior, Ibagué, August 31, 1966, 8–9, in Sumario no. 9437, for homicide, initiated May 12, 1959 [Rovira], Juzgado Primero Superior, Ibagué, AHI. SJ.1.15.1.198–99. *Tribuna* also explicitly made the connection after an August massacre: "Cartas a *Tribuna*," *Tribuna*, August 16, 1959, 3. Cases outside Tolima include memorandum, "Transcripción oficio No. 037017-CE-EM-E2/206," 1–2; "Informe de la Gobernacion sobre los sucesos de Restrepo (V.)," Valle del Cauca Governor Absalón Fernández de Soto and Valle Secretario de Gobierno Mario Hurtado Reina to Amaya Ramírez, September 3, 1959, 2, AGN.MinGob.SG.222.2083.266.

15. Uribe, *Matar, rematar y contramatar*, 13–14, 105–6, introduces the distinction between mobile and localized village (*veredal*) bands. See also Ortiz Sarmiento's suggestive

comments about the relationship between *desplazado* return and armed band (*cuadrilla*) political affiliation, in *Estado y subversión*, 250–51n81.

16. The case was never solved. Ruling, Tribunal Superior, Ibagué, July 9, 1969, Sumario no. 13396, for homicide and personal injuries, initiated May 7, 1959 [Rovira], Tribunal Superior, Ibagué, AHI.SJ.1.17.1.146–53.

17. Uribe, *Matar, rematar y contramatar*, 29–31, 188.

18. Ruling, Juzgado Primero Superior, Ibagué, April 30, 1970, 14, 16, 22, in Sumario no. 1156, cuaderno no. 2, AHI.SJ.1.5.2.14, 16, 22.

19. This paragraph draws primarily on Sumario no. 2445, for multiple homicide and robbery [Rovira], initiated May 9, 1959, Juzgado Cuatro Superior, Ibagué, AHI.SJ.1.5.1.2, 3+, 4+, 6; ruling, Tribunal Superior, Ibagué, September 25, 1960, 4, in Sumario no. 1156, cuaderno no. 2, AHI.SJ.1.5.2.34. In addition to the remainder of these files, see also AHI.SJ.1.5.3.

20. Signalers are described in Guzmán Campos, "Los grupos en conflicto," 182–83.

21. Guzmán Campos, "Tanatomanía en Colombia," 257 ("atrocious"); ruling, Juzgado Primero Superior, Ibagué, April 30, 1970, 18 ("possibly"), in Sumario no. 1156, AHI.SJ.1.5.2.20.

22. Telegram, Parga Cortés to Interior Minister, May 11, 1959, AGN.MinGob. DM.7.52.160; memorandum, Sarmiento R. to Jefe, SIC, 2, "Pacto de paz firmaron en el Valle de San Juan (Tol)," *El Tiempo*, May 19, 1959, 6.

23. Uribe, *Matar, rematar y contramatar*, 85; Sumario no. 9437.

24. Telegram, Vidal Susunaga et al. [Valle de San Juan] to Lleras Camargo, May 29, 1959, AGN.MinGob.DM.7.52.121–22; telegram, Marco Gómez et al. [Ibagué] to Lleras Camargo, June 11, 1959, AGN.MinGob.DM.7.52.62–63; "Graves amenaza [*sic*]," *Tribuna*, July 9, 1959, 5.

25. Petition, Jesús M. Oviedo P. [alias Mariachi] [Planadas (Ataco)] to Lleras Camargo, June 28, 1959, 1–2, AGN.PR.DSP.117.52.69–70. See also minutes of meeting of bipartisan commission to Sumapaz, July 13, 1959, 4–6, AGN.MinGob.DM.7.52.4–6.

26. *Anales 2*, no. 98 (May 2, 1959): 1153–54.

27. *Anales 2*, no. 104 (May 11, 1959): 1231.

28. *Anales 2*, no. 105 (May 12, 1959): 1251 ("chief"); *Anales 2*, no. 106 (May 13, 1959): 1271 ("in Tolima").

29. *Anales* (May 12, 1959): 1246, 1254; *Anales* (May 13, 1959): 1266.

30. *Anales* (May 2, 1959): 1153.

31. Telegram, Miguel Neira et al. [Guamal (Meta)] to Lleras Camargo, May 13, 1959, AGN.MinGob.DM.5.43.93.

32. CER, Acta No. 37, May 27, 1959, 5, AGN.MinGob.DM.3.28.214.

33. Letter, Fermín Ospina Torres, Secretary, National Conservative Directorate, to Prospero Carbonell, Consejero de la Presidencia de la República, August 28, 1959, AGN. PR.SG.308.70.16.

34. No study on the Quindío-Tolima border region presents evidence linking Chispas to the crime, and he is only mentioned once in the voluminous judicial investigation. It is likely that a breakaway band of his followers may have committed the attack on behalf of La Palmita's Liberals. See Ortiz Sarmiento, *Estado y subversión*, 248–50; Arocha, *La violencia en el Quindío*, 157–58, 139–40.

35. *El Clarín* transcript, May 25, 1959, 12:15 P.M. broadcast, AHM.Clarín.6.

36. "¿La Rehabilitación para qué?," *La República*, July 6, 1959, 7.

37. *Something of Value* (United States, 1957) had appeared as *Sangre sobre la tierra* (Blood on the Ground) in late 1957. *El Tiempo,* October 30, 1957, 22.

38. Sánchez G. and Meertens, *Bandits, Peasants, and Politics,* 149; Despatch 728, "Violence and Rehabilitation: Report of Amnesty Tribunal," June 9, 1960, 1, 721.00/6–960, Internal Affairs, reel 1.

39. "Numerosas amnistías fueron solicitidas por la gobernación," *Tribuna,* July 12, 1959, 1, 4.

40. See editions of the *Anales* from May–August 1959.

41. CER, Acta No. 42, July 1, 1959, 3, 6; memorandum, Lleras Camargo et al. to Attorney General, 2.

42. *Calibán,* "Danza de las horas," *El Tiempo,* July 3, 1959, 4.

43. "Los créditos de Rehabilitación se han concedido sin discriminación política: Dicen los 5 gobernadores de departamentos en estado de sitio," *El Tiempo,* June 26, 1959, 1, 19; "'Con mentiras se atiza la violencia desde la capital': Dice el director del liberalismo, Doctor Darío Echandía," *El Tiempo,* June 24, 1959, 1, 14.

44. Memorandum, Lleras Camargo et al. to Attorney General. See also draft, "Declaración del Doctor Jose Gomez Pinzon Jefe de la Oficina de Rehabilitacion," June 17, 1959, 1, AGN.PR.OR.1.2.2.

45. Karl, "State Formation," 228–31.

46. Ibid., 229–33.

47. Villar Borda, *Alberto Lleras,* 244; Karl, "State Formation," 343, 353–56.

48. Memorandum, Guillermo Escobar Alzate, Secretario, Asamblea de Caldas, to Lleras Camargo, October 30, 1959, AGN.PR.SP.31.25.124; "Hay que exigir que la rehabilitación siga en el Tolima," *Tribuna,* July 21, 1959, 5; "Continuar la rehabilitación pidieron en la mesa redonda," *Tribuna,* August 23, 1959, 1; "Peticiones conjuntas," *Tribuna,* August 15, 1959, 6. For the vitriolic Conservative response, see "Defensa de la paz hace un vocero de Ataco, ante las versiones de La República," *Tribuna,* August 21, 1959, 3.

49. Petition, Alfonso Castañeda [Richard] et al., to President et al., September 1, 1959, AGN.MinGob.SG.224.2109.39.

50. A partial exception is César Augusto Ayala Diago: "El origen del MRL (1957–1960) y su conversión en disidencia radical del liberalismo colombiano," *Anuario Colombiano de Historia Social y de la Cultura,* no. 22 (1995): 116, 120.

51. Memorandum no. 81, British Embassy, Bogotá, to Foreign Office, September 11, 1959, 7–8, NAUK.FO 371/139524.

52. See, for example, "Comisión a Chiquinquirá Depto. Boyacá," Agentes Secretos to Jefe, SIC, February 11, 1960, 2–3, AGN.MinGob.DM.12.90.172–73.

53. Despatch 537, "Conversation with Father Vicente Andrade Valderrama, Moral Adviser to the UTC," March 25, 1960, 1, 721.00/3–2560, Internal Affairs, reel 1.

54. Despatch 87, "Joint WeekA No. 32," August 12, 1960, 8, 721.00(W)/8–1260, Internal Affairs, reel 2.

55. Steffen W. Schmidt, "*La Violencia* Revisited: The Clientelist Bases of Political Violence in Colombia," *Journal of Latin American Studies* 6, no. 1 (May 1974): 98n4.

56. "Informe que presentan los directores ejecutivos," 28.

57. "Campesinos con regreso," *El Tiempo,* July 12, 1960, 4.

58. Bourdieu, "The Force of Law," 831.

59. CER, Acta No. 4, September 18, 1958, 3–4.

60. CER, Acta No. 51, September 9, 1959, 3, AGN.MinGob.DM.3.28.297.

61. Fernando Suárez de Castro, "Reforma agraria moderada," *El Tiempo*, March 21, 1959, 4; *Anales* 2, no. 110 (May 18, 1959): 1330; Jaime Callejas Ospina, "La Rehabilitación no puede esperar," *Tribuna*, August 11, 1959, 4, for quote.

62. Memorandum, Gómez Pinzón to José J. Jiménez, Oficina de Rehabilitación, July 24, 1959, 1, AGN.PR.OC.1.6.40; *Anales* 2, no. 106 (May 13, 1959): 1275; Hirschman, *Journeys toward Progress*, 190.

63. CM, Acta No. 33, March 12, 1959, APR.CM.41.314.

64. CER, Acta No. 26, March 4, 1959, 3–4, AGN.MinGob.DM.3.28.151–52; CER, Acta No. 31, April 14, 1959, 4; "No habrá amnistía a partir del 25 de junio," *El Tiempo*, May 26, 1959, 1, 15.

65. Karl, "Century of the Exile."

66. Joint session of Liberal and Conservative Directorates, Ibagué, July 5, 1959, 1, AGN. PR.DSP.117.52.83, for quote; *Anales* 2, no. 188 (September 8, 1959): 2449.

67. CER, Acta No. 55, October 7, 1959, 4, AGN.MinGob.DM.3.28.319, for quote; CER, Acta No. 2, February 1, 1960, 3, AGN.MinGob.DM.12.97.7.

68. *Anales* 2 no. 140 (July 25, 1959): 1745; Secretaría de Información de Palacio, "Boletin de prensa: Actos legislativos 1.959" [1960], 20, AGN.PR.DIP.12.3.155 ("to prevent"); Guillermo Ospina Fernández and Eduardo Ospina Acosta, *Teoría general de los actos o negocios jurídicos* (Bogotá: Editorial Temis Librería, 1980), 228–29 ("deprive[d]"), and the ensuing critique, 228–30.

69. "Sancionada la ley que prohibe el aprovechamiento de la violencia," *El Tiempo*, January 24, 1960, 1 (for quote), 18.

70. *Anales* 2, no. 154 (August 12, 1959): 1931; CER, Acta No. 65, January 11, 1960, 3, AGN. MinGob.DM.3.28.365.

71. CER, Acta No. 65, 3.

72. The foundational decree still invoked Article 121, which limited its geographic scope ("Decreto Numero 0002 de 1.960 [Febrero 4 de 1.960]," 1–2, AGN.MinGob.OJ.141.1110.33–34). Unless otherwise indicated, this section draws on Karl, "State Formation," chapter 4.

73. Eduardo Zuleta Angel, *Memoria del Ministro de Gobierno al Congreso de 1960* (Bogotá: Imprenta Nacional, 1961), 9; petition, Mario Quiroz R. [Belén de Umbría (Caldas)] to Interior Minister, Jan~aury 15, 1961, AGN.MinGob.OJ.134.1044.163, for quote.

74. Memorandum, Rafael Osorio R. to Zuleta Angel, July 1960, 6, AGN.MinGob. DM.9.74.106.

75. José Antonio Tello, Magistrado, Tribunal de Conciliación y Equidad, Cauca, "Informe que rinde el suscrito magistrado del Tribunal de Conciliacion y Equidad del Departamento del Cauca, al Señor Presidente de la Republica, y al Señor Ministro de Gobierno," July 24, 1961, 1, AGN.MinGob.DM.64.500.71.

76. Memorandum, Gómez Pinzón to Director, Banco Cafetero, June 11, 1960, 1, APR. DSP.1960.Oficina del Consejero. See also CER, Acta No. 65, January 11, 1960, 4.

77. The terms are detailed in Augusto Ramírez Moreno, *Memorias del Ministro de Gobierno al Congreso de 1961* (Bogotá: Imprenta Nacional, 1961), 180–81.

78. Karl, "State Formation," 257; Donny Meertens, *Ensayos sobre tierra, violencia y género: Hombres y mujeres en la historia rural de Colombia 1930–1990* (Bogotá: Universidad Nacional de Colombia, Centro de Estudios Sociales, 2000), 200.

79. Karl, "State Formation," 292.

80. "Relacion de las actividades llevadas a cabo por el Tribunal de Conciliacion y Equidad de Pereira, durante el mes de enero de 1.961," February 2, 1961, 5, AGN.MinGob. OJ.134.1044.170.

81. Karl, "State Formation," 249.

82. The process by which this legalistic culture spread deserves further study, but see the pioneering contributions of LeGrand, "Labor Acquisition and Social Conflict," 37–41, 43; Rocío Londoño Botero, *Juan de la Cruz Varela: Sociedad y política en la región de Sumapaz (1902–1984)* (Bogotá: Departamento de Historia, Universidad Nacional de Colombia, 2011), 187–231.

83. Petition, García P. [Peligro] et al. to Junta, 4.

84. Comisión Cuarta, Cámara de Representantes, Acta No. 36, October 16, 1958, 4, AGN.PR.AC.28.1.212; *Anales* 2, no. 145 (July 31, 1959): 1800–1801.

85. CdI, Acta No. 58, September 1, 1959, AHI.CdI.1959, for quote. Other illustrative examples of this sentiment include "Tratamiento preferencial," *Tribuna*, July 7, 1959, 6. This councilman had been the first to propose a folkloric festival, laying the groundwork for Adriano Tribín Piedrahita's advocacy ("Ibague canta a Colombia"). See chapter 3.

86. "La rehabilitación," 25.

87. Letter, Luis Prieto Hurtado, Secretario del Consejero de la Presidencia, to María Guzmán de López [Bogotá], October 1, 1959, AGN.PR.OC.1.3.12; CER, Acta No. 39, June 17, 1959, 6, AGN.MinGob.DM.3.28.225; Comisión Cuarta, Acta No. 36, 4; letter, Gómez Pinzón to Roberto Méndez [Buga (Valle del Cauca)], June 10, 1960, APR.DSP.1960.Oficina del Consejero; *Anales* (September 7, 1959): 2439.

88. Corte Suprema de Justicia, *Gaceta Judicial* 84, no. 2203–5 (October–December 1958): 773–75, 780–85; Guzmán Campos, "Tensión popular," 112, for quote.

89. Corte Suprema de Justicia, *Gaceta Judicial*, 776–78, 782–83.

90. "Condenada la Nación por las masacres de Rionegro, 1949," *El Tiempo*, October 21, 1958, 3. See also "Alarma entre los beneficiarios de la violencia: Condenada la Nación por compra a precio vil," *Tribuna*, October 27, 1960, 1, 7.

91. Corte Suprema de Justicia, *Gaceta Judicial*, 769–70, 786. For an introduction to the doctrine of "responsibility of the state," consult Juan Carlos Henao, "La responsabilidad patrimonial del Estado en Colombia," in *La responsabilidad patrimonial del Estado: Memoria del seminario internacional sobre la responsabilidad patrimonial del Estado* (Mexico, D.F.: Instituto Nacional de Administración Pública, 2000), 108–14.

92. This analysis is informed in part by Armando Gutiérrez Quintero, "La violencia," *El Cronista*, January 3, 1964, 4.

93. Eduardo Nieto Calderón, Gerente General, Banco Popular, to Santa, July 24, 1961, 1, AGN.MinGob.OJ.135.1040.89. Emphasis added.

94. Bourdieu, "The Force of Law," 817, for quotes.

95. Default rates for the previous programs ran at 95 and 65 percent, respectively. *Anales* (September 7, 1959): 2440.

96. Memorandum, Manuel E. Anzola, Subgerente General, Caja Agraria, to Secretario General, Ministry of Treasury and Public Credit, September 6, 1966, 1, AGN.MinGob. DM.73.558.100. A similar institutional aversion to risk had affected colonization and parcelization, two mainstays of rehabilitation under Lleras. Both contemporary officials

and historians have criticized the Agrarian Bank for applying its normal commercial loan criteria across all cases. CER, Acta No. 65, January 11, 1960, 3; Sánchez G., *Guerra y política*, 92–93, 106.

97. Memorandum, Interior Minister Augusto Ramírez Moreno to Caja Agraria Director Augusto Espinosa Valderrama, August 4, 1961, 1–2, AGN.MinGob.DM.23.214.16–17.

98. Despatch 487, "Views of Secretary General of Liberal Party on Certain Political Matters: Communism, President Lleras; National Front; Church," January 22, 1959, 3, 721.001/1–2259, NARA.59.CDF.3000.721.001/1–1355.

99. César Augusto Ayala Diago, *Resistencia y oposición al establecimiento del Frente Nacional: Los orígenes de la Alianza Nacional Popular (ANAPO), Colombia 1953–1964* (Bogotá: Universidad Nacional de Colombia, 1996), 33, 261.

100. Plutonio, "Apuntaciones," *Tribuna*, July 31, 1959, 4.

101. Plutonio, "Derechos desamparados," 4.

102. "¿. . .?," *Tribuna*, September 4, 1959, 1.

103. Despatch 230, "Joint WeekA No. 41," October 14, 1960, 6, 721.00(W)/10–1460, Internal Affairs, reel 1. The state-of-siege governors repeated this stance in September 1961. Memorandum [1961], 2, APR.DSP.1961.5.Orden Publico.

104. CER, Acta No. 23, December 13, 1960, 1, AGN.MinGob.DM.12.97.110.

105. Petition, Jaime Osorio Arroyave [Pereira] to Eduardo Santa, Secretario General, Interior Ministry, January 17, 1962, 1, AGN.MinGob.OJ.144.1132.167.

106. Letter, Alberto Trujillo Escobar [Manizales] to Interior Minister Fernando Londoño y Londoño, April 5, 1962, AGN.MinGob.DM.29.252.155. A similar complaint is José Domingo Tapia Lozano [Girardot] to President Guillermo León Valencia, August 10, 1962, 112, AGN.MinGob.DM.32.273.31–32. See also the discussion in Karl, "Century of the Exile."

107. For an overview, consult Ana María Bejarano and Eduardo Pizarro Leongómez, "From 'Restricted' to 'Besieged': The Changing Nature of the Limits to Democracy in Colombia," in *The Third Wave of Democratization in Latin America: Advances and Setbacks*, ed. Frances Hagopian and Scott P. Mainwaring (Cambridge and New York: Cambridge University Press, 2005). A. Ricardo López has also critiqued historians' overemphasis on these "formal" elements of the National Front. "A Beautiful Class. An Irresistible Democracy," 206.

108. Alape, *Las vidas*, 273; Pizarro Leongómez, *Las FARC*, 180.

109. David Gómez Rojas, *El General Mariachi: Jesús María Oviedo*, 2nd. ed. (Bogotá: Produmedios, 2008), 15–16, 21–22; "Guerrilleros: Al estilo jalisco," *Semana*, September 2, 1958, 39; Andrade, "Detalles ignorados del movimiento," 8, 19; "Serenata de violín ofreció 'Mariachi' a la Investigadora," *El Tiempo*, September 3, 1958, 8. Details about Ataco's microgeography are gleaned from Registraduría Nacional del Estado Civil, *Circunscripciones electorales y división político-administrativo de Colombia 1961*, 3rd ed. (Bogotá: Registraduría Nacional del Estado Civil, 1961), 71.

110. Alape, *Las vidas*, 261, for quote; Gómez Rojas, *El General Mariachi*, 63.

111. Andrade, "Cuál es la situación," 8; Comando General de las Fuerzas de Policía, Estado Mayor F-2, "Boletin semanal informativo no. 3," February 6, 1959, 11, AGN. PR.CM.149.9.20; interview with unnamed Peace Commission members, in Behar, *Las guerras de la paz*, 35; Alape, *Las vidas*, 276; Matta Aldana, *Colombia y las FARC-EP*, 118–19.

112. "'Mariachi' denuncia un nuevo plan subversivo en el Tolima," *El Tiempo*, January 3, 1960, 3 ("We chiefs"); Guzmán Campos, "Semblanza de jefes guerrilleros," 201; Sánchez G.

and Meertens, *Bandits, Peasants, and Politics,* 52–53 ("a sort"); SIC, "Boletin informativo numero 179, September 21, 1958, AGN.PR.SIC.4.5.71; "Plan de rehabilitacion para el departamento del Tolima" [December 1958?], 2, AGN.PR.DSP.111.55.43.

113. Ortiz Sarmiento, *Estado y subversión,* 272n15; Henderson, *When Colombia Bled,* 212; "Quienes promueven la violencia en Rovira," *Tribuna,* July 17, 1959, 1, 2.

114. Despatch 244, "Joint WeekA No. 46," November 18, 1959, 6, 721.00(W)/11–1859, NARA.59.CDF.3000.721.00(W)/5–459; Alape, *Las vidas,* 268.

115. This side of Mariachi's strategy has since been overshadowed by narratives of Fermín Charry's assassination, but pro-MRL Liberals made sure to point it out. "Bandidos de la libertad," *Tribuna,* July 27, 1960, 4. On the early MRL, see Ayala Diago, "El origen del MRL," 97–100.

116. Gómez Rojas, *El General Mariachi,* 64, 66; "El Gobierno envía tropas a Gaitania y Planadas," *El Tiempo,* January 13, 1960, 14.

117. Memorandum, "Sintesis de la comision efectuada por el Mayor Sub-Jefe de Orden Público en la region del sur del Tolima," Major (R) José I. Rodríguez Flórez, Sub-Jefe Sección de Orden Público, SIC, January 18, 1960, 1, AGN.MinGob.SG.226.2124.183; telegram, Huila Governor Felio Andrade Manrique to Oviedo, January 8, 1960, APR.SG.1960.8.Orden Public lico Correspondencia; telegram, Andrade Manrique to Oviedo, January 9, 1960, APR. SG.1960.8.Orden Publico Correspondencia.

118. "'Mariachi' denuncia un nuevo plan subversivo," 3. Alape quotes extensively from this article in *Las vidas,* 261, 268.

119. Gómez Rojas, *El General Mariachi,* 66.

120. On the cattle, see Matta Aldana, *Colombia y las FARC-EP,* 123–26; Martín Camargo, "Bases para una debate parlamentario en defensa del gobierno y el ejercito," October 1964, 1, AGN.MinGob.DM.51.412.83. Marulanda's and Jaime Guarca's reminisces about the shooting appear in Alape, *Las vidas,* 279, 281–82 (for quotes).

121. "Sintesis de la comision," 1.

122. I explore the episode in more detail in "A State in Spite of Itself: Political 'Authority' and the Birth of the FARC in Colombia" (unpublished paper).

123. I draw here on Alape, *Las vidas,* 313–15.

124. In addition to southern Tolima, see "Cambiará radicalmente la situación con las medidas," *El Tiempo,* January 11, 1960, 1, 15; Despatch 355, "Pacification Campaign in Tolima," January 13, 1960, 3, 721.00/1–1360, Internal Affairs, reel 1.

125. Julio Castillo, Coordinador del Sur del Tolima [Planadas], memorandum, "Observación del Coordinador del Sur del Tolima," May 8, 1960, 1, APR.DSP.1960.7.Ministerio Gobierno; "Exodo en Gaitania," *Tribuna,* May 8, 1960, 1, 2.

126. Manuel Marulanda Vélez et al., "Denuncia: Causas que determinaron cambio de posicion de Manuel Marulanda, y excombatientes del Alto Sur del Tolima," July 1960, 1–1+, APR.SG.1960.4.Denuncia. Details about the raid appear in [ex-guerrilleros del] Sur del Tolima, "Peticiones que hacemos al Gobierno," 2; "Delicada situación en el sur del municipio del Ataco," 1, 2.

127. Marulanda Vélez et al., "Denuncia," 1–1+.

128. Ibid., 1+. For "exit," see Albert O. Hirschman, *Exit, Voice, and Loyalty: Responses to Decline in Firms, Organizations, and States* (Cambridge: Harvard University Press, 1970).

129. Palacios, *Between Legitimacy and Violence,* 174.

CHAPTER 5. REFORMIST PATHS, 1960-1964

1. "Informe rendido por los HH.MM. Rodrigo Mendez Lemaitre y Victor Gonzalez, durante la visita al Municipio de Tolu," March 8, 1962, AGN.MinGob.DM.31.262.50–60. Other documents relating to this case are found elsewhere in the same folder, as well as in AGN.MinGob.OJ.137.1063, AGN.MinGob.DM.34.289, and AGN.MinGob.DM.35.299.

2. Ovidio Delgado and Philippe Chenut, "Ernesto Guhl," in *Pensamiento colombiano del siglo XX*, ed. Santiago Castro-Gómez et al., vol. 1 (Bogotá: Pontificia Universidad Javeriana, Instituto Pensar, 2007), 133–34.

3. Airgram A-538, "Joint WeekA No. 8," February 20, 1963, 2, NARA.59.SNF 1963.3870. POL 2–1 COL 2/1/63.

4. Letter, H. J. von Mellenthin to Eduardo Santa, Sección Jurídica, Interior Ministry, March 16, 1961, 1, AGN.MinGob.OJ.137.1063.125.

5. See "Una facultad para América Latina," *El Espacio*, April 12, 1966, 18–19.

6. Álvaro Villarraga S. and Nelson Plazas N., *Para reconstruir los sueños: Una historia del EPL* (Bogotá: Fondo Editorial para la Paz, Fundación Progresar, Fundación Cultura Democrática, 1994), 11.

7. See, for example, República de Colombia, *Memoria del Ministro de Agricultura al Congreso Nacional–1962* (Bogotá: Imprenta Nacional, 1962), viii–ix.

8. This paragraph is influenced by the notion of "revolutionary time," though I choose not to use it in order to emphasize reform as an alternative path to change. Greg Grandin, "Living in Revolutionary Time: Coming to Terms with the Violence of Latin America's Long Cold War," in *A Century of Revolution: Insurgent and Counterinsurgent Violence during Latin America's Long Cold War*, ed. Greg Grandin and Gilbert M. Joseph (Durham and London: Duke University Press, 2010).

9. Letter, German Ambassador A. Mehrmann to Interior Minister Augusto Ramírez Moreno, March 20, 1961, AGN.MinGob.DM.17.151.50.

10. The verbs "to hope" and "to wait" are identical in Spanish (*esperar*). Gerald Martin, *Gabriel García Márquez: A Life* (New York: Alfred A. Knopf, 2009), 159.

11. "Remarks of the President on Departing from El Dorado Airport at Bogota, Colombia," December 17, 1961, JFKL.POF.114.Colombia General 1961.

12. See Joseph Morgan Hodge's recent historiographical review, "Writing the History of Development (Part 2: Longer, Deeper, Wider)," *Humanity: An International Journal of Human Rights, Humanitarianism and Development* 7, no. 1 (Spring 2016): 125–74.

13. "Año del ejecutivo," *Semana*, January 14, 1960, 23.

14. Armando Gutiérrez Quintero, "El Estado intervencionista," *El Cronista*, February 2, 1964, 4; ESAP, "Memorando numero 5," 1.

15. ESAP, "Memorando numero 5," 1 ("solidarity"); Guillermo Nannetti C., "Colombia y el Estado moderno," *El Tiempo*, November 30, 1965, 4 ("manager").

16. Nannetti C., "La Escuela Superior de Administración Pública," Documento no. 50, Conferencia sobre Administración Pública en los Países en Desarrollo [Bogotá], April 15–21, 1963, 5, AGN.CTR.8.1.177.

17. ESAP, "Memorando numero 5," 1.

18. Comité Nacional Agrario (hereafter CNA), Acta No. 1, September 8, 1960, 1, BLAA. CLR.CP.2.1.1.

19. ESAP, "Memorando numero 5," 1.

20. *Mater et Magistra,* encyclical letter of Pope John XXIII, May 15, 1961, http://www
.vatican.va/holy_father/john_xxiii/encyclicals/documents/hf_j-xxiii_enc_15051961_
mater_en.html.

21. *Pacem in Terris,* encyclical letter of Pope John XXIII, April 11, 1963, http://www
.vatican.va/holy_father/john_xxiii/encyclicals/documents/hf_j-xxiii_enc_11041963_
pacem_en.html.

22. Various documents, CUA.USCCB.OGS.190.58; Armando Valencia Ruiz, *Cambiaremos la vida del campo (explicaciones sobre la reforma social agraria de Colombia)* (Pasto: Imprenta Departmental, 1962).

23. Despatch 292, "Joint WeekA No. 45," November 10, 1960, 10, 721.00(W)/11–1060, Internal Affairs, reel 2.

24. "Annual Message to the Congress on the State of the Union," speech by John F. Kennedy, January 30, 1961, http://www.presidency.ucsb.edu/ws/?pid=8045 ("a new"); Despatch 530, "Joint WeekA No. 5," February 3, 1961, 10, 721.00(W)/2–361, Internal Affairs, reel 2 ("a definite policy").

25. Interview with returned Peace Corps Volunteer Joanne Roll, by Robert Klein, June 18, 2005, JFKL.RPCV.OHI.

26. Unless otherwise noted, discussion of Cuba draws on Robert A. Karl, "Reading the Cuban Revolution from Bogotá, 1957–62," *Cold War History* 16, no. 4 (November 2016): 337–58.

27. *Tribuna,* July 14–16, 1959.

28. Alfredo Vásquez Carrizosa, "La ocupación de Cuba," *La República,* July 6, 1960; Manuel Castellanos, "¿Justicia o revolución?," *El Tiempo,* July 13, 1960, 5, for quote; Hirschman, *Journeys toward Progress,* 193.

29. *Quién es quién en Colombia,* 176; Hirschman, *Journeys toward Progress* (see dedication for quote).

30. Hirschman, *Journeys toward Progress,* 194–203; Despatch 268, "Joint WeekA No. 43," October 28, 1960, 8, 721.00(W)/10–2860, Internal Affairs, reel 2, for quote.

31. Karl, "State Formation," 358–59; Hirschman, *Journeys toward Progress,* 195, 212, 213 (for quote).

32. Karl, "Reading the Cuban Revolution."

33. "La ley de reforma agraria," speech by Lleras Camargo, December 13, 1961, in *El primer gobierno del Frente Nacional,* vol. 4, *Agosto de 1961 a agosto de 1962* (Bogotá: Imprenta Nacional, 1962), 95–99; CNA, Acta No. 1, 1, for quote.

34. Matthew Edel, "The Colombian Community Action Program: An Economic Evaluation" (Ph.D. diss., Yale University, 1968), 1:50; "La Escuela Superior de Administración Pública," 18.

35. "La clase campesina," 264–65. See also "106 milliones de pesos sin invertir en Acción Comunal," *El Tiempo,* May 20, 1962, 26.

36. Edel, "The Colombian Community Action Program," 2:283–84.

37. Memorandum, "Sobre la coordinacion de ayuda del Gobierno Nacional y la Alianza para el Progreso y la Accion Comunal" [1963], 2, AGN.MinGob.DM.38.322.74. See also Karl, "State Formation," 567–68.

38. División de Acción Comunal, Sección de Investigación y Planeamiento, "Informe nacional sobre el desarrollo de la comunidad en Colombia presentado a la Secretaria del Consejo Interamericano Economico y Social de la Union Panamericana," April 1963, 4–5, AGN.MinGob.DM.38.321.5–6.

39. Fernando Londoño y Londoño, *Memorias del Ministro de Gobierno al Congreso de 1962* (Bogotá: Imprenta Nacional, 1962), 43.

40. División de Acción Comunal, Sección de Investigación y Planeamiento, "Informe nacional sobre el desarrollo de la comunidad en Colombia, 20–32.

41. Edel, "The Colombian Community Action Program," 1:123, 91–92.

42. Edel, "The Colombian Community Action Program"; Edward Corbett Le Fevre Jr., "A Study of Colombia's Community Development Program, Accion Comunal" (M.A. thesis, Arizona State University, 1966).

43. Edel, "The Colombian Community Action Program," 1:2 (for quote), 135.

44. Ibid., 1:83, 191–92, 227, 271, 2:284. See also División de Acción Comunal, Sección de Investigación y Planeamiento, "Informe nacional sobre el desarrollo de la comunidad en Colombia," 41.

45. Edel, "The Colombian Community Action Program," 1:35–36, 101–2, 104, 106–9, 2:322, 324 (for quote), 325–26, 328–29.

46. "Gómez Pinzón examina la rehabilitación," 11; "Informe que presentan los directores ejecutivos," 28. See also Otto Morales Benítez, *Memoria del Ministro de Agricultura al Congreso de 1961, parte general* (Bogotá: Imprenta Nacional, 1962), xxxix.

47. "Junta de Acción Comunal forman en Rioblanco, T.," *El Espectador,* February 3, 1963, sec. B, 7. See also "Extraordinaria labor cumplen las juntas veredales de Ataco," *El Campesino,* February 11, 1962, 15; "60 juntas comunales tiene Chaparral, Tol.," *El Campesino,* November 8, 1964, 7.

48. Letter, Honorio Pérez Salazar, Secretario, Comité Nacional Agrario, to Interior Minister, February 1, 1961, AGN.MinGob.OJ.135.1040.166, for quote; memorandum, Santa to Pérez Salazar, February 6, 1961, 1–2, AGN.MinGob.OJ.135.1040.164–65; Germán Guzmán Campos, "Etiología de la violencia," in *La violencia en Colombia,* 2:436.

49. "Conclusiones generales del informe sobre desarrollo de Colombia elaborado por la Mision 'Economia y Humanismo'" [1958], 12–13, AGN.PR.SG.303.15.17–18. For an important example from Huila, see Karl, "State Formation," 191–93.

50. See, for instance, Camilo Torres and Berta Corredor Rodríguez, *Las escuelas radiofónicas de Sutatenza, Colombia: Evaluación sociológica de los resultados* (Bogotá: Oficina Internacional de Investigaciones Sociales de FERES, 1961), 7. The self-styled corrective is Hirschman, *Journeys toward Progress,* 21–23.

51. Brett Troyan, "Re-Imagining the 'Indian' and the State: Indigenismo in Colombia, 1926–47," *Canadian Journal of Latin American and Caribbean Studies* 33, no. 65 (2008): 94–95; Troyan, "Gregorio Hernández de Alba," 96–97, 99; memorandum, "Letter from Genaro Payan Regarding Communist 'Enclave' in Colombia," Gerberich to Assistant Secretary of State Roy R. Rubottom and Ernest Siracusa, January 23, 1959, 721.001/1–2359, NARA.59.CDF.3000.721.001/1–1355.

52. Jimena Perry Posada, *Caminos de la antropología en Colombia: Gregorio Hernández de Alba* (Bogotá: Universidad de Los Andes, Facultad de Ciencias Sociales, 2006), 91–92;

Brett Troyan, *Cauca's Indigenous Movement in Southwestern Colombia: Land, Violence, and Ethnic Identity* (Lanham, Md.: Lexington Books, 2015), 128; Troyan, "Gregorio Hernández de Alba," 100; Gregorio Hernández de Alba, "La Republica de Colombia y sus indigenas," April 14, 1964, 1, BLAA.GHdA.1087, for quote.

53. I draw in part here on Catherine Boone, "Property and Constitutional Order: Land Tenure Reform and the Future of the African State," *African Affairs* 106, no. 425 (October 2007): 559, 563–64, 563n15.

54. Ramírez Moreno, *Memorias del Ministro de Gobierno al Congreso de 1961*, 87–88, 233; Hernández de Alba, "La Republica de Colombia y sus indigenas," 1, for quote.

55. Hernández's advocacy for applied anthropology is discussed in Myriam Jimeno, "Consolidación del estado y antropología en Colombia," in *Un siglo de investigación social: Antropología en Colombia*, ed. Jaime Arocha and Nina S. de Friedemann (Bogotá: Etno, 1984), 180; Roberto Pineda Camacho, "La reivindicación del indio en el pensamiento social colombiano," in *Un siglo de investigación social*, 232, 239.

56. Letter, José M. de Armas P. [Bogotá] to President Guillermo León Valencia, September 3, 1962, 1–2, AGN.MinGob.DM.30.255.5–6, for quotes. See also Robert H. Dix, *Colombia: The Political Dimensions of Change* (New Haven: Yale University Press, 1967), 199. Marco Palacios's argument that "economics seemed to be the [decade's] key discipline" applies better after 1966. *Between Legitimacy and Violence*, 174–75.

57. Myriam Ordóñez Gómez, "Formulario de solicitud de beca para estudios en el exterior," January 1963, [5], CUA.USCCB.OGS.190.57.

58. Useful biographical details appear in *Archivo de investigadores de la Universidad Nacional de Colombia: Inventario documental Orlando Fals Borda, 1644–2002* (Bogotá: Universidad Nacional de Colombia, 2004), 23–24. Jaime Arocha, "Antropología propia: Un programa en formación," in *Un siglo de investigación social*, 263–64, offers additional context.

59. Albert O. Hirschman, "Diary: Brazil and Colombia. August 12–September 11, 1957," [2–3], PUL.AOH.57.10.

60. Letter, Orlando Fals Borda to John M. Maclachlan, November 19, 1956, UN. OFB.33.3.67 ("Applied sociology"); letter, Fals Borda to Gaylord M. Couchman, President, and Leo L. Nussbaum, Dean of the College, University of Dubuque, July 12, 1956, 2, UN. OFB.33.1.5 ("After six").

61. Letter, Fals Borda to T. Lynn Smith, February 17, 1958, UN.OFB.33.3.49 ("This is"); letter, Fals Borda to Couchman and Nussbaum, 1 ("mission").

62. Memorandum, "Utilizacion de la sociedad para construccion de escuelas," Fals Borda to Education Minister Reinaldo Muñoz Zambrano, August 1958, UN.OFB.6.2.67–69; "La escuela de Saucio: Una aplicacion practica de desarrollo comunal," speech by Fals Borda, August 31, 1958, UN.OFB.6.2.42–57. Fals details his early intellectual and professional trajectory in Lola Cendales, Fernando Torres, and Alfonso Torres, "'One Sows the Seed, but It Has Its Own Dynamic': An Interview with Orlando Fals Borda," trans. Luis M. Sander, *International Journal of Action Research* 1, no. 1 (2005): 12–19.

63. Written account of Jaime Quijano-Caballero, in Guzmán Campos, *Camilo: Presencia y destino* (Bogotá: Tercer Mundo, 1967), 71–72; "Proclamados objetivos de la Acción Comunal en el país," *El Tiempo*, November 11, 1959, 1, 19; "Fals Borda se retira de Universidad Nacional," *El Tiempo*, July 29, 1970, 22.

64. Gonzalo Cataño, "La sociología en Colombia: Un balance," in *La sociología en Colombia: Balance y perspectivas; Memoria del III Congreso Nacional de Sociología, Bogotá, agosto 20–22 de 1980* (Bogotá: Asociación Colombiana de Sociología, 1981), 54; Fals Borda, "Prólogo," in *La violencia en Colombia* (2005), 1:25; Carlos Miguel Ortiz Sarmiento, "Historiografía de La Violencia," in *La historia al final del milenio: Ensayos de historiografía colombiana y latinoamericana*, ed. Bernardo Tovar Zambrano, vol. 1 (Bogotá: Departamento de Historia, Universidad Nacional de Colombia, 1994), 376–77.

65. Multiple documents, RAC.RG 1–2.S 311.SS 311–S.71.691; López, "A Beautiful Class. An Irresistible Democracy," 110, 119–21; letter, Fals Borda to Leland C. DeVinney, Rockefeller Foundation, May 20, 1960, RAC.RG 1–2.SS 311.SS 311–S.72.692.

66. Newspaper clipping, "Renuncia del Director del Ministerio de Agricultura," n.d., UN.OFB.6.11.2, for quote; Edel, "The Colombian Community Action Program," 1:55.

67. Memorandum of interview, Erskine McKinley, Assistant Director, Social Sciences, Rockefeller Foundation, with Camilo Torres and Antonio Vittorino, Secretary, Department of Sociology, National University, December 1, 1959, RAC.RG 1–2.S 311.SS 311–S.71.691 ("a very intelligent"); Cataño, "La sociología en Colombia: Un balance," 83 ("closest").

68. Interview with Orlando Fals Borda, by Fernando Cubides and Isabel Cristina Duque, in Fernando Cubides, *Camilo Torres: Testimonios sobre su figura y su época* (Medellín: La Carreta Editores and Universidad Nacional de Colombia, 2010), 93–95.

69. Ibid., 92–93.

70. "Detalle de las tareas que desempeñan los profesores e instructores de la Facultad de Sociología, 1962," in *Camilo Torres y la Universidad Nacional de Colombia*, ed. Mario Aguilera Peña (Bogotá: Universidad Nacional de Colombia, 2002), 151–52; interview with Fals Borda, in Cubides, *Camilo Torres,* 100; "Intervención de Camilo Torres en el Comité de Estudios Técnicos de la Reforma Agraria, 1962," in *Camilo Torres y la Universidad Nacional,* 153; Walter J. Broderick, *Camilo Torres: A Biography of the Priest-Guerrillero* (New York: Doubleday, 1975), 116.

71. Speech by Fals Borda, April 6, 1962, 1 ("cited," "*el grito*"), 3 ("a true"), AGN. CTR.2.2.42, 44; "Los jóvenes irrumpen en el panorama mundial," *El Nacional* [Caracas], [April 1961], n.p.; María Cristina Salazar, Cecilia Muñoz, and Carlos Castillo, "Aspectos de la deserción estudiantil en el Departamento de Sociología de la Universidad Nacional de Colombia," *América Latina* [Rio de Janeiro] 11, no. 4 (October–December 1968): 904; "Una facultad para América Latina," 18–19.

72. Studies of modernization theory and the Kennedy administration include Michael E. Latham, *Modernization as Ideology: American Social Science and "Nation Building" in the Kennedy Era* (Chapel Hill and London: University of North Carolina Press, 2000); Nils Gilman, *Mandarins of the Future: Modernization Theory in Cold War America* (Baltimore and London: Johns Hopkins University Press, 2003).

73. "Fals Borda se retira," 22; Mónica Zuleta P. and Alejandro Sánchez L., "La batalla por el pensamiento propio en Colombia," *Nómadas* 27 (October 2007): 130; Fals Borda, "Prólogo," in *La violencia en Colombia,* 1:25, for quote. On pathologies, see Fals Borda, "El conflicto, la violencia y la estructura social colombiana," 436; Fals Borda, "Ciencias sociales, integración y endogénesis," in *Ante la crisis del país: Ideas-acción para el cambio* (Bogotá: Ancora Editores and Panamericana Editorial, 2003), 77–78.

74. Safford and Palacios, *Colombia: Fragmented Land, Divided Society*, 301–3.

75. Edel, "The Colombian Community Action Program," 2:448–49. See also Karl, "State Formation," 549–50. Torres's Louvain thesis on "the proletarization of Bogotá" was eventually published under the Faculty of Sociology's series.

76. Various documents, AGN.CTR.3.2.

77. Pineda Giraldo, *El impacto de la violencia en el Tolima.*

78. Fals Borda, "Soluciones sociales para los problemas del odio y la violencia," October 6, 1960, APR.DSP.1960.7.Min Educacion. Social change in Saucío came about as the result of nearby dam construction, and not partisan violence.

79. Facultad de Sociología, Universidad Nacional de Colombia, "Boletin informativo no. 7," May 1962, 3, AGN.CTR.2.2.31.

80. Fals Borda, field notes, "Cunday, 1962. Abril," 1, 1+ ("the old," "People"), 3, 15 ("Driven"), 22, UN.OFB.25.3.2, 3, 4, 16, 23.

81. Fals Borda, "Cunday, 1962," 22.

82. López, "A Beautiful Class. An Irresistible Democracy."

83. "Camilo explica su retiro de la Universidad," in *Camilo Torres y la Universidad Nacional*, 296.

84. Mario Laserna, *Estado fuerte o caudillo: El dilema colombiano* (Bogotá: Ediciones Mito, 1961), 21, quoted in Miguel Angel Urrego Ardila, *Intelectuales, estado y nación en Colombia: De la Guerra de los Mil Días a la Constitución de 1991* (Bogotá: Universidad Central, Departamento de Investigaciones, and Siglo del Hombre Editores, 2002), 173. Other titles in this vein include Eduardo Santa, *Nos duele Colombia: Ensayos de sociología política* (Bogotá: Ediciones Tercer Mundo, 1962).

85. Despatch 445, "Congressional Elections: The Impact of the Presidential Race," February 12, 1962, 1, 721.00/2–1262, Internal Affairs, reel 2.

86. Karl, "State Formation," 69, 496–98.

87. Interview with Fulton Freeman, by Dennis O'Brien, June 17, 1969, 32 ("He was purely"), 20 ("He was a very interesting"), JFKL.OHI.

88. Despatch 694, "The Political Situation and the President-Elect," June 26, 1962, 3, 721.00/6–2662, Internal Affairs, reel 2.

89. Report, enclosure to airgram, "INR Coffee Study," George A. Ellsworth to Department of State, September 12, 1963, JFKL.NSF.27.Colombia, General 3/63–11/63; Susana Romero Sánchez, "El miedo a la revolución: Interamericanismo y anticomunismo en Colombia, 1958–1965" (M.A. thesis, Universidad Nacional de Colombia, Bogotá, 2007), 232; Karl, "State Formation," 494–96.

90. Karl, "State Formation," 505–10; Airgram A-679, "Joint WeekA No. 16," April 17, 1963, 3, NARA.SNF 1963.3870.POL 2–1 COL 2/1/63, for quote. Valencia's predicament was partially the result of economic policies undertaken by Lleras to ensure the National Front's survival in 1962. Karl, "State Formation," 495. For discussion of the rural ramifications of inflation and falling coffee prices, see Fals Borda, "Cunday, 1962," 22.

91. Interview with Enrique Peñalosa Camargo, by Ronderos, in Ronderos, *Rebelión y amnistía*, 139–40.

92. Airgram A-591, "Joint WeekA No. 11," March 13, 1963, 7, NARA.59.SNF 1963.3870. POL 2–1 COL 2/1/63.

93. Despatch 686, "Lopez Michelsen Elaborates His Position," May 19, 1960, 4, 721.00/5-1960, Internal Affairs, reel 1.

94. Karl, "State Formation," 349–50, 383–84; telegram, "Liberales de Bolivar congratulan a Hernando Villamarin, por su actitud" [1962], UdA.MRL.1.1.116, for quote.

95. This point is suggested by radio transcript, 1962, 3, UdA.MRL.3.21.23. See also Karl, "State Formation," 446–47.

96. Memorandum of conversation, "The López Michelsen View of Elections," March 23, 1960, 1–2, enclosure to Despatch 538, "Election Aftermath—The Lopez Michelsen View," March 28, 1960, 721.00/3-2860, Internal Affairs, reel 1; Karl, "State Formation," 361.

97. Karl, "State Formation," 397–408, 412–18.

98. Fals Borda, "Cunday, 1962," 4, 6.

99. Memorandum of conversation, August 14, 1963, 2, enclosure to Airgram A-135, "Conversation with Orlando Fals Borda," August 29, 1963, NARA.59.SNF 1963.3869.POL 1 COL General Policy Background 2/1/63.

100. For an example from northern Huila, see "Informe de comision del Huila rendido por el Visitador Nacional de Gobierno, Doctor Obduilio Cuadros Prieto" [excerpt], September 15, 1962, 1–3, AGN.MinGob.DM.26.228.6–8.

101. Letter, Peñalosa Camargo to Hirschman, October 29, 1962, PUL.AOH.68.13; memorandum of conversation, enclosure to Airgram A-135, "Conversation with Orlando Fals Borda."

102. Representative flyers linking agrarian reform with (foreign) Communism and violence can be found in AGN.MinGob.SG.225.2115. The wittiest anti-Communist publication is Juan Manuel Saldarriaga Betancur, De la dictadura al comunismo (Medellín: [no publisher], 1962). For the Catholic Church, see Edel, "The Colombian Community Action Program," 2:432; memorandum, "Visit of Mr. Gary MacEoin, National Federation of Coffee Growers of Colombia," August 16, 1961, 1, CUA.USCCB.OGS.195.39.

103. Interview with Peñalosa Camargo, in Ronderos, Rebelión y amnistía, 140.

104. "Somos pueblos sin madurez, pueriles, mal educados, declara Alberto Lleras," El Tiempo, March 20, 1955, 1, 20 (for quote).

105. Letters, Sara Rodríguez de Zuñiga to Interior Minister Fernando Londoño y Londoño, February 12, 1962, 1–2, and February 14, 1962, 1 ("the bandits"), 2 ("keep occupying"), AGN.MinGob.DM.30.253.129–30, 131–32; memorandum, Obdulio Cuadros Prieto, Visitador Nacional de Gobierno, to Director, Caja Agraria, Seccional del Cauca, February 20, 1962, AGN.MinGob.DM.30.253.128. More details of the case appear in Karl, "Century of the Exile."

106. Comando General de las Fuerzas Militares, "Apreciacion de la situacion interna no. 23," October 5, 1961, 3, APR.SG.1961.3.Fuerzos Militares Informe.

107. For further discussion, see Karl, "A State in Spite of Itself."

108. This observation draws on Palacios, Between Legitimacy and Violence, xiv; and letter, Kennedy to Lleras Camargo, January 10, 1962, republished in Villar Borda, Alberto Lleras, 341.

109. Memorandum, Rafael Lizarralde R., alcalde especial, Algeciras, to governor of Huila, November 20, 1964, 3, AGN.MinGob.DM.61.473.21, for quote; memorandum, Ernesto León Díaz L., Personero Municipal, Cajamarca [Tolima], to Valencia, March 16, 1963, 1–2, AGN.MinGob.DM.38.327.64–65.

110. Untitled memorandum [1962?], 4, AGN.MinGob.SG.233.2200.53, for quote; Karl, "State Formation," 576–77.

111. Telegram 690 (Section 1 of 2), November 13, 1965, 1, NARA.59.SNF 1964–1966.2412. POL 13–5 Farm Groups LA 1/1/64. Marc Chernick and Michael Jiménez make a similar argument for the 1970s in "Popular Liberalism, Radical Democracy, and Marxism: Leftist Politics in Contemporary Colombia, 1974–1991," in *The Latin American Left: From the Fall of Allende to Perestroika,* ed. Barry Carr and Steve Ellner (Boulder, Col.: Westview Press, 1993), 69. Karl, "State Formation," 578, discusses other examples.

112. These are detailed in Karl, "State Formation," 529–30.

113. Memorandum, "Sobre el Plan Cafetero de marzo 17 de 1961," April 1, 1961, 4, APR. SG.1961.4.Mn Gobierno, for quote.

114. Edel, "The Colombian Community Action Program," 2:345–46; Steffen W. Schmidt, "Bureaucrats as Modernizing Brokers? Clientelism in Colombia," *Comparative Politics* 6, no. 3 (April 1974): 440; Karl, "State Formation," 531–39.

115. "Líneas básicas sugeridas para coordinación de labores entre la División de Acción Comunal y los Voluntarios de Desarrollo Comunal del Cuerpo de Paz," June 16, 1963, 4, AGN.MinGob.AI.205.1844.46. Emphasis added.

116. Karl, "State Formation," 581–82.

117. These examples come from ibid., 533, 575; Londoño y Londoño, *Memorias del Ministro de Gobierno,* 25.

118. *Anales* 7, no. 107 (November 6, 1964): 1789.

119. Fals Borda, field notes, "Junta de Acción Comunal," July 2 and July 6, 1964, UN.OFB.6.2.9 ("The decadence"), 8 ("Perhaps"), 8+; Fals Borda, field notes, "Acción Comunal. Saucío," July 2, 1964, UN.OFB.6.2.10.

120. Richard Eder, "Colombia Works for Land Reform," *New York Times,* April 8, 1963, 79.

121. Interview with Fals Borda, in Cubides, *Camilo Torres,* 100. See also Broderick, *Camilo Torres,* 185.

122. Francisco Leal Buitrago, "La frustración política de una generación: La universidad colombiana y la formación de un movimiento estudiantil 1958–1967," in *La sociología en Colombia,* 267–76; Cataño, "La sociología en Colombia: Un balance," 60.

123. Broderick, *Camilo Torres,* 134–39; "El padre Camilo Torres se retira de la Universidad Nacional," in *Camilo Torres y la Universidad Nacional,* 268, for quote.

124. *Camilo Torres y la Universidad Nacional de Colombia,* chapter 5.

125. Broderick, *Camilo Torres,* 165–70; Eder, "Colombia Works for Land Reform," 79.

126. Broderick, *Camilo Torres,* 170–73.

127. República de Colombia, *Memoria del Ministro de Agricultura,* lvii.

128. "Camilo explica su retiro de la Universidad," 296.

CHAPTER 6. BOOKS AND BANDITS, 1962–1964

1. Canal Ramírez, "Balance de opinion: Semana 16 al 24 de octubre de 1.957" [October 1957], 4, AGN.PR.DIP.9.5.13.

2. Airgram A-159, "Joint WeekA No. 37," September 12, 1962, 5–6, 721.00(W)/9-1262, Internal Affairs, reel 2; Airgram A-144, "Joint WeekA No. 36," September 5, 1962, 2, 721.00(W)/9-562, Internal Affairs, reel 2, for quote.

3. Palacios, *Between Legitimacy and Violence*, 136; Daniel Pécaut, *Las FARC: ¿Una guerrilla sin fin o sin fines?*, trans. Pedro Lama (Bogotá: Grupo Editorial Norma, 2008), 34.

4. "Propuesta legislación de emergencia," *El Tiempo*, August 23, 1962, 6. The minister's original statement appears in "El discurso del Ministro de Justicia en el Senado," *El Tiempo*, August 25, 1962, 17.

5. Germán Guzmán Campos, "Reflexión crítica," 354. Guzmán places Lleras's visit in 1959, but see *El Tiempo*, January 8, 1960, 1, 22.

6. Orlando Fals Borda, "Prólogo para la presente edición," in *La violencia en Colombia* (2005), 1:20; Guzmán Campos, "Reflexión crítica," 354, for quote; Fals Borda, "Introducción," in *La violencia en Colombia*, 2:29.

7. See also Torres's 1965 explanation of his attraction to Christianity and social science, which Guzmán quotes in his biography, *Camilo: Presencia y destino*, 74. Between Guzmán's two postings in Fresno (1946–50, 1951–58), the parish was served by another Louvaine-trained priest-sociologist. "Perpetuo Socorro," *Diócesis de Líbano-Honda*, accessed June 2, 2015, http://www.diocesisdelibanohonda.com/site/index.php?option=com_contact&view=contact&id=17%3Aperpetuo-socorro&catid=14%3Aparroquias&Itemid=27.

8. Facultad de Sociología, "Boletin informativo no. 7," 3. Guzmán also put his expertise to work for INCORA's Division of Basic Research (Estudios Básicos). "Personas que integran la división de estudios básicos del INCORA," n.d., UN.EG.26.10.

9. Guzmán Campos, "Reflexión crítica," 354–55; interview with Fals Borda, in Cubides, *Camilo Torres*, 97. After a two-year stint on the clemency tribunals, Umaña chose an open post at the Justice Ministry over an offer to join the Conciliation and Equity Tribunal being formed in Ibagué. Karl, "State Formation," 245n24.

10. The label "freethinking" is suggested by "Sin imprimatur," *El Siglo*, September 28, 1962, 4, quoted in Fals Borda, "Introducción," 27. On the contributions of Torres and the Peace Foundation, see interview with Fals Borda, in Cubides, *Camilo Torres*, 97; Germán Guzmán Campos, "Testimonio," in *La violencia en Colombia*, 1:34; Fals Borda, "Prólogo," 32.

11. Guzmán Campos, "Reflexión crítica," 355.

12. Interview with Fals Borda, in Cubides, *Camilo Torres*, 97–98; Ortiz Sarmiento, "Historiografía de La Violencia," 390, for quote. Fals's push for a homegrown brand of intellectual and political action would deepen; for an early expression, see Fals Borda, "Prólogo," 25; later examples include Fals Borda, "Prólogo para la presente edición," 14, 18–20.

13. Cendales, Torres, and Torres, "One Sows the Seed," 24. For a contemporary critique of Fals's "verbalism," see González, *La violencia en Colombia: Análisis de un libro*, 24.

14. Umaña Luna, "El ambiente penal," 327, for quote.

15. Guzmán Campos and Fals Borda, "Algunas consecuencias de la violencia," 325.

16. The generic usage of "*la violencia*" in later Latin American conflicts is also suggestive: Kimberly Theidon, *Intimate Enemies: Violence and Reconciliation in Peru* (Philadelphia: University of Pennsylvania Press, 2013).

17. "Es muy duro para una madre saber que su hijo es malo, dijo progenitora de Desquite," *El Cronista*, March 18, 1964, 8; Fals Borda, "El conflicto, la violencia y la estructura social colombiana," 432, 436, 441 (for quote).

18. Octava Brigada, *De la violencia a la paz* (Armenia: Imprenta Departamental de Caldas, 1965), 15, 24.

19. See Fals Borda's handwritten annotations on the text of the speech that Carlos Echeverri Herrera, dean of the National University's Faculty of Economic Sciences, delivered at the inauguration of the Faculty of Sociology, August 21, 1959, 5, 22+, UN.OFB.33.4.7, 23+.

20. Fals Borda, "Prólogo," 26.

21. The book's disciplinary framework means that this declaration should be taken as a reflection of methodology, rather than an attempt by the *letrados* to dilute the political elite's role in the crisis, as the master narrative of the National Front would suggest. See Fabio Lozano Simonelli, "El reves y el derecho," *El Espectador*, July 12, 1962, 4; Gonzalo Canal Ramírez, "El coronel y la política," *El Tiempo*, November 9, 1962, 5, for further support on this point.

22. Fals Borda, "Prólogo," 20–21, 25 (for quote). While Fals's retrospective account of the 1962 controversy remains unmatched, many of the newspaper articles that he cited are incorrectly dated. I make use of the original articles where possible.

23. Guzmán Campos, "La quiebra de las instituciones fundamentales," 273 ("catastrophe"); Guzmán Campos, "Tensión popular," 57 ("planned").

24. Fals Borda, "Introducción," 25.

25. See, for example, Palacios, *Between Legitimacy and Violence*, 137; Fals Borda, "Introducción," 23.

26. Lozano Simonelli, "El reves y el derecho," 4.

27. Gonzalo Canal Ramírez, "Un libro sobre violencia," *El Tiempo*, July 29, 1962, 5.

28. To my knowledge, this was the first time two sitting congressmen were killed, let alone within a short span. For context, see "Asesinado en Cartago un representante," *El Tiempo*, July 3, 1962, 1, 6; Vicente Laverde Aponte, *Memoria del Ministro de Justicia al Congreso Nacional en sus sesiones ordinarias de 1962* (Bogotá: Talleres Gráficos del Fondo Rotario Judicial, 1962), 655–81.

29. Fals Borda, "Introducción," 23–24.

30. Campo Posada, "Informe sobre la violencia en Caldas," 2; letter, Rep. Cornelio Reyes et al., to Ramírez Moreno and War Minister Maj. General Rafael Hernández Pardo, April 20, 1961, 1, AGN.MinGob.DM.22.192.13.

31. "A las autoridades competentes el caso del Coronel Valencia," *El Tiempo*, November 7, 1962, 18.

32. Jorge Zalamea, "La violencia no es un producto fatal de la supuesta mala indole del pueblo," *La Nueva Prensa*, April 11, 1962, 42. Studies of 1960s banditry constitute one of the most important currents of historiography on twentieth-century Colombian violence. See especially Sánchez G. and Meertens, *Bandits, Peasants, and Politics*; Meertens, *Ensayos*, chapter 2.

33. Various National Police reports, AGN.MinGob.DM.31.267.

34. "Emplazar al Congreso para que apruebe las facultades extras," *La República*, October 2, 1962, 10.

35. "La rehabilitación de la niñez," *El Tiempo*, August 8, 1961, 4 ("children"); Lt. Col. Álvaro Valencia Tovar, "Un criterio militar ante el problema de la violencia en Colombia," *Revista de las Fuerzas Armadas* 3, no. 8 (June 1961): 265 ("moral decomposition"); Guzmán Campos, "La quiebra de las instituciones fundamentales," 306; Guzmán Campos and Fals Borda, "Algunas consecuencias de la violencia," 323.

36. "Víctor Mosquera Chaux, Presidente del Senado," *El Tiempo*, August 1, 1962, 16.

37. Fals Borda, "Introducción," 24 ("underpinned"); "Víctor Mosquera Chaux," 16 ("possibly").

38. "Aquí Bogotá," *El Siglo*, October 3, 1962, 4; Gilberto Arango Londoño, "Motivo de unión," *El Siglo*, October 2, 1962, 4, for quote.

39. Pierre Nora, "General Introduction: Between Memory and History," in *Conflicts and Divisions*, 3.

40. Jesús María Henao and Gerardo Arrubla, *Historia de Colombia para la enseñanza secundaria*, 3rd ed., vol. 1 (Bogotá: Librería Colombiana, 1920), 6, 228 (for quote). This official textbook would go through eight editions between 1916 and 1967.

41. Jaime Arocha and Nina S. de Friedemann, "Prólogo," in *Un siglo de investigación social*, 8; Hirschman, "Diary" [1].

42. Interview with Umaña Luna, by Galindo Caballero and Valencia Cuéllar, in Galindo Caballero and Valencia Cuéllar, *En carne propia*, 145; Fals Borda, "Introducción," 30.

43. González, *La violencia en Colombia: Análisis de un libro*, 7–8, 11, 20. In spite of their flimsy calculations, Fals and Guzmán's figure—180,000 dead from 1949 through 1958, perhaps 200,000 by 1962—was remarkably consistent with estimates made by Canal Ramírez and others in 1958, and indeed with statistics that scholars accepted from the late 1970s onward. As such, it has helped to reinforce those estimates.

44. Fals Borda, "Introducción," 25, for quote.

45. *El Siglo*, September 23, 1962, sec. Suplemento de Divulgación Ideológica, 6–7; *La República*, September 23, 1962, 2–3.

46. Fals Borda, "Introducción," 29. See also Arango Londoño, "Motivo de unión," 4; "Sin imprimatur," 4; "¿Capellán de los bandoleros?," *El Siglo*, September 28, 1962, 4.

47. Letter, Jorge Ucrós [Louvaine] to Torres, January 30, 1963, 1, CTR.10.4.261; letter, Guzmán [Rome] to Torres, March 10, 1963, 1, AGN.CTR.10.4.272, for quotes.

48. "Víctor Mosquera Chaux," 16.

49. "Aquí Bogotá," *El Siglo*, October 2, 1962, 4 ("in the shadow"); "Un libro sectario," *El Siglo*, August 26, 1962, 4 ("raw"); "Crisis de responsibilidad," *El Siglo*, September 25, 1962, 4 ("four hundred"); Fals Borda, "Introducción," 28–29.

50. "Un libro sectario," 4. See also "Otro 'sociólogo' de la violencia," *El Siglo*, October 1, 1962, 4.

51. González, *La violencia en Colombia: Análisis de un libro*, 18.

52. Benigno Acosta Polo, "El prólogo del 'panfleto político,'" *La República*, September 26, 1962, 4.

53. González, *La violencia en Colombia: Análisis de un libro*, 18.

54. "Víctor Mosquera Chaux," 16.

55. Luis Torres Quintero, "Un concepto injusto," *La República*, October 5, 1962, 4.

56. The Liberal position was articulated by López de Mesa, "Un historial de la violencia," 4; and endorsed by Calibán, "Danza de las horas," *El Tiempo*, October 2, 1962, 4. The Conservative response was "Otro 'sociólogo,'" 4.

57. "Un panfleto político," *La República*, September 26, 1962, 4. Lleras had specified it as "an undeclared civil war against the Liberal Party." Lleras Camargo, "La crisis institucional."

58. Roberto Urdaneta Arbeláez, *El materialismo contra la dignidad del hombre: Su impacto en la vida colombiana* (Bogotá: Editorial Lucrós, 1960), 286, quoted in Guzmán Campos, "Antecedentes históricas de la violencia," 39.

59. "Violencia y acetato," *El Siglo,* October 3, 1962, 4, for quote; "Otro 'sociólogo,'" 4; Crayón, "Exposición," *La República,* October 5, 1962, 4.

60. "Visit of Mr. Eric Lambert, Foreign Office Regional Police Advisor to Colombia May 23–June 26" [1962], 8, NSArch.CDP.OPS.OPS—Colombia Misc. Lleras's evolving stance is referenced in Airgram A-649, "Violence in Colombia: A Case Study," May 26, 1964, 12, LBJL.NSF.CF.14 [2 of 2].Colombia Cables Volume I 12/63–7/65 [folder 1].

61. "Violence in Colombia," 14. Emphasis added.

62. Airgram A-109, "Joint WeekA No. 34," August 22, 1962, 2–3, 721.00(W)/8–2262, Internal Affairs, reel 2; "La sensibilidad social presidirá mi gobierno," *El Tiempo,* August 8, 1962, 18; Gonzalo Canal Ramírez, "El bus 120," *El Tiempo,* August 19, 1962, 4, for quote.

63. See various documents, AGN.MinGob.DM.30.254; letter, de Armas P. to Valencia, 1–2 ("technical"); "Valencia no es partidario de la pena de muerte," *El Tiempo,* August 22, 1962, 18; "Emplazar al Congreso," 10.

64. "Joint WeekA No. 34," 2 ("young"); Sánchez G. and Meertens, *Bandits, Peasants, and Politics,* 162–64 ("the most").

65. Airgram A-148, "Special Powers Bill to Combat Violence," September 6, 1962, 1–2, 721.00/9–662, Internal Affairs, reel 2; "El gobierno anuncia batalla final contra los violentos," *El Tiempo,* August 22, 1962, 23, for quotes; CM, September 24, 1962, 3, APR.CM.43.24; "'El país está frenado por la violencia': Eduardo Uribe B.," *La República,* September 26, 1962, 8; "El gobierno desiste de la cuota de desarrollo," *La República,* September 27, 1962, 10.

66. Telegram 343, October 5, 1962, 1, JFKL.NSF.27.Colombia General 10/62–2/63; Telegram 357, October 9, 1962, 2, JFKL.NSF.27.Colombia General 10/62–2/63; memorandum of conversation, "Economic and Political Situation," 4, enclosure to Airgram A-357, "Conversation with Carlos Lleras," December 11, 1962, 721.00/12–1162, Internal Affairs, reel 2.

67. Airgram A-118, "Violence: The 'Great' Debate in the Senate," August 27, 1962, 2, 721.00/8–2762, Internal Affairs, reel 2 ("owlish"); *Anales* 2, no. 148 (August 4, 1959): 1838 ("the Colombian State").

68. "El gobierno anuncia batalla final contra los violentos," 23; "Propuesta legislación de emergencia," 6 ("affirming"); "El discurso del Ministro de Justicia," 17 ("a war").

69. "El discurso del Ministro de Justicia," 17, for quotes; "Propuesta legislación de emergencia," 6.

70. "El país está frenado por la violencia," 8, for quote; Sánchez G. and Meertens, *Bandits, Peasants, and Politics,* 163.

71. "El discurso del Ministro de Justicia," 17.

72. Guzmán Campos, "Reflexión crítica," 355; Fals Borda, "Introducción," 23.

73. Fals Borda, "Introducción," 30; interview with Umaña Luna, in Galindo Caballero and Valencia Cuéllar, *En carne propia,* 145; Airgram A-209, "Joint WeekA No. 40," October 3, 1962, 5, 721.00(W)/10–362, Internal Affairs, reel 2, for quote. The second edition sold out in under three months. "Aparecerá II tomo de 'La violencia en Colombia,'" *El Espectador,* December 21, 1962, 1.

74. "Joint WeekA No. 40," 5. Among the publisher's other owners was Lozano Simonelli. "La editorial Tercer Mundo busca mecenas," *El Tiempo,* February 20, 2001.

75. López de Mesa, "Un historial de la violencia," 18 ("doctrinaire," "precept," "religious fanatics"); "Otro 'sociólogo,'" 4 ("We had," "cannot go"). For other examples, see various articles, *La República*, October 3, 1962, 4.

76. Fals Borda, "Introducción," 23–24 ("mak[ing]," "has been applied"); Marcial, "Doctrina chulavita," *El Siglo*, October 2, 1962, 4 ("I have"); Torres Quintero, "Un concepto injusto," 4 ("there might," "glorious"). The former first lady and sitting senator delivered her comment in that department's capital during a speech honoring Torres Quintero.

77. Canal Ramírez, "El coronel y la política," 5.

78. Despatch 221, "Joint WeekA No. 41," October 10, 1962, 6, 721.00(W)/10–1062, Internal Affairs, reel 2, for quote. The list of participating newspapers appeared in a full-page advertisement in *El Siglo*, October 4, 1962, 4.

79. "Los periódicos adoptan normas contra la violencia," *El Tiempo*, October 5, 1962, 25 ("a national"); "La impunidad: Fuente de la violencia," *El Siglo*, October 5, 1962, 10 ("the press'").

80. "Combatir la impunidad y toda forma de violencia acordaron directores de diarios," *El Siglo*, October 5, 1962, 10. Discussions of this last point include Guzmán Campos, "Reflexión crítica," 356; Tatiana Acevedo, "A la espera de una generación menos angustiada," *El Espectador*, July 19, 2011.

81. Antonio Caballero, "Prólogo," in *Las guerras de la paz*, by Olga Behar (Bogotá: Planeta, 1985), 8, for quote; Ronderos, *Rebelión y amnistía*, 16.

82. Mauricio Torres, *La naturaleza de la revolución colombiana* (Bogotá: Editorial Iquema, 1959), 127; Ramírez Moreno, *Memorias del Ministro de Gobierno al Congreso de 1961*, 7.

83. "Aquí Bogotá," October 2, 1962, 4 ("unwritten"); "Un código moral," *La República*, October 6, 1962, 4 ("This meeting").

84. "Un código moral," 4.

85. Nicolás Buenaventura, "Significado del libro: 'La violencia en Colombia,'" *Documentos Políticos*, October 1962, 43, for quote; Fals Borda, "Introducción," 33. For specific examples, see "Sabía usted que . . .," *La República*, October 8, 1962, 4; "Solo 4 grupos de bandoleros organizados hay en el país," *El Tiempo*, April 21, 1963, 3.

86. "Un código moral," 4.

87. Fals Borda, "Introducción," 33.

88. Letter, Guzmán to Torres, 1. Emphasis in original.

89. Fals Borda, "Prólogo para la presente edición," 20; Fals Borda, "Introducción," 27; interview with Umaña Luna, in Galindo Caballero and Valencia Cuéllar, *En carne propia*, 145.

90. Letter, Lleras Camargo to Eduardo Santos [Rome], August 21, 1962, 1, BLAA.ES. Correspondencia.9.7.654.

91. Fals Borda, "Prólogo para la presente edición," 20–21.

92. Buenaventura, "Significado del libro," 43 (for quote), 44–45, 53; Ramón López, "Cualquiera que sea el camino, el pueblo colombiano vencerá," *Documentos Políticos*, September 1964, 2–3. For familiarity with Fals, see Nicolás Buenaventura, "Mientras llega la hora de la reforma agraria," *Documentos Políticos*, April 1960, 61.

93. Buenaventura, "Significado del libro," 43 (for quote), 44–45, 53; López, "Cualquiera que sea el camino," 2–3.

94. Use of quotation marks for the term "violence" was not uniform, but its adopters included Communist Party secretary general Gilberto Vieira. See, among others,

Buenaventura, "Significado del libro," 44 (for quote), 42; Gilberto Vieira, "Nueva etapa de lucha del pueblo colombiano," *Documentos Políticos*, March 1965, 1.

95. Víctor Eduardo Prado Delgado, *Bandoleros: Historias no contadas* (Ibagué: V. E. Prado D., 2009), 87–101; "50 años de la pesadilla en La Italia," *La Patria*, August 4, 2013.

96. Fabio Lozano Simonelli, "Las dos violencias," *El Espectador*, September 24, 1963, 4.

97. Fernando Guillén Martínez, *Raíz y futuro de la revolución* (Bogotá: Ediciones Tercer Mundo, 1963), 178, 179, 185, 188, 191. The book was published that October.

98. Fals Borda, "Introducción," 13; Eduardo Umaña Luna, "Un problema social: La niñez abandonada," in *La violencia en Colombia*, 2:213 ("[the] children"); Guzmán Campos, "El nuevo antisocial," in *La violencia en Colombia*, 2:363 ("the generation"), 361 ("the new antisocial"), 361n1, 366 ("el neocriminal"), 378, 385; Guzmán Campos, "Sugerencias para una terapéutica," in *La violencia en Colombia*, 2:496. Authorship of the second volume's chapters is less clear than in the first volume.

99. Umaña Luna, "Un problema social," 231 (for quote), 235–38.

100. Guzmán Campos, "Nuevos aspectos del proceso," in *La violencia en Colombia*, 2:297–98; Guzmán Campos, "Etiología de la violencia," 459.

101. Guzmán Campos, "El tratamiento aplicado a la violencia," in *La violencia en Colombia*, 2:484, 461 (for quote).

102. Guzmán Campos, Fals Borda, and Umaña Luna, *La violencia en Colombia*, 2:7 ("norms"); Fals Borda, "Introducción," 42–56. See also Cendales, Torres, and Torres, "One Sows the Seed," 23–24.

103. Guzmán's source was an *El Tiempo* opinion piece summarizing the findings of a 1962 U.S. scientific conference. "Raíces de violencia," *El Tiempo*, July 27, 1963, 4. The original conference report is Alfred H. Rifkin, "Violence in Human Behavior," *Science* 140, no. 3569 (May 24, 1963): 904–6. See also the quotation from the Mexican sociologist Pablo González Casanova, in Guzmán Campos, "Estadísticas de mortalidad," in *La violencia en Colombia*, 2:326.

104. Guzmán Campos, "El tratamiento aplicado a la violencia," 485 ("The problem"); Guzmán Campos, "Etiología de la violencia," 426 ("almost always"). For latent "violence," see Fals Borda, "Introducción," 12; and Guzmán Campos, "Sugerencias para una terapéutica," 496; for "resentment" and "hatred," see, respectively, Guzmán Campos, "Etiología de la violencia," 430, 443.

105. Sánchez G., "La Violencia in Colombia," 792, addresses the thematic but not the chronological unity implied by the term.

106. This latter point is suggested by "Violence in Colombia."

107. The original rhyme is impossible to reproduce in English: "*Colombia es un país de cosas singulares / Dan la guerra los civiles / Y la paz los militares.*"

108. Deas, "Violent Exchanges," 384.

109. "Report of the Colombia Survey Team: Part I," chapter 3, paragraphs 8 (for quotes), 9, 24, 28, 76, 245.

110. Ortiz Sarmiento, *Estado y subversión*, 272n15; Henderson, *When Colombia Bled*, 212; "Quienes promueven la violencia," 1, 2.

111. "La violencia en Colombia," 70.

112. Comando General de las Fuerzas Militares, "Informe complementario no. 8 del cuadro de violencia," February 21, 1961, 2–3, APR.SG.1961.3.Fuerzos Militares Informe, for

quote; Comando General de las Fuerzas Militares, "Informe complementario no. 14 del cuadro de violencia," May 5, 1961, 3, APR.SG.1961.3.Fuerzos Militares Informe.

113. Published programmatic statements include Valencia Tovar, "Un criterio militar," 266–67.

114. Memorandum, "Instrucciones al Embajador de Colombia en Washington sobre ayuda militar" [1961], 4, APR.DSP.1961.4.Relaciones Exteriores.

115. "La violencia en Colombia," 27–38.

116. Interview with Iván Marino Ospina, by Patricia Lara, in Patricia Lara, *Siembra vientos y recogerás tempestades*, 2nd ed. (Bogotá: Planeta, 1986), 73–74. See also Sánchez G. and Meertens, *Bandits, Peasants, and Politics*, 24, 84.

117. Karl, "State Formation," chapter 6; "Colombianos aquí y allá . . .," *Semana*, December 23, 1958, 29; "Agentes subversivos adelantan campaña de descrédito del país," *El Tiempo*, September 20, 1959, 3.

118. Valencia Tovar, *Testimonio de una época*, 365–67, 409–10; interview with Álvaro Valencia Tovar, by Glenda Lariza Martínez Osorio, in *Hablan los generales: Las grandes batallas del conflicto colombiano contadas por sus protagonistas*, ed. Glenda Lariza Martínez Osorio (Bogotá: Editorial Norma, 2006), 71, 38, 45, 50–53, 60–66; Karl, "State Formation," 453–63.

119. The *Armed Forces Journal* (*Revista de las Fuerzas Armadas*) began publication in April 1960, joining existing publications by the army and National Police. Guhl's National War College (Escuela de Guerra) teaching materials, 1960–70, are found throughout UN.EG.7.

120. Capt. Fabio Guillermo Lugo P., "Acción contra la violencia," *Revista de las Fuerzas Armadas* 3, no. 9 (August 1961): 491–500; Karl, "State Formation," chapter 8.

121. "Violence in Colombia," Appendix B, "The Colombian Anti-Violence Plan," 3, for quote; memorandum, "Assessment of Impact of U.S. Civic Action Programs," Appendix B, "Civic Action Cost Comparison—Bolivia," May 4, 1964, 2, LBJL.NSF.Komer.15.Counter-Insurgency Police Program 1964–1965–1966 [2 of 2]; memorandum, "Military Actions for Latin America (U)," Appendix C, November 30, 1961, 67, JFKL.NSF.276.Department of Defense (B), Joint Chiefs of Staff Vol. I, Military Actions for Latin America.

122. "Violence in Colombia," Appendix C, "The Role of the Military Missions," 2, for quote; "The Colombian Anti-Violence Plan;" Leal Buitrago, *El oficio de la guerra*, 81–82.

123. Memorandum of conversation, "Political Situation," August 29, 1962, 1–2, Enclosure 1 to Airgram A-133, "Conversation with Alvaro Gomez Hurtado," August 31, 1962, 721.00/8-3162, Internal Affairs, reel 2, for quote; CM, Acta No. 1, August 27, 1962, APR. CM.43.5–8.

124. Octava Brigada, *De la violencia a la paz*, 25, 47 ("[political]"); Registraduría Nacional del Estado Civil, "Circular Postal No. 228: Producción de cédulas en el mes de Agosto," September 3, 1962, 3, APR.SG.1962.5.Registraduria ("suspect"); Karl, "State Formation," 665–66, 678–79.

125. Waldo Carmona Fitzgerald, "Amplia labor sicológica y de represión viene adelantando el 'Batallón Colombia,'" *El Cronista*, January 17, 1964, 3, for quote; Comité de Solidaridad con los Presos Políticos, *El libro negro de la represión: Frente Nacional 1958–1974* (Bogotá: Editorial Gráficas Mundo Nuevo, 1974), 42, 44; petition, Comité de Mujeres Democratas del Norte del Tolima [Armero] to Valencia and presidential cabinet, March 18, 1964, APR.SG.1964.28.Orden Publico 1964.

126. Octava Brigada, *De la violencia a la paz,* 16, 27, 38, 40.

127. Karl, "State Formation," 680–82.

128. Various National Police reports, AGN.MinGob.DM.43.365; "Solo 4 grupos de bandoleros organizados," 3; memorandum of conversation, Valencia and Ambassador Fulton Freeman, April 3, 1963, 2, JFKL.NSF.27.Colombia General 3/63–11/63, for quote.

129. This last point is raised in Airgram A-432, "Rural Violence in 1963," February 11, 1964, 2, NARA.59.SNF 1964–1966.2047.POL 23 Internal Security Counter-Insurgency COL 1/1/64.

130. Letter, Tolima Governor Alfonso Jaramillo Salazar et al. to Roberto García Peña [*El Tiempo*], January 5, 1963, 3, AGN.MinGob.DM.38.327.307 ("the battle"); telegram, Elvira de Alvarado et al. [Ibagué] to Valencia, March 22, 1963, AGN.MinGob.DM.38.327.7 ("a . . . crusade"); "La pacificación es principal meta del Mingobierno Mendoz," *El Cronista,* August 25, 1964, 1, 2.

131. Airgram CA-11098, Department of State to Embassy, April 20, 1965, 1, NARA.59. SNF 1964–1966.2047.POL 23 Internal Security Counter-Insurgency COL 1/1/6; Karl, "State Formation," 648.

132. Guzmán Campos, "Etiología de la violencia," 444, for quote; Guzmán Campos, "El tratamiento aplicado a la violencia," 470.

133. Telegram 15, U.S. Consulate, Cali, to Department of State, November 5, 1964, 2, NARA.59.SNF 1964–1966.2042.Political Affairs and Relations.

134. By 1965, the project was set to consume half of the government's total budget for civic-action infrastructure projects. Memorandum, "FY 1963 Development Grant Program," March 5, 1963, 1–2, AGN.DNP.110.30.254–55; "Project Agreement between AID and the Ministry of War, an Agency of the Government of Colombia" [1965?], 3–4, AGN.DNP.110.30.110–11.

135. Interview with Víctor Eduardo Prado Delgado, by the author, August 2, 2012; Prado Delgado, *Bandoleros: Historias no contadas,* 101.

136. Sánchez G. and Meertens, *Bandits, Peasants, and Politics,* 95 (for quote), 162, 170–72.

137. Meertens, *Ensayos,* 164–65, 169–70; Sánchez G. and Meertens, *Bandits, Peasants, and Politics,* 100, 182; Prado Delgado, *Bandoleros: Historias no contadas,* 50, 73–79, 92–93, 109–14; Telegram 973, April 28, 1964, NARA.59.SNF 1964–1966.3216.Social Conditions 1/1/64, for quote. The increasing prevalence of sexual violence is suggested by Meertens, *Ensayos,* 160; Policía Nacional, "Informacion general de orden publico no. 152," October 24, 1962, APR.SG.1962.4.Mn Guerra.

138. Departamento Administrativo de Seguridad (hereafter DAS), "Síntesis informes regionales," April 13, 1964, 8, APR.SG.1964.5.Depto Adm de Seguridad.

139. See the discussion in chapter 7.

140. Sánchez G. and Meertens, *Bandits, Peasants, and Politics,* 99, 101; DAS, Seccional Huila, "Informe sobre la cuadrilla de bandoleros dirigida por Hector Perez Gonzalez (a. 'Tres Espadas')," May 19, 1962, 4, AGN.MinGobDM.32.272.78.

141. Meertens, *Ensayos,* 170; Víctor Eduardo Prado Delgado, *Bandoleros: Imágenes y crónicas* (Ibagué: V.E. Prado D., 2010), 89, 96; "Eliminado ayer Desquite," *El Cronista,* March 18, 1964, 1; Prado Delgado, *Bandoleros: Historias no contadas,* 82–83.

142. Valencia Tovar, *Testimonio de una época,* 400–408, 402 ("devoured"); Airgram A-284, "Joint WeekA No. 45," 1–2; Airgram A-388, "Joint WeekA No. 51," December 19, 1962,

4-5, 721.00(W)/12-1962, Internal Affairs, reel 2; "A las autoridades competentes," 1, 18; interview with Fals Borda, in Cubides, *Camilo Torres*, 98-99 ("Of course"). Valencia's report appeared in multiple publications, including "Texto del informe del Coronel Valencia," *El Espectador*, December 19, 1962, 7.

CHAPTER 7. CONFRONTATION, 1963-1966

1. Unless otherwise noted, all quotes and references in this section are drawn from *Riochiquito*. *Le Monde*, October 5-26, 1965, chronicles the Frenchmen's "disappearance," subsequent detention by the Colombian police, and ultimate expulsion from the country.

2. Arturo Alape, *Tirofijo: Los sueños y las montañas, 1964-1984*, 2nd ed. (Bogotá: Editorial Planeta, 1994), 28-29; "Patrullas del Ejército refuerzan la persecución de los bandoleros," *El Espectador*, March 18, 1965, 3. For the later legend, see Arturo Alape, *Las muertes de Tirofijo*, 5th ed. (Bogotá: Seix Barral, 2002).

3. Medófilo Medina, "Las diferentes formas de entender el conflicto armado en Colombia," *Razón Pública*, February 23, 2015, http://www.razonpublica.com/index.php/conflicto-drogas-y-paz-temas-30/8274-las-diferentes-formas-de-entender-el-conflicto-armado-en-colombia.html.

4. Alape, *Las vidas*, 12.

5. See, for example, DAS, Seccional Huila, "Informe especial de inteligencia," April 25, 1964, 4, APR.SG.1964.5.Depto. Adm. de Seguridad.

6. Policía Nacional, "Informacion general de orden publico no. 187," November 22, 1962, 1, APR.SG.1962.4.Mn Guerra.

7. See also González Arias and Marulanda Alvarez, *Historias de frontera*, 90.

8. This point is informed by Peter F. Guardino, *The Time of Liberty: Popular Political Culture in Oaxaca, 1750-1850* (Durham and London: Duke University Press, 2005), 284-86.

9. Hernández de Alba to Mendoza Hoyos, 2.

10. "Informe sobre obras in Belalcázar (Páez); Karl, "State Formation," 207-8.

11. "Así se iniciaron en el país las repúblicas independientes," *El Cronista*, July 8, 1964, 8; "La 'elite' comunista y su 'trabajo' negativo de 1950 al año de 1952," *El Cronista*, July 28, 1964, 1, 7; "Así se iniciaron las primeras escuelas de 'cuadros' comunista en el Tolima," *El Cronista*, August 4, 1964, 5; "Tiro Fijo en el 'Davis,'" *El Cronista*, September 11, 1964, 3; Alape, *Las vidas*, 180, 210-11, 215-16; Alfredo Molano Bravo, "¿Cómo es hoy la república independiente de El Pato?," *El Espectador*, July 12, 2014.

12. "Exilados de la 'República' del Pato hablan sobre andanzas de los 'Rojos,'" *El Cronista*, October 1, 1964, 6; petition, Junta Comunal del Alto Pato [Huila/Caquetá] to Alberto Lleras Camargo, January 23, 1962, 1, APR.DSP.1962.2.Juntas, for quote.

13. Petition, Martín Camargo to Valencia et al., June 6, 1964, 2, APR.SG.1964.28.Orden Publico 1964 #3 ("it loaned"), emphasis in original; José Antonio Moreno, "'El Pato,' otra república independiente, de 'Richard,'" *El Tiempo*, May 30, 1964, 6 ("self-rehabilitation"); Camargo, "Bases para una debate parlamentario en defensa del gobierno y el ejercito," October 1964, 2, AGN.MinGob.DM.51.412.84.

14. Petition, Camargo to Valencia et al., January 18, 1964, 2, APR.SG.1964.28.Orden Publico 1964.

15. "Las parcelaciones voluntarias de la Gobernación del Huila," *Revista Nacional de Agricultura*, April 1965, 42. Darío Fajardo and Héctor Mondragón B., *Colonización y estrategias de desarrollo* (Bogotá: IICA, 1997), 139, offers a useful sketch of area geography.

16. Overall statistics on land redistribution taken from Francisco Cañaveras, "Agropecuaria," *El Cronista*, January 15, 1964, 5. A contemporary estimate of the size of Lara's estate appears in "Polémica sobre la parcelación de la hacienda de 'Balsillas,'" *El Espectador*, April 20, 1965, sec. B, 5. His other ranch, to the southwest, was perhaps two and a half times as large. For contrasting views of Lara, see "Elogio a Oliverio Lara," *Semana*, October 28, 1958, 7; petition, Junta Comunal del Alto Pato to Lleras Camargo, 3.

17. Petition, Camargo to Senator Alberto Galindo et al. [August 1964], 1, AGN.MinGob. DM.49.402.114; flyer [Neiva], "Denunciamos," November 1964, AGN.MinGob. DM.49.402.89; petition, Camargo to Valencia et al., October 29, 1964, 2, AGN.MinGob. DM.49.402.99. Environmental considerations are discussed in "Las parcelaciones voluntarias," 41, 43.

18. Camargo, "Bases para una debate parlamentario," 2–3; Camargo, "Pliego de acusaciones contra los aventureros y provocadores de la violencia sobre las regiones de Guayabero oriente del Huila y Pato Caqueta," July 1964, 1, AGN.MinGob.DM.49.402.77 ("adventurist"); "Dirigente agrario en las repúblicas independientes hace graves revelaciones," *El Cronista*, July 26, 1964, 1, 8.

19. Camargo, "Pliego de acusaciones," 2.

20. Ibid.

21. Petition, Camargo to Ruiz Novoa et al., July 8, 1964, 1.

22. Petition, Camargo to Valencia et al., January 18, 1964, 2.

23. Palomino et al. to Lleras Camargo; Concejo Municipal de Paéz, Resolucion No. 2; letter, Cenon Muñoz V., Rosa Hurtado de Quintero, and J. P. Collo Gutiérrez [Belalcázar] to Senator Víctor Mosquera Chaux, February 15, 1962, AGN.MinGob.DM.33.285.80–81; letter, Mosquera Chaux to Cauca Governor Antonio José Lemos Guzmán, March 18, 1962, 2, AGN.MinGob.DM.33.285.78.

24. Letter, Mosquera Chaux, Rep. Gerardo Bonilla Fernández, and Rep. Tiberio Zuñiga Díaz to Interior Minister Aurelio Camacho Rueda and Ruiz Novoa, October 10, 1963, 1–3, AGN.MinGob.AI.199.1758.188–90.

25. See, for instance, Policía Nacional, "Informe policivo numero 0020, Anexo B, Cuadrillas principales y sus efectivos durante el mes de octubre de 1.963," November 13, 1963, AGN.MinGob.DM.45.376.90.

26. Airgram A-432, "Rural Violence in 1963," February 11, 1964, 5–6, NARA.59.SNF 1964–1966.2047.POL 23 Internal Security Counter-Insurgency COL 1/1/64; "Protestas de los campesinos ante el gobierno por ataque a 'Riochiquito,'" *Voz de la Democracia*, June 6, 1963, 6.

27. Alape, *Tirofijo*, 43, 52–53; Álvaro Delgado, *Todo tiempo pasado fue peor: Memorias del autor basadas en entrevistas hechas por Juan Carlos Celis* (Bogotá: La Carreta Editores, 2007), 174–75, 176 (for quote).

28. Valencia Tovar, *Testimonio de una época*, 458; "Rural Violence in 1963," 5.

29. Movimiento Agrario de Riochiquito, "Renunciamos preparativos de violencia oficial" [1962], AGN.MinGob.DM.34.292.39. See also Movimiento Agrario de Riochiquito, "Asi se desarrolla la violencia en Colombia," December 1962, AGN.MinGob.DM.45.376.193.

30. Dirección General de la Policía Nacional, "Información General de Orden Público," No. 180, 1, November 16, 1962, AGN.MinGob.DM.34.292.36.

31. "Dos cabos y cuatro soldados muertos en asalto a una camioneta en el Huila," *Tribuna*, May 5, 1960, 2; Policía Nacional, "Informacion general de orden publico no. 97," September 15, 1962, 1–2, APR.SG.1962.4.Mn Guerra; "El Ejército rodea la banda de 'Tiro Fijo' en el Tolima," *El Tiempo*, January 23, 1962, 1, 13.

32. Marulanda Vélez et al., "Denuncia," 1–1+; letter, Jaime Amaya and Isauro Yosa [Marquetalia] to Lleras Camargo, February 20, 1962, 1–2, APR.DSP.1962.4.Orden Publico.

33. "Solo 4 grupos de bandoleros organizados," 3.

34. Airgram A-6, "Progress Report on Colombian Internal Defense Plan (IDP)," July 4, 1964, 2, NARA.59.SNF 1964–1966.2047.POL 23 Internal Security Counter-Insurgency COL 1/1/64.

35. "Informe especial de inteligencia," 2. See also Airgram A-6, "Progress Report," 9.

36. "Misión socio económica visitará a Marquetalia," *El Tiempo*, April 25, 1964, 6. For the lawyer Hernando Garavito Muñoz's prior legal work, see Expediente no. 1610, for conspiracy [Villarrica], initiated December 10, 1954, Juzgado Quinto de Instrucción Penal Militar, Villarrica, AHI.SJ.2.7.1.

37. "Misión socio económica visitará a Marquetalia," 6.

38. Ibid.; Airgram A-600, "Joint WeekA No. 18," April 30, 1964, 3, NARA.SNF 1964–66.2042.Joint WeekAs 4/1/64; Germán Guzmán Campos, *La violencia en Colombia: Parte descriptiva* (Cali: Ediciones Progreso, 1968), 422 ("fear," "senile"); "Se desintegró misión de Marquetalia," *El Tiempo*, May 3, 1964, 9 ("the cause").

39. "Se desintegró misión de Marquetalia," 9.

40. "Habrá cambio de estructuras pero por los medios legales," *El Tiempo*, May 28, 1965, 28, for quotes; Airgram A-686, "Ruiz-Valencia Exchange Highlights Problem of Military Intervention," June 12, 1964, NARA.SNF 1964–66.2046.[untitled folder].

41. Memorandum, British Embassy, Bogotá, to Foreign Office, December 12, 1957, 5–6, NAUK.FO 371/126493.

42. "Habrá cambio de estructuras," 28. For the reply of one of Lleras's Liberal justice ministers, see Vicente Laverde Aponte, "El gobierno anterior y la violencia," *El Tiempo*, May 30, 1964, 4.

43. Arenas, *Diario de la resistencia*, 25.

44. "Los Paeces, esclavos de Tiro Fijo," *El Cronista*, July 5, 1964, 3; Arenas, *Diario de la resistencia*, 21, for quote.

45. Arenas, *Diario de la resistencia*, 27; Alfredo Molano Bravo, "La ruta de la cancharina," *El Espectador*, June 21, 2014; interview with Matallana, by Arango Z., in Arango Z., *FARC, veinte años*, 214, for quote.

46. "Confirmada la muerte de 'Richard,'" *El Espectador*, March 26, 1965, 2; Alape, *Las vidas*, 17.

47. Nicolás Buenaventura, "El 'gorila' aunque se vista de seda . . .," *Documentos Políticos*, May 1964, 7; López, "Cualquiera que sea el camino," 1, for quote; C. D. Cruz, Alcibiades

Paredes, and Nicolás Buenaventura, "¿Es la clase obrera vanguardia revolucionaria en Colombia?," *Documentos Políticos,* December 1964, 23; "Llamamiento de los campesinos de Marquetalia," *Documentos Políticos,* May 1964, 85; Alape, *Las vidas,* 284.

48. Stoller, "Alfonso López Pumarejo and Liberal Radicalism."

49. Alape, *Las vidas,* 316–20; *Riochiquito.* This portrayal is seconded by subsequent interviewers: Alape, *Las vidas,* 290, 295, 297; Guillermoprieto, *Looking for History,* 22–23, 25.

50. Alape, *Las vidas,* 285; Karl, "State Formation," 725–27.

51. "Programa agrario de los guerrilleros," in Arenas, *Diario de la resistencia,* 128–34.

52. See Gilberto Vieira, *Organicemos la revolución colombiana! Informe político al IX Congreso del Partido Comunista de Colombia* (Bogotá: [unknown publisher], 1961), 89.

53. See Valencia Tovar, *Testimonio de una época,* 474.

54. "Carta abierta de los colonos y campesinos de Marquetalia al Presidente Doctor Guillermo Leon Valencia," May 20, 1964, APR.SG.1964.28.Orden Publico 1964 #4.

55. Ibid., 2. In an August letter, Marulanda would also ask MRL congressmen to bring formal complaints to the Senate against Valencia and the military, under Article 102. "Tiro Fijo envió carta a parlamentarios del MRL," *El Cronista,* August 4, 1964, 2.

56. This point expands upon observations about the FARC made by Ramírez Tobón, "La guerrilla rural en Colombia," 69–70; and interview with Gilberto Vieira, by Ronderos, in Ronderos, *Rebelión y amnistía,* 141.

57. Jacobo Arenas, *Cese el fuego: Una historia política de las FARC* (Bogotá: Editorial Oveja Negra, 1987), 75; Matta Aldana, *Colombia y las FARC-EP,* 122, 132–33.

58. For debates about the battle, see Robert A. Karl, "Myths of Marquetalia: The State of Colombian Historiography at the FARC's Fiftieth," paper presented at the Thirty-Fifth Latin American Studies Association Congress, New York, May 28, 2016.

59. Alape, *Tirofijo,* 25–27; interview with Manuel Marulanda Vélez, by Arturo Alape, in Alape, *La paz, la violencia,* 276–77; Arenas, *Cese el fuego,* 78.

60. Interview with Marulanda, in Alape, *La paz, la violencia,* 264–65.

61. Moreno, "'El Pato,' otra república independiente," 6.

62. Karl, "State Formation," 710–12; Camargo to Valencia et al., May 11, 1964, APR. SG.1964.28.Orden Publico 1964 #3. Camargo's response to the Communist Party leadership would be published as "Dirigente agrario," 1, 8; a transcription appears in González Arias, *Espacios de exclusión,* 131–36.

63. Petition, Camargo to Galindo et al. [August 1964], 1; petition, Camargo to Valencia et al., May 8, 1964, 2, APR.SG.1964.28.Orden Publico 1964 #3 ("a total change"); petition, Camargo to Valencia et al., January 5, 1965, AGN.MinGob.DM.61.467.31 ("I preferred"); petition, Camargo to Valencia et al., May 11, 1964, APR.SG.1964.28.Orden Publico 1964 #3.

64. Karl, "State Formation," 773–74; telegram, Eduardo Cabrera Dussán, Secretario de Gobierno, Huila, to Asesor General, Interior Ministry, February 11, 1965, AGN.MinGob. OJ.149.1186.80; telegram, Huila Governor Jaime Afandor Tovar to Asesor General, Interior Ministry, March 2, 1965, AGN.MinGob.OJ.149.1186.79; "Auxilio al oriente del Huila viene prestando la Cruz Roja," *El Tiempo,* December 7, 1964, 9; letter, Galindo to Mendoza Hoyos, January 8, 1965, AGN.MinGob.DM.61.467.29.

65. Petition, Camargo to Valencia et al., February 25, 1965, 1; Airgram A-514, "Joint WeekA No. 12," March 19, 1965, 6, NARA.SNF 1964–66.2043.Joint WeekAs 1/1/65, for quote.

66. Maj. Álvaro Meneses Franco, "El Batallón de Infantería Colombia en El Pato, Caquetá," *Revista del Ejército* 5, no. 23 (December 1965): 256, 266; González Arias, *Espacios de exclusión*, 111.

67. Meneses Franco, "El Batallón de Infantería Colombia," 263.

68. Valencia Tovar, *Testimonio de una época*, 458–59.

69. Delgado, *Todo tiempo pasado fue peor*, 175 (for quote), 176–77.

70. Valencia Tovar, *Testimonio de una época*, 459, 466–76. Among other intelligence sources, the army intercepted correspondence establishing the plot; photographs and transcriptions of these letters are reprinted in ibid., 460–65. The stylistic errors, typeface, and signatures match those of other period documents from Marquetalia and Riochiquito.

71. Ibid., 473; Alape, *Tirofijo*, 25–28, 55; interview with Marulanda, in Alape, *La paz, la violencia*, 276; petition, Marcos Pardo Cultochambo [Belalcázar] to Interior Minister, May 20, 1965, 1, AGN.MinGob.DM.64.500.46; DAS, Seccional Huila, "Resumen de informaciones rendidas por el Sr. Raul Echeverry Villegas," February 24, 1965, 3, AGN.MinGob.DM.61.473.65.

72. Alape, *Tirofijo*, 28–34.

73. Memorandum, Hernández de Alba to Mendoza Hoyos, 3; interview with Roll, for quote.

74. "Valencia emplaza a Ruiz N.," *El Espectador*, March 18, 1965, 2, for quote; "Sólo seis agentes vigilaban a Inzá," *El Espectador*, March 20, 1965, 3; Alape, *Tirofijo*, 35.

75. "La farsa sangrienta," *El Espectador*, March 20, 1965, 4; memorandum, Hernández de Alba to Mendoza Hoyos, 1, 3.

76. "Acta numero uno," 2–3; "Informe sobre la situación socio-económica y de orden pública del área de Tierradentro," October 6, 1966, 1–2, DSP.1966.11.Tierradentro; Karl, "State Formation," 286–87; Tello, "Informe," 4, for quote.

77. "Lista de las personas deplazadas"; petition, Miguel Antonio Valencia [Belalcázar] to Interior Minister, May 13, 1965, AGN.MinGob.DM.64.500.51; memorandum, Cauca Governor Alina Muñoz de Zambrano to President Carlos Lleras Restrepo, September 28, 1966, 1–2, APR.DSP.1966.7.Gobernacion del Cauca.

78. "Informe sobre la situación socio-económica," 5; "Acta numero uno," 14–15; "Sistema de auto-defensa en Itaibe contra guerrilleros," *El Campesino*, August 30, 1965, 2.

79. Memorandum, Tesalia [Huila] alcalde Gregorio Quesada Fajardo to Afandor Tovar and Cabrera Dussán, May 8, 1965, AGN.MinGob.DM.61.473.55; memorandum, Feliciano Losada V., Inspector Departamental de Policía [Pacarní] to Afandor Tovar, May 9, 1965, AGN.MinGob.DM.61.473.54; "Acta numero uno," 14.

80. Memorandum, Quesada Fajardo to Afando Tovar and Cabrera Dussán.

81. Movimiento Agrario de Riochito [*sic*], "Mas sangre joven, mas sangre campesina en una nueva provocacion contra Riochiquito," May 7, 1965, AGN.MinGob.DM.61.473.61 ("pimps"); memorandum, Losada V. to Afandor Tovar; Valencia Tovar, *Testimonio de una época*, 482–84; Alape, *Tirofijo*, 57.

82. Delgado, *Todo tiempo pasado fue peor*, 176; Valencia Tovar, *Testimonio de una época*, 484.

83. Alape, *Tirofijo*, 57–58.

84. Valencia Tovar, *Testimonio de una época*, 479–80; Alape, *Tirofijo*, 54.

85. Roberto Romero Ospina, "FARC 1964–2014: Marquetalia, un conversatorio memorable con un documental como pretexto," *Agencia de Noticias Nueva Colombia*, May 27,

2014, http://2014.anncol.eu/index.php/colombia/historia/7011-marquetalia-un-conversato-rio-memorable-con-un-documental-como-pretexto.

86. Telegram 444, September 17, 1965, NARA.SNF 1964-66.2048.POL 23-8 1/1/65; Alape, *Tirofijo*, 55, 60-61, 63; Arenas, *Diario de la resistencia*, 112-13, 116, 122-24; interview with Marulanda, in Alape, *La paz, la violencia*, 279; *Riochiquito*.

87. Telegram, Cenón Muñoz et al. to Valencia, September 20, 1965, APR.SG.1965.23. Orden Publico.

88. Valencia Tovar, *Testimonio de una época*, 378, 488.

89. "San José, (Dolores), realiza con todo éxito Fiestas Pro Paz," *El Cronista*, September 6, 1964, 2; "El producido del Festival Pro Paz se distriburá en obras de primera importan-cia," *El Cronista*, September 9, 1964, 2.

90. Alape, *Tirofijo*, 54.

91. "Jorge Villamil Cordovez, una página del Huila en el Folclor," *El Cronista*, February 8, 1964, 15; letter, Gómez Valderrama to War Minister Gen. Gabriel Rebeiz Pizarro, September 20, 1965, AGN.MinGob.DM.67.520.142-44.

92. Letter, Gómez Valderrama to Rebeiz Pizarro, 1-2. Emphasis in original.

93. "Memorandor [*sic*] obras desarrollo Pato-Guayabero," September 7, 1966, 3-4, APR. DSP.1966.8.Informe Privado Min Obras; Karl, "State Formation," 774-78.

94. Memorandum, "Envío plan socio-economico," November 14, 1965, AGN.MinGob. DM.61.476.29; memorandum, "Medidas orden público," Rebeiz Pizarro to Gómez Valder-rama, November 29, 1965, AGN.MinGob.DM.61.476.50, for quote.

95. Karl, "State Formation," 774-75.

96. Molano Bravo, "¿Cómo es hoy la república independiente de El Pato?"

97. Valencia Tovar, *Testimonio de una época*, 488.

98. Memorandum, Hernandez de Alba to José Elías del Hierro, Director, Caja Agraria, September 14, 1965, AGN.MinGob.AI.203.1816.173, for quote; Karl, "State Formation," 779.

99. Karl, "State Formation," 762, 779; Valencia Tovar, *Testimonio de una época*, 485-86.

100. See especially Marulanda and Arenas's comments in Alape, *Tirofijo*, 26, 80.

101. Memorandum, "Actuación de Incora en Tierradentro," INCORA Director General Enrique Peñalosa Camargo to Interior Minister Misael Pastrana Borrero, [1966], 1-2, APR. DSP.1966.11.Tierradentro. An unspecified number of *desplazados* had been ordered out of Tierradentro to Neiva and other military posts.

102. "Acta Numero Uno," 10 (for quote), 13-14. See also "Informe sobre la situación socio-económica y de orden público del área de Tierradentro," Muñoz de Zambrano to Sixth Brigade Commander Col. Alfonso Velásquez Mazuera, October 6, 1966, 3, APR. DSP.1966.11.Tierradentro.

103. "Acta numero uno," 11-12. See also chapter 3.

104. "Acta numero uno," 7; telegram, Acting Cauca Governor Risberto A. Hurtado to Muñoz de Zambrano, October 17, 1966, APR.DSP.1966.11.Tierradentro.

105. Memorandum, Jorge Osorio Silva, Coordinador, División de Asuntos Indígenas, to Interior Minister Douglas Botero Boshell, May 13, 1969, 1, AGN.MinGob.DM.112.828.1; memorandum, "Programa de Desarrollo del Sur del Cauca," División de Asuntos Indígenas to INCORA Sub-Gerente Jurídico, August 26, 1968, 2, AGN.MinGob.DM.98.735.54; memo-randum, "Reforma administrativa de la División," Hernández de Alba et al. to Interior Min-ister, September 30, 1968, AGN.MinGob.DM.111.820.53-57; Joris Van de Sandt, "Behind the

Mask of Recognition: Defending Autonomy and Communal Resource Management in Indigenous Resguardos, Colombia" (Ph.D. diss., University of Amsterdam, 2007), 73–74. The important implications for regional indigenous politics and identity are discussed in Troyan, *Cauca's Indigenous Movement.*

106. Alape, *Tirofijo,* 78–84; Matta Aldana, *Colombia y las FARC-EP,* 202–4, 214; interview with Guaraca, in Arango Z., *FARC, veinte años,* 163, 164 ("very difficult").

107. Alape, *Tirofijo,* 80–81; Matta Aldana, *Colombia y las FARC-EP,* 207–8; Central Intelligence Agency (hereafter CIA) Directorate of Intelligence, Current Intelligence Weekly Special Report, "Banditry and Insurgency in Colombia," July 22, 1966, 6–7, CIA FOIA.

108. Interview with Guaraca, in Arango Z., *FARC, veinte años,* 163–64; Alape, *Tirofijo,* 80, 83.

109. "Declaración política de la Segunda Conferencia Guerrillera del Bloque Sur," in Arenas, *Diario de la resistencia,* 135–38 (138 for quote).

110. Alape, *Tirofijo,* 27–28, 80 (for quote).

111. Matta Aldana, *Colombia y las FARC-EP,* 214.

112. Manuel Marulanda Vélez, *Cuadernos de campaña,* 3rd ed. (Bogotá: [unknown publisher], 2000), 72–73, 75 (for quote).

EPILOGUE

1. David H. Price, *Cold War Anthropology: The CIA, the Pentagon, and the Growth of Dual Use Anthropology* (Durham: Duke University Press, 2016), chapter 13.

2. The argument first appeared in Samuel P. Huntington, "Political Development and Political Decay," *World Politics* 17, no. 3 (April 1965): 386–430.

3. Cooper, "Conflict and Connection," 1524.

4. Orlando Fals Borda, "Camilo revolucionario: 2a parte," *Alternativa,* April 15, 1974, 30.

5. Germán Guzmán Campos, *El padre Camilo Torres,* 9th ed. (Bogotá: Siglo Veintiuno Editores, 1989), 24.

6. Fals Borda, "Camilo revolucionario," 31, for quote; Juan Gomis, "Perfil de Camilo Torres," in *Retrato de Camilo Torres* (Mexico, D.F.: Editorial Grijalbo, 1969), 51–54.

7. Guzmán Campos, *El padre Camilo Torres,* chapter 5 (72 for "ruling class"); Fals Borda, "Camilo revolucionario," 31 ("the future").

8. Fals Borda, "Camilo revolucionario," 30; Torres, "La violencia y los cambios socioculturales."

9. Guzmán Campos, *El padre Camilo Torres,* 236, for quote.

10. Cataño, "La sociología en Colombia: Un balance," 68–70, 80.

11. Interivew with Umaña Luna, in Galindo Caballero and Valencia Cuéllar, *En carne propia,* 29, 159–61; letter, Guzmán [Mexico City] to Fals Borda, April 5, 1969, UN. OFB.35.5.37–38, for quote.

12. Guzmán Campos, *La violencia en Colombia: Parte descriptiva.* Guzmán also published one of Torres's first biographies, which later appeared as *El padre Camilo Torres.*

13. Guzmán Campos, "Reflexión crítica," 354.

14. Cataño, "La sociología en Colombia: Un balance," 58–59; Broderick, *Camilo Torres,* 240–41.

15. Fals Borda, *La subversión en Colombia: Visión del cambio social en la historia,* Monografías sociológicas, no. 24 (Departamento de Sociología, Universidad Nacional, and Ediciones Tercer Mundo, 1967), 11–14; letter, Fals Borda to Hernando Agudelo Villa, October 10, 1966, 2, UN.OFB.35.3.3.

16. Fals Borda, *La subversión en Colombia,* 15.

17. See Fals's handwritten note on the back of speech by Echeverri Herrera, 22+.

18. Fals Borda, "Lo sacro y lo violento, aspectos problemáticos del desarrollo en Colombia," *La Nueva Prensa,* April 6, 1965, 79–88.

19. Fals Borda, "Violence and the Break-Up of Tradition in Colombia," in *Obstacles to Change in Latin America,* ed. Claudio Véliz (London and New York: Oxford University Press, 1965), 188–205. Fals presented an earlier version of the paper in 1962—perhaps not coincidentally during the early uproar over *La violencia en Colombia.* The paper appeared in print only later: Fals Borda, "The Role of Violence in the Break with Traditionalism: The Colombian Case," in *The Sociologists, the Policymakers and the Public: The Sociology of Development,* vol. 3, Transactions of the Fifth World Congress of Sociology (Louvain: International Sociological Association, 1964), 21–32.

20. Pierre Nora, "Generation," in *Conflicts and Divisions,* 522.

21. Lessie Jo Frazier, *Salt in the Sand: Memory, Violence, and the Nation-State in Chile, 1890 to the Present* (Durham and London: Duke University Press, 2007), 67.

22. Fals Borda, *La subversión en Colombia,* 205.

23. Taussig, *Law in a Lawless Land,* 134; James D. Henderson, *Colombia's Narcotics Nightmare: How the Drug Trade Destroyed Peace* (Jefferson, N.C.: McFarland, 2015), chapter 1. Cf. Grupo de Memoria Histórica, *¡Basta ya!,* 32–33.

24. León Zamosc, *The Agrarian Question and the Peasant Movement in Colombia: Struggles of the National Peasant Association, 1967–1981* (Cambridge and New York: Cambridge University Press, 1986).

25. Fals Borda, *Historia de la cuestión agraria en Colombia* (Bogotá: Fundación Rosca de Investigación y Acción Social, 1975), 126–30.

26. Gilhodès, "Agrarian Struggles in Colombia," 445; Pizarro Leongómez, *Las FARC,* 201.

27. Interviews with Álvaro Fayad and Jaime Bateman Cayón, by Patricia Lara, in Lara, *Siembra vientos,* 94 ("tradition"), 95 ("we"), 97 ("the guerrilla"), 108–9. The Communist Party line appears in CIA Directorate of Intelligence, Intelligence Report, "Foreign and Domestic Influences on the Colombian Communist Party, 1957–August 1966," March 1967, 8–9, CIA FOIA.

28. Interviews with Fayad and Bateman, in Lara, *Siembra vientos,* 64 ("defeat," "convert"), 65, 97 ("[We] conceived"), 98, 112 ("The people"); Ronderos, *Rebelión y amnistía,* 162.

29. Carlos Agudelo, "Daring to Think Is Beginning to Fight: The History of the Magazine *Alternativa,* Colombia 1974–1980" (Ph.D. diss., University of Maryland, College Park, 2007), 63–66, 75.

30. Fals Borda, "Camilo revolucionario," 30–31; and various articles reprinted in Fals Borda, *Historia de la cuestión agraria.* Fals's conceptualization won devotees from the beginning: Torres, for example, was using "La Violencia" in private correspondence by early 1965. Letter, Torres to Ezequiel Guerra [Caracas], March 31, 1965, AGN.CTR.10.4.389. The idea's subsequent dissemination, particularly through the press, deserves further study.

31. Daniel Pécaut, "Reflexiones sobre el nacimiento de las guerrillas en Colombia," in *Violencia y política en Colombia*, 72.

32. Daniel Pécaut, *Crónica de cuatro décadas de política colombiana* (Bogotá: Grupo Editorial Norma, 2006), 295; Medófilo Medina, "Carta abierta a Alfonso Cano," *El Tiempo*, July 14, 2011.

33. Eduardo Pizarro Leongómez, "Las FARC-EP: ¿Repliegue estratégico, debilitamiento o punto de inflexión?," in *Nuestra guerra sin nombre: Transformaciones del conflicto en Colombia*, ed. Francisco Gutiérrez Sanín (Bogotá: Editorial Norma, 2006), 183.

34. Daniel Pécaut, "Presente, pasado y futuro de la Violencia," *Análisis Político* 30 (April 1997): 6; "El conflicto, callejón con salida: Informe Nacional de Desarrollo Humano para Colombia—2003" (Bogotá: United Nations Development Programme, 2003), 53.

35. "Global Study on Homicide 2013" (Vienna: United Nations Office on Drugs and Crime, 2014), 36.

36. Óscar Collazos, "¿Qué es la colombianidad?," *Semana*, December 11, 1980.

37. Gonzalo Sánchez G. and Ricardo Peñaranda, "Presentación," in *Pasado y presente de la violencia*, 9.

38. Arango Z., *FARC, veinte años*; Alape, *La paz, la violencia*; Alape, *Las vidas*; Alape, *Tirofijo*.

39. Sánchez describes his family's experience in Galindo Caballero and Valencia Cuéllar, *En carne propia*, 84–87, 111–17.

40. Palacios, *Between Legitimacy and Violence*, 284.

41. The conference proceedings became *Pasado y presente de la violencia en Colombia*. A second, augmented edition—dedicated to the recently deceased Guzmán—came out in 1991, a third edition in 2007.

42. Sánchez laid out his aims in "Presentación," in *Once ensayos*, 9–10.

43. The book was reissued in 2006.

44. Gonzalo Sánchez G. and Donny Meertens, *Bandoleros, gamonales y campesinos: El caso de la violencia en Colombia* (Bogotá: El Áncora Editores, 1983), 13.

45. Historians would never come to an agreement on La Violencia's starting and end points, but a review of more than thirty works reveals that the largest single portion follow Sánchez's lead.

46. See, for instance, Sánchez G. and Meertens, *Bandoleros, gamonales y campesinos*, 218. The practice became more systematic in the later English translation: Sánchez G. and Meertens, *Bandits, Peasants, and Politics*, 144–45.

47. Sánchez G., "La Violencia in Colombia," 789, originally presented in December 1984. Emphasis in original. The idea has not gone uncontested: see Malcolm Deas, "Algunos interrogantes sobre la relación guerras civiles y violencia," in *Pasado y presente de la violencia*, 1–46; and Pécaut's critique of "the myth of violence's persistence," in "Reflexiones," 89. See also Sánchez's and Deas's subsequent reflections on this issue: Sánchez G., *Guerras, memoria e historia*, 31–32; and Deas, "Violent Exchanges," 349–50, 390–91.

48. Sánchez G., "Prefacio a la segunda edición," in *Pasado y presente de la violencia en Colombia*, ed. Gonzalo Sánchez G. and Ricardo Peñaranda, 2nd ed. (Bogotá: CEREC, 1991), 11.

49. Ibid.

50. "Nadie se salva," *Semana*, August 6, 1987; Gonzalo Sánchez G., "Presentación: Los intelectuales y las comisiones," in *Colombia: Violencia y democracia*, by Comisión de

estudios sobre la violencia, 4th ed. (Bogotá: IEPRI, Universidad Nacional de Colombia and Colciencias, 1995); "Los violentólogos," *Semana*, September 15, 2007.

51. *Colombia: Violencia y democracia*; Jaramillo Marín, *Pasados y presentes de la violencia en Colombia*, 139, 143–45, 153.

52. Sánchez G., "La Violencia in Colombia," 792, for quote. See also Meertens, *Ensayos*, 40.

53. Sánchez G., *Guerra y política*, 36–37.

54. Sánchez G., "La Violencia in Colombia," 804; Meertens, *Ensayos*, 39.

55. Nora, "Generation," 525.

56. See the reports of the Historical Memory Group (from the National Center for Historical Memory), including Grupo de Memoria Histórica, Comisión Nacional de Reparación y Reconciliación, "Recordar y narrar el conflicto: Herramientas para reconstruir memoria histórica" pamphlet (2009), 19 ("a unifying"); Sánchez G., "Prólogo," in *¡Basta ya!*, 16 ("Far").

57. Ley 1448 de 2011, June 10, 2011, *Diario Oficial* (June 10, 2011): 1–33; Grupo de Memoria Histórica, *¡Basta ya!*, 112, for quote.

58. Sánchez G., "Prólogo," in *¡Basta ya!*, 13, for quote.

59. "Acuerdo General para la terminación del conflicto y la construcción de una paz estable y duradera," August 26, 2012, https://www.mesadeconversaciones.com.co/sites/default/files/AcuerdoGeneralTerminacionConflicto.pdf; Jorge Iván González, "Buena noticia: Las FARC ya no son comunistas," *Razón Pública*, October 29, 2012, http://www.razonpublica.com/index.php/conflicto-drogas-y-paz-temas-30/3375-buena-noticia-las-farc-ya-no-son-comunistas.html, for quote.

60. Braun, "¡Que Haiga Paz!," 51–52.

BIBLIOGRAPHY

FILMS

Esta fue mi vereda. Directed by Gonzalo Canal Ramírez (1958; Colombia).
Riochiquito. Directed by Jean-Pierre Sergent and Bruno Muel (1965; France).

INTERVIEWS

Interview with Víctor Eduardo Prado Delgado, by the author, August 2, 2012.

PERIODICALS

Acción Liberal
Agencia de Noticias Nueva Colombia
Alternativa
América Latina [Rio de Janeiro]
Anales del Congreso
Diario Oficial
Documentos Políticos
El Campesino
El Cronista
El Espacio
El Espectador
El Independiente
El Nacional [Caracas]
El Siglo
El Tiempo

Gaceta Judicial
La Nueva Prensa
La Patria
La República
Le Monde
New York Times
Revista de las Fuerzas Armadas
Revista del Ejército
Revista Nacional de Agricultura
Semana
Science
Time
Tribuna
Voz de la Democracia

PUBLISHED WORKS

3'000.000 de colombianos cedulados: 1 plebiscito y 2 elecciones; Diciembre de 1958. Bogotá: Registraduría Nacional del Estado Civil, 1958.

Acevedo Carmona, Darío. "El Pacto de Benidorm o el olvido como antídoto para conjurar los fantasmas del odio y de la sangre." In *Tiempos de paz: Acuerdos en Colombia, 1902–1994*, edited by Medófilo Medina and Efraín Sánchez. Bogotá: Alcaldía Mayor de Bogotá, Instituto Distrital de Cultura y Turismo, 2003.

"Acuerdo General para la terminación del conflicto y la construcción de una paz estable y duradera." August 26, 2012. https://www.mesadeconversaciones.com.co/sites/default/files/AcuerdoGeneralTerminacionConflicto.pdf.

Adelman, Jeremy. *Worldly Philosopher: The Odyssey of Albert O. Hirschman.* Princeton: Princeton University Press, 2013.

"Adriano Tribin Piedrahita o el fundador del Festival Folclorico Colombiano." In *Protagonistas del Tolima siglo XX: Las más importantes personalidades del Tolima desde 1900 hasta 1995.* Bogotá: Pijao Editores, 1995.

Agudelo, Carlos. "Daring to Think Is Beginning to Fight: The History of the Magazine *Alternativa*, Colombia 1974–1980." Ph.D. diss., University of Maryland, College Park, 2007.

Aguilera Peña, Mario, ed. *Camilo Torres y la Universidad Nacional de Colombia.* Bogotá: Universidad Nacional de Colombia, 2002.

Alape, Arturo. *La paz, la violencia: Testigos de excepción.* 3rd ed. Bogotá: Planeta, 1993.

———. *Las muertes de Tirofijo.* 5th ed. Bogotá: Seix Barral, 2002.

———. *Las vidas de Pedro Antonio Marín, Manuel Marulanda Veléz, Tirofijo.* Bogotá: Editorial Planeta, 2004.

———. *Tirofijo: Los sueños y las montañas, 1964–1984.* 2nd ed. Bogotá: Editorial Planeta, 1994.

Amaya Ramírez, Guillermo. *Memoria del Ministro de Gobierno al Congreso de 1959.* Bogotá: Imprenta Nacional, 1959.

Andrade Melgarejo, Diana. "Guadalupe era de Tame pero Villavicencio se impuso: La rehabilitación de los Llanos Orientales, 1948–1957." Undergraduate thesis, Universidad de los Andes, 2009.

Arango Z., Carlos. *FARC, veinte años: De Marquetalia a La Uribe.* 3rd ed. Bogotá: Ediciones Aurora, 1985.

Archivo de investigadores de la Universidad Nacional de Colombia: Inventario documental Orlando Fals Borda, 1644-2002. Bogotá: Universidad Nacional de Colombia, 2004.

Arenas, Jacobo. *Cese el fuego: Una historia política de las FARC.* Bogotá: Editorial Oveja Negra, 1987.

——. *Diario de la resistencia de Marquetalia.* Bogotá: Ediciones Abejón Mono, 1972.

Arocha, Jaime. "Antropología propia: Un programa en formación." In *Un siglo de investigación social: Antropología en Colombia,* edited by Jaime Arocha and Nina S. de Friedemann. Bogotá: Etno, 1984.

——. *La violencia en el Quindío: Determinantes ecológicos y económicos del homicidio en un municipio caficultor.* Bogotá: Ediciones Tercer Mundo, 1979.

Arthur, Paige. "How 'Transitions' Reshaped Human Rights: A Conceptual History of Transitional Justice." *Human Rights Quarterly* 31, no. 2 (2009): 321-67.

Aslanian, Sebouh David, Joyce E. Chaplin, Ann McGrath, and Kristin Mann. "How Size Matters: The Question of Scale in History." *American Historical Review* 118, no. 5 (December 2013): 1431-72.

Ayala Diago, César Augusto. "El cierre del Congreso de 1949." *Revista Credencial Historia* 162 (June 2003). http://www.banrepcultural.org/blaavirtual/revistas/credencial/junio2003/raro.htm.

——. "El origen del MRL (1957-1960) y su conversión en disidencia radical del liberalismo colombiano." *Anuario Colombiano de Historia Social y de la Cultura,* no. 22 (1995): 95-121.

——. "La explosión de Cali: Agosto 7 de 1956." *Revista Credencial Historia* 117 (September 1999): 11.

——. *Resistencia y oposición al establecimiento del Frente Nacional: Los orígenes de la Alianza Nacional Popular (ANAPO), Colombia 1953-1964.* Bogotá: Universidad Nacional de Colombia, 1996.

Behar, Olga. *Las guerras de la paz.* Bogotá: Planeta, 1985.

Bejarano, Ana María, and Eduardo Pizarro Leongómez. "From 'Restricted' to 'Besieged': The Changing Nature of the Limits to Democracy in Colombia." In *The Third Wave of Democratization in Latin America: Advances and Setbacks,* edited by Frances Hagopian and Scott P. Mainwaring. Cambridge and New York: Cambridge University Press, 2005.

Bermúdez, Alberto. *Del Bogotazo al Frente Nacional: Historia de la década en que cambió Colombia.* Bogotá: Tercer Mundo Editores, 1995.

Betancourt E., Darío, and Martha L. García B. *Matones y cuadrilleros: Origen y evolución de la violencia en el occidente colombiano, 1946-1965.* Bogotá: Tercer Mundo Editores, 1990.

Boone, Catherine. "Property and Constitutional Order: Land Tenure Reform and the Future of the African State." *African Affairs* 106, no. 425 (October 2007): 557-86.

Borneman, John. *Political Crime and the Memory of Loss.* Bloomington: Indiana University Press, 2011.

Bourdieu, Pierre. "The Force of Law: Toward a Sociology of the Juridical Field." *Hastings Law Journal* 38 (July 1987): 814-53.

Brands, Hal. *Latin America's Cold War.* Cambridge: Harvard University Press, 2010.

Braun, Herbert. *The Assassination of Gaitán: Public Life and Urban Violence in Colombia.* Madison: University of Wisconsin Press, 1985.

———. "'¡Que Haiga Paz!' The Cultural Contexts of Conflict in Colombia." In *Peace, Democracy, and Human Rights in Colombia,* edited by Christopher Welna and Gustavo Gallón. Notre Dame, Ind.: University of Notre Dame Press, 2007.

———. Review of *Blood and Fire:* La Violencia *in Antioquia, Colombia, 1946–1953,* by Mary Roldán, *Hispanic American Historical Review* 83, no. 3 (August 2003): 596–97.

Broderick, Walter J. *Camilo Torres: A Biography of the Priest-Guerrillero.* New York: Doubleday, 1975.

Buenaventura, Nicolás. *Historia PCC, Tomo II. Cuaderno II: El origen del Frente Nacional (1957–58).* Bogotá: CEIS-INEDO, 1990.

Bushnell, David. *The Making of Modern Colombia: A Nation in Spite of Itself.* Berkeley: University of California Press, 1993.

Caballero, Antonio. "Prólogo." In *Las guerras de la paz,* by Olga Behar. Bogotá: Planeta, 1985.

Caballero Argáez, Carlos. "Nacimiento de un intelectual: Alberto Lleras Camargo en los años veinte del siglo XX." In *Alberto Lleras Camargo y la Universidad de los Andes.* Bogotá: Escuela de Gobierno Alberto Lleras Camargo, Universidad de los Andes, 2007.

Cataño, Gonzalo. "La sociología en Colombia: Un balance." In *La sociología en Colombia: Balance y perspectivas; Memoria del III Congreso Nacional de Sociología, Bogotá, agosto 20–22 de 1980.* Bogotá: Asociación Colombiana de Sociología, 1981.

Cendales, Lola, Fernando Torres, and Alfonso Torres. "'One Sows the Seed, but It Has Its Own Dynamic': An Interview with Orlando Fals Borda." Translated by Luis M. Sander. *International Journal of Action Research* 1, no. 1 (2005): 9–42.

Chalarca, José. *La caficultura en el Huila: Historia y desarrollo.* Bogotá: Comité Departamental de Cafeteros del Huila, 2000.

Chartier, Roger. "The Saint-Malo–Geneva Line." In *Conflicts and Divisions,* edited by Lawrence D. Kritzman, translated by Arthur Goldhammer. Vol. 1, *Realms of Memory: Rethinking the French Past.* New York: Columbia University Press, 1996.

Chernick, Marc W. *Acuerdo posible: Solución negociada al conflicto armado colombiano.* Translated by Juan Fernando Esguerra. Bogotá: Ediciones Aurora, 2008.

Chernick, Marc W., and Michael F. Jiménez. "Popular Liberalism, Radical Democracy, and Marxism: Leftist Politics in Contemporary Colombia, 1974–1991." In *The Latin American Left: From the Fall of Allende to Perestroika,* edited by Barry Carr and Steve Ellner. Boulder, Col.: Westview Press, 1993.

Ciro: Páginas de su vida. Bogotá: Ediciones Abejón Mono, 1974.

Comaroff, John L. "Reflections on the Colonial State, in South Africa and Elsewhere: Factions, Fragments, Facts and Fictions." *Social Identities: Journal for the Study of Race, Nation and Culture* 4, no. 3 (1998): 321–61.

Comité de Solidaridad con los Presos Políticos. *El libro negro de la represión: Frente Nacional 1958–1974.* Bogotá: Editorial Gráficas Mundo Nuevo, 1974.

Canal Ramírez, Gonzalo. *Estampas y testimonios de violencia.* Bogotá: Canal Ramirez, 1966.

Connelly, Matthew. "Taking Off the Cold War Lens: Visions of North-South Conflict during the Algerian War for Independence." *American Historical Review* 105, no. 3 (June 2000): 739–69.

Contraloría Seccional del Tolima. *Anuario estadístico histórico geográfico de los municipios del Tolima 1956*. Ibagué: Imprenta Departmental, 1957.

————. *Anuario estadístico histórico-geográfico de los municipios del Tolima 1958*. Ibagué: Imprenta Departmental, 1960.

Cooper, Frederick. "Conflict and Connection: Rethinking Colonial African History." *American Historical Review* 99, no. 5 (December 1994): 1516–45.

Crenzel, Emilio A. *Memory of the Argentina Disappearances: The Political History of "Nunca Más."* New York: Routledge, 2012.

Cubides, Fernando. *Camilo Torres: Testimonios sobre su figura y su época*. Medellín: La Carreta Editores and Universidad Nacional de Colombia, 2010.

Deas, Malcolm. "Algunos interrogantes sobre la relación guerras civiles y violencia." In *Pasado y presente de la violencia en Colombia*, edited by Gonzalo Sánchez G. and Ricardo Peñaranda. Bogotá: CEREC, 1986.

————. "Violent Exchanges: Reflections on Political Violence in Colombia." In *The Legitimization of Violence*, edited by David E. Apter. London: Macmillan, 1997.

Delgado, Álvaro. *Todo tiempo pasado fue peor: Memorias del autor basadas en entrevistas hechas por Juan Carlos Celis*. Bogotá: La Carreta Editores, 2007.

Delgado, Ovidio, and Philippe Chenut. "Ernesto Guhl." In *Pensamiento colombiano del siglo XX*, edited by Santiago Castro-Gómez, Alberto Flórez-Malagón, Guillermo Hoyos Vásquez, and Carmen Millán de Benavides. Vol. 1. Bogotá: Pontificia Universidad Javeriana–Bogotá; Instituto Pensar, 2007.

Díaz-Callejas, Apolinar. "Memorias actualizadas de un colombiano sentenciado a muerte." *Nueva Sociedad* 100 (April 1989): [1–20].

Dinges, John. *The Condor Years: How Pinochet and His Allies Brought Terrorism to Three Continents*. New York and London: Free Press, 2004.

Dix, Robert H. *Colombia: The Political Dimensions of Change*. New Haven: Yale University Press, 1967.

Echandía, Darío. *Humanismo y técnica*. Bogotá: Editorial Kelly, 1969.

Edel, Matthew. "The Colombian Community Action Program: An Economic Evaluation." 2 vols. Ph.D. diss., Yale University, 1968.

"El conflicto, callejón con salida: Informe Nacional de Desarrollo Humano para Colombia–2003." Bogotá: United Nations Development Programme, 2003.

"El Pacto de Benidorm" and "Pacto de Sitges." In *Tiempos de paz: Acuerdos en Colombia, 1902–1994*, edited by Medófilo Medina and Efraín Sánchez. Bogotá: Alcaldía Mayor de Bogotá, Instituto Distrital de Cultura y Turismo, 2003.

El primer gobierno del Frente Nacional. Vol. 1, *Mayo de 1958–agosto de 1959*. Bogotá: Imprenta Nacional, 1960.

El primer gobierno del Frente Nacional. Vol. 2, *Agosto de 1959–julio de 1960*. Bogotá: Imprenta Nacional, 1960.

El primer gobierno del Frente Nacional. Vol. 4, *Agosto de 1961 a agosto de 1962*. Bogotá: Imprenta Nacional, 1962.

"El sanjuanero." *Alcaldía de Ibagué*. Accessed June 19, 2013. http://www.alcaldiadeibague .gov.co/web2/joomla/index.php?option=com_content&view=article&id=274:el-sanjuanero&catid=16:ibague-capital-musical&Itemid=67.

Fajardo, Darío, and Héctor Mondragón B. *Colonización y estrategias de desarrollo*. Bogotá: IICA, 1997.

Fals Borda, Orlando. *Ante la crisis del país: Ideas-acción para el cambio*. Bogotá: Ancora Editores and Panamericana Editorial, 2003.

———. *Historia de la cuestión agraria en Colombia*. Bogotá: Fundación Rosca de Investigación y Acción Social, 1975.

———. *La subversión en Colombia: Visión del cambio social en la historia*. Monografías sociológicas, no. 24. Departamento de Sociología, Universidad Nacional, and Ediciones Tercer Mundo, 1967.

———. "The Role of Violence in the Break with Traditionalism: The Colombian Case." In *The Sociologists, the Policymakers and the Public: The Sociology of Development*. Vol. 3. Transactions of the Fifth World Congress of Sociology. Louvain: International Sociological Association, 1964.

———. "Violence and the Break-Up of Tradition in Colombia." In *Obstacles to Change in Latin America*, edited by Claudio Véliz. London and New York: Oxford University Press, 1965.

Ferguson, James. *The Anti-Politics Machine: "Development," Depoliticization, and Bureaucratic Power in Lesotho*. Minneapolis: University of Minnesota Press, 1994.

Frazier, Lessie Jo. *Salt in the Sand: Memory, Violence, and the Nation-State in Chile, 1890 to the Present*. Durham and London: Duke University Press, 2007.

Galindo Caballero, Mauricio, and Jorge Valencia Cuéllar. *En carne propia: Ocho violentólogos cuentan sus experiencias como víctimas de la violencia*. Bogotá: Intermedio, 1999.

Gallón Giraldo, Gustavo. *Quince años de estado de sitio en Colombia, 1958–1978*. Bogotá: Librería y Editorial América Latina, 1979.

Galvis Serrano, José A. "El cuartelazo de Pasto." *Revista Credencial Historia* 193 (January 2006). http://www.banrepcultural.org/blaavirtual/revistas/credencial/enero2006/cuartelazo .htm.

García Márquez, Gabriel. "Prólogo." In *Memorias*, by Alberto Lleras Camargo. Bogotá: Taurus, 2006.

"German Guzmán Campos o la paz sin reposo." In *Protagonistas del Tolima siglo XX: Las más importantes personalidades del Tolima desde 1900 hasta 1995*. Bogotá: Pijao Editores, 1995.

Gilhodès, Pierre. "Agrarian Struggles in Colombia." In *Agrarian Problems and Peasant Movements in Latin America*, edited by Rodolfo Stavenhagen. Garden City, N.Y.: Anchor Books, 1970.

Gilman, Nils. *Mandarins of the Future: Modernization Theory in Cold War America*. Baltimore and London: Johns Hopkins University Press, 2003.

"Global Study on Homicide 2013." Vienna: United Nations Office on Drugs and Crime, 2014.

Gómez Rojas, David. *El General Mariachi: Jesús María Oviedo*. 2nd. ed. Bogotá: Produmedios, 2008.

———. *Semblanzas del conflicto colombiano: Esquema de consenso nacional de paz*. Bogotá: Produmedios, 2008.

Gomis, Juan. "Perfil de Camilo Torres." In *Retrato de Camilo Torres*. Mexico, D.F.: Editorial Grijalbo, 1969.

González Arias, José Jairo. *Espacios de exclusión: El estigma de las repúblicas independientes 1955–1965*. Bogotá: CINEP, 1992.

———. "La Violencia en el Huila, 1946–1966." In *Historia general del Huila*, edited by Bernardo Tovar Zambrano and Reynal Salas Vargas. Vol. 2. Neiva: Academia Huilense de Historia, 1996.

González Arias, José Jairo, and Elsy Marulanda Alvarez. *Historias de frontera: Colonización y guerras en el Sumapaz*. Bogotá: CINEP, 1990.

González, Jorge Iván. "Buena noticia: Las FARC ya no son comunistas." *Razón Pública*. October 29, 2012. http://www.razonpublica.com/index.php/conflicto-drogas-y-paz-temas-30/3375-buena-noticia-las-farc-ya-no-son-comunistas.html.

González, S.J., Miguel Angel. *La violencia en Colombia: Análisis de un libro*. Bogotá: Centro de Estudios Colombianos, 1962.

Gran atlas y geografía de Colombia. Bogotá: Intermedio Editores, 2004.

Grandin, Greg. "The Instruction of Great Catastrophe: Truth Commissions, National History, and State Formation in Argentina, Chile, and Guatemala." *American Historical Review* 110, no. 1 (February 2005): 46–67.

———. "Living in Revolutionary Time: Coming to Terms with the Violence of Latin America's Long Cold War." In *A Century of Revolution: Insurgent and Counterinsurgent Violence during Latin America's Long Cold War*, edited by Greg Grandin and Gilbert M. Joseph. Durham and London: Duke University Press, 2010.

Gross, Jan. *Revolution from Abroad: The Soviet Conquest of Poland's Western Ukraine and Western Belorussia*. Expanded ed. Princeton and Oxford: Princeton University Press, 2002.

Grupo de Memoria Histórica. *¡Basta ya! Colombia: Memorias de guerra y dignidad*. Bogotá: Imprenta Nacional, 2013.

Grupo de Memoria Histórica, Comisión Nacional de Reparación y Reconciliación. "Recordar y narrar el conflicto: Herramientas para reconstruir memoria histórica." Pamphlet. 2009.

Guardino, Peter F. *The Time of Liberty: Popular Political Culture in Oaxaca, 1750–1850*. Durham and London: Duke University Press, 2005.

Guerrero, Javier. *Los años del olvido: Boyacá y los orígenes de la Violencia*. Bogotá: Institutional de Estudios Políticos y Relaciones Internacionales, Universidad Nacional de Colombia and Tercer Mundo Editores, 1991.

Guillén Martínez, Fernando. *Raíz y futuro de la revolución*. Bogotá: Ediciones Tercer Mundo, 1963.

Guillermoprieto, Alma. *Looking for History: Dispatches from Latin America*. New York: Vintage Books, 2001.

Gutiérrez Anzola, Jorge Enrique. *Violencia y justicia*. Bogotá: Ediciones Tercer Mundo, 1962.

Guzmán Campos, Germán. *Camilo: Presencia y destino*. Bogotá: Tercer Mundo, 1967.

———. *El padre Camilo Torres*. 9th ed. Bogotá: Siglo Veintiuno Editores, 1989.

———. *La violencia en Colombia: Parte descriptiva*. Cali: Ediciones Progreso, 1968.

———. "Reflexión crítica sobre el libro 'La Violencia en Colombia.'" In *Pasado y presente de la violencia en Colombia*, edited by Gonzalo Sánchez G. and Ricardo Peñaranda. Bogotá: CEREC, 1986.

Guzmán Campos, Germán, Orlando Fals Borda, and Eduardo Umaña Luna. *La violencia en Colombia*. Vol. 1. Bogotá: Taurus, 2005 [1962].

———. *La violencia en Colombia*. Vol. 2. Bogotá: Taurus, 2005 [1964].

———. *La violencia en Colombia: Estudio de un proceso social*. 2nd ed. Vol. 1. Bogotá: Ediciones Tercer Mundo, 1964.

Hartlyn, Jonathan. "Military Governments and the Transition to Civilian Rule: The Colombian Experience of 1957–1958." *Journal of Interamerican Studies and World Affairs* 26, no. 2 (May 1984): 245–81.

Hartog, Hendrik. "Pigs and Positivism." *Wisconsin Law Review* 4 (1985): 899–935.

Henao, Juan Carlos. "La responsabilidad patrimonial del Estado en Colombia." In *La responsabilidad patrimonial del Estado: Memoria del seminario internacional sobre la responsabilidad patrimonial del Estado*. Mexico, D.F.: Instituto Nacional de Administración Pública, 2000.

Henao, Jesús María, and Gerardo Arrubla. *Historia de Colombia para la enseñanza secundaria*. 3rd ed. Vol. 1. Bogotá: Librería Colombiana, 1920.

Henderson, James D. *Colombia's Narcotics Nightmare: How the Drug Trade Destroyed Peace*. Jefferson, N.C.: McFarland, 2015.

———. *La modernización en Colombia: Los años de Laureano Gómez, 1889–1965*. Translated by Magdalena Holguín. Medellín: Editorial Universidad de Antioquia, 2006.

———. *Las ideas de Laureano Gómez*. Bogotá: Tercer Mundo, 1985.

———. *When Colombia Bled: A History of the Violencia in Tolima*. University: University of Alabama Press, 1985.

Hernández Nariño, Homero. "Crónica de un pueblo olvidado de Colombia: Herrera—Sur del Tolima." 2010. http://www.centrodememoriahistorica.gov.co/descargas/memorias_region/cronica_de_un_pueblo_olvidado_herrera_tolima.pdf.

Hirschman, Albert O. *Exit, Voice, and Loyalty: Responses to Decline in Firms, Organizations, and States*. Cambridge: Harvard University Press, 1970.

———. *Journeys toward Progress: Studies of Economic Policy-Making in Latin America*. Garden City, N.Y.: Anchor Books, 1965.

Hobsbawm, E. J. "The Anatomy of Violence." *New Society* 28 (April 11, 1963): 16–18.

———. "The Revolutionary Situation in Colombia." *World Today* 19, no. 6 (June 1963): 248–58.

Hodge, Joseph Morgan. "Writing the History of Development (Part 2: Longer, Deeper, Wider)." *Humanity: An International Journal of Human Rights, Humanitarianism and Development* 7, no. 1 (Spring 2016): 125–74.

Huntington, Samuel P. "Political Development and Political Decay." *World Politics* 17, no. 3 (April 1965): 386–430.

"Ibague canta a Colombia." Accessed June 20, 2013. http://ibaguecantaacolombia.mex.tl/frameset.php?url=/1384680_Ibague-Canta-a-Colombia.html.

James, Daniel. *Resistance and Integration: Peronism and the Argentine Working Class, 1946–1976*. Cambridge and New York: Cambridge University Press, 1988.

Jaramillo Marín, Jefferson. *Pasados y presentes de la violencia en Colombia: Estudios sobre las comisiones de investigación*. Bogotá: Pontificia Universidad Javeriana, 2014.

Jelin, Elizabeth. *State Repression and the Labors of Memory*. Translated by Judy Rein and Marcial Godoy-Anativia. Minneapolis: University of Minnesota Press, 2003.

Jiménez, Michael F. "The Many Deaths of the Colombian Revolution: Region, Class and Agrarian Rebellion in Central Colombia." *Papers on Latin America,* no. 13. Columbia University, Institute of Latin American and Iberian Studies, 1990.

Jimeno, Myriam. "Consolidación del Estado y antropología en Colombia." In *Un siglo de investigación social: Antropología en Colombia,* edited by Jaime Arocha and Nina S. de Friedemann. Bogotá: Etno, 1984.

Joseph, Gilbert M., and Daniel Nugent, eds. *Everyday Forms of State Formation: Revolution and the Negotiation of Rule in Modern Mexico.* Durham and London: Duke University Press, 1994.

Karl, Robert A. "Century of the Exile: Colombia's Displacement and Land Restitution in Historical Perspective, 1940s-60s." *Canadian Journal of Latin American and Caribbean Studies* (forthcoming).

———. "Myths of Marquetalia: The State of Colombian Historiography at the FARC's Fiftieth." Paper presented at the Thirty-Fifth Latin American Studies Association Congress, New York, May 28, 2016.

———. "The Politics of Colombian Development in Latin America's Long 1950s." Unpublished paper.

———. "Reading the Cuban Revolution from Bogotá, 1957–62," *Cold War History* 16, no. 4 (November 2016): 337–58.

———. "State Formation, Violence, and Cold War in Colombia, 1957–1966." Ph.D. diss., Harvard University, 2009.

———. "A State in Spite of Itself: Political 'Authority' and the Birth of the FARC in Colombia." Unpublished paper.

Lara, Patricia. *Siembra vientos y recogerás tempestades.* 2nd ed. Bogotá: Planeta, 1986.

Laserna, Mario. *Estado fuerte o caudillo: El dilema colombiano.* Bogotá: Ediciones Mito, 1961.

Latham, Michael E. *Modernization as Ideology: American Social Science and "Nation Building" in the Kennedy Era.* Chapel Hill and London: University of North Carolina Press, 2000.

Laverde Aponte, Vicente. *Memoria del Ministro de Justicia al Congreso Nacional en sus sesiones ordinarias de 1962.* Bogotá: Talleres Gráficos del Fondo Rotario Judicial, 1962.

Leal Buitrago, Francisco. *El oficio de la guerra: La seguridad nacional en Colombia.* Bogotá: Tercer Mundo Editores and IEPRI, 1994.

———. "La frustración política de una generación: La universidad colombiana y la formación de un movimiento estudiantil 1958-1967." In *La sociología en Colombia: Balance y perspectivas: Memoria del III Congreso Nacional de Sociología, Bogotá, agosto 20-22 de 1980.* Bogotá: Asociación Colombiana de Sociología, 1981.

Le Fevre, Edward Corbett, Jr. "A Study of Colombia's Community Development Program, Accion Comunal." M.A. thesis, Arizona State University, 1966.

LeGrand, Catherine. "Labor Acquisition and Social Conflict on the Colombian Frontier, 1850–1936." *Journal of Latin American Studies* 16, no. 1 (May 1984): 27–49.

Lleras Camargo, Alberto. *Memorias.* Bogotá: Taurus, 2006.

———. *Mi gente.* 3rd ed. Bogotá: Banco de la República, 1976.

———. *Nuestra revolución industrial.* Bogotá: Aedita Editores, 1957.

———. *Reflexiones sobre la historia, el poder y la vida internacional.* Edited by Otto Morales Benítez. Bogotá: Tercer Mundo Editores and Ediciones Uniandes, 1994.

Lombana Silva, Nelson. "Militares sabotean 41 festival folclórico colombiano en Ibagué." *Partido Comnista de Colombia*. June 24, 2013. http://www.pacocol.org/index.php/comite-regional/tolima/4660-militares-sabotean-41-festival-folclorico-colombiano-en-ibague.

Lomnitz-Adler, Claudio. *The Return of Comrade Ricardo Flores Magón*. Brooklyn: Zone Books, 2014.

Londoño Botero, Rocío. *Juan de la Cruz Varela: Sociedad y política en la región de Sumapaz (1902–1984)*. Bogotá: Departamento de Historia, Universidad Nacional de Colombia, 2011.

Londoño, Rocío, and Medófilo Medina. "Eso también explica la muerte de Gaitán: Entrevista con José María Villarreal." *Análisis Político* 38 (December 1999): 55–70.

Londoño y Londoño, Fernando. *Memorias del Ministro de Gobierno al Congreso de 1962*. Bogotá: Imprenta Nacional, 1962.

Long, William J., and Peter Brecke. *War and Reconciliation: Reason and Emotion in Conflict Resolution*. Cambridge: MIT Press, 2003.

López, Abel Ricardo. "'A Beautiful Class. An Irresistible Democracy': The Formation of the Middle Class in Bogotá, Colombia, 1940–1960." Ph.D. diss., University of Maryland, College Park, 2008.

Martin, Gerald. *Gabriel García Márquez: A Life*. New York: Alfred A. Knopf, 2009.

Martínez Osorio, Glenda Lariza, ed. *Hablan los generales: Las grandes batallas del conflicto colombiano contadas por sus protagonistas*. Bogotá: Editorial Norma, 2006.

Marulanda Alvarez, Elsy. *Colonización y conflicto: Las lecciones del Sumapaz*. Bogotá: Instituto de Estudios Políticos y Relaciones Internacionales, Universidad Nacional de Colombia, and Tercer Mundo Editores, 1991.

Marulanda Vélez, Manuel. *Cuadernos de campaña*. 3rd ed. Bogotá: [Unknown publisher] 2000.

Mater et Magistra. Encyclical letter of Pope John XXIII. May 15, 1961. http://www.vatican.va/holy_father/john_xxiii/encyclicals/documents/hf_j-xxiii_enc_15051961_mater_en.html.

Matta Aldana, Luis Alberto. *Colombia y las FARC-EP: Origen de la lucha guerrillera: Testimonio del comandante Jaime Guaraca*. 2nd ed. Tafalla, Spain: Txalaparta, 2008.

Medina, Medófilo. "La resistencia campesina en el sur del Tolima." In *Pasado y presente de la violencia en Colombia*, edited by Gonzalo Sánchez G. and Ricardo Peñaranda. Bogotá: CEREC, 1986.

———. "Las diferentes formas de entender el conflicto armado en Colombia." *Razón Pública*, February 23, 2015. http://www.razonpublica.com/index.php/conflicto-drogas-y-paz-temas-30/8274-las-diferentes-formas-de-entender-el-conflicto-armado-en-colombia.html.

Meertens, Donny. *Ensayos sobre tierra, violencia y género: Hombres y mujeres en la historia rural de Colombia 1930–1990*. Bogotá: Universidad Nacional de Colombia, Centro de Estudios Sociales, 2000.

Misión "Economía y Humanismo." *Estudio sobre las condiciones del desarrollo de Colombia*, 2 vols. Bogotá: Aedita Editores, 1958.

Molano, Alfredo. *Amnistía y violencia*. Bogotá: CINEP, 1980.

———. "La colonización: Voces y caminos." In *Yo le digo una de las cosas . . .: La colonización de la Reserva la Macarena*, edited by Alfredo Molano, Darío Fajardo, and Julio Carrizosa. [Bogotá]: Fondo FEN Colombia, 1989.

———. *Selva adentro: Una historia oral de la colonización del Guaviare*. 2nd ed. Bogotá: El Áncora Editores, 2006.

Molina, Gerardo. *Las ideas liberales en Colombia: 1849–1914*. 12th ed. Vol. 1. Bogotá: Tercer Mundo Editores, 1988.

Morales Benítez, Otto. *Memoria del Ministro de Agricultura al Congreso de 1961, parte general*. Bogotá: Imprenta Nacional, 1962.

———. "Prólogo." In *Reflexiones sobre la historia, el poder y la vida internacional*, by Alberto Lleras Camargo, edited by Otto Morales Benítez. Bogotá: Tercer Mundo Editores and Ediciones Uniandes, 1994.

Morcate Labrada, Flora, and Olimpia Niglio. "La restauración del club campestre de Obregón&Valenzuela en Ibagué: Una experiencia académica." *Arquitectura y Urbanismo* 33, no. 1 (2012): 137–43.

Moyn, Samuel. *The Last Utopia: Human Rights in History*. Cambridge: Belknap Press, 2010.

"Murió el dirigente político conservador del Huila Felio Andrade." *Caracol*, October 14, 2010. http://www.caracol.com.co/noticias/actualidad/murio-el-dirigente-politico-conservador-del-huila-felio-andrade/20101014/nota/1371424.aspx.

Nora, Pierre. "General Introduction: Between Memory and History." In *Conflicts and Divisions*, edited by Lawrence D. Kritzman, translated by Arthur Goldhammer. Vol. 1, *Realms of Memory: Rethinking the French Past*. New York: Columbia University Press, 1996.

———. "Generation." In *Conflicts and Divisions*, edited by Lawrence D. Kritzman, translated by Arthur Goldhammer. Vol. 1, *Realms of Memory: Rethinking the French Past*. New York: Columbia University Press, 1996.

Octava Brigada. *De la violencia a la paz*. Armenia: Imprenta Departmental de Caldas, 1965.

Oquist, Paul H. *Violence, Conflict, and Politics in Colombia*. New York: Academic Press, 1980.

Ortiz Sarmiento, Carlos Miguel. *Estado y subversión en Colombia: La Violencia en el Quindío, años 50*. Bogotá: Fondo Editorial CEREC, 1985.

———. "Historiografía de La Violencia." In *La historia al final del milenio: Ensayos de historiografía colombiana y latinoamericana*, edited by Bernardo Tovar Zambrano. Vol. 1. Bogotá: Departamento de Historia, Universidad Nacional de Colombia, 1994.

Ospina Fernández, Guillermo, and Eduardo Ospina Acosta. *Teoría general de los actos o negocios jurídicos*. Bogotá: Editorial Temis Librería, 1980.

Pacem in Terris. Encyclical letter of Pope John XXIII. April 11, 1963. http://www.vatican.va/holy_father/john_xxiii/encyclicals/documents/hf_j-xxiii_enc_11041963_pacem_en.html.

Palacios, Marco. *Between Legitimacy and Violence: A History of Colombia, 1875–2002*. Translated by Richard Stoller. Durham and London: Duke University Press, 2006.

Pécaut, Daniel. *Crónica de cuatro décadas de política colombiana*. Bogotá: Grupo Editorial Norma, 2006.

———. *Guerra contra la sociedad*. Bogotá: Espasa, 2001.

———. *Las FARC: ¿Una guerrilla sin fin o sin fines?* Translated by Pedro Lama. Bogotá: Grupo Editorial Norma, 2008.

———. "Presente, pasado y futuro de la Violencia." *Análisis Político* 30 (April 1997): 1–43.

———. *Violencia y política en Colombia: Elementos de reflexión*. Edited and translated by Alberto Valencia Gutiérrez. Medellín: Hombre Nuevo Editores, 2003.

"Perpetuo Socorro." *Diócesis de Líbano-Honda.* Accessed June 2, 2015. http://www .diocesisdelibanohonda.com/site/index.php?option=com_contact&view=contact&id=17 %3Aperpetuo-socorro&catid=14%3Aparroquias&Itemid=27.

Perry Posada, Jimena. *Caminos de la antropología en Colombia: Gregorio Hernández de Alba.* Bogotá: Universidad de Los Andes, Facultad de Ciencias Sociales, 2006.

Piccato, Pablo. "Comments: How to Build a Perspective on the Recent Past." *Journal of Iberian and Latin American Research* 19, no. 1 (2013): 91–102.

Pineda Camacho, Roberto. "La reivindicación del indio en el pensamiento social colombiano." In *Un siglo de investigación social: antropología en Colombia,* edited by Jaime Arocha and Nina S. de Friedemann. Bogotá: Etno, 1984.

Pineda Giraldo, Roberto. *El impacto de la violencia en el Tolima: El caso de El Líbano.* Monografías sociológicas, no. 6. Bogotá: Facultad de Sociología, Universidad Nacional de Colombia, 1960.

Pizarro Leongómez, Eduardo. *Las FARC (1949–1966): De la autodefensa a la combinación de todas las formas de lucha.* Bogotá: Tercer Mundo Editores, 1991.

———. "Las FARC-EP: ¿Repliegue estratégico, debilitamiento o punto de inflexión?" In *Nuestra guerra sin nombre: Transformaciones del conflicto en Colombia,* edited by Francisco Gutiérrez Sanín. Bogotá: Editorial Norma, 2006.

Posada, Jaime, and Gonzalo Canal Ramírez. *La crisis moral colombiana.* Bogotá: Antares, 1955.

Prado Delgado, Víctor Eduardo. *Bandoleros: Historias no contadas.* Ibagué: V. E. Prado D., 2009.

———. *Bandoleros: Imágenes y crónicas.* Ibagué: V. E. Prado D., 2010.

———. *Sur del Tolima "terror": Repúblicas independientes, 1962–1965.* Ibagué: V. E. Prado D., 2011.

Price, David H. *Cold War Anthropology: The CIA, the Pentagon, and the Growth of Dual Use Anthropology.* Durham: Duke University Press, 2016.

Puel, Hugues. "Catholicism and Politics in France in the 20th Century." *Oikonomia: Rivista di Etica e Scienze Sociali* (February 2000). http://www.oikonomia.it/index.php /en/2016/56–2001/febbraio-2001/181-catholicism-and-politics-in-france-in-the-20th-century.

Quién es quién en Colombia. 3rd ed. Bogotá: Oliverio Perry Editores, 1961.

Rama, Angel. *The Lettered City.* Translated by John Charles Chasteen. Durham and London: Duke University Press, 1996.

Ramírez Moreno, Augusto. *Memorias del Ministro de Gobierno al Congreso de 1961.* Bogotá: Imprenta Nacional, 1961.

Ramírez Tobón, William. "La guerrilla rural en Colombia: ¿Una vía hacia la colonización armada?" In *Estado, violencia y democracia: Ensayos.* Bogotá: Instituto de Estudios Políticos y Relaciones Internacionales and Tercer Mundo Editores, 1990.

Rappaport, Joanne. *The Politics of Memory: Native Historical Interpretation in the Colombian Andes.* Durham and London: Duke University Press, 1998.

Registraduría Nacional del Estado Civil. *Circunscripciones electorales y división político-administrativo de Colombia 1961.* 3rd ed. Bogotá: Registraduría Nacional del Estado Civil, 1961.

República de Colombia. *Memoria del Ministro de Agricultura al Congreso Nacional–1962.* Bogotá: Imprenta Nacional, 1962.

Robinson, James A. "Colombia: Another 100 Years of Solitude?" *Current History* 112, no. 751 (February 2013): 43–48.

Roldán, Mary. *Blood and Fire: La Violencia in Antioquia, Colombia, 1946–1953*. Durham and London: Duke University Press, 2002.

Romero Sánchez, Susana. "El miedo a la revolución: Interamericanismo y anticomunismo en Colombia, 1958–1965." M.A. thesis, Universidad Nacional de Colombia, Bogotá, 2007.

Ronderos, Carlos. *Rebelión y amnistía: La historia colombiana del siglo XX contada por sus protagonistas*. Bogotá: Espasa, 2003.

Safford, Frank, and Marco Palacios. *Colombia: Fragmented Land, Divided Society*. New York: Oxford University Press, 2002.

Saldarriaga Betancur, Juan Manuel. *De la dictadura al comunismo*. Medellín: [no publisher] 1962.

Sánchez G., Gonzalo. *Guerras, memoria e historia*. 2nd ed. Bogotá: La Carreta Editores, 2009.

———. *Guerra y política en la sociedad colombiana*. Bogotá: El Áncora Editores, 1991.

———. "La Violencia in Colombia: New Research, New Questions." Translated by Peter Bakewell. *Hispanic American Historical Review* 65, no. 5 (November 1985): 789–807.

———. *Los días de la revolución: Gaitanismo y 9 de abril en provincia*. Bogotá: Centro Cultural Jorge Eliécer Gaitán, 1983.

———. "Presentación: Los intelectuales y las comisiones." In *Colombia: Violencia y democracia*, by Comisión de estudios sobre la violencia, 4th ed. Bogotá: IEPRI, Universidad Nacional de Colombia and Colciencias, 1995.

———. "Raíces históricas de la amnistía o las etapas de la guerra en Colombia." In *Ensayos de historia social y política del siglo XX*. Bogotá: El Áncora Editores, 1984.

———, ed. *Once ensayos sobre la violencia*. Bogotá: Fondo Editorial CEREC and Centro Gaitán, 1985.

Sánchez G., Gonzalo, and Donny Meertens. *Bandits, Peasants, and Politics: The Case of "La Violencia" in Colombia*. Translated by Alan Hynds. Austin: University of Texas Press, 2001.

———. *Bandoleros, gamonales y campesinos: El caso de la violencia en Colombia*. Bogotá: El Áncora Editores, 1983.

Sánchez G., Gonzalo, and Ricardo Peñaranda, eds. *Pasado y presente de la violencia en Colombia*. Bogotá: CEREC, 1986.

———. *Pasado y presente de la violencia en Colombia*. 2nd ed. Bogotá: CEREC, 1991.

Santa, Eduardo. *Nos duele Colombia: Ensayos de sociología política*. Bogotá: Ediciones Tercer Mundo, 1962.

Schmidt, Steffen W. "Bureaucrats as Modernizing Brokers? Clientelism in Colombia." *Comparative Politics* 6, no. 3 (April 1974): 425–50.

———. "La Violencia Revisited: The Clientelist Bases of Political Violence in Colombia." *Journal of Latin American Studies* 6, no. 1 (May 1974): 97–111.

Schoultz, Lars. "Urbanization and Changing Voting Patterns: Colombia, 1946–1970." *Political Science Quarterly* 87, no. 1 (March 1972): 22–45.

Secretaría de Agricultura, Departamento del Tolima. *La violencia en el Tolima*. Ibagué: Imprenta Departamental, 1957.

Silva Vargas, Vicente. *Las huellas de Villamil*. Neiva: Fondo de Autores Huilenses, 2002.

Steele, Abbey. "Seeking Safety: Avoiding Displacement and Choosing Destinations in Civil Wars." *Journal of Peace Research* 46, no. 3 (May 2009): 419–30.

Sternhell, Yael A. *Routes of War: The World of Movement in the Confederate South.* Cambridge: Harvard University Press, 2012.

Stoller, Richard. "Alfonso López Pumarejo and Liberal Radicalism in 1930s Colombia." *Journal of Latin American Studies* 27, no. 2 (May 1995): 367–97.

Taussig, Michael T. *Law in a Lawless Land: Diary of a* Limpieza *in Colombia.* Chicago and London: University of Chicago Press, 2005.

Theidon, Kimberly. *Intimate Enemies: Violence and Reconciliation in Peru.* Philadelphia: University of Pennsylvania Press, 2013.

Tirado Mejía, Álvaro. *Aspectos políticos del primer gobierno de Alfonso López Pumarejo, 1934–1938.* Bogotá: Procultura and Instituto Colombiano de Cultura, 1981.

———. *Colombia en la OEA.* Bogotá: Banco de la República and El Áncora Editores, 1998.

Tokatlián, Juan Gabriel. "El acuerdo sobre drogas en La Habana: Un moderado paso radical." *Razón Pública.* June 8, 2014. http://www.razonpublica.com/index.php/conflicto-drogas-y-paz-temas-30/7676-el-acuerdo-sobre-drogas-en-la-habana-un-moderado-paso-radical.html.

Torres, Camilo. "La violencia y los cambios socio-culturales en las áreas rurales colombianas." In *Once ensayos sobre la violencia,* edited by Gonzalo Sánchez G. Bogotá: Fondo Editorial CEREC and Centro Gaitán, 1985.

Torres, Camilo, and Berta Corredor Rodríguez. *Las escuelas radiofónicas de Sutatenza, Colombia: Evaluación sociológica de los resultados.* Bogotá: Oficina Internacional de Investigaciones Sociales de FERES, 1961.

Torres, Mauricio. *La naturaleza de la revolución colombiana.* Bogotá: Editorial Iqueima, 1959.

Troyan, Brett. *Cauca's Indigenous Movement in Southwestern Colombia: Land, Violence, and Ethnic Identity.* Lanham, Md.: Lexington Books, 2015.

———. "Gregorio Hernández de Alba (1904–1973): The Legitimization of Indigenous Ethnic Politics in Colombia." *European Review of Latin American and Caribbean Studies* 82 (April 2007): 89–106.

———. "Re-Imagining the 'Indian' and the State: Indigenismo in Colombia, 1926–47." *Canadian Journal of Latin American and Caribbean Studies* 33, no. 65 (2008): 81–106.

Tribín Piedrahita, Adriano. "Pasión y vida de una apoteosis," n.d. http://www.festivalfolclorico .com/index.php/el-festival.

Urdaneta Arbeláez, Roberto. *El materialismo contra la dignidad del hombre: Su impacto en la vida colombiana.* Bogotá: Editorial Lucrós, 1960.

Uribe, María Victoria. *Matar, rematar y contramatar: Las masacres de La Violencia en el Tolima, 1948–1964.* Bogotá: CINEP, 1990.

Urrego Ardila, Miguel Angel. *Intelectuales, estado y nación en Colombia: De la Guerra de los Mil Días a la Constitución de 1991.* Bogotá: Universidad Central, Departamento de Investigaciones, and Siglo del Hombre Editores, 2002.

Valencia Ruiz, Armando. *Cambiaremos la vida del campo (explicaciones sobre la reforma social agraria de Colombia).* Pasto: Imprenta Departmental, 1962.

Valencia Tovar, Álvaro. *Testimonio de una época.* 2nd ed. Bogotá: Planeta, 1992.

Van de Sandt, Joris. "Behind the Mask of Recognition: Defending Autonomy and Communal Resource Management in Indigenous Resguardos, Colombia." Ph.D. diss., University of Amsterdam, 2007.

Vezzetti, Hugo. *Sobre la violencia revolucionaria: Memorias y olvidos*. Buenos Aires: Siglo Veintiuno, 2009.

Vieira, Gilberto. *Organicemos la revolución colombiana! Informe político al IX Congreso del Partido Comunista de Colombia*. Bogotá: [unknown publisher] 1961.

Villar Borda, Leopoldo. *Alberto Lleras: El último republicano*. Bogotá: Planeta, 1997.

———. "Alberto Lleras y la edad de oro de la OEA." *Revista Credencial Historia* 100 (April 1998).   http://www.banrepcultural.org/blaavirtual/revistas/credencial/abril1998/10001.htm.

Villarraga S., Álvaro, and Nelson Plazas N. *Para reconstruir los sueños: Una historia del EPL*. Bogotá: Fondo Editorial para la Paz, Fundación Progresar, and Fundación Cultura Democrática, 1994.

Villegas, Benjamín, ed. *Alberto Lleras: Antología*. Vol. 3, *El político*. Bogotá: Villegas Editores, 2006.

———. *Alberto Lleras: Antología*. Vol. 4, *El gobernante*. Bogotá: Villegas Editores, 2006.

———. *Alberto Lleras: Antología*. Vol. 5, *El diplomático*. Bogotá: Villegas Editores, 2006.

Walker, Louise E. *Waking from the Dream: Mexico's Middle Classes after 1968*. Stanford: Stanford University Press, 2013.

Westad, Odd Arne. *The Global Cold War: Third World Interventions and the Making of Our Times*. Cambridge and New York: Cambridge University Press, 2005.

Wilde, Alexander W. "Conversations among Gentlemen: Oligarchical Democracy in Colombia." In *The Breakdown of Democratic Regimes: Latin America*, edited by Juan J. Linz and Alfred Stepan. Baltimore and London: Johns Hopkins University Press, 1978.

Zamosc, León. *The Agrarian Question and the Peasant Movement in Colombia: Struggles of the National Peasant Association, 1967–1981*. Cambridge and New York: Cambridge University Press, 1986.

Zea, Germán. *Memorias del Ministro de Justicia al Congreso Nacional en sus sesiones ordinarias de 1959*. Bogotá: Imprenta Nacional, 1959.

Zolov, Eric. *Refried Elvis: The Rise of the Mexican Counterculture*. Berkeley: University of California Press, 1999.

Zuleta Angel, Eduardo. *Memoria del Ministro de Gobierno al Congreso de 1960*. Bogotá: Imprenta Nacional, 1961.

Zuleta P., Mónica, and Alejandro Sánchez L. "La batalla por el pensamiento propio en Colombia." *Nómadas* 27 (October 2007): 124–41.

INDEX

Italic page numbers indicate illustrations.

absolution, 57
Acción Cultural Popular (ACPO). *See* Popular
    Cultural Action
Advanced School of Public Administration, 136,
    146
Afro-Colombians, 145
aggression, biological bases of, 172
Agrarian, Industrial, and Mining Bank: default
    rates at, 112, 264n95; in *desplazado* resettle-
    ment, 107, 208; end of discrimination against
    Liberals by, 77; loan criteria used by, 265n96;
    National Liberal Revolutionary Movement
    on, 68; risk aversion of, 112, 264n96. *See also*
    rehabilitation loans
agrarian question, 107, 125; Torres and, 145
agrarian reform: Cuban influence on, 125; IN-
    CORA in implementation of, 134; landowner
    resistance to, 140; in Law 135 of 1960, 126–29,
    133, 134, 140; under Lleras Camargo, 107, 112,
    123–29, 133; San Silvestre ranch conflict and,
    120–22
Agrarian Reform Law of Cuba (1959), 125
Agriculture Ministry: in cacao cultivation, 187;
    Fals Borda in, 133
alcohol, in Tolima: ban on, 67; taxes on, 91
Alliance for Peace, 92
Alliance for Progress, 124, 126, 134, 187
All-Purpose Teams, 81, 83, 129

Alternativa (magazine), 220–21
Amaya Ramírez, Guillermo, 102, 106–7
amnesty programs: in 1953, 27, 55, 240n48; in
    1958 (proposed), 82, 255n73
Andrade Manrique, Felio: on bandit attacks, 155;
    on cattle rustling, 116; on coffee trafficking,
    98; and cultural festival, 93; pardons by,
    91, 210; in regional politics of creole peace,
    91–92
anthropology, vs. sociology, 131
anti-Communism, 139–40
anti-guerrilla operations, 173
Arciniegas, Germán, 31
Arenas, Jacobo: Camargo compared to, 197;
    death of, 212; in military campaign against
    Marquetalia, 197–200; in Southern Bloc, 203,
    211–13
"armed colonization," 88–89, 258n107
Armed Forces. *See* military
Armed Forces Journal, 281n119
Army of National Liberation (ELN), 216–17,
    218
authoritarianism: in 1950s, 26–29; Benidorm ac-
    cord in transition from, 29; Lleras Camargo's
    response to, 26–27, 28
autodefensas (self-defense forces): in El Pato,
    201–2; in Marquetalia, 199–200; in Riochiq-
    uito, 205–6, 209

309

bambuco, 64, 74, 251n4
Bambuco Pageant, 259n126
bandits: Benidorm accord on, 29; Communists
    as, 184; in Conservative assault on rehabilita-
    tion, 102–3, 157; death of, 177, 180, 184; iden-
    tity of, 156–57; military operations against,
    12, 173–80; number of, 177; resurgence in
    1962 of, 12, 148, 155–58
bank. *See* Agrarian, Industrial, and Mining Bank
beauty queens, 148–50, 207
Belalcázar, regional politics and rehabilitation
    in, 89–90
Benidorm accord (1956), 29–30, 32, 242n70
betrayals, memory of, 55–56, 58
biology, of aggression, 172
Blackblood. *See* Sangrenegra
Black Horseman. *See* Charry Rincón, Fermín
Black March (March of Death, 1965), 202
Bogotá: as "Athens of South America," 18;
    Kennedy's visit to, 122, 126, 134, 143; orphans
    in, 170; Tunjelito neighborhood of, 135
Braun, Herbert, 8
budgets. *See* funding
bus transportation, violence associated with,
    73–74, 99

cacao cultivation, 187, 188
Caja de Crédito Agrario, Industrial y Minero.
    See Agrarian, Industrial, and Mining Bank
Cali, dynamite explosion in, 30
Camargo, Martín, 185–89, *186;* Arenas compared
    to, 197; and Marulanda/Tirofijo, 186; and
    military campaign against El Pato, 201–2;
    in self-rehabilitation of El Pato, 187–89,
    200–201; and Villamil, 188, 189, 208
campesinos, use and meaning of term, 236n34
Canal Ramírez, Gonzalo: attempts to quantify
    displacement, 43; attempts to quantify vio-
    lence, 42–43, 277n43; on roadway homicides,
    161; *This Was My Village,* 42, 71; on *La violen-
    cia en Colombia,* 154–55
Caro, Miguel Antonio, 248n51
cartoons, political, 98, *161*
Castañeda, José Alfonso (Richard), *60,* 91, 186,
    188, 202
Castro, Fidel, 125, 126
casualties: attempts to quantify, 42–43, 245n17;
    military, 177. *See also* homicides
Catholic Church: anti-Communism and, 140; on
    social progress, 124–25; on Torres, 216; on *La
    violencia en Colombia,* 158. *See also* Popular
    Cultural Action

cattle rustling, 116, 117–18, 191
censorship: under Laureano, 26; under Rojas
    Pinilla, 30, 40, 66
Charro Negro (Black Horseman). *See* Charry
    Rincón, Fermín
Charry Rincón, Fermín (Charro Negro [Black
    Horseman]), *70;* assassination of, 114–18, 191;
    pardon for, 91, 210, 259n119; rehabilitation
    of, 88
Charry Samper, Héctor, *161, 162–63,* 165, 166
Chernick, Marc, 234n5, 274n111
children: orphaned, 156, 170; *La violencia en
    Colombia* on, 170
Chispas (Sparks). *See* Rojas, Teófilo
Christianity: in National Investigatory Commis-
    sion, 57, 250n78; Torres on socialism and,
    145. *See also* Catholic Church
chulavitas: Conservative politicians' defense
    of, 164–65; Liberals' fight in Tolima against,
    54–55, 57, 61–62; new wave of, in 1960s, 191
cigarette taxes, 91
Ciro Trujillo Castaño. *See* Trujillo Castaño, Ciro
citizenship: and anti-Communism, 140; Law 19
    of 1958 and, 127; and petitioning of *junta,* 68,
    252n20; political, 4, 127, 140; of provincial
    Colombians, 61; social, 4, 113, 127, 140, 143
civic-military action, 175–79, 190–91
Civil Front, 31–33
civilian-military relations, as challenge for Lleras
    Camargo administration, 35–36
civil service, Sitges pact on, 32
civil war, undeclared, 5, 43, 159–60, 277n57
Clarín, El (radio program), 102–3
"clean" Liberals. See *limpios*
clemency tribunals, 83, 91, 255n76
clientelism, in rehabilitation, 90
Coca-Cola generation, 31
cocaine, 221
coffee cultivation: anti-Communism and, 140;
    decline in prices, 30, 31; violence associated
    with harvests, 72–73, 98
Colombia: *llerismo* in national ethos of, 43–44;
    map of (c. 1960), *xvi;* national ideas of
    violence in, 77–78, 173; social scientists' influ-
    ence on national self-image of, 225
Colombian Institute of Agrarian Reform
    (INCORA): and El Pato *desplazados,* 208;
    in Fals Borda's research in Cunday, 135; on
    indigenous land, 211; landowner resistance
    to, 140; mission of, 134; Torres in, 134, 145,
    146; under Valencia, 138
"colonization, armed," 88–89, 258n107

Comisión Especial de Rehabilitación. *See* Special Rehabilitation Commission

commission on violence. *See* National Investigatory Commission on the Causes and Current Situations of Violence in the National Territory

Communal Action, 127–29; Communism equated with, 140; and disillusionment with reform, 143–44; establishment of, 127; National University in training for, 133; success of, 127–29

Communism: in Cuba, 121, 122; global struggle against, 174; rise of opposition to, 139–40

Communist Party. *See* Communists

Communist Party Congress, Tenth, 212

Communists, 12–13, 182–213; as bandits, 184; difference between Liberals and, 68–69; inevitability of military violence against, 183; Liberal leaders meeting with, 69–71, *70*; Liberal resistance working with, 57–58; Lleras Camargo's peace policy supported by, 86–89; local benefits of collective work by, 87; map of Gran Tolima communities of, *58*; marginality of, 69; and National Investigatory Commission, 57–59, 86–87; rehabilitation of, 86–89, 105; on Rojas/Chispas, 174; selective memory of, 213; in Southern Bloc, 203, 212–13; urban vs. rural, 182–83; on *La violencia en Colombia*, 168. *See also specific communities and members*

Community Action Councils, 127–29; and disillusionment with reform, 143–44; of El Pato, 186, 187; establishment of, 127; number of, 127; of Rioblanco, 129, 142; success of, 127–29

comunes. See Communists

Conciliation and Equity Tribunals, 108–14; Agrarian Bank in work of, 112; challenges facing, 109–10; and Communal Action, 129; establishment of, 108; mission of, 108–9; and state of siege, 113–14; in Tierradentro, 204–5; Zuñiga family before, 142

confession, 57, 250n78

congressional elections: of 1958, 34; of 1960, 105, 115–16, 123, 138–39

Congress of Colombia: on agrarian reform, 126, 133; closure in 1949 of, 26; on land disputes, 107–8; after La Palmita massacre, 101–2; Lleras Camargo as member of, 20; in López's resignation, 23; on rehabilitation, 101–2, 108; shootout on floor of, 25–26; Sitges pact on, 32; Valencia administration speeches of 1962 at, *161*, 161–63, 165; on *La violencia en Colombia*, 155, 164–65

Conservatives: in Benidorm accord, 29–30; constitution of 1863 overturned by, 18; idea of violence of, 29; loss of power in 1930, 19, 25; in National Front, 4; in National Investigatory Commission, 45; as recipients of rehabilitation, vs. Liberals, 84–85, 101–2; rehabilitation criticized by, 101–5, 157; return to power in 1946, 23–25; role in peace initiatives, vs. Liberals, 4; violence as electoral strategy of, 52–54, *53*; on *La violencia en Colombia*, 157–60, 163–65; in War of a Thousand Days, 18. *See also specific elections and members*

consolidation, 207, 209

constitution: of 1863, 18, 111; 1936 reform of, 20, 124; of 1991, 223; Article 16 of, 198; challenges of return to rule under, 32; Sitges pact on, 32

constitutional coup of 1949, 26

construction jobs, 81–82, 88

convivencia (coexistence): in Benidorm accord, 29; breakdowns in, 96–97; in Community Action Councils, 186; in creole peace, 82; Lleras Camargo in, 4, 9, 78, 82, 105, 160, 167; meaning of term, 4; in National Investigatory Commission, 61, 74; petitions as act of, 68; in rehabilitation, 83, 84; in Sitges pact, 32; social scientists' vision of, 11, 133, 171

Córdova, José María, 111

cost of living, 31, 86

coups: of 1944 (attempted), 23, 240n48; of 1949, 26; of 1953, 27, 34; of 1957, 2, 3; of 1958 (attempted), 35–36

creole peace, 10–11, 63–94; challenges to, 96; Communist support for, 86–89; as forgotten peace, 12–13, 169; local priorities in, 65, 86–89; meaning of term, 3, 65; military role in, 173; National Investigatory Commission in, 74–78, *76*; negotiations of 1957–58 in, 66–71; pardon in, 82–83; partisan homicides threatening, 72–73, *73, 75–77*, 98, *99*; regional identity in, 92–94; regional politics in, 65, 89–92; repatriation of *desplazados* in, 65. *See also* rehabilitation

Cuba: Agrarian Reform Law of, 125; Communists suspected of links to, 204

Cuban revolution: Colombian views on, 121, 122, 125; and ELN, 216; Liberal Revolutionary Movement on, 139; Organization of American States on, 126

cultural festivals, 92–94

Cunday, Fals Borda's research in, 135–36, 140, 143

Danger. *See* García, Leopoldo

Deas, Malcolm, 96

deaths. *See* casualties; homicides
declaration of principles of press (1962), 165–67
Decree 0328 (1958), 82–83, 91
democratic transition: challenges facing, 32, 40; National Front in, 4; plebiscite on, 32–33
democratization, third-wave, 3
demonstrations, over presidential election of 1958, 31–32
departmental boundaries, 6
"desarmando los espíritus", 49–50, 61
desplazados: from El Pato, 201–2, 206–8; in evolution of conflict, 54–55; human and economic costs of, 43; National Investigatory Commission on, 52; number of, 43, 52, 245n20; reparations for, 110–12, 208; from Riochiquito, 206, 209–11
desplazados, repatriation of: in El Pato, 207–9; failures of, 74, 99, 101; in Gran Tolima, 99, 101, 106; homicides associated with, 98–99; land disputes in, 106–7; scope of, 65, 71, 251n6, 256n90; second round of, 85–86
Desquite (Revenge), 168–69, 179–80, 184
detention facilities, military, 176
development, Lebret report on, 40–41, 124, 194
developmentalism, global, 11
developmentalist policies: on indigenous population, 130; Law 19 of 1958 in, 127; Law 135 of 1960 in, 126–29; under Lleras Camargo, 81–82, 121; military involvement in, 150; origins of, 11; in rehabilitation, 81–82; of social scientists, 11, 121–23, 130–36; under Valencia, 138, 141
"dirty" Liberals. See *sucios*
displacement. See *desplazados*
drug trade, 221
Dussán, Germán (General Santander), 56, 117, 129, 142
dynamite explosion in Cali, 30

Echandía, Darío: as acting president, 23; career of, 83; on coffee trafficking, 98; and cultural festival, 92–93; on "fishing at night," 98; as governor of Tolima, 75, 83, 85; on land disputes, 107; in rehabilitation, 83–84, 86
economic development. *See* development
economy, Colombian: in 1950s, 30, 31; in 1960s, 138; as challenge for Lleras Camargo administration, 36–37; costs of displacement to, 43; under Rojas Pinilla, 30, 31, 36; under Valencia, 138, 272n90
Edel, Matthew, 128
education, funding for, 81, 242n74

Education Ministry: on causes of violence, 41–42, 245n14; Communal Action under, 127; Fals Borda's presentation to, 132
elections. *See* congressional elections; presidential elections
electoral strategy, Conservative, violence as, 52–54, *53*
El Líbano, 259n126; Guzmán as priest of, 45; retaliation for assassination attempt in, 54
ELN. *See* Army of National Liberation
El Pato, 184–89; Community Action Councils of, 186, 187; displacement from, 201–2, 206–8; as independent republic, 184–87, 200–202; Liberal peace delegation in, 69; military campaign of 1965 in, 201–2; National Investigatory Commission in, 59–60, *60*; rearmament of, 188–89; rehabilitation in, 184–87; self-rehabilitation in, 187–89, 200–201
emergency food aid, 187
emergency powers, Rojas Pinilla's abuse of, 28
"empathetic memory," 218
Equipos Polivalentes. *See* All-Purpose Teams
Espectador, El (newspaper), 18, 28
ethnicity, in causes of violence, 41–42
expectations, created by reform efforts, 123, 146

Fals Borda, Orlando, 11, *131*, 131–37; disillusionment of, 144–45, 215; education of, 132; evolution of views of, 215, 217–18; in exile, 215, 218; "Forbidden History" column by, 220; functionalism rejected by, 134, 135; on "generation of La Violencia," 218, 219, 222; in Gran Tolima, 135–36, 140, 143; Guzmán's influence on, 152; as intellectual leader in sociology, 131–33; in Marquetalia commission, 193–94, 215; at National University, 132–37; personal memories of, in La Violencia, 224; Sánchez influenced by, 222; *Subversion in Colombia*, 218–19; after Torres's death, 217–19; Torres's relationship with, 133, 218; use of term "La Violencia" by, 218, 222; on *la violencia*, definition of, 5, 153; working with the state, 132–33. See also *violencia en Colombia, La*
FARC, 12–13, 219–22; conditions for fighters in, 219–20; in drug trade, 221; establishment of, 10, 212–13; goal of, 213; government cease-fire with, 222, 223; government negotiations with, 225–26; and 19th of April Movement, 220–21; Popular Army added to name of, 221; and *La violencia en Colombia*, 181; La Violencia in origins of, 1, 2
Fernández de Soto, Absalón, 45, 61

festivals: cultural, 92–94; peace, 180, 207
finances. *See* funding
First Guerrilla Conference of the Southern Bloc, 203
First International Symposium on La Violencia, 222, 291n41
fiscal crisis, in Gran Tolima (1958), 91, 258n114
"fishing at night" metric, 98
Folkloric Festival, 93–94
food aid, emergency, 187
"Forbidden History" (Fals Borda), 220
forced displacement. *See desplazados*
forgetting, pact of, 13, 166
forgotten peace, creole peace as, 12–13, 169
Frazier, Leslie Jo, 218
Frente Civil. *See* Civil Front
Frente Nacional. *See* National Front
Fuerzas Armadas Revolucionaries de Colombia. *See* FARC
functionalism, 134–35, 171
funding: for Communal Action, 127; for education, 81, 242n74; for rehabilitation, 79–81, *80*, 104; for *La violencia en Colombia*, 152, 157

Gaitán, Jorge Eliécer: assassination of, 25, 45, 165; and Guzmán, 45; on *país nacional* and *país político*, 16–17
Gaitania, 59, *59*, 88, 115–17, 178
García, Leopoldo (Peligro [Danger]), 54–58, *56*; on betrayals, 55–56, 58; on Communists, 57–58; on development of Liberal resistance, 55–57; in land sales, 142; life of, 51; in National Liberal Revolutionary Movement, 68; on noms de guerre, 55; and Oviedo/Mariachi, 115; in peace negotiations, 67, 68; petition to *junta* submitted by, 68, 252n20; on start of Conservative violence, 54–55
García Márquez, Gabriel, 17, 19, 20, 23, 220
General Santander. *See* Dussán, Germán
generation of La Violencia, 218, 219, 222
generation of midcentury, 31
generation of the state of siege, 31, 218–19
Gilhodès, Pierre, 88
global developmentalism, 11
Gómez, Laureano. *See* Laureano Gómez
Gómez Hurtado, Álvaro: on Plan Lazo, 176; on rehabilitation, 101, 157; on Sitges pact, 32; on *La violencia en Colombia*, 157, 158–59; on Yopal training center, 146, 147
Gómez Pinzón, José: career of, 79; on community action, 128; management of rehabilitation by, 79–80; and regional politics, 91, 92;

and rehabilitation, 83–84, 105; on reparations requests, 110–11
González, Miguel Angel, 158, 159, 163
González, Víctor, 120–22
Good Neighbor policy, 20, 124
Gran Tolima, 6–8; boundaries of, 6–7; civic-military action in, 176–77, 178–79; cultural festival in, 92–94; Fals Borda's research in, 135–36, 140, 143; fiscal crisis of 1958 in, 91, 258n114; Liberal peace delegations in, 66–69; location of Communist communities in, *58*; maps of, *7, 39, 58, 73*; National Investigatory Commission interviews in, 38–39, 50–61; National Investigatory Commission peace-work in, 75–77; National Liberal Revolutionary Movement in, 67–68; partisan homicides of 1957–58 in, *72*, 72–73, *73*, 75–76, *99*; partisan homicides of 1959 in, 98–102, *99*; peace under Rojas Pinilla in, challenges to, 66; petitions to *junta* from, 68, 252n20; regional identity of, 92–94; rehabilitation in, 79, 84–85, 91, 92–94; rehabilitation in, aftermath of, 114–18; repatriation in, 99, 101, 106; scope of displacement in, 43, 52; topography of, 7–8, 173. *See also specific communities*
graves, mass, 52, 54
Greater Tolima. *See* Gran Tolima
Guaraca, Jaime, 87, 212, 213, 258n104
Guerrilla Fighters' Agrarian Program, 197–98
guerrillas: military operations against, 173; in Southern Bloc, 203, 212–13; transition from self-defense to, 200
Guhl, Ernesto, 121–22, 145, 175
Gutiérrez Anzola, Jorge Enrique, 107, 108
Guzmán Campos, Germán, 9–10, 38–62, *51*; Catholic Church's reprimand of, 158; on Communists, 57–59; on development of Liberal resistance, 56–57; educational projects of, 45; in El Pato, 59–60, *60*; evolution of views of, 215, 217; in exile, 158, 167, 215, 217; at First International Symposium on La Violencia, 222; García/Peligro interviews with, 54–58; honorific title given to, 151; influence on direction of commission, 45–46, 50; in La Herrera, 38–39, 52, 57; on La Palmita massacre, 100; in Marquetalia commission, 193, 215; parish of, 45, 151; on peace and reconciliation, potential for, 56–57, 60–61; on peace-making role of commission, 75; reissue of *La violencia en Colombia* in 1968 by, 217; on reports by commission, 77; on Rionegro, 111; Sánchez influenced by, 222; after Torres's

Guzmán Campos *(continued)*
death, 217; on violence as Conservative
electoral strategy, 52–54. *See also* National Investigatory Commission on the Causes and
Current Situations of Violence; *violencia en
Colombia, La*

"haciendo patria", 88, 130
harm, moral and material, 112
helicopters, military, 177, 195
Hernández de Alba, Gregorio: on indigenous
population of Tierradentro, 184–85, 189, 209,
211; influence on Lleras Camargo's indigenous policy, 130; on peace in Latin America
vs. Europe, 21; on Tierradentro massacre of
1950, 130
Hirschman, Albert O., 126, 128, 132
history: vs. memory, 157–59; violence-as-idea
influencing versions of, 209–11
Hobsbawm, Eric, 26
homicides, bandit: decline of, 177, *178*, 180;
partisan homicides surpassed by, 155–56;
resurgence in 1962 of, 12, 148, 155–58
homicides, drug-related, 221
homicides, partisan: 1957–58, in Gran Tolima,
72, 72–73, *73*, 75–76, *99*; 1957–59, national,
72, 72–73, 98, *99*; 1959, in Gran Tolima,
98–102, *99*; 1963, national, 177, *178*; attempts
to quantify, 42–43, 245n17; bandit homicides
surpassing, 155–56; *desplazado* repatriation associated with, 98–99; *La violencia en
Colombia* on number of, 158, 277n43
homicides, roadway: 1958, 73–74, *99*; 1962, 155,
156, 160–61; 1963, 168–69
homogenization, partisan, 54, 107
Huntington, Samuel, 215

Ibagué: cultural festival in, 92–94; interparty relations in, 47–49; massacre of 1958 in, 48–49;
population growth in, 47; topography of, 47
identity, regional, and creole peace, 92–94
INCORA. *See* Colombian Institute of Agrarian
Reform
independent republics, Communist, 88; El Pato
as, 184–89, 200–202; Marquetalia as, 184,
191–200; Riochiquito as, 184, 189–91, 202–7
Indigenous Affairs Division, 130
indigenous population: land of, 130, 204–5, 211;
Lleras Camargo's policy on, 130; in Tierradentro, 89, 185, 189, 204–5, 209, 211
"individualist State," 123

Instituto Colombiano de Reforma Agraria (IN-
CORA). *See* Colombian Institute of Agrarian
Reform
intelligence gathering, by military, 176–77, 203,
287n70
Intelligence Service, Colombian (SIC), 30, 66,
71, 76
inter-Americanism, 21
Interior Ministry: Communal Action under,
127; and El Pato *desplazados,* 208; Lleras
Camargo in, 20; on Peace Corps, 144
international influence, on reform efforts,
121–22, 139–40
International Monetary Fund, 36
Inzá, Marulanda's attempt to seize, 204

Jaramillo Marín, Jefferson, 223, 250n78
Jelin, Elizabeth, 13
Jiménez, Michael, 88, 274n111
job creation, 81–82, 88
John XXIII (pope), 124–25, 140
journalism, Lleras Camargo's career in, 18–19, 28
judicial system, 82–83
junta of 1957–58, 33–34; and Canal Ramírez, 42;
on education funding, 242n74; and Lebret
report, 41; and National Investigatory Commission, 44–45, 46; and peace delegations
in Tolima, 67, 68; petitions submitted to, 68,
252n20
Juntas de Acción Comunal. *See* Community
Action Councils
Justice Ministry, Umaña at, 170, 275n9

Kennedy, John F., 124–26; Alliance for Progress
of, 124, 126, 134; election of, 124; visit to
Bogotá, 122, 126, 134, 143
Kenya, Mau Mau insurgency in, 103

La Herrera: aerial attack on, 38–39, 52, 56;
Guzmán's visit to, 38–39, 52, 57; location of,
38, *39*, 250n83
La Italia, massacre of 1963 in, 168–69, 179
land: indigenous, 130, 204–5, 211; legal reforms
relating to disputes over, 106–9; restrictions
on sales of, 142. *See also* agrarian question
La Palmita, massacre of 1959 in, 98–102, 115,
260n12, 261n34
Lara Borrero, Oliverio, 187–89, 284n16
Laureano Gómez (The Monster): in Benidorm
accord, 29–30, 242n70; enemies targeted by,
34; in exile, 29; family of, 32, 101, 146; Lleras

Camargo's speech defending, 22; López compared to, 22; opposition to López by, 22–23; power in National Front, 34; in presidential election of 1950, 26; on presidential election of 1958, 34–35; return from exile, 33–34; in Sitges pact, 32; on *La violencia en Colombia*, 163–64

Law 19 (1958), 127, 134

Law 124 (1959), 108

Law 135 (1960), 126–29, 133, 134, 140

Law 201 (1959), 107

Laws of the Plains, 171, 213

Lebret, Louis-Joseph: Communal Action influenced by, 129; development report by, 40–41, 124, 194, 244n8; National Investigatory Commission influenced by, 46; and rehabilitation, 81, 83

legal reforms, 96–97, 106–14; on land disputes, 106–9; on reparations, 110–12. *See also* agrarian reform

León Valencia, Guillermo. *See* Valencia, Guillermo León

letrados (men of letters), 11, 130–47; associated with state vs. partisan politics, 121, 129, 132–33; developmentalist policies of, 130–36; disillusionment of, 145–47; emergence of new, 122–23, 129; as focus of study, 5; international influence on, 121–22; Lleras Camargo as, 17–18; in military, 150; in *país letrado*, 17; *país político* against, 136–41; on La Violencia, 211

Liberal Recovery Movement (MRL), 116, 138–39

Liberal Republic, 19–20, 159

Liberal Revolutionary Movement (MRL), 138–39, 190, 192, 193–94

Liberals: in Benidorm accord, 29–30; Communist collaboration with, 57–58; development of armed resistance in, 26, 55–57; difference between Communists and, 68–69; idea of violence of, 78; language of, 16; Lleras Camargo as leader of, 28–29, 66; loss of power in 1946, 23–25; in National Front, 4; in National Investigatory Commission, 45; in peace delegations in Tolima, 66–67; as recipients of rehabilitation, vs. Conservatives, 84–85, 101–2; return to power in 1930, 19, 25; role in peace initiatives, vs. Conservatives, 4; spike in 1950 in violence against, 25–26; in War of a Thousand Days, 18. *See also specific elections and members*

limpios ("clean" Liberals), 58, 66–68, 142

livestock rustling, 116, 117–18, 191

Lleras, Felipe, 18

Lleras, Lorenzo María, 18

Lleras Camargo, Alberto, 9, 15–37, *17*; in Benidorm accord, 29–30, 242n70; as congressman, 20; on democratic transition, challenges of, 32; early life of, 17–20; education of, 18; in exile, 24–27; family of, 18; on Gran Tolima, concern about, 8; on inter-Americanism, 21; as interim president (1945–46), 23–24, 104; as interior minister, 20; journalism career of, 18–19, 28; as *letrado*, 17–18; as Liberal Party leader, 28–29, 66; in López government, 19–23; López's influence on, 19–20; National Investigatory Commission proposed by, 44–46; in OAS, 25–27; on political transitions, 3; retirement after presidency, 167; on Rojas government, 28, 40; in Sitges pact, 32–33; speaking style of, 20; on "undeclared civil war," 5, 277n57; in U.N. founding, 21–22; at University of the Andes, 27; on *la violencia*, 5

Lleras Camargo, Alberto, as president (1958–62): ACPO speech by, 15–16, 19, 37, 127, 244n8; agrarian reform under, 107, 112, 123–29, 133; amnesty under, 82, 255n73; challenges facing, 35–37, 40; on coffee trafficking, 98; Communist support for, 86–89; in *convivencia*, 4, 9, 78, 82, 105, 160, 167; in creole peace, 65; and cultural festival in Tolima, 92–93; election of, 31–35; end of term, 121, 136–38; Fals in administration of, 133; inauguration of, 36, 46–47, 49; indigenous policy of, 130; on land reform, 106–8; and Lebret report, 244n8; on National Investigatory Commission, 77–78; in origins of *La violencia en Colombia*, 211; on peace-work in Tolima, 76–77; in rehabilitation as national policy, 78–86, 103–5; return of *desplazados* under, 251n6; state of siege under, 78–79, *80*, 107–8, 113–14; Valencia compared to, 160

Lleras Restrepo, Carlos, 125–26, 129

llerismo, 43–44

Loaiza, Gerardo, 55–56, 57, 68, 115

loans, rehabilitation. *See* rehabilitation loans

local priorities, in creole peace, 65, 86–89

Lomnitz, Claudio, 87

López, A. Ricardo, 136

López Michelsen, Alfonso, 138–39

López Pumarejo, Alfonso: in Benidorm accord, 30; in exile, 22, 23; family of, 138; influence on Lleras Camargo, 19–20; Laureano compared to, 22; in presidential election of 1934, 19; in

López Pumarejo *(continued)*
    presidential election of 1942, 22; resignation
    of, 23; return to politics in 1956, 28; Revolu-
    tion on the March under, 19–20, 22, 23

"manager State," 123, 137–38, 144–46
March of Death (Black March, 1965), 202
Mariachi. *See* Oviedo, José María
Marín, Pedro Antonio. *See* Marulanda Vélez,
    Manuel
Marquetalia: commission of social scientists in,
    192–94, 215; as independent republic, 184,
    191–200; military campaign of 1964 against,
    192, 195–200, *196, 200*; partial dissolution
    of Communist movement at, 71, 87; peace
    negotiations with Communists of, 69; popu-
    lation of, 253n28; in Southern Bloc, 212
Marulanda Vélez, Manuel (born Pedro Antonio
    Marín; alias Tirofijo [Sureshot]), 10–12, *70;*
    attempts to capture, 192; on cattle rustling,
    117–18; on Charry Rincón's assassination,
    114–15, 117; Ciro's relationship with, 203–4;
    conversion from Liberal to Communist,
    10, 71; as founder of FARC, 10; in Guerrilla
    Fighters' Agrarian Program, 198; Lleras Ca-
    margo administration supported by, 86–87;
    and military assault against Riochiquito, 182,
    206; in military campaign against Marqueta-
    lia, 195–96, 198–200; origin of name, 71, 186;
    pardon for, 91, 210, 259n119; rehabilitation
    of, 87–88; reports of death of, 182; on return
    to armed resistance, 118; in Southern Bloc,
    203, 211–12
mass graves, 52, 54
material harm, 112
Mau Mau insurgency, 103
medical services, in rehabilitation, 92
Meertens, Donny, 103, 162, 179, 222–23
Mellenthin, Hans-Joachim von, 120–22
memory: of betrayals, 55–56, 58; "empathetic,"
    218; vs. history, 157–59; personal vs. national,
    in La Violencia, 224–25; selective, of Com-
    munists, 213; of violence, multiple versions
    of, 149; in *La violencia en Colombia*, 149; in
    work of National Investigatory Commission,
    61–62, 77
memory commission, 224–25
Méndez Lemaitre, Rodrigo, 120–22
military, Colombian: casualties in, 177; civic
    action by, 175–79, 190–91; in consolidation,
    209; counterviolence strategies of, 173–80;
    in creole peace, 173; El Pato campaign of

1965 by, 201–2; in El Pato redevelopment,
    208–9; expansion of portfolio of, 150, 174–76;
    involvement in violence, 61–62; *letrados* in,
    150; Lleras Camargo administration relations
    with, 35–36; Marquetalia campaign of 1964
    by, 192, 195–200, *196, 200*; on nonstop nature
    of violence, 173; Plan Lazo of, 175–80, 188;
    Riochiquito campaign of 1965 by, 182–83,
    190–91, 202–7; and Southern Bloc, 212; Vil-
    larrica campaign of 1955 by, 27, 58, 66, 173; on
    La violencia en Colombia, 180–81, 194
M-19. *See* 19th of April Movement
modernization theory, 134, 175, 215
Molano, Alfredo, 83
Monster, The. *See* Laureano Gómez
Morales Benítez, Otto, 45, *56*, 87, 218
moral harm, 112
Movimiento 19 de Abril. *See* 19th of April
    Movement
Movimiento de Recuperación Liberal (MRL).
    See Liberal Recovery Movement
Movimiento de Revolucionario Liberal. *See*
    Liberal Revolutionary Movement
Movimiento Liberal Nacional Revolucionario
    del Sur del Tolima. *See* National Liberal Rev-
    olutionary Movement of Southern Tolima
MRL. *See* Liberal Recovery Movement; Liberal
    Revolutionary Movement
murders. *See* homicides
music, *bambuco*, 64, 74, 251n4
mystique, around reform, 124, 126

napalm, 27
Nasa people, 195, 203, 209
National Coffee Federation, 77, 140, 253n24
national ethos, *llerismo* in, 43–44
National Front: Civil Front replaced by, 33;
    Conservative assaults on, 101; in democratic
    transition, 4; *desplazados* at start of, 43; end
    of, 220; mission of, 4; in start of La Violencia,
    225. *See also specific elections, parties, and
    politicians*
national ideas of violence, 77–78, 173
National Investigatory Commission on the
    Causes and Current Situations of Violence in
    the National Territory, 44–62; as antecedent
    to truth commissions, 50, 62, 77; archive of,
    151, 217; Christian practices in, 57, 250n78;
    classified status of findings of, 45; and Com-
    munists, 57–59, 86–87; creation of, 44–46;
    dates of work, 50, 77; on displacement, 52;
    evolution of work, 3, 61; García/Peligro's

interviews with, 54–58; goal of, 3, 44, 46; Guzmán's influence on direction of, 45–46, 50; members of, 45–46, 56; methodology of, 46, 50; open interviews in rural areas by, 38–40, 50–51; on peace and reconciliation, potential for, 56–57, 60–61; as Peace Commission vs. Violence Commission, 61; peacemaking role of, 3, 61, 74–78, 76; recommendations of, 77–78; report by, lack of, 77, 150; in *La violencia en Colombia*, 150–52, 171

National Liberal Revolutionary Movement of Southern Tolima: establishment of, 67–68; Guzmán's meeting with, 75; rehabilitation loans to, 84; on reparations, 110; statutes of, 171, 213

National University of Colombia, sociology department at, 132–37, 145–46, 147

nation-making, role of violence in, 9

Neiva: Camargo in rehabilitation in, 187–89; cultural festival in, 93–94, 259n126

newspapers, 1962 declaration of principles by, 165–67. *See also* censorship; *specific publications*

19th of April Movement (M-19), 220–22, 223

noms de guerre: of Communists, 71; in Liberal resistance, 55

Nora, Pierre, 157, 224

Northern Festival, 259n126

OAS. *See* Organization of American States

observation, sociology's shift from functionalism to, 134–35

Office of Rehabilitation, 79–85, 110

Operation Sovereignty, 207

Oquist, Paul, 245nn17,20

Organization of American States (OAS): on Cuban revolution, 126; establishment of, 25; Fals Borda in, 132; Lleras Camargo in, 25–27

Orientación (radio program), 34, 35

orphans, 156, 170

Ortiz, Carlos Miguel, 152–53

Ospina Pérez, Mariano: family of, 164; Laureano's opposition to, 34; and rehabilitation, 103, 105; state of siege under, 26, 111

Oviedo, José María (Mariachi), 115–17, 129, 266n115

pacification, by military, 150, 160, 177

país letrado (lettered country), 17. See also *letrados*

país nacional (national country): definition of, 16; Gaitán on, 16–17

país político (political country): definition of, 17; Gaitán on, 17

Palacios, Marco, 10

Pan-American Union, 24

pardon program, 82–83, 91, 103, 186, 210

Parga Cortés, Rafael, 66–69; Communists meeting with, 69, 70; and cultural festival, 92–93; as governor of Tolima, 92–93; and La Palmita massacre, 101; Liberal resistance meeting with, 66–67; on Oviedo/Mariachi, 115

Parra, Ignacio (Revolución), 55, 253n20

Partido Comunista de Colombia (PCC). *See* Communists

past, the: history vs. memory of, 157–59; as interchangeable with present, 160; newspaper pact prohibiting coverage of, 166–67

Pasto uprising (1944), 23, 240n48

paz criolla. See creole peace

PCC (Partido Comunista de Colombia). *See* Communists

peace: future of, 226; inseparability of violence and, 2; lack of formal process for, 65; Liberal vs. Conservative roles in initiatives for, 4; map of important sites of, 39, 76; vs. pacification by military, 150, 160, 177. *See also* creole peace

Peace Commission. *See* National Investigatory Commission on the Causes and Current Situations of Violence in the National Territory

Peace Corps, 144

peace festivals, 180, 207

peasants, use and meaning of term, 236n34

Pécaut, Daniel, 221

Peligro (Danger). *See* García, Leopoldo

People's Bank, 256n84

Perón, Juan Domingo, 30

petitions: to *junta* of 1957–58, 68, 252n20; from Marquetalia, 198–99

Piñeda Castillo, Roberto, 255n76

Plan Lazo (Snare), 175–80, 188, 192, 209

"Platform for a Movement of Popular Unity," 216

plebiscite, of 1957, 32–33

political cartoons, 98, *161*

political culture, as challenge for Lleras Camargo administration, 37

political parties. *See* Communists; Conservative; Liberals

political transitions, expanded definition of, 3. *See also* democratic transition

politicians, as focus of study, 5. *See also specific people*

Popular Cultural Action (ACPO), Lleras Camargo's speech at, 15–16, 19, 37, 127, 244n8
Prado Delgado, Víctor Eduardo (Vipradel), 179, 180, 195
presidential elections: of 1930, 19, 22; of 1934, 19; of 1938, 22; of 1942, 22; of 1946, 23–24; of 1949/1950, 25–26, 83; of 1958, 30–35, 72; of 1962, 121, 137, 139, 189–90; of 1970, 220
press coverage, 1962 declaration of principles on, 165–67. See also specific publications
Primera Conferencia Guerrillera del Bloque Sur. See First Guerrilla Conference of the Southern Bloc
prison sentences, 83
Programa Agrario de los Guerrilleros. See Guerrilla Fighters' Agrarian Program
Pro-Peace of Progress Carnival, 259n126
property: legal reforms relating to, 106–9; nexus of violence and, 43, 44, 96, 110. See also land
protests, over presidential election of 1958, 31–32
provincial Colombians: citizenship of, 61; as focus of study, 5. See also rural areas
public services, devolution of, 127
public works construction, 81–82, 88

Quintero Luna, Gentil, 69, 91, 253n24

race, in causes of violence, 41–42
Ramírez Tobón, William, 258n107
Ranching Development Fund, 91, 256n84
reconciliation, National Investigatory Commission on potential for, 56–57, 60–61
reform efforts, postrehabilitation, 120–47; Communism equated with, 140; disillusionment with, 123, 136, 141–47; essential features of, 120–22; expectations created by, 123, 146; international influences in, 121–22, 139–40; origins of, 123–26; país político in, 136–41; sociologists' involvement in, 131–36. See also agrarian reform; legal reforms; rehabilitation
regional identity, and creole peace, 92–94
regional politics, in creole peace, 65, 89–92
regional scale, 6
rehabilitation, 78–92; aftermath of, in Tolima, 114–18; of Communists, 86–89, 105; Conservative assault on, 101–5, 157; definition and use of term, 79, 81; devolution and end of, 104–5, 108, 113, 116; in El Pato, 184–89; establishment as national policy, 78–86; funding for, 79–81, 80, 104; Liberal vs. Conservative recipients of, 84–85, 101–2; local priorities in, 86–89;

reconsideration in 1964–65 of, 183–84; regional politics in, 89–92; scaling back of, 96
rehabilitation loans, 83–85; budget for, 84, 104; to Charry Rincón, 88; end of, 103–4; establishment and expansion of, 83–84; geographic distribution of, 80, 84; to Guaraca, 258n104; Liberal vs. Conservative recipients of, 84–85; number and size of, 84; as reparations, 112, 208; to Rojas/Chispas, 84, 85, 102, 103, 157
reparations, 110–12, 208
repatriation. See desplazados, repatriation of
repression, debate over responsibility for, 159–60
República, La (newspaper), 103, 165, 166
"responsibility of the state," 111–12
"Return of José Dolores, The" (Villamil Cordovez), 63–65, 71, 85, 92
Revenge. See Desquite
Revolución. See Parra, Ignacio
revolution: in Liberal Revolutionary Movement, 138–39; as means vs. end, social scientists on, 122; Torres on obligation of, 216
Revolutionary Armed Forces of Colombia. See FARC
"revolutionary time," 267n8
Revolution on the March, 19–20, 22, 23, 124
Richard. See Castañeda, José Alfonso
Rioblanco: Community Action Council of, 129, 142; development of Liberal resistance in, 55–57; García/Peligro on life in, 51, 54–57
Riochiquito: autodefensa in, 205–6, 209; desplazados from, 206, 209–11; as independent republic, 184, 189–91, 202–7; military assault of 1965 in, 182–83, 190–91, 202–7; National Investigatory Commission in, 86–87; in Southern Bloc, 212
Rionegro, Conservative attack of 1949 on, 111
road construction, 82, 88, 178–79, 282n134
roadway assaults. See homicides, roadway
Rojas, Teófilo (Chispas [Sparks]): as bandit, 156–57; Communists on violence of, 174; and La Palmita massacre, 102, 115, 261n34; Oviedo/Mariachi's support of, 115; rehabilitation loan to, 84, 85, 102, 103, 157
Rojas Pinilla, Gustavo: abdication of, 32; attempt to extend presidency of, 30–32; and Benidorm accord, 30; censorship under, 30, 40, 66; economy under, 30, 31, 36; Lebret report to, 40–41; Lleras Camargo's criticism of, 28, 40; peace under, challenges to, 66; return from exile, 79; state of siege under, 27–28, 40, 66
Roosevelt, Franklin D., 20
Rovira, mass grave in, 52, 54

Ruiz Novoa, Alberto, *161*, 162, 175–76, 180, 194–95
rural areas: Canal Ramírez's study of, 42; Community Action Councils in, 127–29; development of Liberal resistance in, 55–57; gaps in urban understanding of, 37; Guzmán's study of, 38–40; Law 135 of 1960 in, 126–29; migration to urban areas from, 135; resurgence of violence-as-practice in, 39; vs. urban areas, Communists of, 182–83. *See also* National Investigatory Commission on the Causes and Current Situations of Violence
rustling, cattle, 116, 117–18, 191

Sánchez G., Gonzalo, 222–23; on end of pardons, 103; Guzmán's influence on, 222; on meanings of violence, 4; publications of, 222, 291n41; on rehabilitation, 81; on Ruiz Novoa's congressional speech, 162; on Three Horsemen, 179; on La Violencia, 5, 222–25
Sangrenegra (Blackblood), 168, 180, 184
San Silvestre ranch (Tolú), 120–22
Santander. *See* Dussán, Germán
Santander, Francisco de Paula, 18
Santos, Eduardo, 19, 23, 26, 27, 66
Saucío, Fals Borda in, 132, 144–45
scale, importance of, 5–6
Second Guerrilla Conference of the Southern Bloc, 212–13
Second Republic: Communists on, 69; establishment of, 33; military role in, 36; use of term, 33, 144
"second violence," 169, 173–75, 190, 207
self-defense forces. See *autodefensas*
self-rehabilitation: in El Pato, 187–89, 200–201; in Riochiquito, 190–91
Semana (magazine): on construction jobs, 82; on *convivencia*, 37; establishment of, 24; on *llerismo*, 44; on Morales Benítez, 45; on urban areas, 86; on violence-as-practice, 155
Servicio de Inteligencia Colombiana (SIC). *See* Intelligence Service, Colombian
Seventh Guerrilla Conference, 221
SIC. *See* Intelligence Service, Colombian
siege, state of, 26–28; declaration in 1944 of, 28; declaration in 1949 of, 26, 111; end in 1958 of, 78–79; generation of, 31, 218–19; under Lleras Camargo, 78–79, *80*, 107–8, 113–14; under Rojas Pinilla, 27–28, 40, 66
Siglo, El (newspaper): attacks on López in, 22; censorship in, 26; on Liberal repression of Conservatives, 160; on *La violencia en Colombia*, 157, 158, 159, 164

Simonelli, Fabio Lozano, 154, 169, 278n74
Sitges pact (1957), 32–33
social citizenship, 4, 113, 127, 140, 143
socialism, Torres on, 145
social scientists: Conservatives as, 158; developmentalist policies of, 11, 121–23, 130–36; disillusionment of, 123, 136, 141, 144–47, 215–16; on expectations created by reform, 123; first published use of term "La Violencia" by, 218, 222; government-commissioned report in 1987 by, 223–24; influence on national self-image, 225; in Marquetalia commission, 192–94, 215; on revolution as means vs. end, 122; on violence-as-idea, 149, 221–22; as *violentólogos*, 223–25. *See also specific people*
socioeconomic conditions: Lebret report on, 40–41; link between violence and, 41–42
socioeconomic development. *See* development
sociology, Colombian, 131–36; Fals Borda as intellectual leader of, 131–33; functionalism in, rejection of, 134–35, 171; institutionalization of, 132–33; at National University, 132–37, 145–46, 147; observation in, rise of, 134–35. *See also* social scientists
"solidarity State," 123
Sorzano González, Hernando, 101–2
Southern Bloc, 203, 212–13
Soviet Union, Cuban ties with, 125
Sparks. *See* Rojas, Teófilo
Special Rehabilitation Commission, 79–83, 104, 108, 254n57
state, the: "individualist," 123; "manager," 123, 137–38, 144–46; responsibility of, 111–12; "solidarity," 123; use and meaning of term, 234n14
strikes: general, of 1958, 31; student, of 1962, 145–46
structuralism, in *La violencia en Colombia*, 152–53
student protests, 31
student strike of 1962, 145–46
Study on Colombia's Development Conditions (Lebret), 41
Subversion in Colombia (Fals Borda), 218–19
sucios ("dirty" Liberals), 58
Supreme Court, 111
Sureshot. *See* Marulanda Vélez, Manuel
Susunaga, Pedro, 95

Tacumá, Teodoro, 57, 77
Tarzán, 168, 180
Taussig, Michael, 8

taxes, alcohol and cigarette, 91
Tecnócrata, El (magazine), 130
This Was My Village (film), 42, 71
Three Horsemen, 168–69, 177, 179–80, 184
Tiempo, El (newspaper): on bus massacres, 73–74; on Camargo, 200; censorship in, 26; closure in 1955, 28; on "fishing at night," 98; on Kennedy, 124; Lleras Camargo at, 19; on National Investigatory Commission, 46; Peligro's interviews with, 55; political cartoons in, 98, 161; on rehabilitation, 103, 149; on repatriation, 106; on Sitges pact, 32; on Supreme Court ruling on state involvement in violence, 111; on La violencia en Colombia, 155, 164, 165
Tierradentro: Conciliation and Equity Tribunal in, 204–5; consolidation of, 209; indigenous population of, 89, 185, 189, 204–5, 209, 211; massacre of 1950 in, 89, 130, 204; rehabilitation in, 89–90
Time (magazine), 30, 36
Tirofijo (Sureshot). See Marulanda Vélez, Manuel
Tolima. See Gran Tolima
Tolú, San Silvestre ranch in, 120–22
topography: of Gran Tolima, 7–8, 173; of Ibagué, 47
Torres Restrepo, Camilo, 131, 133–37; at Advanced School of Public Administration, 136, 146; alienation of, 146, 147, 215–17; death of, 217–19; on disillusionment with reform, 147; in ELN, 216–17, 218; Fals Borda's relationship with, 133, 218; Guzmán's letters to, 158, 167; in Marquetalia commission, 193; at National University, 133–35, 145–46; in origins of La violencia en Colombia, 151, 152; on revolution as obligation, 216
torture, by military, 176
transitions, political, expanded definition of, 3. See also democratic transition
Tribín Piedrahita, Adriano, 92–93, 264n85
Tribuna (newspaper), 113, 125, 167
Tribunales de Conciliación y Equidad. See Conciliation and Equity Tribunals
truce of 1957–58, 65–78; deepening of, 71–78; negotiations for, 66–71
Trujillo Castaño, Ciro: autodefensa's campaign against, 205–6, 209; and election of 1962, 190; Lleras Camargo administration supported by, 86–87; Marulanda's relationship with, 203–4; and military assault in Riochiquito, 182, 190–91, 202–6; pardon for, 91, 210,

259n119; size of forces of, 190; in Southern Bloc, 212; Valencia Tovar's negotiations with, 202–6
truth commissions, 50, 62, 77, 224

Umaña Luna, Eduardo: career of, 152, 169–70, 275n9; in Marquetalia commission, 193–94. See also violencia en Colombia, La
underdevelopment. See development
United Front of the Colombian People, 216, 217
United Nations (U.N.): Charter of, 21, 238n24; establishment of, 21–22
United States: in Alliance for Progress, 124; on anti-guerrilla operations, 173; Good Neighbor policy of, 20, 124
United States Embassy: on agrarian reform, 126; on banditry, 148; on civic-military action, 175; on Communal Action, 143; on Lleras Camargo, 34, 35; on López Michelsen, 138; on Rojas Pinilla, 30, 32; on Valencia, 137, 138; on La violencia en Colombia, 163, 180
Universal Declaration of Human Rights (1948), 124
University of the Andes, 27
urban areas: gaps in understanding of rural areas, 37; interparty relations in, 47; migration from rural areas to, 135; repatriation from, 86; vs. rural areas, Communists of, 182–83
Uribe Uribe, Rafael, 185

Valencia, Guillermo León, 161; approach to violence, 160–63, 194–95; consolidation under, 207, 209; on Cuban involvement with Communists, 204; developmentalist policies under, 138, 141; El Pato redevelopment under, 208; lack of preparation for presidency, 121, 137–38; Laureano's opposition to, 34; Lleras Camargo compared to, 160; Marquetalia's petition to, 198–99; on military's Plan Lazo, 176, 177; in presidential election of 1958, 31, 34; in presidential election of 1962, 121, 137, 139
Valencia, Miguel, 205, 209
Valencia Dussán brothers, 89–90, 130
Valencia Tovar, Álvaro: in consolidation, 209; military successes of, 175; in Plan Lazo, 175; in Riochiquito negotiations, 202–6, 209; on La violencia en Colombia, 180
Valle de San Juan, massacre of 1960 in, 95–96
Vatican, 124
Venezuela, fall of dictatorship in, 33
Vieira, Gilberto, 279n94
Villamil Cordovez, Graciela, 253n24

Villamil Cordovez, Jorge, *93*; and Camargo, 188, 189, 208; in Ibagué cultural festival, 92–94; and peace festivals, 180; on return of *desplazados* to El Pato, 206–8; "The Return of José Dolores," 63–65, 71, 85, 92; success of musical career of, 207

Villarrica, military campaign of 1955 in, 27, 58, 66, 173

violence *(la violencia)*: capitalization of, 170; meanings of, 4–5, 153–54; quotation marks used with, 11, 153, 168, 169, 279n94; redefinition of, 153, 169; as "technique of violence," 5, 153; vs. La Violencia, use of terms, 5, 12, 153, 223; *La violencia en Colombia* in transition to La Violencia from, 153, 172

violence, in Colombia: attempts to quantify scope of, 42–43, 245n17; Benidorm accord on, 29; as Conservative electoral strategy, 52–54, *53*; discrete periods of, recognition of, 169; discussion in 1950s of causes of, 41–42; inseparability of peace and, 2; link between socioeconomic conditions and, 41–42; map of important sites of, *39*; memory of, multiple versions of, 149; newspaper pact on coverage of, 165–67; prominence of reputation for, 1; "second," 169, 173–75, 190, 207; Sitges pact on, 32. *See also* homicides

violence-as-idea, 9–13; Conservative version of, 29; definition of, 9; and *desplazados* from Riochiquito, 209–10; diverse sources of similar ideas, 172–73; expanding notions of, 9, 11–12; Liberal version of, 78; military version of, 173–79; national versions of, 77–78, 173; remembrance of history influenced by, 209–11; social scientists on, 149, 221–22; in Southern Bloc, 212; in *La violencia en Colombia*, 11–12, 153–54, 171–72

violence-as-practice, 9–13; in bandit assaults, 148, 155–58; as challenge for Lleras Camargo administration, 37; definition of, 9; resurgences of, *39*, 155; in Southern Bloc, 212; spread of, 10; transformations of, 11, 155

Violence Commission. *See* National Investigatory Commission on the Causes and Current Situations of Violence in the National Territory

violencia, la. See violence

Violencia, La, 222–25; dates of, 222–23, 225, 291n45; dissemination of concept, 220; first capitalization of, 170; first published use of term in social science, 218, 222; generation of, 218, 219, 222; origins and development of concept, 1–2, 5, 12, 169, 211; personal vs. national memories in, 224–25; Sánchez on, 5, 222–25; vs. Second Republic, use of terms, 33; start of academic study of, 222; as temporal concept, 2, 5, 172, 222–23; vs. *la violencia,* use of terms, 5, 12, 153, 223; *La violencia en Colombia* in transition from violence to, 153, 172

violencia en Colombia, La (Guzmán Campos et al.), 11–12, 148–81; anticlimax of, 165, 180; on civic-military action, 177–78; Communists on, 168; Conservative attacks on, 157–60, 163–65; on Conservative responsibility for violence, 154, 159; epilogue to, 2; at First International Symposium on La Violencia, 222; funding for, 152, 157; on homicide numbers, 158, 277n43; intellectual pluralism of, 152–53; intellectual responses to, 154–55; on link between peace and violence, 2; meanings of "violence" in, 153–54; memory vs. history in, 157–59; military on, 180–81, 194; origins of, 150–52; press declaration of principles and, 165–67; prologue to 2005 edition of, 167; reissue in 1968 of, 217; second edition of, 163–64; second volume of, 149, 153, 170–73, 177–78, 219; success of, 2, 152; in transformation of violence to La Violencia, 153, 172; and Valencia's approach to violence, 160–63; violence-as-idea in, 11–12, 153–54, 171–72; writing of, 151–52, 170–71

violentólogos, 223–25

Vipradel. *See* Prado Delgado, Víctor Eduardo

Walker, Louise, 10

War Ministry: and El Pato *desplazados,* 208; and Marquetalia commission, 192, 193; on *La violencia en Colombia,* 180. *See also* military

War of a Thousand Days, 18, 185

women, as domesticating corrective, 148

World Bank, 36

World War II, 21

Yopal, training center in, 146, 147

Zuñiga, David, 141–42

Zuñiga, Sara, 141–42

CPSIA information can be obtained
at www.ICGtesting.com
Printed in the USA
LVOW11s0406230917

549713LV00002B/2/P